IN-DEPTH UNDERSTANDING

The MIT Press Series in Artificial Intelligence

Artificial Intelligence: An MIT Perspective, Volume I: Expert Problem Solving, Natural Language Understanding, Intelligent Computer Coaches, Representation and Learning edited by Patrick Henry Winston and Richard Henry Brown, 1979

Artificial Intelligence: An MIT Perspective, Volume II: Understanding Vision, Manipulation, Computer Design, Symbol Manipulation edited by Patrick Henry Winston and Richard Henry Brown, 1979

NETL: A System for Representing and Using Real-World Knowledge by Scott Fahlman, 1979

The Interpretation of Visual Motion by Shimon Ullman, 1979

A Theory of Syntactic Recognition for Natural Language by Mitchell P. Marcus, 1980

Turtle Geometry: The Computer as a Medium for Exploring Mathematics by Harold Abelson and Andrea diSessa, 1981

From Images to Surfaces: A Computational Study of the Human Early Visual System by William Eric Leifur Grimson, 1981

Robot Manipulators: Mathematics, Programming and Control by Richard P. Paul, 1981

Computational Models of Discourse edited by Michael Brady and Robert C. Berwick, 1982

Robot Motion: Planning and Control edited by Michael Brady, John M. Hollerbach, Timothy Johnson, Tomas Lozano-Perez, and Matthew Mason, 1982

In-Depth Understanding: A Computer Model of Integrated Processing for Narrative Comprehension by Michael George Dyer, 1983

IN-DEPTH UNDERSTANDING

A Computer Model of Integrated Processing for Narrative Comprehension

Michael George Dyer

The MIT Press
Cambridge, Massachusetts
London, England

This book was printed and bound in the United States of America.

Publisher's note: This format is intended to reduce the cost of publishing certain work in book form and to shorten the gap between editorial preparation and the final publication. Detailed editing and composition have been avoided by photographing the text of this book directly from the author's typescript or word-processor output.

This dissertation was presented to the Faculty of the Graduate School of Yale University on May 1982.

An appendix has been added which includes a pedagogical parser, along with exercises.

This work was supported in part by the Advanced Research Projects Agency under contract NOO14-75-C-1111 and in part by the National Science Foundation under contract IST7918463.

Library of Congress Cataloging in Publication Data

Dyer, Michael George.
  In-depth understanding.

  Bibliography: p.
  Includes index.
  1. Artificial intelligence—Mathematical models.
  2. Comprehension—Data processing. I. Title.
  Q335.D93 1983   001.53′5   83–7926
  ISBN 0–262–04073–5

Table of Contents

Series Foreword

Artificial intelligence is the study of intelligence using the ideas and methods of computation. Unfortunately, a definition of intelligence seems impossible at the moment because intelligence appears to be an amalgam of so many information-processing and information-representation abilities.

Of course psychology, philosophy, linguistics, and related disciplines offer various perspectives and methodologies for studying intelligence. For the most part, however, the theories proposed in these fields are too imcomplete and too vaguely stated to be realized in computational terms. Something more is needed, even though valuable ideas, relationships, and constraints can be gleaned from traditional studies of what are, after all, impressive existence proofs that intelligence is in fact possible.

Artificial intelligence offers a new perspective and a new methodology. Its central goal is to make computers intelligent, both to make them more useful and to understand the principles that make intelligence possible. That intelligent computers will be extremely useful is obvious. The more profound point is that artificial intelligence aims to understand intelligence using the ideas and methods of computation, thus offering a radically new and different basis for theory formation. Most of the people doing artificial intelligence believe that these theories will apply to any intelligent information processor, whether biological or solid state.

There are side effects that deserve attention, too. Any program that will successfully model even a small part of intelligence will be inherently massive and complex. Consequently, artificial intelligence continually confronts the limits of computer science technology. The problems encountered have been hard enough and interesting enough to seduce artificial intelligence people into working on them with enthusiasm. It is natural, then, that there has been a steady flow of ideas from artificial intelligence to computer science, and the flow shows no sign of abating.

The purpose of this MIT Press Series in Artificial Intelligence is to provide people in many areas, both professionals and students, with timely, detailed information about what is happening on the frontiers in research centers all over the world.

Patrick Henry Winston
Michael Brady

Preface

It takes a great deal of knowledge and processing to understand narrative text. BORIS attempts to understand just a few very complicated stories as deeply as possible in contrast to the approach of skimming a great number of stories. As a result, the BORIS project has had to deal with little explored areas concerning knowledge interactions, expectation failures, multiple perspectives, and multiple levels of abstraction, including thematic patterns. Novel representational problems have also been addressed. For instance, unlike previous story understanders, BORIS contains a representational system of AFFECT primitives for dealing with the affective reactions of narrative characters.

Understanding narratives "in depth" means being able to do more than simply extract the facts of a narrative and infer causal connections between them. An in-depth understander must be able to recognize what was memorable about a narrative, what episodes were of significance, and what the point of the narrative was -- that is, why the narrative was worth telling in the first place. Finally, if a narrative is significant in some way, then the process of in-depth comprehension should result in indexing the narrative in memory so that it will come to mind in appropriate future situations.

At this point in time, people are the only information processors able to understand and appreciate the significance of complex narratives. Consequently, the process model embodied in BORIS is based on numerous subject protocols over tasks involving title selection, text summarization, and question answering. For instance, experimental evidence suggests that subjects process text in a highly integrated manner. Syntactic, semantic, and episodic processes arise as each word or phrase is encountered. Therefore, BORIS takes the same theoretical approach.

The thesis presented here represents an initial attempt to specify and model those knowledge constructs, inference strategies, and memory search processes which are prerequisite for in-depth understanding.

Acknowledgments

First, I would like to thank my thesis advisor, Professor Wendy Lehnert, who served as overseer of the BORIS project and without whom this thesis would have been impossible. She supported me through rough times and that is when it counts. Wendy also helped me organize the chaos of multiple problems (that is BORIS) into a coherent thesis.

I also want to thank the other readers on my committee, Professor Bob Abelson and Professor Roger Schank, who both made valuable comments and suggestions on the final draft of this thesis. Professor Abelson has been a source of constant support throughout my years at Yale. He has also directed a number of experiments on thematic structures in BORIS. Professor Schank has been the architect of an environment at the Yale Artificial Intelligence Lab which is conducive to excellence in research. BORIS is built on numerous theoretical constructs developed by Professor Schank and his previous students.

Very special thanks go to Margot Flowers, who made many valuable contentful, editorial, and stylistic suggestions to this dissertation. Margot was the first to read many of the chapters which follow.

Over the years a great number of individuals at the Yale A.I. lab have contributed to the BORIS project. Without their efforts BORIS would still be sitting on the launching pad. I'm pleased here to be able to acknowledge each in turn:

Tom Wolf was central in the design and implementation of the most recent version of BORIS, and made important contributions to BORIS parsing integration and question answering. Pete Johnson was central in earlier versions of BORIS and made important contributions to BORIS memory and processing structures. No one could ask for better co-programmers and co-researchers than Tom and Pete.

Mark Burstein also made major contributions to earlier versions of BORIS, and was involved in the design of MOP overlays and event assimilation. Marty Korsin, CJ Yang, Lewis Johnson, and Mark Tanner worked a great deal on various BORIS parsers. Margot Flowers provided a number of LISP utilities for BORIS, including output and file access functions.

Steve Harley, Mark Tanner, and Judith Lempert worked on the English generator for BORIS. This generator is based upon code from Rod McGuire's generator. Hence Rod served as the ultimate advisor on all issues regarding English generation.

A number of researchers in psychology have also contributed to the BORIS project. Colleen Seifert (under the guidance of Professors McKoon, Ratcliffe, and Abelson) designed and ran an number of significant, novel experiments on BORIS memory structures, specifically TAUs. Scott Robertson conducted experiments on memory modifications during question answering. Brian Reiser worked on narrative summarization and Plot Units in BORIS. Steve Minton designed and ran a number of experiments on interpersonal structures in BORIS, while Jill Fain experimented with scenario maps. I also want to thank Ira Roseman, who has conducted a number of significant experiments on emotions, and who was kind enough to read and offer useful comments concerning my chapter on the role of AFFECT in BORIS. Andrew Ortony (at the Center for the Study of Reading) was also kind enough to read and offer suggestions on a final draft of the AFFECT chapter.

Others were particularily helpful in my first years: Dr. Chris Riesbeck taught me how to parse. Professors Drew McDermott and Dave Barstow expanded my A.I. horizons outside of natural language. processing. Discussions with Professor Mallory Selfridge and with Larry Birnbaum on parsing were very worthwhile and served as a source of much inspiration.

Among those who have helped make my stay at the Yale A.I. Lab both interesting and memorable are: Valerie Abbott, Bill Bain, Prof. John Black, Prof. Jaime Carbonell, Greg Collins, Ernie Davis, Natalie Dehn, Prof. Jerry DeJong, Ann Drinan, Konrad Dyer, Glen Edelson, Bill Ferguson, Patti Oronzo, Linda Fusco, Jim Galambos, Tom Galloway, Dr. Anatole Gershman, Dr. Ray Gibbs, Prof. Rick Granger, Abraham Gutman, Chris Hammond, Dr. Shoshanna Hardt, Ed Hovy, Dr. Dave Johnson, Prof. Janet Kolodner, Prof. Mike Lebowitz, John Leddo, Stan Letovsky, Jeff Lowney, Steve Lytinen, Beth Marshburn, Judy Martel, Kay Parady, Tony Passera, Rich

Plevin, John Ruttenburg, Steve Salzburg, Udi Shapiro, Dr. Steve Shwartz, Steven Slade, Prof. Elliot Soloway, and Michael Wilk.

One reason the Yale A.I. Lab is a great place to work is that it receives tremendous systems support from the Yale Tools group. This group is lead by John O'Donnell, who is the best facilities director anyone could ask for. Other systems "wizards" I've relied on, who have created numerous utilities, and who I would like to thank, are: Steve Wood, who created the nifty Z screen editor; John Ellis, who created MUF (Multiple User Forks) and SM (the Session Manager); Nat Mishkin, who expanded the capabilities of Yale TLISP and built the windowing package, and Bob Nix, who contributed to Z and other tools. The type fonts for this thesis result from Bob's work on a scribe-driver for the Yale laser printer.

In addition, I want to thank a number of individuals outside of Yale, who have, at one time or another in the past, had a great influence on me. They are: Prof. Neil Jones, Prof. Henry Lundsgaarde, Prof. Steven Muchnick, Prof. Hans Penner, Prof. Jerome Rothstein, Prof. Henry Selby, and Prof. Doug Tuggle.

Finally, this work was supported in part by the Advanced Research Projects Agency under contract NOO14-75-C-1111 and in part by the National Science Foundation under contract IST7918463.

IN-DEPTH UNDERSTANDING

CHAPTER 1

The Meaning of In-Depth Understanding

1.1 BORIS -- A Computer Program

The theory of narrative comprehension presented here is implemented within BORIS, a computer program. BORIS is able to answer questions about a narrative in order to demonstrate that it has read and understood it. Thus BORIS also incorporates a theory of memory search and retrieval for question answering.

What follows is an actual understanding and question answering session with the BORIS program running on a narrative concerning a divorce (called DIVORCE-1). Input to the program is in lower case; output in uppercase. BORIS receives the English shown here as verbatim input and produces verbatim English below as output:

I/O Behavior on DIVORCE-1

```
*(BORIS 'DIVORCE-1)

PROCESSING PARAGRAPH 1:

    Richard  hadn't heard from his college roommate Paul
    for years.  Richard had  borrowed  money  from  Paul
    which  was  never paid back.  but now he had no idea
    where to find his old friend.  When a letter finally
    arrived  from  San Francisco, Richard was anxious to
    find out how Paul was.

READY TO ACCEPT Q/A:

    What happened to Richard at home?
    RICHARD GOT A LETTER FROM PAUL.

    Who is Paul?
    RICHARD 's FRIEND.
```

Did Richard want to see Paul?
YES, RICHARD WANTED TO KNOW HOW PAUL WAS.

Had Paul helped Richard?
YES, PAUL LENT MONEY TO RICHARD.

Why didn't Richard pay Paul back?
RICHARD DID NOT KNOW WHERE PAUL WAS.

How did Richard feel when the letter appeared?
RICHARD FELT GLAD BECAUSE PAUL AND HE WERE FRIENDS.

PROCESSING PARAGRAPH 2:

Unfortunately, the news was not good. Paul's wife
Sarah wanted a divorce. She also wanted the car,
the house, the children, and alimony. Paul wanted
the divorce, but he didn't want to see Sarah walk
off with everything he had. His salary from the
state school system was very small. Not knowing who
to turn to, he was hoping for a favor from the only
lawyer he knew. Paul gave his home phone number in
case Richard felt he could help.

READY TO ACCEPT Q/A:

What was the letter about?
PAUL AND SARAH WERE GETTING A DIVORCE.

Did Paul write Sarah?
NO, IT WASN'T SARAH, IT WAS RICHARD
WHO GOT THE LETTER.

Why was Paul upset about the divorce?
PAUL AND SARAH WERE FIGHTING OVER
THE FAMILY POSSESSIONS.

What did Paul do for a living?
PAUL WAS A TEACHER.

What did Sarah want?
SARAH WANTED TO HAVE THE CAR AND THE HOUSE AND
THE KIDS AND THE ALIMONY.

Why did Paul write to Richard?
PAUL WANTED RICHARD TO BE HIS LAWYER.

PROCESSING PARAGRAPH 3:

Richard eagerly picked up the phone and dialed.
After a brief conversation, Paul agreed to have
lunch with him the next day. He sounded extremely
relieved and grateful.

READY TO ACCEPT Q/A:

Why did Richard call Paul?
RICHARD WANTED TO ARRANGE A MEETING WITH PAUL.

Did Richard contact Paul?
YES. RICHARD CALLED PAUL.

How did Richard contact Paul?
BY PHONE.

How did Paul feel when Richard called?
PAUL WAS HAPPY BECAUSE RICHARD AGREED TO BE PAUL'S
LAWYER.

PROCESSING PARAGRAPH 4:

> The next day, as Richard was driving to the restaurant, he barely avoided hitting an old man on the street. He felt extremely upset by the incident, and had three drinks at the restaurant. When Paul arrived Richard was fairly drunk. After the food came, Richard spilled a cup of coffee on Paul. Paul seemed very annoyed by this so Richard offered to drive him home for a change of clothes.

READY TO ACCEPT Q/A:

Why did Richard eat out with Paul?
RICHARD WANTED TO DISCUSS THE DIVORCE CASE WITH PAUL.

What happened to Richard on the way
to the restaurant?
RICHARD ALMOST RAN OVER AN OLD MAN.

Why did Richard get drunk?
RICHARD WAS UPSET ABOUT ALMOST RUNNING OVER
THE OLD MAN.

What happened at the restaurant?
RICHARD SPILLED COFFEE ON PAUL.

How did Richard feel when the coffee spilled?
RICHARD WAS UNHAPPY.

Why did Richard spill the coffee?
RICHARD WAS DRUNK.

When did Richard almost hit the old man?
WHILE RICHARD WAS DRIVING TO THE RESTAURANT.

Where did Richard have lunch with PAUL?
AT A RESTAURANT.

PROCESSING PARAGRAPH 5:

> When Paul walked into the bedroom and found Sarah
> with another man he nearly had a heart attack. Then
> he realized what a blessing it was. With Richard
> there as a witness, Sarah's divorce case was shot.
> Richard congratulated Paul and suggested that they
> celebrate at dinner. Paul was eager to comply.

READY TO ACCEPT Q/A:

> Why did Richard drive Paul home?
> SO PAUL COULD CHANGE HIS CLOTHES.
>
> What happened to Paul at home?
> PAUL CAUGHT SARAH COMMITTING ADULTERY.
>
> How did Paul feel?
> PAUL WAS SURPRISED.
>
> Why did Sarah lose her divorce case?
> SARAH COMMITTED ADULTERY.
>
> Why did Richard congratulate Paul?
> PAUL WON THE DIVORCE CASE.

TEXT PROCESSING COMPLETED ON: DIVORCE-1

1.2 What BORIS Is Up Against

This section is included to give the reader some idea of the kinds of problems that arise in almost any fragment of narrative text. In this case the examples which appear below are taken from DIVORCE-1. Each problem raised in this section will be addressed at some point in the thesis, once a sufficient theoretical foundation has been developed.

(a) Richard hadn't heard from his college roommate Paul in years.

Here BORIS is told a non-event. What should BORIS do with this? Simply storing an event as not having occurred is inadequate. For instance, when people read: "John walked into the room and Mary was not there." they infer that John wanted to see Mary and had been expecting her there. They do not simply store in memory the fact: FALSE [LOC [MARY,OFFICE]].

(b) ... which was never paid back.

This phrase also refers to a non-event, but what is its effect on processing? Many readers said that Richard was willing to help Paul because Richard felt obligated to Paul. Therefore, this non-event must be understood in terms of the relationship between Paul and Richard. In addition, it should be noted that this phrase never explicitly mentions WHO failed to pay WHAT to WHOM, yet people never notice this, and automatically fill on these roles from knowledge of loans and their repayment.

(c) ... but now he had no idea where to find his old friend.

How do we go about parsing an expression like (c) and once parsed, how do we represent its semantics? That is, we must determine what representation the parser should produce. The word "had" does not refer to physical possession. The word "old" does not refer to the age of Richard's friend. How do we represent the meaning of "finding" someone? Also, we must understand the connection between (b) and (c), that finding Paul is an enabling condition for paying him back.

(d) When a letter finally arrived from San Francisco ...

People assume that the letter is from Paul even though this is never explicitly stated.

(e) Unfortunately, the news was not good.

What effect does "unfortunately" have on processing and how is it represented?   Furthermore, people assume that the entire second paragraph in DIVORCE-1 refers to information contained in the letter and that Richard is reading this letter.   But we are never explicitly told: "Richard began to read and the letter stated the following: ..."

(f) Paul's wife Sarah wanted a divorce.

How do we represent a divorce in memory?   At the very least, it must refer both to marriage and to the legalities required in terminating a marriage.   Otherwise the subsequent mention of a lawyer would make no sense.

(g) ... but he didn't want to see Sarah walk off with everything he had.

Parsing and representation here is complex.   Representing "walk off" as physical movement is inadequate.   Similarly, "see" does not refer here to literal vision.   Nor can "everything" be taken too literally.   Metaphors and suggestive references must be handled with care.

(h) His salary from the state school system was very small.

What does (h) have to do with the story?   People immediately realize the connection between a small salary and lawyers' fees, alimony, etc.   But BORIS must explicitly establish this connection.

(i) Not knowing who to turn to, he was hoping for a favor from the only lawyer he knew.

How are "who to turn to", "hoping", "favor", "only" to be parsed and represented?   Here BORIS must know about lawyers in order to understand why "lawyer" has been mentioned.   Notice, also, that the story never explicitly states that Richard is the lawyer being referred to, yet people automatically make this inference.

(j) Richard eagerly picked up the phone and dialed.

The story never explicitly states who Richard dialed or engaged in conversation. Furthermore, protocols of individuals indicate that many people infer at this point that Richard will agree to be Paul's lawyer.

(k) He sounded extremely relieved and grateful.

What is to be done with affects such as "relieved" and "grateful"? People use their knowledge of these affects to assign an appropriate referent to "he". Most people immediately assume that "he" is Paul, not Richard.

(l) ... he barely avoided hitting an old man on the street.

BORIS must realize that "hitting" here refers to a vehicle accident rather than a fist fight.

(m) When Paul arrived Richard was fairly drunk.

The story never explicitly states where it is that Paul has arrived. People nevertheless interpret Paul's arrival in terms of their arrangement to meet. But how?

(n) ... so Richard offered to drive him home for a change of clothes.

Why did Richard make this offer? Why does Paul have to change clothes? Connections must be made between these events to answer such questions.

(o) When Paul walked into the bedroom ...

What is Paul doing in the bedroom and how did he get there? Most scene changes are made only implicitly in narratives. Nor are we explicitly told that Richard drove Paul home, only that he offered to.

(p) ... and found Sarah with another man he nearly had a heart attack.

The story never explicitly states that Sarah was having an affair. This must be inferred, along with Paul's probable reaction. Only then does it make sense for "heart attack" to denote surprise, and not a cardiac arrest.

(q) Then he realized what a blessing it was.

What is "blessing"? What is the effect of this sentence on processing, and what is constructed in memory?

(r) With Richard there as a witness, Sarah's divorce case was shot.

BORIS needs to know something about witnesses to successfully understand this sentence. Also, the word "case" here is not a container or unit of measurement, as in "case of beer", and "was shot" is metaphorical.

(s) Richard congratulated Paul and suggested they celebrate at dinner.

How do we represent "congratulated" and why does Richard make his suggestion? BORIS must understand why congratulations are in order. But the story never explicitly states that Paul has won, simply that Sarah has lose. The implication is clear, but must be inferred nonetheless.

1.3 Knowledge and Memory for Comprehension

As the excerpts above suggest, understanding narrative text is a complicated task, requiring the interaction of many disparate sources of knowledge. The story DIVORCE-1 requires the following abstract constructs to represent its conceptual content: object primitives [Lehnert and Burstein, 1979] [Lehnert, 1979], scripts [Cullingford, 1981], [DeJong, 1979a] settings [Dyer and Lehnert, 1980], goals [Wilensky, 1978a], plans [Schank and Abelson, 1977], affects [Roseman, 1979], themes [Wilensky, 1978b], interpersonal relationships [Schank and Abelson, 1977], physical states [Schank, 1975], events [Dyer, 1981a], social acts [Schank and Carbonell, 1979],

MOPs [Schank, 1982a], and TAUs [Dyer, 1981b]. This thesis deals with issues of knowledge representation, knowledge application, memory instantiation, memory search and processing interactions within multiple knowledge source domains.

To understand narratives, one must have knowledge about the actions and situations which arise within them. A story involving a divorce, for instance, would be incomprehensible to one who did not already know something about divorces. But what does knowledge of divorce look like and how is it organized? Any theory of narrative understanding must include a theory of knowledge representation for the kinds of things narratives deal with.

But a representational system alone is not enough. A theory of narrative comprehension must also include processing knowledge -- i.e. knowledge which determines when and how representations are to be used. For instance, when we read:

> Paul wanted to change his clothes. When Paul
> walked into the bedroom...

we use our knowledge about clothing in order to understand why Paul went into the bedroom. To do this, we must know: a) to change clothes one must obtain new clothes, b) clothes are commonly kept in one's bedroom, c) to obtain an object, one must be near that object, and d) this may require walking into the room containing the desired object. There are other things we also know about clothes -- e.g. clothes are bought at stores, and they cost money. But this particular knowledge happens to be irrelevant in the example above. So a theory of narrative processing must explain how knowledge is organized during processing so that only knowledge relevant to the situation at hand will be applied.

These processes of comprehension must construct in episodic memory [Tulving, 1972] a conceptual representation of the narrative. Memory for a narrative will be composed of instantiations of many different knowledge structures that must be causally connected. For instance, when people read about a husband who catches his wife being unfaithful, they do not immediately think of lawyers. However, if a lawyer is mentioned next:

> After George caught his wife committing adultery
> George decided that he needed a lawyer.

they are not surprised. In contrast, consider the following fragment:

> After George caught his wife committing adultery
> George decided that he needed a basketball player.

In this case people become very confused because they can not find any relationship between adultery and basketball players.

In addition, access links must also be built for subsequent use by search and retrieval processes, particularly during question answering. If narrative episodes can not be appropriately accessed, then the result of the narrative comprehension process will be of little use.

Finally, narrative episodes do not reside in isolation in memory. When we read a narrative, often a related narrative will come to mind [Schank, 1982b]. This indicates that both narratives are being processed and indexed in a like manner at some level in episodic memory. Often, the level of indexing is at a very abstract level, dealing with very general themes. When this occurs, a story may remind a reader of another story which shares little at the content level, and yet is typified or characterized at a more abstract level by the same themes.

1.4 Natural Language Processing: Some Background

Research in text processing has grown explosively in the past ten years. Consequently, no effort is being made here to review all potentially relevant literature. Instead, the following section is intended to give the reader a perspective from which the scope and aims of the BORIS project can be examined.

1.4.1 Early Semantics-Based Approaches

Some of the earliest semantics-based approaches to natural language processing were represented by the SHRDLU [Winograd, 1972] and MARGIE [Schank, 1975] systems:

SHRDLU engaged in an interactive dialog concerning a micro-world of blocks. It could answer questions about blocks and carry out simple commands, such as "Pick up the red pyramid on a blue block." SHRDLU represented the meaning of a sentence in terms of a procedure to carry out a set of actions within the blocks micro-world. For instance, "the red pyramid on a blue block" would translate into a program to examine each block until a blue one was found, and then check to see if a red pyramid was on top of it, and if not, continue searching for another blue block, etc. Unfortunately, this approach of procedural representation made it difficult to represent the meaning of a sentence outside the context of a pre-specified micro-world.

In contrast, MARGIE was based on a representational system intended to be independent of any particular micro-world. This representational system was based on a fixed set of primitive semantic ACTS which were related by a number of Conceptual Dependencies (CD)[1] [Schank and Abelson, 1977] [Schank, 1973]. MARGIE was composed of three modules: ELI [Riesbeck, 1975], MEMORY [Rieger, 1975], and BABEL [Goldman, 1975]. ELI parsed English sentences, producing CD representations. MEMORY then generated all of the inferences which arose from the conceptual representations produced by ELI. These inferences were themselves represented in CD. Finally, BABEL [Goldman, 1975] generated paraphrases by expressing each CD in English.

There were several novel aspects to MARGIE. First, ELI was driven by semantic rather than syntactic concerns. Second, ELI used the notion of "expectations" to aid in its conceptual analysis. That is, lexical items would access CD structures. Associated with each structure would be one of more expectations for what might follow. For instance, the primitive ACT of INGEST represented knowledge about putting substances inside one's body (such as eating, smoking, etc.). One expectation associated with INGEST looked for the occurrence of an edible object. When an expectation was satisfied, the expected entity would be connected to the CD structure associated with the expectation and an instantiation of an INGEST conceptualization would be built in memory.

Expectations are one way of representing an active context. Among other things, this active context can be used to aid in

---

[1]For a brief discussion of CD theory, see appendix II.

disambiguating word senses. For instance, an expectation associated with INGEST arising from "ate" in the following sentence:

> John ate a hot dog.

will select the food meaning of "hot dog" (rather than a canine with a high fever). However, MARGIE had great difficulty handling more than one sentence at a time. This occurred because MEMORY generated every possible inference it could. Since each inference would generate a CD, and since that CD had many potential inferences associated with it, very quickly MEMORY would be overcome by a combinatorial explosion of inferences. There seemed to be no way of constraining inferences to just those which were relevant to the text at hand.

1.4.2 Script-Based Understanding

The combinatoric problem was partially solved by the notion of a script [Schank and Abelson, 1977]. Scripts[2] contain pre-arranged causal chains which represented stereotypic actions associated with a given setting. For instance, a restaurant script includes the knowledge that people sit down, order, eat, tip, pay, and then leave. Once a script has been activated, the relevant inferences, concerning actions to follow, are acquired for free. A computer program, SAM [Cullingford, 1978], used scripts to understand simple stories. For instance, given the story:

> John went to a restaurant. He ordered lobster from
> the waitress. He left a big tip and went home.

SAM could use its script to fill in the relevant information not explicitly stated within the story. For example:

> Q: What did John eat?
> A: Lobster.

---

[2]Similar work has been conducted with the more general notion of a frame [Minsky, 1975] [Minsky, 1977] [Charniak, 1978].

Q: Who brought the lobster to John?
A: The waitress.

The restaurant script contains information the the diner usually eats what he orders and that the food is usually brought by a waitress or waiter. Thus SAM knew that John ate lobster even though the story had never explicitly mentioned this fact.

1.4.3 Goal-Based Understanding

The strictly script-based approach of SAM had serious limitations. These limitations were a natural consequence of what scripts had been originally designed to accomplish. Since scripts were intended to capture only very stereotypic knowledge, they lacked intentionality. For instance, although SAM knew that the waitress brought food to the diner, SAM did not know **why** she did this. As a result SAM was incapable of handling stories in which the characters' mental states lead them to deviate from the actions predicted by the script.

In order to understand novel situations when they occurred, therefore, it was necessary to track the goals and plans of the characters in the story. This approach was taken by PAM [Wilensky, 1978b], a program which explained the action of a character by using the character's goals to infer a plan which the character was using to achieve his goal. Consider the following text handled by PAM:

Willa was hungry. She picked up the Michelin Guide and got into her car.

A script-based program like SAM would be unable to connect up these three events unless it already had some HUNGER-READ-MICHELINE-GUIDE-DRIVE script. However, readers understand that Willa is using the Michelin guide to locate a restaurant to drive to even though it is the first time they have encountered this text. Instead of relying on a script, PAM used general knowledge about goals and plans to infer causal connections between physical actions. Regarding the story above, this knowledge included:

The goal of hunger is satisfied by eating.
One plan for eating is the restaurant script.
Michelin Guides tell the location of restaurants.
One plan for getting somewhere is to drive there.

PAM encoded general relationships between goals and plans. Furthermore, most scripts in PAM were represented as plans. Any action by a character was explained once PAM found a plan (compatible with the character's goals) of which that action was a part. By concentrating on inferences which connected up only goals and plans, PAM avoided some of the combinatoric problems that had arisen in MARGIE's mode of inference.

1.4.4 Text Skimmers

Both SAM and PAM tried to understand everything they read. They examined every word and attempted to build up as complete a set of causal and intentional connections as possible. Each program was capable of answering questions about stories read in order to demonstrate their comprehension.

In contrast, the text skimmers FRUMP [DeJong, 1979b] and IPP [Lebowitz, 1980] represent a different processing philosophy. Instead of answering questions about the text, each program displays its understanding by constructing a summary which represents the "gist" of a story. Unlike SAM and PAM, both FRUMP and IPP ignore words in the text. The resulting memory of a story often missed events and situations which occurred within the story.

Both these programs read numerous stories on the UPI (United Press International) news wire. FRUMP contains over 50 "sketchy" scripts, concerning such things as: earthquakes, kidnappings, visiting dignitaries, labor strikes, and breaking diplomatic relations.

These programs operate in a "top-down" manner. Once a knowledge structure is referred to in the text, this structure directs subsequent parsing strategies. For instance, when FRUMP finds a story which involves one of its scripts, it uses that single script to guide its analysis of the text. Given an earthquake "sketchy" script, FRUMP can extract from a UPI story the time, place, magnitude and number of casualties caused by the quake. Everything else, however, will be ignored.

Instead of knowing a little about many things, IPP knows a lot about one domain -- i.e. terrorism. IPP contains specific knowledge structures on extortion, kidnappings, bombings, skyjackings, shootings, etc. and their relations to one another. Unlike FRUMP, IPP maintains a long-term episodic memory of the stories it has read, and uses this memory as a basis for making generalizations about terrorism. For instance, if IPP reads several stories about attacks against the British by the IRA, then IPP will make the generalization that terrorist attacks in Britain are normally caused by the IRA.

The top-down approach of fulfilling prior expectations and selectively ignoring information not conforming to these expectations gives both systems a good deal of robustness. The main negative consequence is that unusual or unexpected information is often missed and not incorporated into a final memory representation of the story. This approach is adequate, however, for the task of extracting a sparse summary for stories.

1.5 In-Depth Understanding

In contrast to the text skimmers, BORIS attempts to understand narratives as deeply as possible. For BORIS, understanding a narrative "in-depth" means the following: 1) reading in a careful mode rather than skimming, 2) handling narratives which involve multiple interacting knowledge sources, 3) parsing text in an integrated fashion, where memory search and construction processes are evoked on a word-by-word basis, and 4) recognizing the key thematic patterns which characterize a narrative at very abstract levels.

Careful Reading -- BORIS reads each sentence (or phrase) in a left-to-right manner, without backing up over the text. Unlike skimmers, BORIS attempts to construct a complete representation of a narrative, including all physical events and mental states, along with the causal connections between them. As a result, BORIS operates in a very bottom-up manner. Processing is directed more from information arising in the input than from pre-determined expectations. Expectations in BORIS are encoded in the episodic memory of the narrative read thus far and are activated by search processes. This bottom-up approach gives BORIS the capability of noticing unusual events, which are often missed by exclusively top-down processing approaches. It is the unusual and unexpected events, including the mistakes and failures of the characters, which often make a story memorable. By their very nature, such events can not be predicted in a top-down manner.

Multiple Knowledge Domains -- Earlier systems at Yale were largely "dedicated" to handling one or two knowledge structures. MARGIE dealt with Conceptual Dependency structures, SAM with scripts, PAM with goals and plans, FRUMP with sketchy scripts, OPUS [Lehnert and Burstein, 1979] [Lehnert, 1979] with knowledge about object primitives, etc. However, no single program existed which was capable of handling stories involving the interactions of all these different sources of knowledge, including novel sources, such as the affective reactions of narrative characters.

An initial attempt to handle complicated narratives had been made by simply applying ELI, PAM and SAM in a "round robin" fashion. This approach failed because ELI, PAM, and SAM each operated in isolation from one another and each lacked knowledge about how various knowledge structures interacted.

Parsing Integration and Unification -- ELI parsed sentences in isolation and then passed them to SAM or PAM. As a result, any information in SAM or PAM which could have helped ELI in its parsing tasks remained unavailable. It does not appear that people process text in separate phases [Marslen-Wilson et al., 1978] [Tyler and Marslen-Wilson, 1977]. Instead, they perform memory manipulations and inference tasks on a word-by-word basis.

With the advent of FRUMP, parsing was integrated with other processes to the extent that sketchy scripts in FRUMP directed the parsing task. Since the creation of FRUMP other projects at Yale have stressed the notion of integrated processing.

BORIS is a highly integrated system. All memory search, instantiation, and inference tasks occur as side-effects of a single, unified parsing process which occurs on a word-by-word basis. Furthermore, narratives questions are parsed by the same processes which handle the narratives themselves. One natural consequence of this integration is that BORIS often knows the answer to a question before it has completely understood the question. Another natural consequence is a "Loftus Effect" for narratives [Loftus, 1979] [Loftus,

1975]. That is, asking a question about a narrative may cause the memory of the narrative to be altered.

Thematic Level of Analysis -- Understanding a narrative "in depth" involves recognizing the moral or point of a narrative. This is analogous to being able to characterize the theme of a narrative in some appropriate way, as in selecting an apt title or adage for it.

In BORIS, abstract thematic patterns, such as hypocrisy, are handled by memory structures called TAUs (Thematic Abstraction Units). These structures arise when expectation failures occur, causing episodes to be organized around errors in planning. As such, they contain an abstracted intentional structure, which represents situation-outcome patterns in terms of: the plan used, its intended effect, why it failed, and how to avoid (or recover) from that type of failure in the future. This information is often expressed in terms of an adage, such as "the pot calling the kettle black", and is abstracted from the specific content making up the episodes that each TAU organizes. This abstraction allows each TAU to organize episodes (which share the same failures in planning) across widely differing contexts. TAUs account for the phenomena of cross-contextual remindings, and serve as a way of sharing planning information in new domains.

1.6 Methodology, Scope, and Aims

As natural language programs tackle more complicated narratives, it becomes harder to characterize their domain of applicability. A simple metric, such as "this program correctly reads all stories 100 words or less in length" is unattainable. Therefore, it is important to briefly discuss the approach to natural language processing being taken in the BORIS project.

Psychological Validity -- Currently, people are the only examples of systems capable of understanding complicated narrative text. Therefore, BORIS tries to mimic the behavior exhibited by people who have performed the task of reading various narratives such as DIVORCE-1.

Specifically, subjects were asked to read a given narrative. After a short amount of time or an intervening task subjects were asked to answer questions about the narrative. Two weeks later they were asked to recall the narrative in as much detail as possible. Others subjects were given the opposite task of first recalling the narrative and then two weeks later answering questions about the narrative. This data was then used to guide program design decisions.

Experience with BORIS has also lead to a number of psychological experiments made concerning various knowledge structures used in BORIS [Lehnert and Robertson, 1981], [Lehnert, Black, Robertson, 1982], [Seifert, 1981]. These experiments lend support to approaches taken in BORIS and will be discussed later.

Generality -- Since BORIS is not a skimmer, but rather an in-depth understander, it is not practical to hook BORIS up to the UPI wire, as was done for FRUMP. It might be quite some time before a story appears on the UPI wire which contains interactions of the same knowledge structures utilized in BORIS. However, a program which only reads one story might be open to the criticism of being ad hoc.

To demonstrate that the principles embodied in BORIS are general, BORIS is able to understand stories which are different than DIVORCE-1, but yet involve the same kinds of knowledge structures. For example, BORIS was able to read DIVORCE-2 (below) without any additional knowledge than was needed for DIVORCE-1.

DIVORCE-2

George was having lunch with another teacher and grading homework assignments when the waitress accidentally knocked a glass of coke on him. George was very annoyed and left refusing to pay the check. He decided to drive home to get out of his wet clothes.

When he got there, he found his wife Ann and another man in bed. George became extremely upset and felt like going out and getting plastered.

At the bar he ran into an old college roommate David, who he hadn't seen in years. David offered to buy him a few drinks and soon they were both pretty drunk. When George found out that David was a lawyer, he told him all about his troubles and asked David to represent him in court. Since David owed George money he had never returned, he felt obligated to help out.

Later, David wrote to Ann, informing her that George wanted a divorce. Her lawyer called back and told David that she intended to get the house, the children and a lot of alimony. When George heard this, he was very worried. He didn't earn much at the junior high school. David told him not to worry, since the judge would award the case to George once he learned that Ann had been cheating on him.

When they got to court, David presented George's case, but without a witness they had no proof and Ann won. George almost had a fit. David could only offer George his condolences.

If one compares DIVORCE-1 and DIVORCE-2, it should be clear that they share many of the same knowledge structures. Both DIVORCE-1 and DIVORCE-2 make use of knowledge about divorce, lawyers, bedrooms, drinking, letters, phones, driving, friendship, etc. However, these two narratives also differ at many different levels: lexical, syntactic, semantic, and episodic.

Lexical/Syntactic Level

Different lexical phrases and syntactic constructs are used to describe similar events:

1. Spilling liquid:

> DIVORCE-1: Richard spilled a cup of coffee on Paul.

> DIVORCE-2:   ...the waitress accidentally knocked a glass of coke on him.

2. Discovering adultery:

> DIVORCE-1: When Richard walked into the bedroom and found Sarah with

another man...

DIVORCE-2:   He found his wife and
another man in bed.

Semantic Level

1. In DIVORCE-1, Richard learns that Paul needs a lawyer
after having read a letter from Paul. In DIVORCE-2, David learns
that George needs a lawyer after bumping into George at a bar. In
neither narrative is the reader told explicitly that the lawyer has
agreed to take the case. This fact must be inferred. In each story this
inference is evoked by a different event:

DIVORCE-1: Richard eagerly picked up the phone
and dialed.

DIVORCE-2: ...he felt obligated to help out.

2.   In both stories one character spills liquid on another.
However, the consequences are very different:

In DIVORCE-1 it is Richard who spills something
on Paul, thus causing Richard to drive Paul home.

In DIVORCE-2 it is the waitress who spills
something on George in DIVORCE-2, causing
George to refuse to pay the check and then drive
himself home.

Notice that it would make no sense in DIVORCE-1 for Paul to
refuse to pay the check. This is a result of the different social
relationships in each story between the spiller to the one being spilled
on.

Episodic Level

Both stories differ greatly in terms of the ordering and outcome
of events. For instance:

1. Discovering adultery:

In DIVORCE-1 Richard catches his

wife in bed at the end of the narrative.

In DIVORCE-2 George catches his wife toward the beginning of the narrative.

2. Emotional Responses:

In DIVORCE-1 Paul "almost has a heart attack" when he discovers his wife in bed.

In DIVORCE-2 George's "near fit" is the result, instead, of losing the divorce case.

3. Final Outcomes:

In DIVORCE-1 the husband wins although the characters never actually get to court.

In DIVORCE-2 the characters all appear in court and the husband loses.

It can be rather difficult to make up narratives which share exactly the same knowledge structures contained in DIVORCE-1, yet involve interestingly different interactions. Thus DIVORCE-2 both lacks some structures contained in DIVORCE-1 while containing some new knowledge not included in DIVORCE-1. Because of this, it was necessary to add some knowledge and processing rules to BORIS before DIVORCE-2 could be handled. Where the same knowledge structures are used, however, no changes were necessary.[3] Given the dramatic differences between these two narratives, the success of BORIS in handling both stories seems to indicate that BORIS has achieved a level of generality.

---

[3]For examples of BORIS answering questions concerning DIVORCE-2, see appendix sections I.5 and I.6.

1.7 A Guide to the Reader

The organization of this thesis is based on the assumption that a reader's attention diminishes through time. I've tried to construct this thesis so that the major points and larger brush strokes are made toward the beginning of the thesis, while the more detailed, minor brush strokes occur toward the end. In addition, each chapter contains a section discussing related work. This organization is appropriate in a broad-based thesis dealing with interactions among many sources of knowledge.

The thesis is divided into four major parts. Part I deals with the role of abstract themes in narratives: i.e. Chapter 2 presents TAUs, which both account for one class of cross-contextual remindings during narrative comprehension, and supply an abstract level at which narratives can be characterized in terms of planning situations involving expectation failures. Chapter 3 discusses a categorization scheme of planning metrics. This scheme provides the foundation for the recognition of a large class of TAUs. Finally, chapter 4 presents a system of AFFECT representation and processing, including a discussion of how TAUs and AFFECTs are related.

Part II examines issues of process integration and their consequences for memory retrieval during question answering: Chapter 5 compares the way BORIS parses text at narrative comprehension time with parsing at question understanding time, and the resulting effects on episodic memory. Chapter 6 contains an overview of how different knowledge sources in BORIS interact during comprehension along with an overview of processing control.

Part III deals with a number of specific knowledge structures used in BORIS: Chapter 7 presents a system of intentional links which are used to build up larger knowledge structures and discusses their role in answer retrieval. This chapter also introduces MOPs (Memory Organization Packets) [Schank, 1982a] and their role in knowledge representation. Chapter 8 compares MOPs with scripts and examines a number of related MOP structures, including CONTRACTs and LEGAL-DISPUTEs. Chapter 9 discusses the representation of space and time through the use of scenario mapping, while Chapter 10 deals with the role of the interpersonal level in narratives.

Part IV consists of an overview of what has been covered: Chapter 11 contains a detailed, annotated trace of BORIS reading DIVORCE-2, along with some sample question-answering and English generation traces. Finally, chapter 12 contains a summary of major claims, along with current BORIS limitations and a number of directions for future research.

The reader who wants an overview should read just Parts I, II, and the conclusions chapter. The reader who is interested in how specific knowledge structures were represented and applied in BORIS should also read chapters 7,8,9, and 10. Finally, those who want to know some of the nitty gritty concerning how everything came together can examine the annotated traces in chapter 11 of part IV. At the end of chapter 11 are included some program 'specs' concerning the current BORIS implementation.

Appendix I contains copies of various stories read by BORIS for easy reference, along with sample questions and answers generated by BORIS. The last section in appendix I lists the major memory structures currently implemented in BORIS.

Appendix II contains a brief discussion of Conceptual Dependency theory, including scripts, plans and goals. Readers totally unfamiliar with the Yale school of natural language processing can refer to this appendix in order to gain an initial introduction to the theoretical material upon which this dissertation was built.

Appendix III contains both a description and implementation of McDYPAR, a micro version of DYPAR (Dyer's Parser). McDYPAR is a demon-based conceptual analyzer written in TLISP, a dialect of LISP at Yale. In addition to implementation code, Appendix III includes a sample lexicon, sample execution trace, sample demon definitions, and a set of exercises for expanding the capabilities of McDYPAR.

PART I. RECOGNIZING NARRATIVE THEMES

There is more to understanding narratives in depth than being able to later answer questions of fact and causality. In-depth understanding entails recognizing what is interesting in a narrative; grasping the moral, point, or significance or a narrative; recognizing what makes it memorable -- including why, in the first place, it was a narrative worth telling. This deep level of analysis depends upon the recognition of thematic patterns in narratives. In this part of the thesis we present a class of thematic structures which are based upon abstract planning situations, and examine how such structures are recognized during narrative processing. We also explore the role of affect in narratives and its relationship to these thematic structures.

CHAPTER 2

Thematic Abstraction Units

2.1 Introduction

People often rely on common sayings or adages, when asked to summarize or title stories. Why do adages often serve as an effective way of characterizing a story? In this chapter we will present a memory construct, called a TAU, which serves as a basis for story characterization by means of cross contextual remindings and the recall of adages.

When asked to characterize the following story:

MINISTER'S COMPLAINT

In a lengthy interview, Reverend R severely criticized President Carter for having "denigrated the office of president" and "legitimized pornography" by agreeing to be interviewed in Playboy magazine. The interview with Reverend R appeared in Penthouse magazine.

readers often responded[4] with adages such as:

Adg-1: The pot calling the kettle black.
Adg-2: Throwing stones when you live in
a glass house.

Clearly, these adages are an effective characterization of MINISTER'S COMPLAINT. But how do we recognize this fact? By what process does an 'appropriate' adage come to mind, and to what purpose?

---

[4]Some of these responses were elicited in protocols. Other adages were generated spontaneously by subjects during summarization experiments.

Furthermore, when supplied with an adage and a context, some individuals experience remindings from episodes in their lives. For instance, one individual was first presented with the following:

context: EDUCATION

Adg-3: Closing the barn door after
the horse has escaped.

and then asked to recall some episode from his life. He experienced this reminding:

ACADEMIA

Years ago, I was at University U-1, where I could never get the facilities I needed for the research I wanted to do. So I decided to apply to University U-2, which offered a much better research environment. When the chairman learned I had been accepted to U-2 and was actually leaving U-1, he offered to acquire the facilities I had wanted. By then, however, my mind was already made up.

Several observations are worth making here: First, for adage Adg-3 to have initiated this reminding, the ACADEMIA episode must have somehow been indexed in long-term memory in terms of some abstract situation characterized by that adage. Furthermore, this indexing could not have had anything to do with the specific semantic content of the adage, since Adg-3 ostensibly concerns a farmer, a horse and a barn door. In contrast, ACADEMIA involves a chairman, a researcher, and university facilities.

To account for such phenomena, I will present a class of knowledge constructs, called TAUs (Thematic Abstraction Units), which share similarities with other representational systems under development at Yale, such as Schank's TOPs [Schank, 1980] and Lehnert's Plot Units [Lehnert, 1982a] [Lehnert, 1982b].

2.2 Thematic Abstraction Units

TAUs were first developed in the context of BORIS [Dyer, 1981b] [Lehnert, Dyer et al., 1982], where they serve a number of purposes: First, they allow BORIS to represent situations which are more abstract than those captured by scripts, plans, and goals as discussed in [Schank and Abelson, 1977]. Second, TAUs contain processing knowledge useful in dealing with the kinds of planning and expectation failures that characters often experience in narratives. Finally, TAUs also serve as episodic memory structures, since they organize events which involve similar kinds of planning failures.

In general, TAUs arise when expectation failures occur due to errors in planning. As such, they contain an abstracted planning structure, which represents situation-outcome patterns in terms of: (1) the plan used, (2) its intended effect, (3) why it failed, and (4) how to avoid (or recover) from that type of failure in the future. If we abstract out this planning structure from both the BARN-DOOR and ACADEMIA episodes, we get the following TAU:

TAU-POST-HOC

(1) x has preservation goal G active
   since enablement condition C unsatisfied.
(2) x knows a plan P that will keep G
   from failing by satisfying C.
(3) x does not execute P and G fails.
   x attempts to recover from the failure
   of G by executing P.
   P fails since P is effective for C,
   but not in recovering from G's failure.
(4) In the future, x must execute P when G
   is active and C is not satisfied.

(adage: Closing the barn door after the horse.)

TAU-POST-HOC captures the kind of planning failure that occurred for both the farmer who lost his horse, and the chairman who lost a graduate student. If the ACADEMIA story were told to an actual farmer who had lost his horse under the same planning circumstances, that farmer might well be reminded of his own experience. Whether this occurs or not, however, depends on what other episodes are in long-term memory and what features are shared between them. Notice, for instance, that both BARN-DOOR and ACADEMIA share goals at some level. That is, both the farmer and the chairman had a goal requiring proximity on the part of another entity. Since these features are shared, one experience has a better chance of causing a reminding of the other to occur. For instance, the farmer would have recalled the HIRED HAND episode below before recalling the BARN-DOOR episode because of their shared features:

HIRED HAND

The hired hand always wanted a raise, but the farmer would not grant it. Finally, the hired hand got an offer to work at a neighbor's farm. When the farmer found out, he offered the hired hand a nice raise, but it was too late.

Although these episodes (i.e. HIRED HAND, ACADEMIA, BARN-DOOR) share the same TAU, HIRED HAND and ACADEMIA have more indices in common. One possible organization for them appears below:

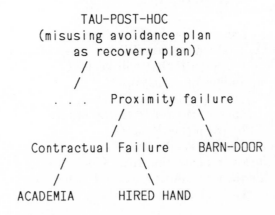

In this way TAUs can account for cross-contextual remindings (as in the case of BARN-DOOR and ACADEMIA).

Principle 1

```
+--------------------------------------------+
| TAUs organize   cross-contextual   episodes |
| which involve similar failures in planning. |
+--------------------------------------------+
```

Episodes are often related in memory because they share the same abstract planning error even though they differ in content. However, cross-contextual remindings can occur only where episodes are organized under the same TAU, yet do not share content features. Where content is shared, the "closer" episode will be recalled.[5] Consider the following episode:

IRANIAN EMBASSY

While holding 52 US hostages in Iran, the Iranian government condemned the take-over, by terrorists, of its embassy in Great Britain. "This is a violation of international law", protested Iran.

A reader was spontaneously reminded of this episode while reading MINISTER'S COMPLAINT (page 27). Again, there is little in common between these stories at the content level. IRANIAN EMBASSY is about politics, while MINISTER'S COMPAINT is about pornography. However, at the abstract planning level, they both share the following TAU:

---

[5]This does not imply that BARN-DOOR can't remind one of episodes unrelated to TAU-POST-HOC. Clearly, other indexing methods will be operating at the same time. The farmer may recall BARN-DOOR simply in terms of "experiences I have had with horses". Of course, this kind of indexing can not lead to cross-contextual remindings.

TAU-HYPOCRISY

x is counter-planning against y
x is trying to get a higher authority z to
    either block y's use of a plan P-1
    (or to punish y for having used P-1)
    by claiming that P-1 is an unethical plan
y claims that x has used an unethical plan P-2
    similar to P-1
therefore, x's strategy fails

(adage: "The pot calling the kettle black.")

In the case of MINISTER'S COMPLAINT, x is Reverend R, y is President Carter, and the third party is 'public opinion'. In the case of IRANIAN EMBASSY, x is the Iranian militants, y is the British terrorists, and the third party is 'world opinion', such as the United Nations.

As argued in [Schank, 1980], the reminding process is useful for the following reason: Once a situation has caused one to be reminded of an episode, all of the expectations associated with that episode become available for use in making predictions about what will occur next. In the case of TAUs, their associated expectations include advice on either how to avoid making the error predicted by the TAU, or on what alternative plan can be used to recover from the error once it has been made. The ability to store cross-contextual episodes make TAUs very general and powerful mechanisms. Once an episode has been indexed under a TAU, its recovery/avoidance heuristics become available for use in completely different situations. Thus, planning advice learned in one context can help processing in other contexts, if the experience was recognized in terms of an appropriate TAU in the first place.

2.3 Bad Planning is Widespread

An examination of adages reveals that many are concerned with planning failures. That is, adages advice us either how to recover from a failure, or how to recognize and thus avoid future failures. Often this advice is given implicitly, simply by describing situations in which certain planning errors lead to goal failures. In most cases, adages capture what has been called meta-planning [Wilensky, 1980a] -- i.e. planning advice on how to select or use plans in general. For example, some adages deal with the need for checking enablement conditions before plan execution:

> Adg-4: Don't count your chickens
> before they're hatched.

Other adages stress choosing less costly avoidance plans over more costly recovery plans:

> Adg-5: A stitch in time saves nine.

or weighing the risks involved with the goal to be achieved:

> Adg-6: If it ain't broke, don't fix it.
> Adg-7: The cure can be worse than the disease.

Many plans require cooperation or coordination with others. This can simplify planning but complicate plan execution:

> Adg-8: Two heads are better than one.
> Adg-9: Too many cooks spoil the broth.

Some plans involve selecting an appropriate agent:

> Adg-10: The blind leading the blind.
> Adg-11: Who pays the piper calls the tune.

Timing, enablement conditions, cost, plan coordinations, and agents are just a few of the areas in which plans can go wrong. Other areas, for example, include counter-planning against a foe,

> Adg-12: Cut off your nose to spite your face.

anticipating planning failures when using high risk plans,

> Adg-13: Don't burn bridges behind you.

the timing of plans,

Adg-14: The early bird catches the worm.

and tradeoffs between short-term and long-term planning strategies:

Adg-15: If you can't lick 'em join 'em.
Adg-16: Don't bite the hand that feeds you.
Adg-17: Honesty is the best policy.
Adg-18: Live by the sword, die by the sword.

Any story that involves these kinds of planning failures will end up being indexed under a TAU which contains abstract planning advice (and can often be expressed in natural language by an adage.) When a related story is read and indexed under that TAU, its associated adage may come to mind. For instance, a story about how a ghetto riot protesting bad economic conditions resulted in black businesses being burned, would be indexed under TAU-GREATER-HARM,[6] with an adage such as Adg-12 above possibly coming to mind.

Principle 2

```
+-------------------------------------+
| TAUs are characterized  by adages,  |
| which provide planning information  |
+-------------------------------------+
```


Plans and plan failures cut across all knowledge domains. This is because we are always choosing plans, adjusting old plans to new situations, recovering from errors in planning, finding explanations for why a plan failed, etc. Furthermore, we have a large storehouse of heuristic plans, and there are many ways a plan can go wrong: You can't execute one plan until you have the right enablements satisfied; plan components must be executed in the right order; plans require agents, etc. This large and complex domain serves as a perfect terrain in which to index many episodes.

---

[6]TAU-GREATER-HARM is described more fully in the next chapter.

Many of these adages give what may appear to be superficial advice. It may seem strange that memories should be organized around such 'obvious' rules for planning, but then again, how often do we fail in our plans because we have violated some adage? How often, for instance, have we failed because we acted before we planned? ("Look before you leap.") How many times have we gotten into trouble for being late? When have we initiated a plan, only to discover we had miscalculated the amount of effort or the side-effects involved? ("Easier said than done.") How often have we delayed executing a simple plan, only later having to execute a more costly plan? The answer is: "very often". These adages are common because they point out the kinds of planning errors people are always making. By definition, plans which failed were "bad" plans. Good planners at the very least follow the general planning advice represented in the adages of their culture.

2.4 TAU Implementation

The implementation of TAUs in BORIS has lead to the following kinds of questions: How do TAUs function during story understanding? Specifically, what aspects of narratives do TAUs serve to represent and how are TAUs recognized while a narrative is being read? Furthermore, once TAUs are instantiated in episodic memory, what connections exist between them and other knowledge structures, and how and when are TAUs searched?

I will address these questions in the context of DIVORCE-1, which contains a number of TAUs:

2.4.1 TAU-DIRE-STRAITS

In DIVORCE-1 the following situation occurs: Richard, a lawyer, receives a letter from an old friend Paul. Paul's wife Ann is divorcing him and Paul is very worried that he will lose his house and children. At this point, DIVORCE-1 reads:

> Not knowing who to turn to, he [Paul] was hoping
> for a favor from the only lawyer he knew. Paul
> gave his home phone number in case Richard felt he

could help.

Richard eagerly picked up the phone and dialed. After a brief conversation, Paul agreed to have lunch with him the next day.   He sounded extremely relieved and grateful. ...

In order to process these paragraphs, the BORIS program accesses a TAU called TAU-DIRE-STRAITS, which contains the following pattern:

TAU-DIRE-STRAITS

x has a crisis goal G.
x has experienced a planning failure
  (i.e. x can't resolve the crisis by himself).
x seeks a friend y to be his agent
  (since y knows what plans to execute).

(adage: "A friend in need is a friend indeed.")

In addition, TAU-DIRE-STRAITS contains the following affective expectations:

x is uncertain whether x
  will be able to help.
If y agrees to help
  Then x will have a positive
    affect toward y
  Else x will have a negative
    affect (possibly toward y).

Using TAU-DIRE-STRAITS, BORIS is able to parse, represent, and connect up these story fragments:

Not knowing who to turn to... the only lawyer he knew... in case Richard felt he could help...   He sounded extremely relieved and grateful.

In addition, it is relatively easy for BORIS to determine that the pronoun in:

He sounded extremely relieved and grateful.

refers to Paul rather than to Richard. BORIS does this by using its knowledge about the meanings of "relieved" and "grateful" in the context of the affective predictions arising from TAU-DIRE-STRAITS.[7]

2.4.2 TAU-CLOSE-CALL

Consider the situation which arises in paragraph four of DIVORCE-1:

> ... as Richard was driving to the restaurant he barely avoided hitting an old man on the street. He felt extremely upset by the incident, and ...

Since Richard did not actually hit the old man, at first glance we might be tempted to represent this non-event in Conceptual Dependency as:

```
                        o              +-> old man
    Richard <=/=> PROPEL <---VEHICLE <--|
                                       +-< unknown
```

Here $<=/=>$ indicates a negative 'mode' associated with the primitive act of PROPEL. However, this is inadequate since the inferences arising from such a mode are very different than those in DIVORCE-1. Consider the following situation:

> ST-1:   Richard did not run over an old man.
> Richard was very upset.

This situation is also represented by the same Conceptual Dependency diagram shown above. However, people who read ST-1

---

[7]The representation and processing of affects and their relationship to TAUs is discussed in detail in chapter 4.

get the impression that Richard intended to kill the old man, but then something went wrong. Thus, Richard's intentional state is important. Compare this to the following passage:

> ST-2: Richard was driving to a restaurant and **barely avoided** stopping at a Baskin Robins. He felt extremely upset by this.

ST-2 sounds odd because Richard can stop at a Baskin Robins anytime simply by an act of volition. In order to 'make sense' of this situation people have to postulate outlandish circumstances, such as Richard being obese and having trouble staying on a diet.

In order to represent Richard's highway experience in DIVORCE-1, BORIS uses a knowledge structure called TAU-CLOSE-CALL. It has the following structure:

> TAU-CLOSE-CALL
>
> x experiences a major
>   preservation goal G.
> G was caused by an event
>   not intended by x.
> G turns out to be 'fleeting'
>   (so a recovery plan P is not needed).
>
> (adage: "Miss by an inch as good as a mile.")

In addition, TAU-CLOSE-CALL contains the following affect information:

> x feels surprised
> (since the event was unintended).
> x feels fear/worry
> (since the event motivates a
>   major preservation goal).
> x feels relief and residual tension
> (since the goal turns out to be
>   fleeting).

BORIS uses TAU-CLOSE-CALL both to instantiate VEHICLE-ACCIDENT (without erroneously representing the accident as having actually occurred) and to connect the fleeting PRESERVE-HEALTH goal with Richard's negative affect. These connections are then used later to answer the question:

> Q1: What **almost** happened to Richard
>   on the way to the restaurant?
> A1: He nearly ran over an old man.

which is distinct from question Q2:

> Q2: What **didn't** happen to Richard
>   on the way to the restaurant?
> A2: Richard wasn't kidnapped by Martians.

It is clear from these examples that "almost happened" can not be semantically processed in the appropriate way without the corresponding TAU.

2.4.3 TAU-REG-MISTAKE

At the restaurant, the following situation occurs:

> Richard spilled a cup of coffee on Paul. Paul seemed very annoyed by this so Richard offered to drive him home for a change of clothes.

In order to understand why Richard makes this offer to Paul, BORIS must know many mundane facts, including:

> What "spilling" means.
> How liquids affect clothes.
> That people don't like to be uncomfortable.
> Where clothes are kept.
> Etc.

In addition to these facts, BORIS must also be able to figure out how both Paul and Richard may feel about this incident, and what kind of response each may make. Again, Richard's intentional state is important. Consider the following alternate versions:

V-1:   Richard picked up a cup of coffee and deliberately poured it over Paul's head.   Richard felt embarrassed.

V-2: Richard spilled coffee on Paul. Paul was very annoyed, so Richard bought himself another cup.

Neither version makes sense. In V-1, Richard performed the action intentionally, while in V-2 Richard's response was designed to achieve his own goals, rather than Paul's goals. Clearly, these passages make little sense because they violate our expectations regarding how people will respond when a goal violation occurs.

To capture these expectations, BORIS employs a knowledge structure called TAU-REG-MISTAKE, which contains the following information:

TAU-REG-MISTAKE

x (the schlemiel) causes
  an unintended event E.
E motivates a preservation
  goal G on the part
  of y (the schlimazel).
If x and y have a positive
  interpersonal relationship,
Then x is motivated to serve as an
  agent for y in recovering G.

In addition, TAU-REG-MISTAKE also possesses the following affective expectations:

If x and y have a positive
  interpersonal relationship
Then x will feel regret, guilty,
  embarrassment, etc.
y will feel upset and angry at x.

When BORIS realizes that Richard has inadvertently caused a PRESERVE-COMFORT goal on the part of Paul, it activates TAU-REG-MISTAKE.   This structure predicts that Richard will do something to help Paul recover this goal. Since driving home achieves an enablement condition on changing clothes, Richard's offer is connected to the 'spill-mistake' bound to TAU-REG-MISTAKE. This can then be accessed to answer the question:

Q2: Why did Richard offer to drive Paul home?
A2: Richard had spilled coffee on Paul's clothes.

2.4.4 TAU-RED-HANDED

When Paul arrives at home to change his clothes, he discovers his wife in bed with another man. BORIS uses setting information associated with BEDROOMs to infer that Sarah is having sex with another man. Sexual involvement causes BORIS to check relationship information. At this point BORIS determines that Sarah is violating the marriage contract.[8]   However, there is more to this passage than the recognition that Sarah has been committing adultery. Paul has walked in on Sarah right in the middle of the act. We expect shock on the part of Paul, followed by anger. From Sarah's point of view, we expect surprise, embarrassment, and possibly feelings of guilt.

These affective expectations are represented in TAU-RED-HANDED, which also contains the following information:

TAU-RED-HANDED

x is committing a violation V
   of a contract (between x and y,
   where y may be society)
x requires secrecy to achieve V
y directly ATTENDs (eyes or ears) to V
x suffers a goal failure
   with respect to V
x and y now have an explicit
   goal conflict (where y may
   retaliate)

(adage: "Caught red-handed.")

---

[8]Settings are treated in chapter 9 while contracts are discussed in chapter 8.

Once BORIS has inferred that Sarah has committed a violation, it checks to see if the other partner in the contract is aware of the violation. If this character has discovered the violation directly, then BORIS activates TAU-RED-HANDED. Now the affective knowledge associated with TAU-RED-HANDED is used to disambiguate the segment highlighted below:

> When Paul walked into the bedroom and found Sarah with another man **he nearly had a heart attack.**

as meaning surprise rather than cardiac arrest.

TAUs are useful, not only because they provide a representation for situations which arise, but also because they are accessed by processes associated with other knowledge structures. Consider the following question:

> Q1: Why did Paul think he had won the case?
> A1: Because he had caught Sarah committing adultery.

Answering this question involves a considerable amount of knowledge about judges and what influences their decisions. For example, to apply the following rules of jurisprudence,[9]   processes will search to see if TAU-RED-HANDED is active.

> rr1: If x and y are engaged in a contract
>   and the judge has proof that
>   x violated the contract,
>   Then the judge will award the case to y.

> rr2: If y wants to prove that
>   x has violated a contract,
>   Then a witness to the violation
>   is a good form of evidence.

---

[9]Legal reasoning is discussed in section 8.6.4.

Thus, Paul thinks he will win because TAU-RED-HANDED supplies to the judge proof that Sarah has violated the marriage contract.

2.4.5 TAU-HIDDEN-BLESSING

After Paul catches Sarah, the story reads:

> Then he realized what a blessing it was. With Richard there as a witness, Sarah's divorce case was shot.

This passage is handled by BORIS with the aid of TAU-HIDDEN-BLESSING. It contains the following information:

> ### TAU-HIDDEN-BLESSING
>
> x experiences a goal failure, caused
>   by an event E.
> x has a realization (i.e. an MBUILD in
>   Conceptual Dependency notation)
>   that E also enables (or causes)
>   another goal to succeed.
>
> (adage: "Every cloud has a silver lining.")

When BORIS reads that Paul has realized Sarah's adultery is a "blessing", it activates TAU-HIDDEN-BLESSING. This knowledge structure expects to hear of a goal that has been achieved by the same event which caused a prior goal failure. So, when BORIS hears that Sarah's divorce case "was shot", it examines Sarah's goal failure to see if this implies a goal success for Paul. If a goal failure for Paul had followed the episode involving adultery, then BORIS would have been confused. Consider:

> Then Fred realized what a blessing his wife's death was. Now Fred could kill himself.

Here, people's expectations for a goal success are strong enough that they imagine scenarios in which Fred's suicide achieved some goal of Fred (e.g. Fred is a terminal cancer patient in great pain, who has been staying alive to take care of his invalid wife).

TAU-HIDDEN-BLESSING also has the following affective expectations:

First, x feels negative affects.
Then, x feels positive affects.

This information is used to answer questions which presume that a character feels positively about an event which has thwarted that character's goal:

Q2: Why was Paul happy that Sarah
     was cheating on him?
A2: He realized that Sarah's divorce
     case was shot.

2.4.6 Searching TAUs During QA

Since TAUs arise in situations where deviations have occurred, they tend to refer to the more interesting events in stories. BORIS makes use of this fact during question answering. For example, BORIS interprets the question: "What happened at SETTING?" as: "What interesting event occurred at SETTING?". In order to answer this question, BORIS first searches for TAUs associated with the specified setting. Therefore, the question:

Q3: What happened at the restaurant?

will be answered with:

A3a: Richard spilled a cup of coffee on Paul.

rather than with:

A3b: Richard and Paul talked about the case.

Likewise,

Q4: What did Richard do on the way
     to the restaurant?

will be answered with:

A4a: He almost ran over an old man.

rather than:

A4b: He drove a car.

2.5 Recognizing TAUs: An Overview

In order for BORIS to use TAUs in constructing an episodic memory of a narrative, BORIS must be able to recognize TAU-related situations when they occur. In this section we present an overview of the issues involved in recognizing TAUs. In the next chapter, a recognition scheme for TAUs based on expectation failures and planning errors will be discussed in greater detail.

In general, the recognition of TAUs is complex because they can not be processed in a predictive fashion (i.e. relying on prior expectations). This is because TAUs represent unusual and/or idiosyncratic situations. For instance, consider the recognition TAU-RED-HANDED. This construct represents the situation in which a character's plan fails during its execution because the plan required secrecy and its execution has been observed by another individual.

In DIVORCE-1, BORIS must first infer from the context that Sarah is committing a violation. To do so, BORIS uses the following rules:

cr1: If x has sexual contact with y
        and x is involved in a marital
        contract with z
     Then infer a contractual violation
        of the "sexual fidelity rule"
        in the marriage contract

cr2: If x has violated the rule of a contract
        between x and y
     Then check to see if y is aware of
        the violation.

Sometimes, however, the lexical items themselves cause TAU-RED-HANDED to be activated. Consider the following:

John caught Billy using the typewriter.

Here, the word "caught" activates the information associated with TAU-RED-HANDED, and many people find themselves inventing a scenario in which Billy is John's son, who was forbidden to play with his father's expensive typewriter. Other terms (especially those referring to affects) may also activate TAUs directly. For example, "guilty" also causes TAU-RED-HANDED to be checked.

TAU-DIRE-STRAITS is also idiosyncratic, since it represents the situation of being in trouble and having a friend come to the rescue when no one else will help. Such situations can not be predicted ahead of time. Thus, TAUs must be recognized in a very 'bottom-up' fashion. This means that the recognition of a TAU must occur as a natural consequence of tracking those aspects of a narrative which make up many of the key features which cause TAUs to be accessed.

What are some of the key features which comprise TAUs? Clearly, plans are important. Almost every event in a narrative involves both the plans and goals of a character, but not every event gives rise to a TAU. If TAUs are to be accessed, other aspects must be monitored as well.

For one thing TAUs have a strong affective component. The characters concerned experience strong emotions, such as: guilt, jealousy, anger, fear, relief, etc. For instance, in TAU-POST-HOC it is the futility of the recovery plan, combined with the feeling of "if only I had done things differently" that helps provide an access "key" to this TAU. A sudden change in affect may also indicate the presence of a TAU. In TAU-HIDDEN-BLESSING, for instance, the character experiences a strong negative affect followed immediately by a strong positive affect. More will be said about the relationship between TAUs and affects in chapter 4.

In addition, people store TAUs very differently in their memories, depending on their point of view. For example, being the schlimazel in TAU-REG-MISTAKE is a different experience than being the schlemiel. Likewise, the person caught 'red handed' will index that episode differently than than the individual who came upon him.

Finally, the intentionality of the character involved constitutes an important access key. In most TAUs, the character has experienced an expectation violation: the event that occurred was not intended by the character. This can happen in several ways. In TAU-REG-MISTAKE, a character simply performs an action that was accidental. Accidents often lead to goal failures, and for this reason, accidents are inherently interesting. Likewise, TAU-CLOSE-CALL arises from accidental circumstances.

Goals may be achieved unintentionally. A character may have intended to achieve a goal by means of one plan, only to have it achieved in an unanticipated way. This happens in TAU-HIDDEN-BLESSING, where a goal failure turns out to achieve another goal in a fortuitous manner.

In addition, goals thought to have been achieved may actually fail. In such cases we have violations of beliefs (i.e. expectations about either future or past events). For example, suppose that DIVORCE-1 had ended in the following way:

NEW PAINT

Paul was so sure that he would win the divorce case that he went ahead and had the entire house painted. However, when he got to court, the judge awarded the house and a lot of alimony to Sarah. Was Paul upset!

This situation is captured by the following TAU:

TAU-UNSUPPORTED-PLAN

x has a goal G1
x formulates plan P1 to achieve G1
x believes that P1 will succeed
 so X initiates plan P2 for achieving G2
 based on the belief that G1 has been
 (or will be) achieved
G1 fails, since P2 depended on G1
 P2 fails and therefore G2 also fails

(Adages:

Don't cross bridges until you come to them.

Don't count your chickens before their hatched.)

In this case, a character experiences a goal failure because he executed a plan based on a false expectation. Therefore, in order to recognize TAUs, the reasons for why plans have failed must be examined. This examination of the cause of a failure is central to the recognition of the appropriate TAU. For each kind of planning failure there is an associated TAU, whether or not there exists an adage to characterize it.

Thus, some of the key components used in recognizing TAUs are: (1) fortuitous goal achievements or goal failures, (2) violations of expectations or beliefs, (3) strong affective reactions, (4) accidental or unintended actions, and (5) and examination of the reasons for plan failures. In the next chapter, a recognition scheme for TAUs based on expectation failures and planning errors will be discussed in more detail.

2.5.1 Tracking the Reasons Plans Fail

Whenever a story is being read, the goals and plans of the characters must be constantly monitored. Whenever a plan is chosen, the reader judges the plan in terms of its likelihood of success. Consider the following story:

DRUNK AND LAMPPOST

A drunk was looking for his lost keys under a lamp post. When asked where he had lost them, he pointed to a location in the darkness. When asked why he was looking here, the drunk replied: "This is where the light is."

This story is memorable because of the bad planning it contains. If we analyze the story at the goal/plan level, we find the following kind of structure:

```
Goal G1 = Drunk wants to sleep.
  |
Plan P1 = Go to bed.
  |
Goal G2 = Drunk wants to enter his home.
  |
Plan P2 = Use keys to unlock door.
  |
xxx <---- BLOCKED-BY keys lost in LOC1
  |
Goal G3 = Obtain keys.
  |
Plan P3 = SEARCH (ATTEND eyes to LOC1)
  |  |
  |  |
  |  Goal G4 = Be at LOC1
  |
xxx <---- BLOCKED-BY lack of light
  |
Goal G5 = Get light
```

The drunk could have chosen a reasonable plan associated with a goal at any other level and the story would have turned out 'normal'. Below are different possible stories, each depending on a plan chosen to achieve a goal at each different level:

```
At G1 level:

    The drunk lost his  keys in the dark.
    So he went to sleep in the park.

At G2 level:

    The drunk lost his keys in the dark.
    So he crawled in through the window.

At G3 level:

    The drunk lost his keys in the dark.
    So he went to a locksmith.
```

```
At G4 level:

    The drunk lost his keys in the dark.
    So he borrowed a flashlight from a neighbor.
```

However, the drunk chose a plan to achieve 'get light' which simultaneously blocked the already achieved goal G4 of 'be at LOC1'. Now if the drunk realizes this and goes back to LOC1, he will have unblocked the proximity condition G4 only to have re-blocked the lighting condition G5.[10]

The advice implicitly mentioned in the DRUNK AND LAMPPOST is:

> Don't choose a plan (needed to unblock one enablement condition) which will automatically block another (already satisfied) enablement condition.

There is no common adage for this (that I'm aware of), yet this is a TAU nonetheless. Anyone who reads a story involving this type of planning error, and who knows the DRUNK AND LAMPPOST story, will be reminded of it. This is especially true if the story being read uses the plan of SEARCH.

The important point is that unless the plans are being tracked, this TAU could not be accessed, and the point of the story would have been lost. We would only know that the drunk had a goal failure, but not why. Why he did is the point of the DRUNK AND LAMPPOST story [Schank, 1982b].

---

[10]This situation is analogous to a similar error in planning which Sussman's HACKER [Sussman, 1975] made while stacking blocks. In both cases, a form of 'thrashing' occurs because the achievement of one enablement condition simultaneously blocks another enablement condition.

2.5.2 Capturing the Point of a Story

So far the BORIS project has emphasized the use of TAUs in narrative comprehension. Much work remains to be done in modeling remindings during comprehension. This is important for extracting the 'moral' or point of a story. A computer program which can only answer questions of fact about IRANIAN EMBASSY (on page 31), such as:

Q: How many Americans are being held in Iran?
A: Fifty-two.

Q: Who seized the Iranian embassy in Britain?
A: Terrorists.

Q: What did the Iranians do?
A: They protested the take-over.

is missing the point of why the IRANIAN EMBASSY is of interest. The point of IRANIAN EMBASSY is TAU-HYPOCRISY, and that's where it should be remembered in long-term memory, rather than just under "things I know about Iran" or "embassy events I have read".

Principle 3

```
+--------------------------------------+
| TAUs   represent one   kind of story |
| point   and   account for what makes |
| some narratives memorable.           |
+--------------------------------------+
```

Actually, there is no such thing as 'the' moral of a story when the story is complex. Stories have many morals, each one arising from an expectation failure which gives rise to a TAU that then serves as an index into memory. Consider the following narrative:

JOB TROUBLES

Fred had a good-paying job but he wanted even more money. He lied to his boss about the amount of work he had done, hoping to get a raise. His boss found out he had lied and got mad. Fred told his boss to go to hell, so his boss fired him.

Nobody would hire Fred because of his bad reputation, so Fred became very poor. He was desperate. He pleaded with his friend Wayne to help him find a new job. Wayne used his influence to obtain a good job for Fred. But once Fred had a secure job, he then completely snubbed Wayne.

JOB TROUBLES contains a number of TAUs; therefore, it can be characterized by a number of adages. Some of these appear below:

1. Honesty is the best policy.
2. Don't bite the hand that feeds you.
3. A friend in need is a friend indeed.
4. Once you've outlived your usefulness,
   you're discarded.

Any one of these can serve as a point or moral of JOB TROUBLES. Thus, JOB TROUBLES will be remembered in terms of the TAUs characterized by these morals. One consequence of this is that narratives with many TAUs will be more interesting and better remembered than narratives containing none or only a few TAUs.

2.6 TAU Experiments

What is the psychological validity of TAUs? Do people have TAUs "in their heads" and, if so, how do they use them? Some initial exploratory experiments [Seifert, 1981] [Seifert et al., 1982] indicate that people use TAUs both to organize and comprehend narratives.

In one experiment [Seifert, 1981], subjects read groups of stories each sharing the same TAU, but differing in content. Subjects were able to generate new stories, using completely different contexts, yet capturing the same planning structure specified by each TAU.

In a follow-up experiment, different subjects were asked to sort the resulting stories generated from the first experiment. A cluster analysis [Johnson, 1967] revealed a strong tendency for subjects to sort stories together by TAUs. Where stories shared the same content (but not the same TAUs) they were still sorted by TAUs (rather than by content).

Specifically, eight subjects (group G1) were asked to read three stories, each of which had been written to illustrate a different TAU, appearing below. Each is illustrated here only by an appropriate adage:

1. TAU-HYPOCRISY (The pot calling the kettle black.)

2. TAU-INCOMPETENT-AGENT (The blind leading the blind.)

3. TAU-UNSUPPORTED-PLAN (Counting chickens before they're hatched.)

Each subject was then asked to generate (for each story read) a novel story containing a similar structure. The twenty-four stories generated by this scheme were then presented to another group (G2) of twenty subjects. The novel stories appeared in any one of four different random orders. Each subject in group G2 was asked to sort these stories into groups with "similar plots". Subjects were not told how many groups to form, but a guideline of 2 to 6 groups was suggested.

A hierarchical clustering analysis [Johnson, 1967] revealed how strongly related were pairs of stories. This analysis produced three clearly defined clusters, each corresponding to a specific TAU. Furthermore, every pair of stories within a given cluster had been sorted together by a minimum of at least nine subjects. Examples of the stories generated by subjects from group G1 are presented below:

TAU-HYPOCRISY

Story-5: Mark always complained about how unfair it was to others in the class when someone cheated on exams. When his physics class had their next exam, Mark 'checked' his answers with those of the person next to him.

TAU-INCOMPETENT-AGENT

Story-16:   Richard was anxious to get a teaching job. However, his friend (who was still out of work) told him don't be anxious to take the first job offered. Rich had one job offered him. He refused. He never got offered another teaching job and had to be placed on welfare.

TAU-UNSUPPORTED-PLAN

Story-21:   Paul had just completed his interview for a position as an orderly in a nearby hospital. He was so encouraged by the interview that he went out and bought an orderly uniform. The next day he received a phone call saying that he had not been selected for the position.

In some cases, stories containing different TAUs shared similar contexts. Certain stories, for instance, described school situations; other stories dealt with crimes; others involved sports, etc. Notice that Story-16 and Story-21 above each involve job hunting. As a result, they could have been grouped together. However, when two stories shared similar content, but differed according to their TAUs, subjects systematically sorted the stories into groups by shared TAUs.

As a result of this initial experiment, it appears that subjects are able to both generate and recognize stories which share the same kind of abstract thematic units, irrespective of story content.

2.7 Comparison With Related Work On High Level Structures

We have stated that TAUs capture one class of themes -- i.e. those involving errors in planning. What other classes of knowledge exist at the thematic level? Are TAUs as abstract as one can get? What other thematic patterns and processes might be invoked during comprehension?

A number of other researchers have also been working on high level knowledge structures and examining their role in both planning and comprehension. Related research is briefly discussed below, where it is compared with TAUs.

2.7.1 TAUs and TOPs

One researcher concerned with the issue of cross-contextual remindings and its relationship to thematic knowledge is Schank [Schank, 1982b], who has developed a theory of TOPs (Thematic Organization Packets). TOPs are defined in terms of goal situations and appear to be even more abstract than TAUs. For example, both "Romeo and Juliet" and "West Side Story" share as a common theme the TOP of MG;OO, which stands for the situation of "Mutual Goal; Outside Opposition". One of the reasons people are reminded of "Romeo and Juliet" when they read (or view) "West Side Story" is that both are indexed by the same TOP.

Another example of a TOP is PG;EI ("Possessive Goal; Evil Intentions"). PG;EI captures the notion of someone gradually taking more and more control of some object while claiming to be satisfied with each new acquisition. The theme of PG;EI is exemplified in Hitler taking country after country before World War II. However, PG;EI is not restricted to political imperialism, but may occur in other contexts, such as sports, education, interpersonal relationships, etc. For instance, the escalating demands of a blackmailer are also captured by PG;EI.

TOPs and TAUs share a number of features. They both serve to index cross-contextual episodes in memory. In addition, both structures involve expectation failures. However, there are a number of differences between TOPs and TAUs. The main differences are ones of abstraction and emphasis. TOPs are intended to represent goal interactions. Furthermore TOPs appear to be even more abstract than TAUs and are designed to be the highest indexing scheme in memory. As a result, only a limited number of TOPs are supposed to exist. In contrast, since people employ a very extensive system of planning information, there exist a great number of TAUs in memory, one for each type of planning error. In fact, TAUS appear to serve as an indexing scheme used by TOPs. So the relationship of TOPs to TAUs is analogous to that between goals and plans.

For instance, while the goal situation of "Romeo and Juliet" is captured at the most abstract level by MG;OO, there exist other themes at the planning-failure level. One such theme is represented by TAU-ALLIED-DECEPTION, which among other things contains the following planning advice:

> If you're counter-planning with plan P
>   involving DECEPTION (i.e. MTRANSing
>   false information) against your foes
> Then be sure that you do not deceive
>   any of your allies with plan P
>   (by informing your allies of P
>   before P is executed).

TAU-ALLIED-DECEPTION arises in "Romeo and Juliet" when Juliet chooses to fool her opponents with a false report of her death. However, she fails to make sure that her ally Romeo will not also by fooled by the same false report. As a result, she deceives Romeo also.

Just as different plans may be used to achieve the same goal, different TAUs may index distinct TOPs. For instance, the theme of imperialism, represented by PG-EI, commonly includes a TAU component, represented by TAU-APPEASEMENT. This TAU is characterized by the following adage:

> Adg: Give 'em an inch and they'll take a mile.

At first glance it may appear that TAU-APPEASEMENT must always be associated with the goal of recurring acquisition of physical possessions, as desired by the imperialist. However, consider the following story:

PHILANDERER

> Each time Betty caught John with another woman,
> he promised he'd be true, so Betty forgave him.

Here, Betty is experiencing a planning failure because she is using a plan involving appeasement. This plan is reasonable when executed for the first time. However, once it has failed, it's subsequent use is foolish. Thus, TAU-APPEASEMENT characterizes the theme of PHILANDERER even though John's goal does not involve gaining control of objects possessed by Betty (as characterized in PG;EI).

A strict division between TOPs and TAUs is impossible to

maintain because goals and plans can't really be treated separately. Plans can not be discussed in complete isolation from the goals they are intended to achieve. Likewise, goals can not be discussed without regard to the kinds of plans they give rise to. As a result, there will be some overlap between the thematic situations which both TOPs and TAUs attempt to capture.

2.7.2 TAUs and Meta-Planning

Since TAUs carry advice about how to avoid (or recover) from planning errors in general, TAUs may be characterized as containing meta-planning information. Recently, Wilensky [Wilensky, 1980a] has argued for the need of a meta-planner which would know how to select plans, how to coordinate plans, etc. An example of a Wilensky meta-plan is GOAL-PIGGY-BACKING, in which plan P1 is chosen over plan P2 if P1 can achieve more than one active goal simultaneously. Notice that GOAL-PIGGY-BACKING may be characterized by the adage:

Adg: Killing two birds with one stone.

Like the theory of TAUs, Wilensky's meta-planning system contains advice on forming alliances, computing the cost of various plans, etc. However, TAUs and meta-planning differ in the perspective that each takes.

Wilensky approaches narrative comprehension from a problem-solving perspective. He views understanding narratives in terms of a problem solver which can choose an appropriate plan to achieve a goal without experiencing failure [Wilensky, 1980a]. In contrast, TAUs were arrived at by noticing that story readers often characterize stories in terms of adages, and that the same characterization would often be made for stories involving completely different contexts. TAUs take their inspiration from Schank's work on TOPs, cross-contextual remindings, and failure-driven memory [Schank, 1982b] [Schank, 1982a].

Schank has argued that episodic memory is organized, not around planning successes, but rather around their failures [Schank, 1981]. Learning occurs only where failures have occurred. TAUs are more often characterized by adages which describe situations involving failures rather than successes. Consider TAU-POST-HOC which contains the adage: "Closing the barn door after the horse has escaped." This adage characterizes a situation in which a failure has occurred. In contrast, "Killing two birds with one stone" (in GOAL-PIGGY-BACKING) refers to a situation in which one has planned successfully.

Of course, positive and negative advice are simply two sides of the same coin. One becomes a successful planner by both a) following good meta-planning practice and b) avoiding past meta-planning errors. The theories of both TOPs and TAUs claim that memory is organized around remembering failures rather than remembering successes. If a success has occurred, then nothing new has to be built in memory because successful plans can be reconstructed from general meta-planning and planning information. In contrast, failed plans will be of interest since they can not be reconstructed from general meta-planning knowledge.[11]   Associated with a failed plan will be an episode in memory. When a planning error occurs, remindings are experienced. Therefore, the theories of TOPs and TAUs emphasize the organization of episodes in memory as a result of planning, while Wilensky's meta-planning theory emphasizes the way in which plans are formulated and executed in the first place. Clearly, all of these approaches are complementary.

2.7.3 TAUs and Plot-Units

Another theory involving high-level knowledge structures is the system of Plot Units developed by Lehnert [Lehnert, 1982a]. Examples of Plot Units are: RETALIATION, COERCED AGREEMENT, HONORED REQUEST, and FORTUITOUS PROBLEM RESOLUTION.   Plot Units are also abstract representational structures because they deal not with specific goals, plans, and events, but rather with the general effect of events on the mental states of characters. Instead of containing specific goals and plans, Plot Units are made up of configurations of positive events (+), negative events (-), and mental states (M).   For instance,

---

[11]Schank is not the first to emphasize the importance of failures in planning. For instance, Sussman's HACKER program [Sussman, 1975] used its mistakes as a basis for improved planning. However, it is Schank who has pointed out the consequences of failure for episodic memory organization.

FORTUITOUS PROBLEM RESOLUTION represents the following situation:

```
        +--> (-) ---+
        |           | m
    t   |     (M) <--+
        |
        +--- (+)
```

This is a case in which a negative state (-) motivates a mental state (i.e. active goal) on the part of a character, but then some positive event (+) terminates the negative state. For example, FORTUITIOUS PROBLEM RESOLUTION[12] arises in DIVORCE-1 when Paul wins his divorce case, not through any plan of his own, but because by chance he catches Sarah committing adultery.

Plot Units seem to fall in between TOPs and TAUs. Some Plot Units, such as HIDDEN BLESSING (i.e. a negative states leads to a positive state) and REGRETTABLE MISTAKE are similar to TAUs in BORIS. Other Plot Units, such as EXCHANGE, are related to MOPs[13] as implemented in BORIS. What is important about Plot Units is that they provide a level of abstraction in which various event interactions can be "chunked". In these chunks the details are ignored, thus revealing overall important, major configurations that are useful in dealing with summarization tasks.

Currently, a number of Plot Units have been implemented in BORIS and are being used to represent and generate narratives summaries [Lehnert, 1982a] [Lehnert, 1982b] for DIVORCE-1 and DIVORCE-2.

------

[12]Lehnert's Plot Units seem to share some similarity with Wilensky's theory of "internal story points" [Wilensky, 1980b].

[13]MOPs are discussed in chapters 7 and 8.

2.8 Very Large Thematic Patterns

It is clear from work on TAUs, TOPs, meta-planning, and Plot Units that the domain of high level thematic structures is extensive. From our limited discussion here it is also evident that all four approaches are complimentary, rather than conflicting. Can all thematic structures be captured by the theories presented here, or do there exist other levels of thematic processing?

In order to gain insight into human memory organization for narratives, we have asked subjects to perform various tasks, such as question answering, paraphrasing, and summarization. At one point we also asked subjects to select an appropriate title for various narratives. For instance, in the case of DIVORCE-1, one individual immediately came up with the following title:

> "An old man saves a divorce."

This title refers to an even larger pattern than those represented in the TAUs we have discussed so far. We call this particular pattern FORTUITOUS-RESOLUTION-CHAIN. It refers to the ironic situation that Paul would not have won his case if a sequence of things hadn't "gone wrong". The structure of FORTUITOUS-RESOLUTION-CHAIN is a 'chain' of unintended events, each enabling an unintended event which follows it:

> unintended event --> ...
> unintended event --> ...
> ---> major goal achievement

In DIVORCE-1, the specific events instantiated within FORTUITOUS-RESOLUTION-CHAIN are:

If Richard hadn't almost hit the old man,
   he wouldn't have gotten drunk.
If he hadn't gotten drunk,
   he wouldn't have spilled the coffee,
If he hadn't spilled the coffee
   Paul wouldn't have gone home early.
If Paul hadn't gone home early,
   he wouldn't have caught his wife
   and thereby win the divorce case.

If such larger structures exists, then it should be possible to ask questions about them and perform search and retrieval on them. For example:

Q: Why was Paul so lucky?
A: If Richard hadn't spilt the coffee
   Paul wouldn't have caught Sarah in bed.

Q: What was ironic about Paul winning
   the divorce case?
A: It wasn't Richard's ability as a lawyer,
   but his drunken ineptness which lead
   to Paul winning his case.

Q: Why was Sarah's behavior hypocritical?
A: Sarah wanted all of the family possessions
   while at the same time she was the one
   committing adultery.

What other thematic 'chains' are people capable of abstracting from narratives? Consider a story in which a character suffers a major goal failure because a series of smaller enablement conditions each fail. We call this situation an ENABLEMENT-FAILURE-CHAIN, which contains the following structure:

enablement failure --> ...
enablement failure --> ...
--> major goal failure

An example of this structure appears in the following adage:

For wont of a nail the horseshoe was lost.
For wont of a horseshoe the horse was lost.
For wont of a horse the rider was lost.
For wont of a rider the message was lost.
For wont of the message the battle was lost.

There are several issues, regarding these larger patterns, which require more research. For instance, notice that FORTUITOUS-RESOLUTION-CHAIN is made up of TAUs. This fact appears to be significant. Furthermore, such larger patterns appear to act as indices into memory. That is, a person might be reminded of the "for wont of a nail" maxim while reading a story with this same type of enablement failure chain. Also, both of these structures have an ironic element, which is significant and should also be captured.

2.9 Conclusions

In this chapter I have presented a class of abstract knowledge constructs, called TAUs, which organize episodes around failures in planning. TAUs perform the following major functions in narrative comprehension:

- TAUs represent abstract situations in which failures in planning have occurred.

- Narratives are indexed abstractly by TAUs in addition to being indexed by their content.

- TAUs account for at least one form of cross-contextual reminding phenomena.

- TAUs have avoidance and/or recovery information associated with them. This information is often expressed in the form of a common adage.

- TAUs may carry expectations concerning the affective reactions of narrative characters.

- Since stories are indexed in terms of planning errors, TAU information often captures the moral or point of a story.

Finally, since TAUs represent unusual and/or idiosyncratic situations, they must be recognized in a 'bottom-up fashion', as a natural consequence of tracking the key features used in indexing TAUs. Key features are: plans, expectation and belief failures, abstract goal outcomes, accidental events, strong affective reactions, point of view, and the reasons for plan failures. The next chapter contains a scheme for recognizing TAUs which is based on expectation failures and planning errors.

CHAPTER 3

Recognizing TAUs

3.1 Introduction

In the last chapter we established how TAUs capture a deep level of understanding, one which is thematic in nature. Furthermore, we pointed out that TAUs define a class of very abstract knowledge structures, each representing situations involving errors in planning. In this chapter we address in greater depth a key issue concerning TAUs, namely:

> How are those thematic patterns, which are embodied as TAUs, recognized during text processing?

The recognition of TAUs is central for the following reason: Unless each TAU can be activated and applied at the appropriate moment during processing, its existence in memory will be of little use. If a TAU is not recognized, then its planning information, for either error avoidance or recovery, will not be available when needed.

Before discussing a scheme for thematic recognition, three observations must be made:

> 1. The thematic level is not absolutely essential to factual comprehension, and there can be disagreement from person to person on which themes are applicable in a given narrative.

Since TAUs capture a class of thematic patterns, and since these themes are very abstract, it is possible to understand a narrative at the content level while missing some point at the thematic level. For instance, we doubt if Khomeini (or other radical Arabs) ever recognized TAU-HYPOCRISY as a theme in the IRANIAN EMBASSY story (page 31). Why is this the case? Clearly, TAU-HYPOCRISY involves the legitimacy (or illegitimacy) of various plans. Since Khomeini did not feel that taking over the US embassy in Tehran was

morally wrong, he could not foresee the irony westerners would notice
as he accused the terrorists in Britain of wrong-doing.   So plan
LEGITIMACY is an essential component in the recognition of this
theme.

Similarly,   the   theme   TAU-UNJUST-ROLE-REVERSAL
(characterized by the adage: "Adding insult to injury") was
recognized by some individuals who read DIVORCE-1, but not by
others.   Those who noticed this theme felt that Sarah was unjustified
in trying to get all of the family possessions, including a lot of
alimony, when it was she, not Paul, who had been committing
adultery.   That is, Sarah acted as if Paul had been the violator of the
marriage contract, rather than herself.   Again, the recognition of this
TAU depends on an analysis of plan LEGITIMACY.   As a result, plan
LEGITIMACY which must be monitored during comprehension (and
planning) if one class of TAUs is to be recognized.

> 2.   Some individuals will recognize a given TAU in
> time to avoid making the error characterized by it,
> while other individuals are not reminded of the
> TAU until after their plan has already failed and
> their expectations have been violated.

This fact can be explained as a natural consequence of the way
in which TAUs are learned, constructed, and accessed in memory.
When an individual makes a novel error in planning, an associated
TAU is created which captures the situation surrounding it at the
most abstract level possible.   In addition, an analysis is made
concerning why the plan may have failed and what to do about it in
the future.   This information is then associated with the appropriate
TAU.

In the previous chapter we stated that TAU application is
triggered whenever failures occur.   However, if TAUs are recognized
only whenever their entire thematic patterns are satisfied, one could
recognize TAUs only after failures are made.   As a result, error
recovery might improve through time but error avoidance would never
be possible.

Instead, access to TAUs must be dynamic and must vary
according to different plan experiences.   The sooner one attempts to
recognize a given TAU, the more processing effort must be expended.
This occurs because a greater number of TAUs are potentially

applicable when TAU recognition is attempted early on, since only a portion of an entire thematic pattern has be satisfied. As a result, attempts at early recognition of TAUs will result in more false matches. So access to TAUs varies according to a trade-off between error avoidance and recognition effort. This trade-off can be optimized by following two dynamic access adjustment strategies:

> If the goal to be achieved has IMPORTANCE < NORM
>   and the situation arises infrequently
> Then don't build access links to the associated TAU
>   until most of the thematic pattern has been
>   recognized (possibly after a failure has occurred)

> If the goal to be achieved has IMPORTANCE > NORM
>   or the situation occurs frequently
> Then build access links to the associated TAU
>   as early as possible (i.e. before a failure
>   has occurred)

Given identical circumstances, the same TAU may be triggered much earlier in individual X than in individual Y. This implies both a) that X will make errors less often and b) that X also will check more often for potential TAUs which turn out not to be applicable.[14]

> 3. TAU recognition and application is by nature
>   more complicated than the recognition of concrete
>   knowledge structures, such as specific scripts, plans,
>   or goals.

TAUs are much more abstract than scripts, and unlike scripts,

---

[14]Goal importance and goal frequency assessments occur in all planning situations. For instance, I have difficulty remembering to buy a new can of tennis balls because, in such cases, playing with slightly dead balls only causes minor inconvenience during play. In contrast, I once locked my keys in my car years ago and was stranded several hours while waiting for the auto club to come. After that single experience I always check my pocket for keys before I slam any car door. Similarly, it becomes important to avoid errors in planning when achieving a goal that is active on a daily basis; for example, making an effort to wash the dishes right after meals so they won't pile up.

TAUs index cross-contextual situations. These facts are reflected in the different ways in which TAUs and scripts must be recognized. Since scripts usually involve a sequence of stereotypic activities in the service of a specific goal, the mention of a setting, initiating activity, or the main goal of a script will often serve to trigger it. In contrast, TAUs are not associated with any specific activity, goal, or setting. Rather, TAUs are triggered as the result of abstract goal/plan analysis. This analysis depends on a) failures which result during planning, b) the types of plans being used to achieve a given type of goal and c) a categorization scheme based on potential failure points in planning.

3.2 Activating The Recognition Process

Since episodes can be indexed in terms of TAUs, and since TAUs represent planning errors, it is clear that a major aspect of TAU recognition depends on the ability to recognize planning errors when they arise. There are three situations which indicate that a planning error may have occurred: a) goal failures, b) expectation failures and c) planning choices. These are discussed below.

3.2.1 Goal Failures Activate TAUs

Most goals are achieved, maintained, or altered as the result of active planning processes. Therefore, the occurrence of a failure indicates that a potential error may have been made in the plan intended to deal with that goal situation. It is interesting to note that TAUs will be built even if the failure was outside of the planner's control. Although a planner cannot control providence, he will still try to alter his own planning strategies in the future. The ability to do so rests on a capacity to recall the situations surrounding any goal failure even if the failure was not the direct result of an error in planning.[15] Consider the following story:

LOOK-ALIKE

Harry wanted to escape from his alimony payments, so he took the place of a look-alike who was away on vacation. It turned out that the look-alike was wanted by gangsters for gambling debts. Now Harry was in fear for his life.

The LOOK-ALIKE story concerns a character who, while successfully avoiding one goal failure, as an unpredicted side-effect of his plan ends up suffering from a more serious goal crisis. This pattern is captured by TAU-MADE-WORSE, and is characterized by the adage:

Adg: Out of the frying pan and into the fire.

TAU-MADE-WORSE is recognized once the plan has caused a goal failure after having achieved the original goal which had initiated the original plan. Whenever a goal failure occurs, the situation prior to that failure is examined and TAU recognition rules are applied. In this case, the rule is:

tr.1   If the previous goal
         was a preservation goal G
         and the active plan was intended by G
      Then activate TAU-MADE-WORSE

This is only one possible rule. Others will be discussed below.

After the planner experiences this kind of failure, what the planner learns as a result will become an enablement condition specific

---

[15] A study [Terr, 1981] of the Chowchilla, California children who were kidnapped together on a bus and held underground revealed that each child had created an 'explanation' of what the child believed he had done wrong, which had 'lead' to the child's kidnapping. Their explanations involved superstitions concerning the use of specific objects, the weather that day, etc. These children then anxiously avoided similar situations in the future.

to the plan of "switching identities", which is therefore not cross-contextual in nature. The TAU, however, remains cross-contextual in nature, since any story involving TAU-MADE-WORSE will be indexed under that TAU, even though it may have nothing to do specifically with switching identities, alimony, or gambling debts.

3.2.2 Expectation Failures Activate TAUs

Each active planning structure contains a number of expectations about the outcomes predicted for various courses of action. If an action fails to lead to a predicted outcome, then an expectation failure has occurred, and may be the result of an error, either in planning or in plan implementation. Expectation failures also indicate the potential for an error before it has actually occurred.

Expectations often involve predicting the behavior of others in response to a given planner's actions. If the other characters respond in an unanticipated way, then this also constitutes an expectation failure. In such cases the failure may or may not be the result of an error on the part of the planner. However, a planner can only attempt to improve on his own planning mistakes. Therefore, failures due to the actions of others will also index TAUs in episodic memory. Consider the following story:

CAR AFLAME

> Henry came upon an over-turned automobile with a driver unconscious at the wheel. The car was on fire and Henry barely managed to drag the driver from the wreck before the car burst into flames. A month later, Henry was sued for having injured the driver's back when pulling him out of the wreck.

When an individual heard this story he was reminded of a newspaper story he had read years before, concerning a rapist in central park:

CENTRAL PARK

> While walking through central park, Linda was attacked by a rapist. However, she managed to

fight him off with a pen knife she carried in her purse. Later, the rapist filed charges against her for assault with a deadly weapon.

What both CAR AFLAME and CENTRAL PARK share at the thematic level is an expectation violation concerning the way another character should behave in response to the main character's course of action. This violation is represented by TAU-UNJUST-RETALIATION. In each case, the other character treated the planner's actions in isolation from the surrounding circumstances. In CAR AFLAME, the driver used the following plan to response to Henry:

If x causes a goal failure for y
Then x may retaliate against y.

In isolation, this rule is perfectly reasonable. If someone wrenches your back, you have a right to retaliate. However, taking into account the outer context, Henry expected the driver to be grateful for having saved the driver's life.

In CENTRAL PARK, the rapist also used the retaliation plan above. However, given the outer context of self-defense against assault, Linda expected the rapist to feel guilt. Thus, CENTRAL PARK is also captured by TAU-UNJUST-RETALIATION.

A related TAU is TAU-UNJUST-ROLE-REVERSAL. Consider the following story:

WOLF AND CRANE

A wolf had a bone stuck in his throat. He promised to reward the crane if the crane would use its long beak to remove the bone. Once the bone was removed, the crane asked for a reward. The wolf told the crane that the crane should thank him for not having eaten the crane while his head was in the wolf's mouth.

Here the crane has experienced an expectation failure. The crane expected the wolf to respond with gratitude. Instead, the wolf reversed roles, demanding that the crane be grateful to the wolf.

When a character violates the expectations of another character, the basis of the expectation is examined. In the stories above, the expectations arise from knowledge structures concerning RETALIATIONs and FAVORs.[16] Associated with these structures are TAU recognition rules that are activated when those structures are violated. For instance, if a return favor is predicted but fails to occur, then the following rules are activated:

> tr.2 If the one obligated to return the favor
> responds by causing a goal failure
> on the part of the other character
> Then activate TAU-UNJUST-RETALIATION

> tr.3 If the one obligated to return
> the favor demands a return favor
> from the other character
> Then activate TAU-UNJUST-ROLE-REVERSAL

False beliefs constitute a class of expectation failures, involving disputed knowledge states. Character actions are based on knowledge states. Planning errors often occur when a planner bases his plan on a false belief. When we read about a character's plan, we assess the knowledge state the plan is based on. If the character's beliefs violate the reader's knowledge state, then the reader will be cued for a potential planning error.

3.2.3 Planning Choices Activate TAUs

If TAUs were recognized only after actual failures had occurred, planners would never be able to avoid future failures. Therefore, a large component of TAU recognition involves analyzing the potential for errors at each point that planning decisions are made, even though a failure may not yet have occurred. It is this planning decision analysis which gives the planner the ability to avoid subsequent errors in the future. Since the same planning analysis used in real-time planning is active during text analysis, the planning choices of narrative characters can elicit recall of a TAU for the reader before

---

[16]FAVOR is discussed in chapter 10.

the entire TAU is encountered in the text.

It is important to note that an error in planning may be recognized even in those cases in which the associated goal is achieved. For instance, if a very costly plan is used to achieve a minor goal, when less costly plans are available, then a planning error has still occurred, even though the major goal has been achieved. This situation is characterized by the adage "Killing a fly with an elephant gun" and will be discussed in more detail below.

Recognizing that a failure has occurred is not enough, however. Even if a TAU is applicable, we must be able to select which TAU correctly characterizes the overall situation. We must have a method of distinguishing one TAU from another. TAUs differ according to a) the kinds of planning errors which were made and b) the abstract goal/plan situation surrounding the error. Thus, in order to recognize the appropriate TAU, one must have the following information available:

1. The plan being selected or used to achieve a given goal.

2. Information about the plan, in the form of a) restrictions upon its use, b) the number of times that a plan has been used in the past, and c) how well, or badly, the plan has fared each time in achieving various goals.

3. General knowledge about the tradeoffs involved in choosing one plan over another.

It is the analysis of these three aspects of planning situations that distinguish one TAU from another. Therefore, TAU recognition is based on categorizing planning errors along the three dimensions mentioned above. Whenever a plan is selected, these three dimensions are analyzed. If the surrounding plan type, plan restrictions, and tradeoffs match a past error, then the appropriate TAU will be recognized.

Most of the time, standard plans are selected to achieve standard goals. In such cases, no expectations are violated, so TAU recognition is not attempted. Whenever a plan choice deviates from a expected plan choice, TAU recognition processes are activated.

So TAU recognition depends on both a) a deviation from

expected planning procedures and b) a categorization of classes of planning failures. The deviation indicates the potential for a TAU to occur, while the categorization scheme supplies a method by which the appropriate TAU can be selected. These planning categories are presented in the section which follows. TAU recognition rules are associated with each category. When we notice a plan which falls within that category the recognition rules are applied. These rules then either a) determine whether a specific TAU is applicable, or b) discriminate between various potential TAUs. If a number of disjoint rules fire, then more than one TAU may be recognized for the same episode.

Once a TAU has been recognized, the specific content of the episode will determine where the episode resides in memory with respect to other episodes indexed under that TAU. For instance, both of the following stories are indexed in terms of TAU-POST-HOC:

PATCO

> After having been decertified by the federal government, the Professional Air Traffic Controllers Organization (PATCO) decided to end their strike in an attempt to regain their jobs. However, the FAA no longer took notice of any actions taken by a now defunct union.

QUITS SMOKING

> After learning that he had incurable cancers in each lung, Joe decided to quit smoking.

In each case, a planner has applied a prevention plan when it is no longer effective. However, the PATCO story will be indexed closer to HIRED-HAND and ACADEMIA (page 28) because they all involve job hiring.[17]   QUITS SMOKING, on the other hand, will be indexed

---

[17]The issue of indexing by content is a complex one, and will not be discussed here. Instead, see [Kolodner, 1980].

with other TAU-POST-HOC stories involving P-HEALTH goals. [18]

3.3 A TAU Categorization Based on Planning Metrics

Planning rarely occurs in isolation from an overall planning context. A planning context includes those alternative courses of action the planner could have taken while attempting to achieve some goal. For instance, if a planner selects a weak plan P1 to achieve a goal, this normally constitutes a planning error. However, if P1 turns out to be the only course of action available to him, then it no longer constitutes a planning error. Therefore, the assessment of a planning error must be sensitive to surrounding circumstances.

A planner is always making decisions during planning and plan execution. Planning errors normally involve mistakes in judgment, made at some point during planning or plan execution, which usually lead to goal failures. These judgements and decisions are based on a number of planning metrics. These metrics consist of information about various plans, usually accumulated through past experience with each plan. In some cases, each metric possesses a static value; in other cases, the values must be computed dynamically. As plans are applied to different situations, the values of their metrics undergo adjustment. However, the list of metrics themselves is relatively fixed, and is used as the basis for recognizing planning errors when they arise.

Associated with each metric is an context-free piece of planning advice involving how the metric is to be used. This advice determines how plans should be evaluated, when assuming that other metrics need not being taken into consideration. For instance, all things being equal, a planner should alway select a low risk plan over a high risk plan.

Below are briefly listed 11 planning metrics which serve as a basis for recognizing planning failures, along with information about how each metric is to be evaluated:

_____

[18]P-HEALTH stands for "preservation of health". Preservation goals are only active when threatened. See appendix II or [Schank and Abelson, 1977].

PLANNING METRICS

1. ENABLEMENT -- Necessary preconditions before a plan can or should be executed. This includes such things as a) when a plan should be executed, and b) the correct order in which various sub-portions of a plan must be executed before proceeding to the next sub-portion. Choose plans with all enablements satisfied over plans with some enablements not yet satisfied.

2. COST -- Resources used during plan execution, including time, money, physical and mental effort, etc. Select low cost plans over high cost plans.

3. EFFICACY -- The perceived capability of a plan to achieve a particular goal. This is usually based on the past performance of a plan under various circumstances and in the service of differing goals. Adopt effective plans over weak plans.

4. RISK -- The potential of negative side-effects during plan execution, or the dangers involved in using a particular plan if something goes wrong. Elect low risk plans over high risk plans.

5. COORDINATION -- The ability to successfully divide a single plan between multiple planners to achieve a common goal. Choose plans that are well-coordinated over plans which lack organization.

6. AVAILABILITY -- The number of plans which are currently available for achieving a current goal, including the flexibility of altering a current plan or selecting a new plan in the face of a potential planning failure. The more options available, the more able the planner is to recover from an error while planning. Pick a plan with many options over plans with few options.

7. LEGITIMACY -- The perceived judgment by any important party concerning the correct ethical use of a

given plan in a given situation. Adopt legitimate plans before illegitimate plans.

8. AFFECT -- Emotional responses to plan failure (or success) and its effect on subsequent planning. Prefer plans which respond to goal outcomes over plans which are selected during states of heightened emotion.

9. SKILL -- The ability of a planner to correctly execute a known plan, based on a 'scorecard' of past use. Choose well-practiced plans over novel plans.

10. VULNERABILITY -- In counter-planning situations, the planner must be able to take into account the potential of retaliation from his opponents. When counter-planning, adopt plans less vulnerable to retaliation over plans more vulnerable to attack.

11. LIABILITY -- In alliance situations, the planner must take into account the obligations created by accepting help from his allies. When giving or receiving aid, choose plans which incur less indebtedness to one's allies over plans which leave one more obligated.

Planning decisions are based, not only on a single metric in isolation, but also on tradeoffs between various metrics. As a result, some overlap between planning metrics is unavoidable. For instance, planning RISK could be treated as a form of planning COST. However, it is possible to select a plan with a perceived low RISK but very high COST. Likewise, a very cheap plan to implement may not be a very safe one. The metrics of EFFICACY and EXPERIENCE are also related. Usually, well-used plans are more effective plans, but this may not always be the case.

Principle 4

```
+-------------------------------+
| TAU  recognition  is  based   |
| on eleven planning metrics.   |
+-------------------------------+
```

What follows is a discussion of each planning metric, along with a) sample stories that contain planning errors concerning each metric, b) the TAUs which arise, c) any associated adages, and d) related rules of activation.

3.3.1 ENABLEMENT

The success of each plan often depends on one or more necessary preconditions. Such preconditions are numerous and can not all be mentioned here. Instead, we will just briefly discuss a few planning errors based on enablement conditions:

SECRECY -- Many DECEPTION plans require SECRECY. In such cases the planner must successfully keep others from learning about the planner's activities. This often involves blocking the ability of others to ATTEND to him. In DIVORCE-1, for example, Sarah wanted to both have an affair with another man and at the same time win a lot of alimony in court. This goal required that Paul not know that she was committing adultery. Readers of DIVORCE-1 assumed that Sarah was surprised by Paul's sudden return home to change his clothes. This inference was made because readers assumed that Sarah's plan required secrecy.

A common failure in SECRECY-based plans involves thinking that SECRECY is being maintained when it is not. This type of planning failure is represented by the following TAU:

TAU-SELF-DECEPTION

    x has a goal G involving counter-planning
      against y
    x selects a plan P to block an enablement
      condition C1 on y (involving ATTEND)
    x executes plan P but
      this results in enablement
      condition C2 being blocked for x
    x falsely believes that C1 is also blocked for y
    y's counter-plan is successful and x's goal fails

Consider the following story:

OSTRICH

An ostrich was being chased by a tiger. The ostrich needed a place to hide, so he put his head in a hole in the sand. Since he couldn't see the tiger, he thought the tiger couldn't see him either. The tiger found him and he was eaten.

This story was created from the adage:

Adg: Hiding one's head in the sand.

When the OSTRICH story was read to a Taiwanese student, the student recalled the following chinese adage:

Adg: Don't cover your ears when stealing the town bell.

which refers to the following story:

TOWN BELL

A thief wanted to steal the town bell. He sneaked into town at night and attached the bell to his belt. As he moved the bell began to ring, so the thief put his hands over his ears. Since he couldn't hear the bell, he thought he was safe. However, the townspeople awoke from the ringing and caught him.

Both OSTRICH and TOWN BELL have a number of elements in common:

1. The plans in both episodes involve SECRECY -- i.e. blocking the act of ATTENDing. In the first episode, however, it is ATTEND(eyes), while in the second, it is ATTEND (ears).

2. In both episodes, the plan fails because the planner deceives himself into thinking that his opponent's ability to ATTEND is blocked simply because his own ability to ATTEND is blocked.

In both stories, the plan fails because the planner has allowed himself to choose an easier plan by deceiving himself into thinking that the plan is sufficient. However, in both cases the same fundamental enablement condition has been violated. Thus, TAU-SELF-DECEPTION is triggered by two factors: 1) a missing enablement condition and 2) a false belief on the part of the planner.

Notice that these two stories share little at the level of goals. The ostrich has a P-HEALTH goal, while the thief has a D-CONT goal.[19]   One goal is justifiable (i.e. self-preservation) while the other goal involves an evil intention (i.e. thievery). The key similarity between these two episodes occurs at the planning level.

TIMING -- Some enablement conditions concern the time when plans are initiated. The best plan will fail if it is executed too late:

> Adg: Closing the barn door after the horse
>   has escaped.

For an example of a timing-based error, see the discussion of TAU-POST-HOC in section 2.2.

If plans are executed too late, they may not fail, but it may make their cost much higher. Consider the following story:

MISSING SHINGLE

> John noticed that his roof was leaking due to a missing shingle. However, he ignored it, figuring that it could be fixed anytime. A week later, when he decided to replace the shingle, he discovered that the loose water had caused extensive damage to the entire ceiling.

This situation is captured by the following TAU:

---

[19]D-CONT stands for "delta-control" -- i. e. a goal to change who has control of an object. See appendix II.

TAU-TOO-LATE

x has p-goal G active with
    recovery plan P1 available
    at COST C1
x delays applying P1 to G
x discovers that P1 will no longer
    achieve G and that P2 must
    be used, but COST C2 of P2
    is much greater than C1

Associated adages:

   Adg: A stitch in time saves nine.
   Adg: Nip it in the bud.

A key element in recognizing **TAU-TOO-LATE** is the fact that the planner has needlessly delayed using an available plan. The use of TIMING in planning is complex and includes: a) the DURATION before a plan is initiated, b) the DURATION taken for each portion of a plan, c) the DURATION expended in between the execution of one plan portion and the next. A mistake in timing at any point can lead to the failure of the plan.

Some plans will fail if they're executed too soon, before necessary enablement conditions are satisfied. Recall TAU-UNSUPPORTED-PLAN and the NEW PAINT episode (page 47).

NEED -- A fundamental precondition for the execution of any plan intended to achieve a goal is that the goal in fact be an active one. Consider the following story:

NEW YORK ELEPHANTS

John saw his friend Bill carrying an elephant gun in New York City. When he asked Bill what the gun was for, Bill replied it was to keep elephants away. John then noted that there aren't any elephants in New York City. "You see, my plan is working!" responded Bill.

This situation is captured by TAU-NO-NEED. Whenever a plan

is initiated to achieve a preservation goal, a check must be made to see if the goal is currently active. There is no point in calling for a doctor if one is not sick. As with TAU-SELF-DECEPTION, TAU-NO-NEED is triggered by the occurrence of both a missing enablement condition and a false belief.

AGENCY -- The last planning precondition we will consider here is AGENCY. Many plans require agents. In such cases, one should select an agent who has the necessary qualification and skill to execute the necessary plans. Consider the following story:

PIERCED EARS

Lulu wanted to have her ears pierced. Lulu asked her friend, Wanda, who had never pierced anyone's ears, to perform the operation for her. Lulu now has two badly infected earlobes.

The theme of this story is represented by the following TAU:

TAU-INCOMPETENT-AGENT

x has goal G active
x needs agent of type A to achieve G
x selects incompetent agent y
y has planning failure
    and G is not achieved for x

associated adage:

Adg: Letting a blind man lead you.

Plans which require agents have associated with them the types of agents required. When we read that Lulu wants her ears pierced, we build expectations that Lulu will either a) go see a doctor, b) go see a cosmoeologist or dermatologist, or c) go to someone who has successfully pierced ears in the past. When we read that Lulu has chosen Wanda, TAU recognition rules associated with AGENCY(PIERCE-EAR) are applied to see if Lulu is a competent agent. Since she is not, TAU-INCOMPETENT-AGENT is activated.

3.3.2 COST

In addition to ENABLEMENTS, every plan also has a COST associated with it, which includes a) the mental and physical effort required to execute the plan and b) various additional resources, such as time, material goods, and money. Consider the following story:

FACE LIFT

Bill had an acne pimple on his chin. He decided to
go see a plastic surgeon and have his face lifted.

Here we have a very minor goal involving P-APPEARANCE(FACE). There are a number of plans which involve little cost and are also efficacious:

1. Lance the pimple.
2. Apply acne medication.
3. Use cosmetics to hide it.

However, Bill chooses a plan, which although efficacious, involves great COST in comparison with the seriousness of Bill's facial condition. This planning failure situation is represented by TAU-TOO-COSTLY, which has associated with it the following adage:

Adg: Killing a fly with an elephant gun.

The rule for recognizing TAU-TOO-COSTLY is:

tr.4 If the COST of a plan is higher than normal
and if there are other efficacious plans
available with lower cost,
Then activate TAU-TOO-COSTLY

It is interesting to note that we perceive Bill as having made an error in planning even though Bill actually achieved his goal. The fact that a TAU is still recognized in this case shows that TAUs are associated with planning errors which usually lead to goal failures (but not always).

If Bill had chosen any of the standard plans to achieve his P-APPEARANCE(FACE) goal, TAU recognition rules would not have been activated. It is the fact that our expectations concerning Bill's predicted actions were violated that made us examine Bill's chosen plan more closely. Since PLASTIC-SURGERY is a high cost plan for use with serious P-APPEARANCE goals, TAU recognition rules associated with COST are applied.

3.3.3 EFFICACY

Associated with each plan is the kind of goal which the plan can be normally expected to achieve. The ability of a plan to achieve a given goal is referred to as the plan's EFFICACY.

Whenever a plan is selected, the associated goal is examined and the EFFICACY of the plan (with regard to that goal) is computed. If the plan is not very efficacious and other, more effective plans are available, then a planning error has been made. Consider the following story:

TWO ASPIRIN

> The doctor told George that, probably due to smoking, he had developed a malignant tumor in one lung. George decided to take two aspirin and get a good night's sleep.

Here, George's behavior is very odd. To make sense of TWO ASPIRIN readers are forced to imagine a scenario in which George's behavior is an act of despair or reckless bravado. When we first read about George's condition, we realize that George has a serious P-HEALTH goal. Efficacious plans in this case include chemotherapy and/or surgery. Taking two aspirin, while satisfying the normal principle of choosing low-cost plans first, is not very efficacious. The planning situation represented in TWO ASPIRIN is captured by TAU-TOO-WEAK, which is characterized by the following adage:

Adg: Stalking a rhino with a pea shooter.

TAU-TOO-WEAK is the opposite situation characterized by TAU-TOO-COSTLY since here the planner has chosen a cheap, but ineffective plan over more costly, but effective plans. The recognition rule for TAU-TOO-WEAK is:

tr.5 If a plan P is chosen with a low EFFICACY
      in regard to goal G, and other
      more effective plans are available,
      and G is an major goal
  Then activate TAU-TOO-WEAK

3.3.4 RISK

In addition to the COST of each plan there are associated
RISKs, which represent the chance that executing a plan will create
undesirable side-effects or lead to an undesirable failure. For instance,
if a goal has already been achieved and its failure would be very
undesirable, then it is foolish to undertake a high RISK plan just in
order to add a minor improvement to an already satisfactory
situation. Consider the following story:

GAMBLING MAN

Harold had won $1000 dollars by betting on "Fleet
Foot" at the track. This was just what he needed
to pay off his gambling debts to the mob. However,
Harold was so sure that "Snail Pace" would win in
the next race that he bet all he had on it. Now
Harold is in hiding from the mob's hit men.

Harold's error was in executing a high RISK plan simply to
improve an already satisfactory goal situation. This planning error is
represented by TAU-TOO-RISKY and characterized by the following
adage:

Adg: A bird in the hand is worth two in the bush.

Goal subsumption states [Wilensky, 1978a], [Wilensky, 1978b]
are characterized by states in which recurring goals are satisfied. For
example, marriage subsumes recurring sex and companionship goals; a
job subsumes recurring financial goals, etc. Since subsumption states
satisfy many goals over a long period of time, they are usually very
important. Therefore, the use of high RISK plans, just with the
intent to improve subsumption states, is very foolish. Consider the
following story:

WHALING SPREE

Whalers Inc. was making millions of dollars each year by harpooning whales and selling their blubber. However, Whalers Inc. was not satisfied, so they developed new methods by which they could increase their kill by a factor of a hundred. When whales became extinct, Whalers Inc. went bankrupt.

This story is characterized by the adages:

Adg: Killing the goose that lays golden eggs.
Adg: Casting dirt into the well that gives you water.
Adg: Eating the seed that is for sowing.

Each subsumption state has an associated production rate, based on the nature of the producing source. In the story above, the production rate is based on the natural reproductivity of whales. In other cases, subsumption states may depend on an authority who controls the rate of subsumption. Consider the following story:

CREDIT CARD

John had a good job but he wanted more money. One night he was found using the company's credit card for personal use. As a result, John's boss fired him. Now John is broke.

Here John's subsumption state depended on John's boss. To gain a marginal increase in financial return, he jeopardized the major portion of his income. This story is characterized by the following adage:

Adg: Biting the hand that feeds you.

One major subsumption state is that of HEALTH. Few goal achievements can be enjoyed if this subsumption state has failed in some way. Therefore, high risk plans should never be used when it involves P-HEALTH. Consider the following story:

BAD VISION

Aunt Betty had minor cataracts forming which

blocked her vision slightly. She hear about a new operation in which her corneas could be replaced by pig skin. She was warned that the operation was illegal in the USA because it often resulted in corneal damage. However, she insisted on having the operation. She flew to a clinic in Mexico where they operated on both her eyes. Now Betty is completely blind.

The subsumption goal need not involve P-HEALTH:

CAR IMPROVEMENT

Freddy owned an old car that ran beautifully except for an occasional funny sound in the motor. Freddy decided to have a mechanic tear the motor apart in order to eliminate that sound. The sound is now gone, but Freddy's car is always stalling.

These stories are captured by TAU-LEAVE-ALONE and is illustrated by the following adages:

Adg: The cure is worse than the disease.
Adg: Leaving well enough alone.
Adg: If it ain't broke, don't fix it.

Each of these adages refers to the error of employing high RISK plans for a marginal improvement in a satisfactory goal state. Whenever a plan is selected to improve an existing goal state, the risk of the plan is assessed. If the risk is high, then TAU-TOO-RISKY is activated.

Notice that TAU-TOO-RISKY is **not** activated in cases where a crisis goal has been activated and low risk plans are unavailable. Consider the following story:

TRANSPLANT

A rare disease had permanently damaged Hank's heart. He had only days to live. His one hope was a transplant operation that only had a one in ten chance of success. Hank took that chance. He died during the operation.

In TRANSPLANT, no TAU is activated even though the plan involves a very high risk and the plan ends up failing. Thus, planning metrics cannot be considered in isolation; planning metrics interact. The issue of planning metric interactions is discussed later.

3.3.5 COORDINATION

When two planners are pursuing the same goal for their mutual benefit, care must be taken to insure that their actions are coordinated. This requires that each planner know what aspect of a coordinated plan each planner is responsible for. Consider the following story:

LOST MOVIE

Alfred and George both decided to go to the movies. Alfred thought that George would drive and Alfred would treat. However, George had assumed that Alfred would give him a ride and that he would treat. Each waited for the other to pick him up. By the time they realized what had happened, it was too late to see the movie.

Here, the goal of E-ENTERTAINMENT(MOVIE) requires a plan involving a) getting both individuals to the movie on time and b) paying for both tickets. In addition to checking enablements of HAVE-TRANSPORTATION and HAVE-MONEY, there are D-KNOW goals involving resource sharing. Since George and Alfred are confused over who's responsible for which part of the plan, a failure results. This case of "mixed signals" is captured by TAU-UNCOORDINATED, which has the following adages associated with it:

Adg: A horse with two masters will starve.
Adg: The right hand not knowing what the
        left hand is doing.
Adg: Too many cooks spoil the broth.

TAU-UNCOORDINATED is activated by the mention that each planner assumes planning responsibility without checking with the other planner.[20]

3.3.6 AVAILABILTY

Whenever a plan is chosen, there is always the possibility that the plan may fail. In such cases, the planner may respond in a number of ways, depending on the goal state, the cause of the failure, the planner's available resources, etc. In general, the planner may:

1. Abandon his goal permanently.

2. Try the same plan again at another point in time (when enablement conditions may have changed).

3. Abandon this plan and select another plan.

Associated with each goal are a number of standard plans. For some goals a great many plans may be available. To achieve other goals there may only be a few appropriate plans. The more important the goal, the more need for many planning options in the case that the current plan has failed. This is represented by the planning principle that important goals require more planning options. Some plans of action, however, have the negative side-effect of eliminating the potential use of other currently available plans. Consider the following story:

YALE APPLICATION

Bill didn't like the college he was attending, so he decided to try a transfer to Yale. While waiting for Yale's notice of acceptance or rejection, he let his course work slide. Bill found out that he had flunked all his college courses on the same day that he got a rejection notice from Yale. Now Bill is working as a bellhop.

---

[20]Again we see that false beliefs serve as a recognition component in TAUs. However, a detailed treatment of belief systems [Abelson, 1979] [Abelson, 1973] is beyond the scope of this thesis.

In the event that his application to Yale was not approved, Bill's major option was to stay at his current college. However, Bill failed to maintain this an an option. As a result, his major goal of getting an education was thwarted. YALE APPLICATION is characterized by a number of adages:

Adg: Painting oneself into a corner.
Adg: Burning your bridges behind you.
Adg: Not keeping all your doors open.
Adg: Keeping all your eggs in one basket.

These adages are associated with TAU-FEW-OPTIONS, which among other things, contains the following advice:

If plans P1 and P2 are available to achieve G
  and the execution of P1 would restrict
  the OPTIONs left if P1 fails
Then choose P2 over P1.

TAU-FEW-OPTIONS is activated by the following rule:

tr.6 If x applies a high risk plan P1
       in an attempt to achieve goal G
       and x eliminates a major recovery
       plan P2 for use if P1 fails
     Then activate TAU-FEW-OPTIONS

Some plans may be used recurrently. Other plans, however, are restricted in how often they may be used. When a plan can be used depends on a number of conditions:

Resource Consumption -- For instance, plans which consume a limited resource can only be used as long as the resource is available. Consider the following story:

COLD BOY SCOUT

Johnny Cubscout played all day long with his waterproof matches, having fun watching them flare up. When the rain storm came and he needed to start a fire, the normal matches were wet and Johnny was out of waterproof matches. He caught a bad case of pneumonia.

The planner in this story has violated the following principle:[21]

    If a plan consumes a limited resource
    Then do not use the plan to achieve
       minor goals, or it will be unavailable
       when needed for a major goal.

Other situations involving the waste of resources are illustrated by adages such as:

    Adg: Throwing good money after bad.
    Adg: Casting pearls before swine.

Perseverance Limitations -- Resources limitations are but one form of the AVAILABILITY metric. For example, the plan of APPEASEMENT may work successfully against an opponent who wants something. However, if giving in to the goal of an opponent doesn't stop the opponent's counter-plans, then the plan of APPEASEMENT should not be used again. In this case the AVAILABILITY of the plan decreases with repetition because of the perseverance of the opponent's counter-plan. This error is characterized by the following adage:

    Adg: Give 'em and inch and they'll take a mile.

Knowledge States -- Some plans lose their effectiveness through use because other planners adapt to them. For instance, plans involving DECEPTION achieve their goals by using false information to motivate other characters to take actions which achieve one's own goals. DECEPTION may be tried once or twice against the same party, but soon the same opponents will cease to be fooled by false information. Consider the following story:

WORKING LATE

---

[21]In case the reader is reminded at this point of "The boy who cried wolf" (as was my thesis advisor), then be patient. The relationship between this story and resource limitations will be discussed shortly.

> John was having an affair with a beautiful woman.
> When John came home late he would tell his wife
> Betty that he had been forced to work after hours
> at the office. The next time John was late Betty
> called the office and got no answer. Was John in
> trouble that night when he gave the usual excuse!

John's planning error is in using an identical deception plan repeatedly.

3.3.7 LEGITIMACY

The LEGITIMACY of a plan involves the perceived ethics of its use in various situations. Large numbers of planning situations exist involving LEGITIMACY since people commonly resort to illegitimate plans in order to achieve their goals. For instance, it is illegitimate to retaliate with extreme force in a minor goal competition situation:

BATTERED WITH BAT

> The little old lady yelled insults at the professional
> baseball player during the 5th inning, so he smashed
> her over the head with his heaviest bat.

Many plans, such as those involving murder, extortion, theft, etc. are considered illegitimate in most situations. These plans are often effective initially, but their use results in one's opponents resorting to similar types of counter-plans. This situation is described by the following adage:

Adg: Who lives by the sword dies by the sword.

Another planning situation involving LEGITIMACY is that of TAU-HYPOCRISY, discussed in section 2.1.

3.3.8 AFFECT

An important element in planning is the ability to recover from planning failures. Whenever a failure occurs, the planner will usually experience a number of AFFECT states.[22]   If the planner reacts to these AFFECT states instead of reacting to the failure, then his ability to recover will be hampered. For instance, the adage:

Adg: No use crying over spilt milk.

refers to the negative consequence of emotional reactions on subsequent plan recovery. Sorrow is not the only emotion which can influence planning. Consider the following story:

COLD FEET

John had been jilted by a pretty girl when he was younger. Now he had a crush on Mary, who was very cute. John wanted to ask Mary to the dance, but was afraid that she would turn him down also. So he never asked her. Later, he found out that Mary had been waiting for his call.

John's past failure has made him fearful. This fear keeps him from making any attempt to date Mary. As a result, he suffers a needless failure. This situation is captured by TAU-TOO-CAUTIOUS and is characterized by these associated adages:

Adg: Nothing ventured, nothing gained.
Adg: Once burnt, twice shy.
Adg: Who is bitten by a snake is afraid of an eel.

If a goal will fail with certainty unless some plan is attempted, then avoiding plan execution through fear of failure constitutes a planning error. This abstract plan situation is the opposite of that characterized by TAU-TOO-RISKY, in which a goal is already satisfied but a risky plan is executed anyway just for minor improvements.

---

[22]Chapter 4 treats AFFECT in depth.

3.3.9 SKILL

An important aspect of plan execution is the skill the planner. Skill usually develops from experience at executing a plan more than once, and in a wide range of circumstances. Associated with each plan is the number of times it has been tried, in which situations, and the successes and/or failures experienced. If a plan is novel, it will lack this information, which may be vital in correctly applying it. Consider the following story:

SHOWDOWN

> After reading a lengthy book on how to execute a "fast draw", the marshal's son, Seth, challenged El Bandito to a showdown. El Bandito shot Seth in the hand before Seth's gun had cleared his holster. Seth is lucky to be alive and only missing a few fingers.

This story is characterized by a number of adages:

Adg: An ounce of practice is worth a pound of theory.
Adg: Practice makes perfect.
Adg: Easier said than done.
Adg: He jests at scars who never felt a wound.

Here, the planner mistakenly assumed that knowledge about a skill was sufficient. Seth knew the plan, but the plan was novel to him in the sense that he had never executed it. The more important a goal, the more essential that "tried and true" plans be used first. Novel plans should be tried on minor goals, where a failure will not have serious consequences.

The situation of using a novel plan is represented by TAU-INEXPERIENCED. Whenever a plan is chosen, if the plan requires skill, then past experiences with the plan are examined. If experience with the plan in the active situation is non-existent or meager, then TAU-INEXPERIENCED is activated.

3.3.10 VULNERABILITY

Much planning knowledge deals with counter-planning [Carbonell, 1979] against opponents in goal competition situations. A key principle of counter-planning involves balancing the harm one can cause one's opponent against the resulting harm which one may experience in return: Don't cause yourself more harm than you can cause your opponent. There are two ways in which the cost of a counter-plan can be computed:

1. Compute the normal cost of the plan in effort, time, resources, etc.

2. Compute the potential harm which may result from any predictable retaliatory counter-plans on the part of one's opponent.

It is not necessary that one's opponent use an identical counter-plan in retaliation. The important point is that the planner who is most vulnerable should avoid counter-plans which will lead to retaliation in the area of vulnerability. Consider this story:

FROZEN ASSESTS

To teach the United States a lesson, Iran cut off its already limited supply of oil to the USA. Whereupon, the USA froze over 4 billion dollars worth of Iranian assets, causing severe financial hardship to Iran.

Here, Iran has attempted to hurt the USA financially when Iran is more vulnerable to financial retaliation by the USA. This situation is characterized by the following adage:

Adg: Don't throw rocks if you live
in a glass house.

The theme characterized by this adage is TAU-VULNERABLE. It is activated by the following rule:

tr.7 If x is using a counter-plan P
      which is intended to thwart y's goal G,
    Then examine knowledge of y's available
      counter-plans and if y has P
      available to retaliate
      then activate TAU-VULNERABLE

The cost of a counter-plan does not have to involve a direct retaliation on the part of one's foe. If the direct side-effect of a plan causes more harm to the planner than to the foe, the plan is foolish. Consider the following stories:

GHETTO RIOTS

Blacks wanted to protest the bad living conditions within the inner city, so they rioted. As a result, their own homes and businesses were destroyed, and outsiders became more afraid to invest in the area.

ANGRY SUICIDE

Mary caught her boyfriend Bill cheating on her. She was so mad at Bill that she decided to kill herself so that he would feel guilty.

In both cases, the negative side-effects of plan execution outweigh the goal benefits obtained in executing the retaliatory plan. This planning error is characterized by TAU-GREATER-HARM, which is illustrated by the following adage:

Adg: Cutting off one's nose to spite one's face.

What is the difference between TAU-VULNERABLE and TAU-GREATER-HARM? In TAU-VULNERABLE, the planner has to correctly anticipate the potential reaction of his opponent to his counter-plan. In TAU-GREATER-HARM, the planner has to take into account the negative side-effects of a retaliatory plan, without regard for the opponent's reactions. Thus, TAU-VULNERABLE is a refinement of TAU-GREATER-HARM. The issue of TAU refinement will be discussed later.

3.3.11 LIABILITY

Many plans are achieved by forming alliances or contracts. These contracts incur obligations on both parties. One should choose plans with minimal contractual obligations over plans with undesirable liabilities. There are many different kinds of plan liabilities. One liability is illustrated by the following adage:

Adg: Who pays the piper calls the tune.

Other liabilities result from creating alliances or obtaining agents who make use of illegitimate plans. Consider the following story:

THREE PUNKS

Antonio was an honest businessman. One day his daughter Maria was raped by three punks. The police couldn't prove anything against the three punks, so Antonio went to Brandoni, the godfather of the mafia, to obtain revenge. Now Antonio must let the mafia use his business as a front for illegal narcotics. Antonio is very unhappy.

This story is characterized by a short-term success with an illegitimate ally resulting in a long-term loss due to unwanted obligations. This situation is illustrated by the following adages:

Adg: You cannot touch pitch without getting defiled.
Adg: If you lie down in the mud, you come up dirty.

3.4 TAU Interrelationships

As stated in section 2.5.2, a story can be indexed in terms of more than one TAU. This happens for two reasons:

1. Multiple planning errors occur in many stories, as in the "boy who cried wolf" (see below).

2. Some TAUs are refinements or generalizations of other TAUs.

Consider this version of the "boy who cried wolf":

CRYING WOLF

The boy was bored watching his sheep, so he cried "wolf! wolf!". When the hunters came to rescue his sheep, they found him laughing at them. The next day, a real wolf appeared and began eating his sheep, so he cried "wolf! wolf!". This time the hunters thought the boy was joking, so they didn't appear and he lost all his sheep. When the hunters found out what had happened, they told the boy that it "served him right".

There are three planning errors the boy made in this story: First, he violated a LIABILITY metric. That is, he treated his allies badly, so that they weren't willing to help him later on when he needed them. Second, he violated an AVAILABILITY metric by using DECEPTION more than once against the same group of hunters. The first time his plan worked, but once the hunters had been deceived with the same misinformation, the plan was no longer effective in achieving the same response a second time. Finally, the boy violated a trade-off principle associated with limited availability plans -- that such plans should be saved for use in achieving major, not minor, goals. The boy in CRYING WOLF used up his deception plan to achieve a minor entertainment goal rather than saving it for an important P-HEALTH(sheep) goal. Likewise, in COLD BOY SCOUT the planner wasted a limited resource (needed for building an important fire) simply to satisfy a trivial entertainment goal.

A story may also be indexed by multiple TAUs in cases where two TAUs are related to one another directly. Recall the CAR IMPROVEMENT story (on page 87) which was captured by TAU-LEAVE-ALONE. What is the difference between TAU-LEAVE-ALONE and TAU-MADE-WORSE? The difference between these TAUs is that TAU-MADE-WORSE involves planning to avoid negative crisis goals while TAU-LEAVE-ALONE involves planning in positive situations when the major goal is already satisfied. So these TAUs share the same general structure, but differ with respect to the goal situation.

When structures are shared between TAUs, the rules that recognized them serve as discrimination rules. The nature of these discriminations can be revealed by analyzing the adages which characterize them. For instance, at first glance the adages:

> Adg: Burning bridges behind you.
> Adg: Counting chickens before they're hatched.

appear to have little in common. However, in both "burning bridges" and "counting chickens", the planner has assumed plan success and so does not have a recovery plan available. The major difference, then, between TAU-FEW-OPTIONS and TAU-UNSUPPORTED-PLAN is that in "counting chickens" (i.e. TAU-UNSUPPORTED-PLAN) the planner has also gone ahead and made new plans based on the success of his initial plan, while in "burning bridges" the planner has restricted his recovery options in the face of a RISKY plan. The assumption of success (i.e. the false belief) is the same, but the planning metrics differ. In TAU-UNSUPPORTED-PLAN, the plans need not be risky at all.

As a result of the similarities between these two TAUs, the story YALE APPLICATION (on page 89), which was treated above under TAU-FEW-OPTIONS, might also be indexed under TAU-UNSUPPORTED-PLAN. This additional indexing will occur if the reader assumes that Bill's bad grades were a result of not bothering to work because Bill was already sure that he'd been accepted into Yale. Since a planner won't anticipate failure (and thus prepare recovery options) if he already assumes a goal success, TAU-FEW-OPTIONS often arises in situations also characterized by TAU-UNSUPORTED-PLAN.

Whenever an initial state of affairs, based on an erroneous assumption, can lead to distinct planning errors, multiple TAU recognition rules will be activated. Clearly, TAU interrelationships is an area for more future research.

3.5 Planning Metric Tradeoffs

As stated earlier, planning metrics do not operate in isolation. Although a high cost plan is worse than a low cost one, if the goal is important and the high cost plan is more efficacious, then choosing a high cost plan would not constitute an planning error. If a plan is very risky, but is the only one available, then again there is no error in planning. Thus, planning metrics are interrelated in a number of ways. Some of these interrelationships can be represented in terms of tradeoffs between goal importance, plan availability, and other planning metrics. Some of these tradeoffs are listed below:

td.1 The more important the goal, the more important to select plans with high EFFICACY, even if it violates other metrics -- i.e. plans with high COST, high RISK, high LIABILITY, etc.

td.2 The less important the goal, the more reasonable to choose plans with low EFFICACY, such as novel plans.

td.3 Minor, trivial goals should not be pursued with high COST, or high RISK plans.

td.4 Plans which have low AVAILABILITY and are EFFICACIOUS for achieving important goals should not be used to achieve minor goals.

3.6 The Point of Planning Metrics

Every plan has resource usages, timing constraints, and other preconditions. All of these constraints constitute a form of cost involved in using a plan. The goal which a plan can achieve is the benefit obtained. So errors in planning could be simply discussed in terms of a "cost/benefit" analysis. But what would we have gained? Nothing would be solved, other than stating the obvious. What is important, from the point of building a process model, are the following questions:

- What are the specific costs?
- What are the benefits?
- How are they calculated in different situations?

The scheme presented in this chapter is based on a categorization of planning metrics. Each metric has to be taken into account.   In addition, there are metric interactions.   Metrics are attached to and calculated for each plan.   Processes then examine each metric for plan misuse.   When metrics are violated in certain ways, these violations trigger memories.

Are the metrics presented here the 'right' ones? Some metrics may overlap somewhat and others may be too general.   This is an area in need of future research.   What is useful about the specific planning metrics presented here is that they provide a level of generalization and analysis which is free from (and yet arises out of) specific plans.   For instance, the metric of VULNERABILITY can have many possible causes. Maybe the planner is vulnerable in terms of resource use, or lost allies, or some enablement condition, etc. So theme recognition is based on generalization processes that abstract out these categories from more content-oriented information associated with specific goals and plans.

Thus VULNERABILITY is not a simple property attached to a plan, but is rather calculated from our knowledge of the strength's of the planner's opponents. What makes us look for this information is the fact that VULNERABILITY is known to be an important aspect of counter-planning.   We must already have recognized that the planner is in a goal competition situation and that the plan he selected is a counter-plan.   Once this much has been noticed from the content of the situation, then RETALIATION is a predictable abstract plan response.   Since the metric of VULNERABILITY is associated with RETALIATION, TAU recognition processes are then activated to check for negative side-effects. If the negative side-effects are greater than the goal achieved, then a TAU is built.

3.7 Conclusions

In this chapter we presented a general recognition scheme for TAUs based on categorizing TAUs according to 11 planning metrics, which include COST, RISK, AVAILABILITY, ENABLEMENTS, etc. These are summarized below, along with associated TAUs:

```
Planning Metrics                TAUs
-----------------               ----

  ENABLEMENT      TAU-POST-HOC,   TAU-UNSUPPORTED-PLAN
  COST            TAU-TOO-COSTLY, TAU-MADE-WORSE
  EFFICACY        TAU-TOO-WEAK, TAU-INCOMPETENT
  RISK            TAU-TOO-RISKY, TAU-LEAVE-ALONE
  COORDINATION    TAU-UNCOORDINATED, TAU-ALLIED-DECEPTION
  AVAILABILITY    TAU-FEW-OPTIONS, TAU-APPEASEMENT
  LEGITIMACY      TAU-HYPOCRISY, TAU-UNJUST-RETALIATION
  AFFECT          TAU-TOO-CAUTIOUS, TAU-HIDDEN-BLESSING
  SKILL           TAU-INEXPERIENCED, TAU-DIRE-STRAITS
  VULNERABILITY   TAU-VULNERABLE, TAU-GREATER-HARM
  LIABILITY       TAU-LIABLE, TAU-IMPLICIT-CONTRACT[23]
```

We have argued that TAU recognition processes are activated by the occurrence of either a) goal failures, b) plan failures, or c) expectation failures, (which include false beliefs). Of these, expectation failures are the most important TAU activators since they allow a planner to recognize a TAU (and thus access its error avoidance advice) before a goal failure actually results. Whenever an unexpected planning choice is taken, therefore, TAU recognition rules are activated. Which recognition rules are tried depends on the eleven planning metrics. The recognition rules make use of these planning metrics in order to assess the appropriateness of a given planning judgment. Associated with each metric are both context-free and context-sensitive (i.e. metric tradeoffs) rules which give the planner the ability to decide whether a planning error has been made. As a result, this system of planning metrics serves as an indexing scheme for TAU categorization, selection, and recognition.

---

[23]TAU-IMPLICIT-CONTRACT is discussed in section 12.3.

CHAPTER 4

The Role of AFFECT in Narratives

4.1 Introduction

This chapter presents a theory of AFFECT, developed in BORIS [Dyer, 1983], to deal with issues of processing and interaction between thematic sources of knowledge, such as interpersonal themes (IPTs) and TAUs.

Descriptions of the emotional states of characters, and the emotional reactions of characters to the situations they encounter, occur with frequency in narratives of any complexity. Why is this the case? What purpose does the mention of a character's emotional response serve in terms of its effect upon the way readers process narrative text?

The representation and processing of emotions has largely been ignored by story understanding systems. This is due in part to the kinds of stories which understanders, such as SAM [Cullingford, 1978], PAM [Wilensky, 1978b], FRUMP [DeJong, 1979b], and IPP [Lebowitz, 1980] were intended to handle. The stories these programs read were essentially action oriented. In contrast, BORIS [Lehnert, Dyer et al., 1982], [Dyer, Wolf, Korsin, 1981], [Dyer, 1981b], [Dyer, 1981a], [Dyer, 1981c], [Lehnert, 1981] reads more complicated narratives, where interpersonal themes (IPTs) and expectation failures (TAUs) must be taken more into account. These thematic elements are often revealed through affective reactions.

Consider DIVORCE-1. This narrative contains numerous references to the emotional reactions of its characters. These affective segments are highlighted in boldface below:

DIVORCE-1

Richard hadn't heard from his college roommate Paul for years. Richard had borrowed money from Paul which was never paid back, but now he had no idea where to find his old friend. When a letter finally arrived from San Francisco, Richard was **anxious** to find out how Paul was.

Unfortunately, the news was not good. Paul's wife Sarah wanted a divorce. She also wanted the car, the house, the children, and alimony. Paul wanted the divorce, but he didn't want to see Sarah walk off with everything he had. His salary from the state school system was very small. Not knowing who to turn to, he was **hoping** for a favor from the only lawyer he knew. Paul gave his home phone number in case Richard felt he could help.

Richard **eagerly** picked up the phone and dialed. After a brief conversation, Paul agreed to have lunch with him the next day. He sounded extremely **relieved** and **grateful.**

The next day, as Richard was driving to the restaurant he barely avoided hitting an old man on the street. He felt **extremely upset** by the incident, and had three drinks at the restaurant. When Paul arrived Richard was fairly drunk. After the food came, Richard spilled a cup of coffee on Paul. Paul seemed **very annoyed** by this so Richard offered to drive him home for a change of clothes.

When Paul walked into the bedroom and found Sarah with another man he **nearly had a heart attack.** Then he realized what a blessing it was. With Richard there as a witness, Sarah's divorce case was shot. Richard **congratulated** Paul and suggested that they **celebrate** at dinner. Paul was **eager** to comply.

In order to have a viable theory of affective descriptions in narratives, the following issues must first be addressed:

- How are affective aspects of narratives represented in memory and how are these memories accessed?

- How are affects recognized and what consequences do affects have on inferencing and other processes?

- What are the relationships between affective states and other knowledge structures?

4.2 Representing Emotions

In BORIS, emotional reactions are represented by a knowledge structure called an AFFECT. This structure is used to trace the emotional states of narrative characters at the moment that emotional reactions are experienced. Each AFFECT is constructed out of six basic components:

1.   STATE -- This component holds a primitive state of emotional arousal which is either positive (POS) or negative (NEG). In general, a NEG emotion signals a goal failure while a POS emotion indicates goal success.

2.   CHAR -- Indicates which character in the narrative is feeling the primitive emotion.

3.   G-SITU -- Refers to the goal situation which gave rise to the primitive emotional state. The major information an AFFECT carries is a goal situation which describes the success, failure, or activation of a goal, along with other information, such as agency and expectations. These are discussed below.

4.   TOWARD (optional) -- Primitive emotions can be directed at another character. For example, "anger" and "guilt" can arise from goal situations involving other characters.

5.   SCALE (optional) -- Characters can feel an emotion at various levels of intensity. Currently, BORIS only supports two levels: >NORM and <NORM. For example, "furious" and "ecstatic" are represented with STATEs being NEG and POS, respectively, and with SCALE set to >NORM. One the other hand, "mildly annoyed" or

"hardly upset" are captured by SCALE set to <NORM.[24]

6. E-MODE (optional) -- Goal situations can either refer to the expectations characters have about likely future outcomes, or to the expectations of characters concerning outcomes which are on-going. In the former case, E-MODE is set to EXPECTED, while in the latter, E-MODE may be UNEXPECTED.

One reason AFFECTs are important is because they implicitly convey information about goals [Wilensky, 1978b]. Although AFFECTs do not mention specific goals, they do describe abstract goal situations which are currently active. For example, in BORIS the affective descriptor "joy" indicates that a character has achieved some goal, while "sad" indicates a character's goal has failed. More complicated goals situations involve the intervention of other characters in pursuit of a goal (as in the case of agency). Hence "grateful" implies that some goal of x has been achieved by means of another character y, while "anger" directed by x toward y implies that y has caused a goal failure for x. The directionality of AFFECT can also be reversed. If a goal of x has failed due to y's actions, then y may feel "guilt". Alternatively, y may feel something akin to "pride" after having brought about a goal success for x.

In each of these cases, affective descriptors say nothing about specific goal content, but instead serve to reveal abstract goal circumstances.

Principle 5

```
+------------------------------------------+
| Affective reactions reveal underlying |
| goal situations at an abstract level. |
+------------------------------------------+
```

---

[24]To handle a broader range of differences in emotional intensity, a numerical scale could be used. However, the current, three-way value system of <NORM, (norm) and >NORM so far is adequate for the kinds of narratives BORIS has dealt with.

A portion of the BORIS lexicon appears in the table below. It contains a number of affective descriptions and their corresponding conceptual structures. Affect information is represented declaratively while abstract goal situations are captured by active processes, called demons. [25]

BORIS Affect Lexicon

lexicon	affect info.	goal situation
happy joyous glad	(AFFECT STATE (POS) CHAR x G-SITU (a))	(a) Goal of x achieved
unhappy upset sad	(AFFECT STATE (NEG) CHAR x G-SITU (b))	(b) Goal of x thwarted or suspended or preservation goal active
grateful thankful	(AFFECT STATE (POS) CHAR x G-SITU (c) TOWARD y)	(c) y caused goal situation (a) to occur

---

[25]Demons control their own processing. They can delay their execution until certain conditions have been satisfied. Demons are described in chapter 6.

```
annoyed        (AFFECT              (d)   y caused goal
angry              STATE (NEG)             situation (b)
furious            CHAR   x               to occur
                   G-SITU (d)
                   TOWARD  y)
```

- - - - - - - - - -

```
hopeful        (AFFECT              (e)   Goal of x
                   STATE (POS)             is active
                   CHAR   x
                   G-SITU (e)
                   E-MODE  (EXPECTED))
```

```
fearful        (AFFECT              (f)   P-goal (i.e.
worried            STATE (NEG)             preservation
                   CHAR   x               goal) is
                   G-SITU (f)             active
                   E-MODE  (EXPECTED))
```

```
surprised      (AFFECT              (g)   A goal is
shocked            STATE  pos/neg          achieved or
                   CHAR   x               thwarted
                   G-SITU (g)
                   E-MODE  (UNEXPECTED))
```

- - - - - - - - - -

```
relieved       (AFFECT              (h)   Situation (f)
allayed            STATE (POS)             was active but
                   CHAR   x               p-goal failure
                   G-SITU (h))            avoided
```

```
disappointed   (AFFECT              (i)   Situation
                   STATE (NEG)             (e) was active
                   CHAR   x               but goal is
                   G-SITU (i)             now thwarted
```

- - - - - - - - - -

```
proud          (AFFECT              (j)  goal of y
smug               STATE (POS)           achieved
                   CHAR   x              by x
                   G-SITU (j)
                   TOWARD  y)


guilty         (AFFECT              (k)  goal of y
ashamed            STATE (NEG)           thwarted
embarrassed        CHAR   x              by x
regretful          G-SITU (k)
                   TOWARD  y)


         - - - - - - - - - -


ecstatic       (AFFECT              (l)  important
                   STATE (POS)           goal of x
                   CHAR   x              achieved
                   G-SITU  (l)
                   SCALE  (>NORM)


hardly sad     (AFFECT              (m)  minor
                   STATE (NEG)           goal of x
                   CHAR   x              thwarted
                   G-SITU  (m)
                   SCALE  (<NORM)
```

In this lexicon more complicated AFFECTs are represented by partial decomposition into more basic AFFECTs. For instance, "gratitude" refers to goal situation (c), which itself accesses the simpler AFFECT of "joy" (goal situation (a) in the lexicon). Thus, "gratitude" represents an abstract situation in which x feels "joy" due to the fact that y has achieved x's goal.

In addition to joy, sadness, anger, gratitude, guilt and pride, BORIS handles descriptors such as "shock", "hope", "disappointment" and "relief". In BORIS these affective descriptors refer to abstract goal situations involving character expectations. For instance, a "hopeful" character expects happy outcome (e), while a "worried" character expects an unhappy outcome (f).

If a character feels "shock" or "surprise" (goal situation (g)), then we know this character had not anticipated the associated goal situation. In the case of "surprise" or "shock", however, the goal may have been either achieved or thwarted. As we can see from these examples:

    ex1: When John heard he'd won
          the lottery he almost had a fit.

    ex2: John was shocked to find out
         his car had been stolen.

in the case of "shock", whether the primitive emotion is POS or NEG must be determined by inference from contextual information.

"Relief" and "disappointment" involve more complex goal situations than "hope" or "fear". Consequently, like "gratitude" and "anger" they are also partially decomposed into their more primitive counterparts. In BORIS, "relief" indicates that a narrative character x at one point had an active goal, which x expected would fail. Instead, the goal either did not fail, or was then actually achieved. To capture this situation, the positive AFFECT which represents "relief" (situation (h) in the lexicon above) refers back to the AFFECT structure described by "worry" (situation (f)). So a character who feels POSITIVE "relief" is one who at some point felt NEGATIVE "worry". Conversely, "disappointment" is represented by an initial expectation that a goal would be achieved (e) which then actually ends up being thwarted (i).

4.3 Affective Connections

Although each AFFECT has a precise meaning in BORIS, their corresponding English words do not.[26] That is, people are 'sloppy' in

---

[26]There need not be a one-to-one correspondence between AFFECT structures and natural language terms. For instance, the emotional feeling y experiences after having achieved a goal for x can not be captured exactly by any single English word (e.g. consider "fulfilled", "satisfied", "proud", "gratified", "smug"). Likewise, the English word "smug" may refer either to x achieving one of x's own goals or to x achieving y's goal.

their use of emotional descriptors. For instance, "upset" can refer to either situations: "unhappy" (b), "angry" (d), "worried" (f) or "guilty" (k) in the lexicon above. This occurs because "unhappy", "angry", "fearful" and "guilty" all share the same NEGATIVE state of arousal.

As we've just seen, AFFECTs enter into standard relationships with one another. If we read that a character feels 'relieved', then we should be able to infer that this character (at some earlier point) may have felt "fearful". Likewise, if we read that a character is "fearful", then we should know that the character is also "unhappy". These AFFECT interrelationships are represented in diagram D4.1 below:

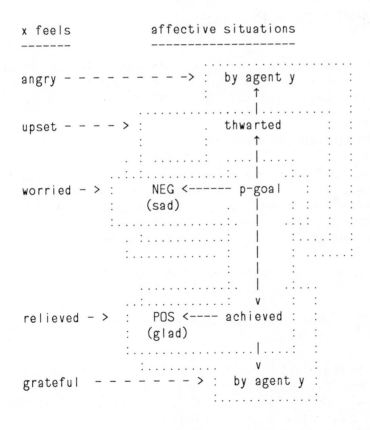

```
x feels                 affective situations
-------                 --------------------

                          ...........................
angry - - - - - - - - -> :   by agent y             :
                        :          ↑                :
        .................:         |              . :
upset - - - - > :           .   thwarted          : :
                :         :        ↑               : :
              . : .............   ..|......         : :
          ..: :.............       |         :  .:. :
worried - > :       NEG <------ p-goal        :  : :
          :         (sad)        .  |          :  : :
          :...................:.... |          :  : :
            :  :.............      . |        :......:
            :  :.............        |        :  .....:
            :  :.............        |        :  : .:
               :............... .    |        :  : :
             ..:.............:       v        : :
relieved - > :       POS <---- achieved  :    : :
             :       (glad)              :    : :
             :....................|.....: :
               :............. .   v        :
grateful  - - - - - - - > :   by agent y   :
                          :...............:
```

Diagram D4.1

Here, each affective description is represented by a "layer". Since some affective descriptions 'subsume' others, their layers overlap. Vertical arrows point to increasingly complicated goal situations.

BORIS uses this subsumption information to match emotional descriptions against emotional expectations. For instance, if "grateful" is expected, but the text says "relieved", the match will still be successful since gratitude 'subsumes' relief. Likewise, if "angry at" is expected, but the text reads "upset", the expectation will still be satisfied.

4.4 AFFECTs in Processing

In addition to carrying expectations, affective descriptions influence processing in two ways: 1) they trigger inferences and 2) they help construct memories. These influences are discussed below.

4.4.1 Cognition and Arousal

The BORIS approach to processing emotions separates the cognitive level (i.e. goal situations) from the level of emotional arousal [Mandler, 1981] [Mandler, 1975] [Schachter, 1966] [Schachter and Singer, 1962]. For example, when BORIS reads that a character x is angry with another character, BORIS infers two facts:

1. x is in a negative state of arousal.
   (i.e. the emotional primitive NEG)

2. x thinks that y has caused one of x's
   goals to fail.

It is important to realize that inferences arise from both levels: At the cognitive level, x may retaliate against y, using counter-plans [Wilensky, 1978b] [Carbonell, 1979]. At the arousal level, x may perform some action designed to reduce the negative state of arousal. This action may have little or nothing to do with recovering from the goal situation which has occurred.

For example, in DIVORCE-1 Richard almost ran over an old man. Since Richard never actually hurt the old man, the p-goals (i.e. preservation goals) triggered by this 'close call' were only active momentarily. However, Richard was left in a negative state of arousal. This motivated Richard to want to reduce that state -- in this case, by drinking alcohol. Without representing his emotional arousal, there would be no way of causally connecting Richard's drinking to the near accident. Thus, affective states can motivate goals. This causal connection is represented in BORIS by a bi-directional affect link,[27] which appears in diagram D4.2 below:

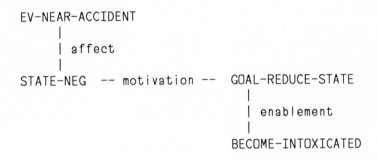

```
EV-NEAR-ACCIDENT
      |
      | affect
      |
STATE-NEG  -- motivation --  GOAL-REDUCE-STATE
                                  |
                                  | enablement
                                  |
                             BECOME-INTOXICATED
```

Diagram D4.2

This affect link is used by BORIS when answering the question:

Q: Why did Richard get drunk?
A: Richard was upset by almost
   having run over an old man.

Other inferences arise from the emotional reactions of characters. Consider the first sentence in the third paragraph of DIVORCE-1:

Richard eagerly picked up the phone and dialed.

---

[27]Other causal connectives are discussed in chapter 7.

Subject protocols indicate that most individuals have already inferred Richard will be Paul's lawyer by the time they have finished reading this sentence. But where did this inference come from? Nowhere does the story explicitly state that Richard will represent Paul. Yet the same inference would not be made if the story had read:

Richard morosely picked up the phone and dialed.

The inference that Richard will help Paul is supported by the word "eagerly". But how?

BORIS contains a number of affect interpretation rules and affect response rules. The interpretation rules map certain lexical items into AFFECTs while the response rules relate these AFFECTs to other knowledge structures. For instance, "eagerly" is interpreted by the rule:

> af1: If x is ACTOR of an ACT
>   which is modified by "eagerly"
>   Then interpret as:
>   "x feel POS affect while x do ACT"

while "morosely" is interpreted:

> af2: If x is ACTOR of an ACT
>   which is modified by "morosely"
>   Then interpret as:
>   "x feel NEG affect while x do ACT"

The affect response rules relate affects to other knowledge structures. For instance, rule ar1 below:

> ar1: If x ASK y to serve as agent for x
>   and y has POS affect
>   Then y has the goal of being x's agent.

> ar2: If x ASK y to serve as agent for x
>   and y has NEG affect
>   Then y has the goal of not being x's agent.

combines Paul's request for a lawyer with the affect arising from "eagerly" to lead BORIS to infer that Richard wants to be Paul's

lawyer.[28]   The cognitive level is represented by the cognitive
component G-SITU, which is important since it carries a description
of a character's goal situation. This information is used by BORIS in
several ways, one being to resolve pronominal references. Consider
again the third paragraph of DIVORCE-1:

> Richard eagerly picked up the phone and dialed.
> After a brief conversation, Paul agreed to have
> lunch with him the next day.   He sounded
> extremely relieved and grateful.

Who does "he" in the third sentence refer to? Richard could
conceivably be grateful that Paul agreed to have lunch with him.
However, people who read DIVORCE-1 assume that "he" refers to
Paul. The reason is that Paul (not Richard) is the one in trouble, and
it is Paul who asked Richard to be his agent. Therefore, Paul is the
one who should be grateful to Richard. As we can see, resolving "he"
requires knowing: a) the cognitive states of both Paul and Richard,
and b) what "grateful" and "relieved" mean at the cognitive level.
When BORIS sees that "he" is bound to the CHAR slot in an
AFFECT, it searches for an active character whose goal situation
matches the G-SITU associated with that AFFECT.   Therefore,
Richard is rejected as a potential referent and Paul is chosen instead.

The separation of the primitive arousal level from the cognitive
level is also important for recognizing expectation violations. Consider
the following:

> John was miserable when he learned that he had
> won the lottery.

There are two possible interpretations of this sentence: a) either John
was miserable prior to winning the lottery and now this news will
cheer him up, or b) John didn't want to win the lottery for some other
reason (e.g. John was in hiding and now the mafia will find him). In
either case, there is a discrepancy between AFFECT state and goal

---

[28]This situation is actually a bit more complicated, since "picked up the
phone" must be understood as an enablement for Richard to communicate his
agreement to Paul.

situation. This discrepancy causes us to want to find an explanation for the discrepancy. The point here is that, without both arousal and cognitive levels of affective knowledge, these discrepancies would go unnoticed.

4.4.2 AFFECT Intensity and Modality

The SCALE component is used by BORIS to determine the importance of the goal involved. For example, if x is "peeved" at y, then probably y caused x only a minor goal failure. If x is "furious", however, then y probably caused a very important goal of x's to fail. Therefore, the SCALE component interacts with other AFFECTs in the following ways:

> as1: If x achieves a major goal for y
> Then y will feel a gratitude >NORM

> as2: If x causes y a major goal failure
> Then x will feel guilt >NORM
> and y will feel anger >NORM

Instead of reading about Paul:

> Not knowing who to turn to, he was hoping for a
> favor from the only lawyer he knew.

suppose DIVORCE-1 had stated:

> Paul had picked Richard at random out of all of the
> lawyers listed in the yellow pages.

In this case, it would sound odd to hear that Paul was "extremely" relieved or grateful, since Richard was not the only available agent for Paul. This example also demonstrates how SCALEs and E-MODEs interact, which is captured by the following kinds of rules:

> as3: If x expects an important goal to fail
> and the goal is achieved
> Then x will feel relief >NORM.

as4: If x expects a minor goal to
be achieved and it fails
Then x will feel disappointment < NORM

If Paul were guaranteed a favor from Richard, then Paul would
not be so grateful. But since Paul is "hoping" for a favor, he cannot
be certain that Richard will help him. Therefore, Paul experiences a
feeling of gratitude and relief which is > NORM.

4.4.3 AFFECTs and Norm Deviations

During processing, norm violations initiate special processing.
For example, when BORIS reads:

Paul's salary from the school was very small.

it builds the following structure:

(OCCUPATION
    ACTOR Paul
    CLASS (TEACHER)
    LOCATION (INSTITUTION
            FUNCTION (EDUCATION))
    SALARY (SCALE IS (<NORM)))

As BORIS constructs the '<NORM', it tries to understand its
significance. One way to do this is by checking for a current
AFFECT associated with the ACTOR in this structure. BORIS uses
the following deviation rule to infer that Paul has an active P-
FINANCES (preserve finances) goal:

ad1: If x is the ACTOR in a knowledge
structure which has an attribute (ATTR)
and ATTR is >NORM or <NORM
and the current AFFECT of x is NEG
Then find a preservation goal G enabled by
ATTR and assume that G is active

This deviation rule works in many situations. Consider the
following case:

Mary was worried. She was overweight.

Here BORIS will infer that Mary has a PRESERVE-HEALTH goal active since PRESERVE-HEALTH is enabled by maintaining normal weight. In contrast, if the sentence had read:

Mary was happy that she was overweight.

then no preservation goal would be inferred.

4.5 Affective Empathy and Interpersonal Themes

Characters don't always react emotionally because they have experienced a direct goal failure or goal success. Often, a character will react emotionally because of what another character has experienced. These reactions are empathetic, and help specify the relationship existing between two characters in a narrative. Consider the following sentence from DIVORCE-1:

S-a: Unfortunately, the news was not good.

How is "unfortunately" to be represented and what is its effect on processing? Here, it is clear that "unfortunately" should be interpreted as:

Richard is negatively aroused because of some goal situation affecting Paul.

But what if the passage had read:

S-b: Fortunately, the news was not good.

Now, the natural effect upon the reader is to assume that Richard does not like Paul. The same result would be achieved by:

S-c: Unfortunately, the news was good.

but not by:

S-d: Fortunately, the news was good.

What is going on here?

In each of these cases, Richard is being emotionally influenced by the goals for which Paul has experienced success (or failure). In each case, BORIS's ability to make the correct interpretation is based on its knowledge of interpersonal themes [Schank and Abelson, 1977] as they relate to empathetic reactions. These relationships are represented in the following table:

Empathy Table

Y has a goal FAILURE	Y has a goal SUCCESS	interpersonal theme
X feels NEG	X feels POS	IPT-FRIENDS(X,Y) (goal accord)
X feels POS	X feels NEG	IPT-ENEMIES(X,Y) (goal conflict)

This Empathy Table encodes, among others, the following rules:

em1: If x and y are friends,
and y has a goal failure
Then x will experience a NEG AFFECT

em2: If y has a goal failure
and x experiences a POS AFFECT
Then either x and y are enemies,
or they are in conflict over this goal

As shown in the table above, situations of negative empathy arise from the interpersonal theme[29] of IPT-ENEMIES.   These situations are signaled by such words as "jealous", "spiteful" and "resentful".

Combining this general empathy knowledge with specific AFFECTs gives BORIS the following knowledge:

em3: If x and y are enemies
      and x causes y a goal failure,
      Then x may feel "smug"
      rather than "guilty"

em4: If x causes y a goal failure
      and x feels "smug",
      Then x and y are probably enemies

em5: If x achieves a goal for y
      and x and y are enemies
      Then y may feel "resentful"
      toward x

For example, in DIVORCE-1 Richard accidentally spilled coffee on Paul.   Since BORIS knows that Richard and Paul are friends, BORIS expects Richard to feel guilty.   However, if the story had read:

... Richard spilled a cup of coffee on Paul.   Richard felt very pleased.

this would have signalled a violation of their interpersonal theme.

4.6 ACEs

Empathetic situations also arise when a character x expresses,

---

[29]Interpersonal themes receive more treatment in chapter 10.

either to himself, or to another character y the reaction x feels concerning a goal situation affecting y. These situations are represented in BORIS by ACEs (Affect as a Consequence of Empathy). Below are the ACEs which exist in BORIS:

```
                      ACE                theme
                      ---                -----

commiserate       x MTRANS      (IPT-FRIENDS x y)
condole              TO  y
                     that [goal failure (y)
                             causes:  x feel NEG ]


felicitate        x MTRANS      (IPT-FRIENDS x y)
congratulate         TO  y
                     that [goal success (y)
                             causes:  x feel POS ]


envy              x MTRANS      (IPT-ENEMIES x y)
jealous              TO  y/x
spiteful             that [goal success (y)
                             causes: x feel NEG ]


gloat             x MTRANS      (IPT-ENEMIES x y)
                     TO  y/x
                     that [goal failure (y)
                             causes: x feel POS ]


reassure          x MTRANS
                     TO y
                     that [y should feel POS
                             in spite of active p-goal
                             or goal failure]
```

```
caution        x MTRANS
warn             TO y
                 that [y should feel NEG
                       in spite of goal success]
```

ACEs commonly occur in narratives involving interpersonal relations. For example, at the end of DIVORCE-1 Richard congratulates Paul. BORIS uses ACE-FELICITATION to interpret this as Richard telling Paul that Richard feels happy because Paul has won his divorce case. If DIVORCE-1 had ended:

> Paul laughed at Sarah and then left with Richard,
> as Sarah was hurling insults at him.

BORIS would use both ACE-GLOAT and ACE-ENVY to interpret this situation.

Empathetic situations also occur in DIVORCE-2 (appendix I.5). Unlike DIVORCE-1, DIVORCE-2 contains a courtroom scene. In this scene the judge sides with the wife. When George loses the case, we read:

> David could only offer George his condolences.

Here, BORIS uses ACE-COMMISERATION to interpret this to mean that David has told George that David feels badly because George has lost the case. So ACEs are important because:

```
                    Principle 6

        +---------------------------------------+
        | ACEs capture the empathetic aspect |
        | of interpersonal relationships.    |
        +---------------------------------------+
```

There are other forms of empathetic interaction. Instead of x telling y about how x feels, x can tell y how y should feel. In DIVORCE-2, the following sentence appears in paragraph four, just before the courtroom scene:

> David [the lawyer] told George [the husband] **not to worry,** since the judge would award the case to George once he learned that Ann [George's wife] had been cheating on him.

Here, George has a negative AFFECT and David is telling George that he should have a positive AFFECT (and why). This is represented in BORIS by ACE-REASSURANCE.

Application of ACE-REASSURANCE (and ACE-WARNING) is more complex than other ACEs since these ACEs are usually followed by a reasoning chain which one character uses to convince the other of his point of view. Thus, ACE-WARNING and ACE-REASSURANCE both imply a difference in beliefs (held by the characters) about the future outcome of a goal situation. In the example above from DIVORCE-2, David's reasoning chain involves the use of several reasoning rules:

> Contract rule:
>   If x alone violated a rule
>   in a contract between x and y
>   Then side with y in a legal dispute

> Witness rule:
>   If x wants to prove to z
>   that y committed a violation
>   Then an eye-witness to the violation
>   is convincing.

The resulting chain of reasoning becomes connected to the ACE-REASSURANCE in episodic memory. Reasoning is discussed in more detail in section 8.6.4.

Among philosophers of language, some constructs represented as ACEs in BORIS are treated within the framework of speech acts [Austin, 1975] [Searle, 1969]. For instance, Austin categorizes "congratulate" and "condole" within the speech act class of "behahitives", while Searle describes these terms as "expressives". There is some disagreement as to how certain terms should be categorized within various speech act taxonomies [Bach and Harnish,

1979] [McCawley, 1979].   Clearly, ACEs only capture a small portion of what is a very complex domain. For instance, one can go through the formality of congratulating someone else without really feeling glad for the other's success. It is still useful, however, to infer from this ACE that a goal success has occurred.

From a process point of view, then, what is important are the ways in which various affect-related constructs interact with one another; the expectations they trigger; the goals and themes they reveal; the kinds of memories and causal connections they help construct, etc.   ACEs are used in BORIS to organize basic expectations concerning goals, affect, empathy, and interpersonal themes.

4.7 AFFECTs and Episodic Memory

Subject protocols indicate that people can not directly access events when given the description of a character's AFFECT.   For example, the question:

Q: When did Paul feel angry?

is very difficult for most people to answer. Subjects try to answer this question by chronologically 'scanning' through the story until they encounter an event in which Paul might have become angry. Likewise,

Q: When did Richard feel surprised?

is answered by scanning until an event is encountered which would have surprised Richard.

These protocols are in keeping with experimental work by Robinson on autobiographical memory [Robinson, 1976].   In his experiments, subjects were prompted with object, activity, and affect terms in order to elicit recall of personal episodes. In general, subjects experienced much more difficulty in recall when prompted with affect terms than when prompted with either object or activity terms.

In the context of narratives, AFFECTs do not serve the same

kind of indexing functions to episodic memory that event-related structures do because a given character can experience many AFFECTs throughout a narrative -- i.e. one for each goal situation. For instance, Richard was surprised to receive a letter from Paul; to almost run over an old man; to have coffee spill on him, etc. In competing goal situations the same character may feel many conflicting AFFECTs at the same time. Consider the case in which Paul catches Sarah in bed. Subjects infer AFFECTs of shock, anger, joy, sadness and relief on Paul's part.[30]   So in order to effectively retrieve these AFFECTs some additional indices must be provided, such as events, settings or specific goals. Consequently, AFFECTs do not themselves hold memories in BORIS. Instead, AFFECTs are usually reconstructed from instantiated goal situations and the memory structures which refer to them. The next section discusses the reconstruction of AFFECTs from TAUs.

Bower and his colleagues have argued that emotions do play a role in indexing memories [Bower et al., 1981]. In their experiments, hypnotized subjects were induced to feel happy (or sad) by imagining various positive (or negative) situations. They were then asked to learn word-lists while in the given emotional state. Later, subjects were asked to recall the same word-lists, again while in a hypnotically induced mood. Word-list recall was better when the subjects were in the same mood during recall as they had been when the list was first learned. Furthermore, subjects who read a story while in a sad mood paid more attention to sad sections in the story and recalled more about sad characters.

The Bower et al. experiments provide evidence that the emotional state of the reader influences memory indexing and memory recall. However, it is **not** the intention of the BORIS program to model the reader's mood. That is, BORIS does not in any way 'feel' happy or sad while processing a narrative. Instead, BORIS simply monitors and infers AFFECT information from the emotional reactions of characters in a narrative. The distinction between feeling emotions and reading about the emotions of others is important and must be kept clearly in mind.

------

[30]Each of these AFFECTs arises from a different perspective. The issue of multiple perspectives is discussed in chapter 8.

4.7.1 AFFECTs Help Built TAUs

AFFECTs are rarely instantiated in BORIS' episodic memory. Instead, the occurrence of an affective reaction usually helps create other memory structures from which AFFECTs can later be reconstructed. The structures most closely related to AFFECTs are TAUs, which were discussed in chapter 2.

Briefly, TAUs arise whenever characters suffer expectation failures or goal failures due to errors in planning. For example, whenever a character accidentally causes a goal failure on the part of another character, TAU-REG-MISTAKE is instantiated. In DIVORCE-1, TAU-REG-MISTAKE is instantiated when Richard spills coffee on Paul. This structure is then used in understanding Richard's attempt to mollify Paul by offering to drive him home.

Likewise, whenever a character is relying on a plan requiring secrecy to achieve a goal and this plan fails as the result of an eye-witness, TAU-RED-HANDED is instantiated. In DIVORCE-1, TAU-RED-HANDED is instantiated when Paul catches Sarah in bed with another man. Since TAU-RED-HANDED predicts an AFFECT of "surprise", it is used to help disambiguate the phrase "he nearly had a heart attack" in DIVORCE-1 to mean "surprise" (rather than "cardiac arrest").

```
                    Principle 7

   +----------------------------------------------+
   | AFFECTs  help  signal  themes  involving |
   | planning errors and expectation failures. |
   +----------------------------------------------+
```

Since TAUs arise from failures, they are often signalled by the occurrence of an affective reaction. So AFFECTs help create memory structures indirectly by often indicating the presence of TAUs.

The only time an AFFECT must be instantiated explicitly in memory occurs when it motivates a goal directly at the arousal level. For instance, the NEG AFFECT that resulted from Richard's nearly hitting an old man directly motivated Richard's goal of drinking. In this case, a link was built between the AFFECT and this goal (see section 4.4.1). Even so, there is no way to directly access this emotional state. Rather, this AFFECT can only be accessed by first retrieving the goal which it motivated, or the event which gave rise to the AFFECT in the first place.

4.7.2 Answering AFFECT Questions

Once memories have been built with the aid of AFFECTs, BORIS is able to access these structures in order to answer questions concerning the affective reactions of the characters. Below are some of the AFFECT-related questions which BORIS has answered for DIVORCE-1:

```
Q1: How did Richard feel when the letter appeared?
RICHARD FELT GLAD BECAUSE PAUL AND HE WERE FRIENDS.

Q2: Why was Paul upset about the divorce?
PAUL AND SARAH WERE FIGHTING OVER
THE FAMILY POSSESSIONS.

Q3: How did Paul feel when Richard called?
PAUL WAS GRATEFUL BECAUSE RICHARD AGREED
TO BE PAUL'S LAWYER.

Q4: Why did Richard get drunk?
RICHARD WAS UPSET ABOUT ALMOST RUNNING
OVER THE OLD MAN.

Q5: How did Richard feel when the coffee spilled?
RICHARD WAS EMBARRASSED.

Q6: How did Paul feel when he caught his wife
with another man?
PAUL WAS SURPRISED.

Q7:  How did Richard feel when Paul won the case?
A7:  RICHARD WAS HAPPY ON PAUL'S BEHALF.
```

In most of these questions, the answer is reconstructed from the knowledge structure which was built when the situation (referred to in the question) was originally processed.   AFFECTs can be reconstructed from the following knowledge structures:

Structure	Used in Question
GOALs	Q2
TAUs	Q3, Q5, Q6
ACEs	Q7
IPTs	Q1

For example, when Richard spilled the coffee, TAU-REG-MISTAKE is built (see section 2.4). This structure represents BORIS's knowledge about social blunders and how each role (i.e. SCHLEMIEL and SCHLIMAZEL) will feel about the blunder. The character bound to SCHLEMIEL should feel embarrassed while the SCHLIMAZEL is expected to be angry. Unless the characters' reactions violate these expectations there is no reason to instantiate a specific emotional state in episodic memory. So when we answer Q5, we look for the default AFFECT associated with SCHLEMIEL in TAU-REG-MISTAKE. Likewise, the answer to Q6 is reconstructed from knowledge about TAU-RED-HANDED. Since TAU-RED-HANDED involves the failure of secrecy, the AFFECT of "surprise" can be reconstructed.

Question Q3 is answered by access to another TAU, TAU-DIRE-STRAIGHTS, which represents the situation in which a character's goal may fail because he has difficulty finding an agent to execute a plan he is incapable of executing himself. So TAU-DIRE-STRAITS captures Paul's situation in DIVORCE-1 of "not knowing who to turn to" and "hoping for a favor from the only lawyer he knew". Once Paul is instantiated as the one in need of an agent in TAU-DIRE-STRAIGHTS, the AFFECTs of "worry" and "hope", followed by "gratitude" (or possibly "disappointment") are predicted.

Question Q2 is reconstructed from Paul's goal, using the rule:

grl: If x has a goal G1 which
      is in competition with
      y's goal G2
   Then x will feel a NEG AFFECT
   (possibly directed TOWARD y)

which states that characters in goal competition situations often experience negative AFFECTs, including anger at their competitors. Since a divorce involves competition over family possessions, we can infer that both Paul and Sarah will feel upset and anger at one another.

Question Q7 is also reconstructed. We know that Paul feels happy to win his case since this achieves his goal. But how does Richard feel? Retrieval of this episode reveals an instantiation of the empathetic structure, ACE-FELICITATION. If x has congratulated y, then x must also feel a positive AFFECT. Therefore, the answer to Q7:

A7: Richard was happy on Paul's behalf.

is inferred from ACE-FELICITATION.

The answer to Q1 is inferred from knowledge of interpersonal themes, using the rule:

irl: If x and y have a positive IPT
    Then x and y will feel a POS
      AFFECT when interacting
      on an interpersonal level.

which represents the principle that friends make each other happy by keeping in touch with one another. More will be said about processing at the interpersonal level in chapter 10.

Question Q4 does not directly refer to an AFFECT. However, its answer involves an AFFECT because the goal of drinking was motivated directly by an affective state. As we saw earlier in section 4.4.1, the negative AFFECT on the part of Richard motivated Richard to want to reduce this state by drinking alcohol. Since this could not be reconstructed from another knowledge structure, BORIS instantiated it by means of an affect link (see diagram D4.2). This link is then used to retrieve the answer to question Q4.

4.8 Comparison With Other Work

PARRY [Colby, 1973] [Colby, 1975] [Colby, 1981] represents the other major language processing model to deal with issues of affect. PARRY was developed by Colby to model symptoms of paranoia. Colby's model ran in a conversational mode and used relatively simple syntactic and semantic patterns to analyze input from a human interviewer. As part of its response mechanism, PARRY monitored a set of numerical variables which represented emotional states of ANGER, FEAR, and MISTRUST. For instance, if FEAR was low and ANGER was high then PARRY would ignore the interviewer's inputs and generate verbal assaults.

These affect-variables interacted according to a set of numerical computations. For example, as FEAR increased MISTRUST would also rise according to the following formula:

```
MISTRUST <-- MISTRUST + (.5 x FEAR x (20 - MISTRUST))
```

PARRY's affect component is very limited and was originally designed to function as but one other influence on response generation. Affect-variables in PARRY served as an "interrupt system" for normal processing. They were intended to model the effect on processing of 'feeling' an emotion or being in a given emotional state. In contrast, BORIS is designed only to understand the conceptual significance of affective reactions on the part of narrative characters. To do so BORIS employs a representational system which relates AFFECTs to one another through decomposition and shared inferences. BORIS is not intended to model emotional states or experiences themselves.

This is an important distinction, since much work on AFFECTs in psychology deals with the physiological [Izard, 1971] [Izard, 1977], psychological [Mandler, 1975] [Strongman, 1978] [Cofer, 1972] and philosophical [Dennett, 1978] complexity of the emotional experience itself. The AFFECT theory in BORIS is more modest in scope since it is designed to deal with one task domain -- i.e. modeling the comprehension processes of narrative readers. Consequently, every design decision in the BORIS AFFECT model was made strictly for processing reasons [Lehnert, 1981].

Consider the division in BORIS between the (POS/NEG) state of arousal and the cognitive level. A number of psychologists

[Schachter, 1966] [Schachter and Singer, 1962] [Mandler, 1981] have made a similar division. In their case it was done in order to capture some of the physiological aspects of emotion. This is not the case in BORIS, which maintains an analogous division on representation and processing grounds alone. From a representational point of view, the POS/NEG state of arousal serves to distinguish relief from disappointment, joy from sorrow, gratitude from anger etc. From a processing point of view, the arousal level captures a set of inferences not handled at the cognitive level. For example, suppose we read a narrative about a character Joe who is fired by his boss. Joe then goes home and kicks his dog. Joe's act of animal abuse can only be explained at the arousal level since Joe's dog has no direct relationship to Joe's job. Similarly, people often avoid an individual who is very angry, even though they were not the cause of his goal failure. We know that such an individual may "take out" his anger on those around him.[31]   Actions resulting from the arousal level are often "irrational" in the sense that aroused individuals often later regret whatever they said or did while in their heightened state.

Another important part of a process model of AFFECT in the narrative domain is the interaction between AFFECT and other knowledge sources. Affective reactions do not occur in a vacuum but rather are initiated by narrative events and character concerns. In this thesis we have examined the interactions between AFFECTs and other knowledge sources, specifically GOALs, TAUs, and IPTs.

4.8.1 Roseman's Model

The approach to processing emotions, which has been taken in BORIS, derives much of its inspiration from a paper by Roseman [Roseman, 1979]. In that paper, Roseman developed five dimensions along which emotions could be categorized:

1. MS: Motivational State -- A division between what a character wants and does not want (i.e. a dimension of desirability).

2. SS: Situational State -- Whether a character gets what

---

[31]Likewise, a POS state of arousal may lead to hugging a stranger.

he wants or not (i.e. a dimension of outcomes).

3. PR: Probability -- What events will definitely occur versus what only may occur.

4. AG: Agency -- Whether the character who is feeling the affect, some other character, or impersonal circumstances were responsible for an outcome.

5. LE: Legitimacy -- Whether a character perceives an outcome to be deserved or undeserved.

By using these dimensions, for example, Roseman can represent the emotion of fear as:

$$MS(+) \ SS(-) \ PR(-)$$
or
$$MS(-) \ SS(+) \ PR(-)$$

So fear involves the chance that what you do not want may occur, or that what you do want may not occur. Similarly, guilt is:

$$MS(+/-) \ SS(+/-) \ AG(\text{self}) \ LE(-)$$
or
$$MS(-/+) \ SS(-/+) \ AG(\text{self}) \ LE(-)$$

which represents attaining something you wanted but didn't deserve, or failing to bring about something undesirable which was deserved.

BORIS captures the emotions discussed in [Roseman, 1979] by combining a cognitive level with a primitive state of arousal. Roseman's dimensions of desirability (MS), outcome (SS), probability (PR), and agency (AG) are handled in terms of abstract goal situations in BORIS, while the arousal element in BORIS does not seem to have any direct analog in Roseman's system.

Instead of the dimension of 'certainty', BORIS uses an expectation component (i.e. E-MODE). This allows BORIS to represent "surprise", which is considered in Roseman's model as a component of all emotions and unrelated to his five dimensions. The E-MODE is also used in BORIS to handle "relief" and "disappointment". Roseman does not mention "disappointment" in

[Roseman, 1979] and he handles "relief" as a negative motivational state that was not attained. In contrast BORIS handles "relief" as an active preservation goal that was expected to fail but was actually achieved.

Currently BORIS does not implement a dimension of 'legitimacy' for AFFECT processing. This would require more sophisticated knowledge about cultural values and norms. Instead, whether a character feels guilt or not depends on interpersonal themes (IPTs). If characters x and y are enemies, then x will feel that it is legitimate to thwart y's goals. If the characters have a positive IPT, then a NEG AFFECT is expected when one thwarts the other's goals. Also, expressions of "envy" (where x feels NEG because y has achieved a goal) and "felicitation" (where x feels POS because y has achieved a goal) are treated in terms of empathy (i.e. ACEs) arising from interpersonal themes. Expressions of empathy are not dealt with in Roseman's paper.

Furthermore, in Roseman's system, "liking/loving" and "disliking/hating" are treated just like any other emotion. In BORIS, however, a distinction is drawn between AFFECTs and IPTs. An AFFECT represents a short-term emotional reaction to specific goal situations while an IPT represents a set of attitudes existing between characters over a long period of time. In BORIS, "like/love" and "dislike/hate" are represented in terms of IPT-FRIENDS, IPT-ENEMIES, and IPT-LOVERS [Schank and Abelson, 1977]. As we saw earlier, the activation of IPT-ENEMIES (versus IPT-FRIENDS) causes a global reinterpretation of the types of AFFECT reactions expected. By making this distinction, BORIS can represent a character x who is momentarily angry with a wife normally loved by x, or momentarily grateful to an enemy normally despised by x.

Roseman made some finer discriminations [Roseman, 1982] than were needed in BORIS. For instance, Roseman distinguished "regret" from "guilt" along the dimension of legitimacy. According to Roseman's model one feels "regret" when one does not deserve a negative outcome, and "guilt" when one deserves a negative outcome.

In BORIS, "guilt", "embarrassment", and "regret" all refer to the same goal situation of x feeling NEG because x has thwarted a goal of y. From a processing point of view, what distinguishes these descriptors is not so much the goal situation, but other aspects surrounding the goal situation. These aspects include planning reactions and ethical judgements. For instance, "guilt" on the part of x implies that y may not yet know that x has thwarted a goal of y's. In contrast, "embarrassment" on the part of x implies that others were eye-witnesses to the goal violation. "Regret" contains a further inference that the character who caused the violation may plan to appease the victim whose goal was violated.

Once plans are taken into account, the domain of AFFECT interpretation widens. Consider the following text:

> Fred was painting the kitchen floor. Boy, did Fred feel stupid when he realized that he had painted himself into a corner!

Clearly Fred is feeling some emotion in this case. However, is it reasonable to call feeling "stupid" an emotion? From a processing point of view, "stupid" here means:

> x has a NEG AFFECT as the result of a goal failure caused by a error in planning which could easily have been avoided.

Other AFFECT related words also may refer to the planning surrounding a goal situation. Consider the following story:

> Kevin had lost his keys. He tried to get in through the window but they were all shut. Kevin then called a locksmith but it was after 5pm. Kevin was very frustrated but still felt determined.

Here, the word "frustrated" means:

> x has a NEG AFFECT as a result of a goal failure after having tried more than one plan to achieve the goal.

while the term "determined" means:

> x will continue to both plan (and execute plans) in order to achieve an active goal.

In order to fully comprehend the meanings of frustration or

determination in the above text, BORIS needs to be able to represent long-term plan situations, such as perseverance in the face of repeated plan failures [Lehnert, 1982a].   Likewise, affects of jealousy and disappointment play important roles in plot structures concerning revenge.   Affects of smugness and pride may refer to x achieving a goal before y within some competitive context. So AFFECTs not only serve to define goal situations, but may also supply additional information about planning and plot structures in narratives. This is an area for future research.

4.8.2 Scope of BORIS AFFECT Model

What is the scope of the BORIS AFFECT model for narrative text? Instead of looking at how affects are felt or experienced, Davitz examined the use of affective terms in English. His survey [Davitz, 1969] of Roget's thesaurus resulted in approximately 400 words dealing with emotions.   These he ultimately mapped down to 50 affect-related terms, selected by Davitz for their coverage of the vocabulary of emotion. The terms he arrived at are listed below:

Admiration	Delight	Gratitude	Panic
Affection	Depression	Grief	Passion
Amusement	Determination	Guilt	Pity
Anger	Disgust	Happiness	Pride
Anxiety	Dislike	Hate	Relief
Apathy	Elation	Hope	Remorse
Awe	Embarrassment	Impatience	Resentment
Boredom	Enjoyment	Inspiration	Reverence
Cheerfulness	Excitement	Irritation	Sadness
Confidence	Fear	Jealously	Serenity
Contempt	Friendliness	Love	Shame
Contentment	Frustration	Nervousness	Solemnity
	Gaiety		Surprise

Affect Vocabulary, Davitz [1969]

From the BORIS perspective, many of these items should be

handled in terms of distinct knowledge sources.[32]   Amusement, boredom, and enjoyment involve entertainment goals [Schank and Abelson, 1977]. Affection, contempt, dislike, friendliness, hate, and love are handled by BORIS in terms of interpersonal themes. Affect-terms which cannot be handled by the current BORIS model include those dealing with planning situations (determination, frustration, impatience) and attitudes or belief systems (admiration, awe, reverence, solemnity).

The remaining affect-terms listed above fall within the scope of the BORIS model. For instance, "confidence" can be represented as a positive AFFECT resulting from the expectation that a goal will be achieved, while "pity" can be represented as an expression or feeling of empathy for the victim of a goal failure.[33]

4.9 Conclusions

If we review the affective reactions of the characters in DIVORCE-1 we can see that almost every important event in the story is signaled by an AFFECT (either implicitly or explicitly):

---

[32]Some items may require multiple, overlapping sources of knowledge. See chapter 8.

[33]Some affect-terms are unusual because they are so specific in meaning. For instance, "grief" defines a negative AFFECT caused by a specific goal failure -- i.e. the loss of a positive interpersonal relationship through death. Other examples of such affect-terms are "lovesick" and "homesick".

Affective Reactions

Richard (R)	Paul (P)	Events
anxious		R gets letter
unhappy (empathy)	worried but hopeful	P gets divorced needs lawyer
	relieved and grateful	R takes case
surprised and upset		R nearly has car accident
guilty	angry	R spills coffee
	surprised and upset	Sarah caught
happy (empathy)	happy	P wins case

This makes sense, since any event of importance to a character will cause an affective reaction on the part of that character.

```
                   Principle 8

        +----------------------------------------+
        | Affective reactions signal situations  |
        | that are important to individuals.     |
        +----------------------------------------+
```

The importance of an event is not intrinsic to the event itself, but to the effect it has on the goals of each character. For example, a character will not be upset to lose an object unless he has the goal of possessing that object. So the goals of each character must be monitored, and one way to do this is by means of AFFECTs. An inappropriate affective response indicates that the goal we initially thought was active is not really active (or vice versa). For instance, if a millionaire loses his wallet, but is not upset, then there is no point in the reader expecting a plan to find the wallet. In contrast, if a child loses a penny and starts to cry, then the reader will expect the child (and possibly the parents) to do something about it.

Notice that understanding the intentional significance of the emotions of narrative characters does not in any sense require an experiential knowledge of emotions. In fact, getting a computer program to feel emotions appears to be a formidable task [Dreyfus, 1972] [Dennett, 1978] [Sloman and Croucher, 1981].

The theory of AFFECT developed in BORIS has had to deal with issues of processing and knowledge interactions with other knowledge structure classes, an example being the interaction between TAUs (which hold planning and expectation failures) and the affective reactions they predict. BORIS affect theory is oriented towards understanding the intentional significance of affective reactions by inferring their corresponding cognitive structures.[34] That is, the importance of emotions in narratives arises from the cognitive structures they signify. These structures reveal the goals of the characters, the goal outcomes they expect versus what actually occurs, and the longer-term relationships which are active between the characters themselves.

As we have shown, AFFECTs are important for both processing and memory. For processing, they help resolve pronominal references, supply active expectations, and trigger inferences. For memory, the mention of AFFECTs causes the creation of memory structures which help organize events for subsequent search and retrieval. Memory

---

[34]Some psychologists, for instance [Zajonc, 1980], argue that affective judgments precede in time the cognitive processes which are assumed by other researchers to constitute the basis upon which these affective judgments are being made. Whether or not this is the case, experience with BORIS strongly supports the claim that AFFECT processing, for narratives at least, is highly cognitive in nature.

structures containing affective reactions are exactly those structures which capture events of greatest importance to the characters involved.

PART II. PROCESS INTEGRATION AND MEMORY INTERACTIONS

This part is concerned with processes: their control, coordination and interaction. Parsing processes during narrative comprehension, retrieval processes during question answering, memory modification processes and reconstructive search processes are interdependent in a number of ways. These interdependencies are examined in chapter 5. What processes 'look like' in BORIS, where they come from, and how they are controlled is specifically addressed in chapter 6.

CHAPTER 5

Integrated Processing with a Unified Parser

5.1 Introduction

BORIS is an integrated natural language understanding system for narratives. In an integrated system, processes of event assimilation, inference, and episodic memory search occur on a word-by-word basis as parsing proceeds. "Parsing" here refers to the task of building a conceptual representation for each natural language expression. In addition to being integrated, the BORIS parser is also a unified parser. The same parser is used both at story understanding time and question answering time. This chapter explores some of the consequences which arise when the same parser serves both tasks. For instance, one such consequence is that BORIS often knows the answer to a question before it has completely understood the question.

5.2 Background

Early natural language programs at Yale used a single parser which operated in isolation from other conceptual processes. The parser would first map each sentence into its Conceptual Dependency (CD) representation [Schank and Abelson, 1977], which a script applier (SAM [Cullingford, 1978]), plan applier (PAM [Wilensky, 1978b]), or question answerer (QUALM [Lehnert, 1978]) would then interpret. For a time, it was hoped that a single parser could be constructed to serve as a "front-end" for every new project taking natural language as input.

But eventually it became clear that this type of modularity had its drawbacks. With an isolated parser, other process knowledge arising from the parsing task could never be made available as an aid in the natural language understanding task itself. Strict modularity was abandoned with the creation of FRUMP [DeJong, 1979b], which relied heavily on scriptal knowledge to direct its parsing processes. Since the creation of FRUMP, every parser at Yale has been integrated to a greater degree -- each trying to make use of task and domain specific knowledge as an aid to the parsing process.

To date, BORIS is the most integrated parsing project at Yale. BORIS runs as a single module: all tasks of event assimilation, inference, memory search and question answering occur as an integral part of the parsing process. Or to it put another way, parsing in BORIS is integrated into all other processes which are needed for narrative comprehension. This chapter discusses some of the issues and consequences that arise from an integrated approach to text processing.

5.3 Integrating Parsing With Memory Search

Our interest in making BORIS more integrated first arose within the task domain of question answering (QA). An informal analysis of question answering protocols revealed that people were making use not only of general syntactic, semantic and lexical knowledge to parse a question, they were also making use of episodic knowledge -- i.e. the information specifically contained within the story they had read. This made perfectly good sense. If people understand in context, then of course they would make use of the story itself as a context for understanding a question about the story. All this episodic information is available after a story has been processed, so why not use it to help parse questions?

For instance, suppose we read the following story:

> Richard hadn't heard from his friend Paul in years.
> He owed Paul money which he had never returned,
> because he didn't know where Paul lived. Then he
> got a letter from Paul asking him to represent Paul
> in a divorce case.

Now, if we are asked:

Q: Why hadn't Richard paid Paul back?

we will think of the following answer:

A: Richard didn't know where Paul lived.

Suppose, however, the story had been:

> Richard hadn't heard from his friend Paul in years.
> Paul had killed Richard's wife and Richard vowed
> that he would get back at him if it was the last
> thing he ever did, but Paul had escaped to
> Argentina.

Now if asked:

Q: Why hadn't Richard paid Paul back?

we do not interpret the question to mean: "Why had Richard not returned money to Paul?" Now we understand "pay back" in terms of revenge.

The expression "pay back" cannot be disambiguated by means of general semantic, syntactic or lexical knowledge. The only way "pay back" can be understood in the question above is by searching episodic memory while the question is being parsed. This view of the question understanding process has four major consequences:

(1) Integrated parsing changes our perspective on what it means to understand a question. It no longer means building a representation of the question in isolation of the narrative context. Understanding a question now involves finding a referent for the question in episodic memory. In the terminology of a prior question answering model [Lehnert, 1978], the parser is now also involved in memory search for an answer key. This means that the representation of a question is no longer just a Conceptual Dependency [Schank and Abelson, 1977] diagram but includes pointers into episodic memory -- i.e. references to episodic instantiations of higher level knowledge structures [Schank et al., 1980].

Principle 9

```
+------------------------------------------+
| The process of understanding a question  |
| cannot be separated  from  the  process  |
| of searching episodic memory.            |
+------------------------------------------+
```

(2) By viewing parsing and episodic search as an integral process, specific knowledge contained within the narrative becomes available to aid in the parsing process itself. As we have already seen with the example of "pay back", this integrated approach makes disambiguation easier.

Principle 10

```
+------------------------------------------+
| Integrating  parsing and  memory search  |
| makes parsing tasks easier.              |
+------------------------------------------+
```

(3) Since an integrated parser starts searching episodic memory immediately (as soon as the first word of the question is parsed), it is now possible to retrieve the answer to the question before its parse is finished. This may sound magical, but in fact people do it all the time. People search memory to find an answer as soon as possible, and then they monitor the rest of the question to make sure that no presuppositions have been violated. For example, given the following story:

> On a night when there was a full moon, John took Mary for a walk along the river. There he kissed her and asked her to marry him. She was so surprised that she was left speechless.

when asked the question:

Q: Who kissed Mary by the river when the moon
    was full?

most people recall the answer "John" by the time they have processed
the first three words in the question. The rest of the question is
simply monitored to make sure that any presuppositions in the
question do not violate knowledge of the story. Earlier Yale systems
would have first parsed the question in its entirety before attempting
any search for an answer.

Principle 11

```
+------------------------------------------+
| In an integrated parser, the answer to   |
| a question  may be  known  before  the   |
| question has been completely parsed.     |
+------------------------------------------+
```

In the case of verification questions, the processes of
understanding the question and finding the answer are equivalent.
For instance, in order to understand the question:

Q: Had Richard borrowed money from Paul?

BORIS must find a referent to this event in memory. If the event is
found while parsing the question, then the answer will be "yes". If a
memory referent cannot be found, then the answer will be "no". In
either cases, the answer is known the moment the question is
understood. At this point, additional search heuristics may be applied
to return an elaboration, such as:

A: Yes. When they were in college.

(4) In those cases when an answer is not found before the
question has been fully processed, subsequent answer retrieval will be
faster in an integrated system. This effect is the result of having
searched episodic memory during question understanding. Since the
parser has already searched episodic memory, the answer retrieval
phase is already partially accomplished by the time the parse phase is

completed.

Principle 12

```
+-------------------------------------------+
| Integrated parsing of questions results |
| in more efficient answer retrieval.     |
+-------------------------------------------+
```

5.4 Parser Unification

BORIS did not start out as a single module. Largely for pragmatic reasons, early versions of BORIS had two parsers. One was called DYPAR [Dyer, 1982] and was used to parse natural language questions about narratives. The other was a version of CA [Birnbaum and Selfridge, 1981]. The CA parser was used to analyze sentences occurring within narratives and produce a Conceptual Dependency representation for each. At story understanding time, a separate event assimilation module accepted these Conceptual Dependencies as input and constructed an episodic memory of the events in the narrative.

The integrated approach to parsing questions was sufficiently successful in BORIS for us to consider this approach for parsing narrative sentences at story understanding time. An additional motivation rose from our belief that two distinct parsers are not psychologically valid. It seems most unlikely that people would use one cognitive apparatus for answering questions which is fundamentally different from the mechanism used for understanding stories.

Because earlier parsers operated in isolation of episodic memory, parser unification had never been an issue. When a parser does not interact with any other processes during sentence analysis, it is trivial to use the same parser to produce Conceptual Dependency representations for both questions and narrative sentences. Parser unification only becomes tricky when parsing procedures are integrated with other memory manipulations.

Recall that the CA parser produced a Conceptual Dependency representation as output and the event assimilator then had the task of building episodic memory from each Conceptual Dependency input. Since the CA parser worked in isolation, it was up to the the event assimilator to apply top-down expectations across sentence boundaries in order to 'knit' events together into a cohesive episodic memory for the narrative. For example, whenever the parser failed to fill a role binding (because of ellisions), or whenever there was a need to interpret a Conceptual Dependency structure in terms of a higher level of knowledge, the event assimilator would step in. However, this approach posed a fundamental problem for parser unification.

A unified parser cannot rely on an event assimilation module to aid in the parse for the following simple reason: Once the narrative has been completely processed, event assimilation expectations no longer exist. These expectations arose as each sentence in the narrative was being read. When the comprehension task is complete and the entire narrative has been processed, there are no more active expectations. But the description of any event which occurred in a narrative may appear within a subsequent question about that narrative. So the QA parser has to be able to parse event descriptions which were parsed at story-understanding time, but without the help of an event assimilation module. It is important to have a QA parser which can work after all active story expectations have terminated.

In fact, the question answering parser (DYPAR) was parsing event descriptions successfully without relying on an event assimilation module. As we have already stated, it accomplished this by searching episodic memory during the parse. Thus, the solution seemed clear: unify the two parsers both by eliminating the event assimilator and by augmenting the QA parser to build episodic memory during its parsing process. This was accomplished, yielding a completely integrated system in which there is a single parser scheduling all processing for both story understanding and question answering.

Specifically, this complete integration was achieved by bottom-up processing techniques. Active processes called "demons" are associated with lexical and phrasal entities. In addition to syntactic and semantic sentence analysis, these demons also search and construct episodic memory.

Although these demons cannot be expected to know about the specific content of episodic memory, they do know enough about the structural principles of episodic memory to search it and determine how each lexical entity should be interpreted. This is done by finding an appropriate knowledge structure in memory, and activating processes associated with that knowledge structure. Memory search demons associated with lexical items ultimately determine which knowledge structure to apply.

Principle 13

```
+-------------------------------------------+
| Memory  access  and  parsing  are  two  |
| sides  of  the  same  coin:    parsing  |
| organizes memory access.                |
+-------------------------------------------+
```

To get an idea of how parsing can entail access to episodic memory, consider the following short story, with two alternative endings:

> Bill was very jealous of his wife Mary. He decided to hire George, a private detective, to keep an eye on her. George took his miniature camera with him to the school where Mary worked.

> E1: There, George found Mary with another teacher.

> E2: There, George found Mary with another man.

In E1, the inference is that Mary is also a teacher. However, the inference in E2 is not that Mary is also a man. The inference to be made about E2 is that Mary is with a man other than her husband Bill (versus other than George).

In addition, if E1 had been read in isolation, it would not be clear whether it is George or Mary who is also a teacher. Interpretive inferences in these cases depend on what immediately precedes and follows "another", and the relationship between George and Mary.

The moment "another" finds the object it is modifying, it activates demons to search episodic memory for the needed interpersonal information.[35]

5.4.1 Event Explanation

Integration in BORIS has resulted in a system which is more explanation-based than expectation-based. Each input must search memory in order to explain itself, instead of relying on some "top-down" process to grab it and interpret it. In BORIS, most expectations [Riesbeck and Schank, 1976] are encoded implicitly within the structure of episodic memory, rather than being active processes which poll the input. Because expectations in BORIS fall into a fixed number of classes, each class can be represented declaratively in terms of the kinds of memories which are being constructed.

For example, when BORIS reads:

S1: The teacher examined the student.

"examined" is represented as:

```
EV-1:  (D-KNOW ACTOR x
                OBJECT (STATE OF y)
                INSTRU (ATTEND TO y))
```

BORIS tries to 'explain' EV-1 in the following way:

> To explain an event E, use whatever bottom-up knowledge is associated with the event to decide where in memory to search. Once a knowledge structure (KS) is found, apply whatever processing is associated with that KS to E. This may result in building new structures (or connections) in episodic

---

[35]The word "another" appears in two narratives BORIS has processed. In DIVORCE-2, BORIS infers that a character is a teacher. In DIVORCE-1, BORIS infers marital infidelity. For a trace of DIVORCE-2, see chapter 11.

memory.

For instance, BORIS knows that the object bound to the ACTOR slot in EV-1 could tell it where to search. Since x is bound to RT-TEACHER (role theme information about teachers), BORIS searches knowledge structures associated with RT-TEACHER. Within RT-TEACHER are pointers to other memory structures (e.g. EV-GIVE-TEST in M-EDUCATION), which will match the description of EV-1. Consequently, EV-1 will be 'explained' in terms of M-EDUCATION. This particular search heuristic will also work correctly in other cases, such as:

S2: The doctor examined the student.

which refers to a rather different situation than the one described by S1.

When the semantics of the input sentence fails to constrain the memory search, episodic memory is searched according to recency. At story understanding time, "focus" lists are maintained of the most recently accessed knowledge structures. The first structure which matches the input is then used to interpret the input. This is similar in spirit to having explicit expectations poll the input according to recency. Thus, the explanation-based approach compares favorably with having expectation-driven techniques.

When is an event fully 'explained'? This is a difficult issue which ultimately depends on the beliefs and interests that a reader brings to the subject matter being read. A satisfactory explanation for one person may seem superficial to another. The intelligence of a reader depends on the depth of explanation sought and what is appropriate given the surrounding circumstances [Carbonell, 1979] [Schank, 1979].

In earlier versions of BORIS, two different approaches were tried:

- Once one knowledge structure has been found which matches the input, then the input has been explained.

- Exhaustively apply every knowledge structure to the input.

In either approach, a given knowledge structure can itself invoke other knowledge structures.

But there are weaknesses with each of these strategies. The first approach is inadequate for an understanding system which supports multiple perspectives [Lehnert, Dyer et al., 1980] [Lehnert, Dyer et al., 1982] [Dyer, 1981a] because the explanation process will terminate after only one perspective is found. For example, in DIVORCE-1, two characters (Richard and Paul) agree to meet at lunch for the following reasons: a) they haven't seen each other for years, and b) Richard is a lawyer and Paul wants Richard to represent him in the divorce case. Their meeting, therefore, has more than one perspective:

> At the scriptal level, a restaurant meal is occurring.
>
> At the thematic level, a suspended friendship is being renewed.
>
> At the role level, a lawyer and a client are meeting to discuss a legal case.

The second approach solves the multiple perspective problem by examining every active knowledge structure in order to explain a given input. However, this creates a very unfocussed system, which will always be considering lots of irrelevant knowledge structures. This approach, therefore, is inherently inefficient.

Here is the current approach used in BORIS:

> An event has been completely 'explained' once it has been analyzed at several specific levels -- scriptal, goal/plan, thematic, and role.

According to this approach, the following sentence:

> Richard borrowed money from his friend Paul to buy a car.

is analyzed in terms of the following levels:

```
  script           goal/plan              thematic
+--------+    +-------------------+    +----------------+
| borrow |    | instrument to     |    | doing a favor  |
| object |    | possessing a car  |    | for a friend   |
+--------+    +-------------------+    +----------------+
```

Once an event has been analyzed in terms of each level, the processing for that event terminates.

5.4.2 Parsing in Different Modes

Although both narrative sentences and questions are parsed by the same program, there are several situations in which the "mode" of understanding (question answering versus story understanding) requires the parser to behave differently.

Tokenization -- Whenever the parser encounters a reference to an object primitive, a setting, or a character, memory is searched to find out if the object already exists in episodic memory. In story-understanding mode, the failure to find a referent results in the creation of a new token in memory. However, during question answering, a failure to find a referent results in abandoning any attempt to find an answer. Instead, a 'complaint' is generated to point out that a referent could not be found. For example, given a story about two characters, Richard and Paul, and a question about George, BORIS would respond:

> Q: What does George do for a living?
> A: I don't recall any mention of a character
>   named George in the story.

So processes which govern tokenization must be sensitive to the narrative task being performed.

Presupposition Checking -- During story understanding, if a knowledge structure in episodic memory is referenced and the role bindings created during the parse fail to match the bindings already in memory, this indicates that a new instantiation must be built. For example, in DIVORCE-1, Richard receives a letter from Paul. If a letter were subsequently mentioned as having been written by another character (say Sarah), then BORIS would create a new instance of a letter knowledge structure in memory.

During question answering, the parser also checks the role bindings presumed by the question against the actual bindings maintained in episodic memory. In this case, however, a failure of roles to match indicates a false presupposition. So BORIS rejects the question and corrects the false presupposition. For instance:

> Q: Why did Sarah write to Richard?
> A: It was Paul, not Sarah, who wrote to Richard.

But people sometimes fail to notice false presuppositions. In such cases the presupposition can become incorporated into their memory model of the narrative. This effect will be discussed more fully in section 5.5.

Question Words -- In any narrative or question, words like "who", "what", "why", "where", etc. must be handled in special ways. If such a word is encountered during question answering, it is assumed to initiate a request for information. During story understanding however, different demons process these words when they occur at clause boundaries. So if a question is encountered while the story is being comprehended, it will be treated as a rhetorical question, and no attempt will be made to answer it.

Local Contexts -- Another difference between story understanding and question answering modes arises from the use of local contexts in story understanding and question answering tasks. Local contexts are represented by the memory created for events immediately prior to some event currently being explained. Consider the following sentence from DIVORCE-1:

> Richard had borrowed money which was never paid back, but now he didn't know where to find his old friend.

The parse of the first clause causes the knowledge structure M-BORROW to be built, within which the event EV-RETURN-OBJ is marked as violated. The second clause, however, is understood with the help of a local M-BORROW context. As the parser produces a representation of Richard's goal failure (not knowing where to find Paul), the following rule is activated:

Negative event rule:

> If a negative event E2 occurs,
>   and the local context contains a
>   violation of a prior event E1
> Then see if E2 is an enablement condition for E1
>   and if so, create a link: <E1 blocked-by E2>
>   as an explanation of the violation.

Thus, 'not knowing where to find Paul' is understood as the explanation for 'never having paid Paul back' by using the above rule, along with enablement information supplied by M-BORROW.

A different kind of local context exists during question answering. In this case, the local context contains the last question asked, along with its answer.[36] Consider the following question and its alternative answers:

> Q: Did Richard know where to find his
>   old friend?
>
> A1: Yes, they met at a restaurant.
> A2: Yes, Paul had written to Richard.
> A3: No. Richard hadn't heard from
>   Paul in years.

Although this question contains information similar to its narrative

---

[36]One use of local context during question answering is to handle situations such as:

```
Q1:   Who wrote Richard a letter?
A1:   Paul.
Q2:   Why?
```

where both the previous question (Q1) and answer (A1) are needed to understand a subsequent question (Q2).

counterpart, BORIS will find answers A1 and A2 before A3 because the local context provide constraints differing from those used during story understanding.

More specifically, there is no direct access to all of Richard's knowledge states in BORIS. Instead, BORIS is forced to search a scenario map (see chapter 9) in order to see if Paul and Richard ever interacted with one another. However, understanding the question:

Q: Why hadn't Richard paid Paul back?

accesses M-BORROW directly (as it was accessed at story understanding time). Next the <blocked-by> link, which was constructed during the comprehension phase, is retrieved by an interference search [Dyer and Lehnert, 1980]. This results in the answer:

A: Richard didn't know where Paul lived.

One natural consequence of the different uses of local context in story understanding and question answering is that it is difficult to understand a question about an event which required a local context when being understood at story understanding time.

5.5 Memory Modification During QA

As parsing became unified and integrated in BORIS, an unanticipated situation arose during question answering: asking BORIS certain questions created episodic memory modifications. At first we thought this effect was a 'bug' in the program, and the difference in parsing modes (see section 5.4.2) was set up in an attempt to eliminate it.

But on further reflection, there is no reason to believe that people only construct memories during narrative comprehension, any more than they only search memories during question answering. In fact, psychological experiments by Elizabeth Loftus [Loftus, 1979] [Loftus, 1975] have demonstrated that the process of asking questions can modify the memory of eyewitnesses. Preliminary experiments performed at Yale [Lehnert and Robertson, 1981] [Lehnert, Black,

Robertson, 1982] [Robertson, Lehnert, Black, 1982] show that the Loftus effect occurs in the case of narratives as well. It follows that memory modification during question answering is a natural consequence of a unified and integrated parser.

How do memory modifications during question answering actually occur? If we assume that the mode of processing (as described in section 5.4.2) determines when new memories can be built, then memory modification depends on "fooling" an understanding system in question answering mode to think that it is operating in story understanding mode. This naturally occurs if the understander assumes that whoever is asking a question knows something about the narrative and may impart this information within the question. Questions normally convey information by means of presuppositions. For example, suppose we read a story about John going to some unidentified store, and then we are asked:

Q: When did John go to buy groceries?

Here, the questioner presupposes that John went specifically to a grocery store. If we believe that the questioner knows something about John's activities, then we will accept being told new information in the question. This is similar to having heard originally that John went "grocery shopping". So modification of old information during question answering depends on:

1. An acceptance (by the answerer) that the questioner may know something about the situation under examination.

2. New information supplied in the presupposition of the question.

Here is an example of a memory modification during question-answering which occurred in BORIS: At the end of paragraph four in DIVORCE-1, Richard had spilled coffee on Paul and as a result offered to drive Paul home for a change clothes. At this point, BORIS was asked the following questions:

Q1: Why did Paul go home?
A1: So he could change clothes.

Q2: Why did Paul change his clothes?
A2: Because they were wet.

Since BORIS expected Paul to arrive at home and change his clothes, and since the questions presupposed that these events had actually occurred, BORIS's memory was altered as a result of parsing Q1 and Q2. At this point episodic memory had instantiated both the event of arriving home and changing clothes (which were never explicitly mentioned in DIVORCE-1).

The process of understanding a question may also build novel access links to episodic memory. In DIVORCE-1, for instance, the event of Paul writing a letter is never explicitly stated. Therefore, no access link to this event exists in episodic memory. When BORIS is first asked:

Q: Did Paul write to Richard?

the explicit mention of "write" causes BORIS to search the knowledge structure M-LETTER and infer that this event must have occurred. At this point, BORIS builds a direct access link to the event EV-WRITE in M-LETTER. The next time BORIS is asked a question regarding this event, memory retrieval will be faster, since the access link now exists. Thus, asking questions about reconstructed events creates indices for access, so subsequent retrieval of an answer to a similar question is faster.

In BORIS, memory modification can occur because the processes which add information to an event description are the same processes which check presuppositions. For example, if a narrative sentence states "John got a letter from Mary" then a letter-event must be instantiated with the bindings: $<$sender $=$ Mary$>$ and $<$receiver $=$ John$>$. In order to determine that this is not a reference to a new letter-event, memory search processes must search to see if another letter-event exists with different bindings. Now suppose that BORIS is asked: "Why did John get a letter from Mary?". Again we must search memory for a letter-event which shares these bindings. So presupposition checking and role-binding instantiations are performed at the same point during both story understanding and question answering. However, if a question presupposition clearly violates our memory, we will complain. So the question: "Why did John kill Mary?" -- in a story about John and Mary getting married -- will not be accepted.

The experiments in [Lehnert and Robertson, 1981] indicate that memory modifications during question answering are more likely to occur when the presuppositions in the question do not violate any important script, plan or goal information in the narrative. Modifications during question answering depend on what information was built in memory during narrative comprehension, and how strongly presuppositions conflict with it. If absolutely everything stated (or inferable) in a narrative were explicitly instantiated, then presupposition checking would always notice new information assumed in a question. However, if memory is largely *reconstructed* from more general information, then it is difficult for a presupposition-checker to distinguish new information from old -- as long as the new does not violate anything on purely reconstructive grounds.

Principle 14

```
+-----------------------------------------+
| For QA-time  memory modifications to |
| occur, memory must be reconstructive.|
+-----------------------------------------+
```

There is good evidence that human memory is largely reconstructive [Bartlett, 1932] [Anderson and Bower, 1973]. For example, Spiro et al. [Spiro, Esposito, Vondruska, 1978] used the following experimental materials in a series of reading experiments:

(A) The karate champion hit the block.

(B) The block broke.

(C) He had had a fight with his wife earlier. It was impairing his concentration.

The following claims were made about reconstructive memory:

1. If only (A) and (B) were first presented, then (B) could be reconstructed from (A), so (B) would not be instantiated in memory. Therefore, a later presentation of (C) would cause people to falsely assume that (B) had not occurred, and memory of (B) would be degraded.

2. If (C) were presented before (A) and (B), then (B) could not be easily reconstructed. Therefore, (B) would be explicitly instantiated, so memory of (B) would not be degraded.

These claims were supported by the experimental data. Whenever people could infer the consequence of an antecedent they did not have to instantiate it, since it was reconstructable. This meant that false information about reconstructable events is more likely to be integrated into an existing memory representation.

5.6 Memory Reconstruction in BORIS

In keeping with the reconstructive claims espoused in Spiro et al. [Spiro, Esposito, Vondruska, 1978], the BORIS system tries to follow a simple principle:

Principle 15

```
+------------------------------+
| Don't instantiate  anything |
| which can be reconstructed.  |
+------------------------------+
```

Whenever a knowledge structure is successfully applied in interpreting an input, a memory instantiation is created (or updated), in which the following information is stored:

1. A pointer to the knowledge structure which was activated (If we don't instantiate this, BORIS wouldn't know what had happened versus what had not happened.)

2. Any role bindings (so that BORIS can recall who did what to whom).

3. Scenario information (so that an event can be placed in a spatio-temporal relationship with other events)

4. "How far" along in the knowledge structure BORIS has progressed.

5. Any higher level goals which this knowledge structure has either achieved, or intends to achieve.

6. Any violations or deviations of this knowledge structure.

Therefore, any event central to a script, scenario, or goal is instantiated. By definition, violations and deviations can not be reconstructed, so they are instantiated. For instance, when BORIS reads a narrative in which George is having coffee at a restaurant, the fact that someone served the coffee is reconstructable from knowledge in a restaurant script. However, if BORIS reads that the waitress spilled coffee on George, then the spill-event must be explicitly instantiated as a violation of EV-BRING-FOOD in M-RESTAURANT and a violation of EV-DO-SERVICE in M-SERVICE. Chapter 8 discusses this example in more detail.

5.7 Conclusions

In a completely integrated system, both parsing and memory processes require a fresh examination. Our experience suggests that one way to proceed is by building fully integrated systems in which a single parsing process invokes all comprehension tasks on an on-going basis.

This chapter has discussed some consequences arising from unifying parsing for both question answering and narrative comprehension in an integrated system such as BORIS. Two major consequences are:

• Answers to questions may be known before questions have been completely understood.

- Asking questions may modify episodic memory by augmenting it with new information contained within the questions.

These phenomena resemble the type of behavior people exhibit when reading and answering questions about narratives, and they deserve further experimentation in both the computational environment and the psychology laboratory.

CHAPTER 6

The Process of Comprehension

6.1 Introduction

To understand complicated narratives like DIVORCE-1 and DIVORCE-2 many different processes must be organized and coordinated. In this chapter I will present an overview of the process model of narrative comprehension which is implemented in BORIS. This overview deals with the following issues:

- How are processes represented and what determines when a process is to be applied?

- What processing tasks must be performed during comprehension?

- How are those processes coordinated which deal with knowledge interactions?

6.2 Demons and Processing Control

In BORIS, all process knowledge is implemented in the form of demons [Dyer, 1982]. Demons fall within the class of production systems [David and King, 1977] [Waterman and Hayes-Roth, 1978] [Anderson, 1976] [Newell, 1973] [Riesbeck and Schank, 1981] and are a generalization of Riesbeck's requests [Riesbeck and Schank, 1976]. Demons implement a form of delayed processing. Demons wait until their test conditions are satisfied, at which point they fire and execute their actions. Each live (active) demon is in charge of its own life cycle, deciding how long to stay alive and when to die. A demon usually kills itself whenever one of the following situations occurs: a) the demon has performed its task, b) the demon notices that some other demon has already accomplished the same task, or c) the demon decides that its test condition no longer has any chance of being satisfied.

Several demons may be assigned the same task, with each one attempting to accomplish it by different heuristic methods. In this way, even if one demon fails another may still succeed, resulting in a more robust system. Once one demon has succeeded, competing demons notice this and kill themselves. As a result, the number of demons active at any time remains small, and this results in efficient processing.

Demons may also "spawn" other demons, thus forming more complicated processing structures, such as a "discrimination tree" of demons. (For more detail, see [Dyer, 1982] or appendix II.) As each demon is spawned, it may be assigned a priority, which determines the order in which demons are tested. In general, unless priorities override the default order, demons are tested according to recency. Finally, demons take arguments, which are bound to corresponding demon parameters at the time the demons are spawned. As a result, processing code is easily shared between demons and many instantiations of the same demon (using different arguments) may be active at the same time. [37] The algorithm below describes the basic control cycle of BORIS, including demon interpretation:

---

[37]BORIS demons are not to be confused with demons in [Charniak, 1972]. Problems with Charniak-style demons are cogently discussed in [Charniak, 1975].

Top-level BORIS Algorithm

LOOP-UNTIL finished narrative
Set READING-MODE to SU

LOOP-UNTIL finished PARSING a paragraph
  Examine next WORD:
    IF WORD is recognized directly in the lexicon
      or is part of a recognizable phrase
        in the phrasal lexicon
      or its root and suffix are recognized
        by morphological analysis
    THEN create a conceptual node (CON)
      and add this CON to Working Memory (WM)
      IF WORD is ambiguous
      THEN set CON node to NIL
        and spawn disambiguation demons
          associated with the word in the lexicon
      IF WORD is unambiguous
      THEN bind CON node with its Conceptualization
        and spawn its associated demons
    ELSE mark WORD as unknown and ignore

  Interpret Demons:
    LOOP-UNTIL no more active demons fire
      FOR each Demon do
        If KILL condition is true
        Then destroy Demon
        If TEST condition is true
        Then execute Demon ACTIONs
          (including spawning other demons)
          and afterwards destroy Demon
        Else Demon remains alive
    END-LOOP [on demons]
  END-LOOP [on paragraph]

Set READING-MODE to QA

LOOP-UNTIL finished a QA session
  PARSE a Question (as during SU above)
  (If the CONCEPTUAL-ANSWER not found
    before PARSE is completed
  Then execute any remaining search demons
  spawned during the parse)

  GENERATE English response (using both the
    CONCEPTUAL ANSWER and PARSE result as input)
END-LOOP [on QA]

END-LOOP [on narrative]

BORIS reads each narrative sentence (or narrative question) word by word in a left-to-right order. Associated with each word (phrase, root, or suffix) in the lexicon are conceptualizations and attached demons. When a lexical item is recognized, the associated conceptualization is placed into a Working Memory and its associated demons are spawned and attached to it.

There are two basic differences between episodic memory and working memory: 1) Working memory becomes inaccessible after each sentence has been incorporated into episodic memory. Thus, demons which search working memory are essentially searching only the most recent active context. 2) Working memory represents the bindings created between word senses, while episodic memory contains the resulting memory structures after inferential processes have occurred.

If a word is ambiguous, then disambiguation demons are spawned. It is their job to select an appropriate conceptualization for the lexical item under consideration [Small, 1981]. Whenever a lexical entity is disambiguated in terms of a CD (Conceptual Dependency) structure [Schank, 1975], or whenever a CD structure is reinterpreted in terms of a higher level of knowledge (such as a MOP[38] or TAU), demons associated with that new knowledge structure will end up being spawned and attached to it. Thus, the process of comprehension may be abstractly characterized as a cycle of knowledge structures spawning processes which build new knowledge structures, where both demons and knowledge structures initially arise from lexical input:

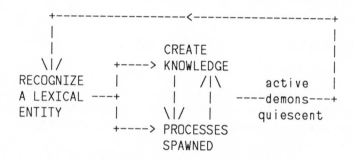

```
     +-------------------<-------------------+
     |                                       |
     |                   CREATE              |
    \|/         +----> KNOWLEDGE             |
RECOGNIZE        |        |   /|\      active |
A LEXICAL ---+   |        |    |    ----demons---+
ENTITY       |   |       \|/   |    quiescent
             +----> PROCESSES
                    SPAWNED
```

Knowledge/Process Creation Cycle

By now it should be clear that all important processing is controlled by demons. This makes it difficult to outline a simple control structure for processing in BORIS. Only by describing the classes of demons which exist in BORIS, and the functions they perform, can we arrive at a clear picture of the corresponding process model of narrative comprehension implemented within BORIS.

Demons in BORIS may be divided into two broad categories: a) demons which deal with interactions between knowledge structures and b) task-oriented demons which perform all of the other jobs necessary for building episodic memories, such as role bindings and word sense disambiguation.

---

[38]MOPs stand for "Memory Organization Packets" and are discussed in chapters 7 and 8.

6.3 Knowledge Interaction Demons

There are seventeen different knowledge structures used by BORIS. These structures must be recognized, instantiated and connected to one another in appropriate ways. How is this done?

It would be prohibitive for BORIS to check every potential knowledge interaction combination. For instance, the number of simple pairwise combinations for n elements is:

$$PAIR\text{-}COMB\ (n) =\ n!\ /\ (2\ *\ (n\text{-}2)!)$$

Given seventeen knowledge elements there would be over 130 pairwise combinations for BORIS to monitor. For n-ary combinations greater than two the potential interactions would be even more explosive.

6.3.1 Knowledge Dependencies

Instead of this "brute force" approach, BORIS makes use of dependencies to delimit the number of knowledge interactions which must be monitored:

Knowledge Dependency Graph

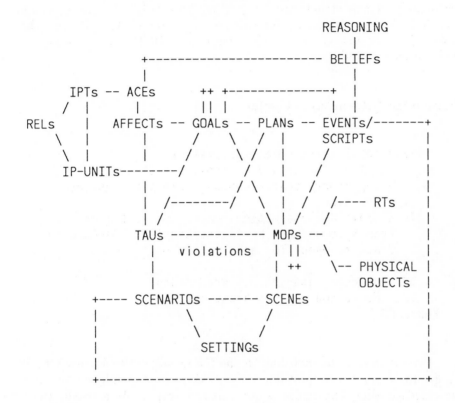

Some of the nodes in this graph have already been discussed somewhat (i.e. TAUs, GOALs, PLANs, AFFECTs, ACEs). The other knowledge structures, such as IPTs, IP-UNITs, RELs, and RTs, are used to represent knowledge about interpersonal themes, interpersonal actions, relationships and social roles. These structures are discussed in part III, along with SETTING information.

There are twenty-eighty knowledge interactions which BORIS must monitor, represented by the links in the above graph. Consequently, BORIS only monitors about one fourth of all potential knowledge interactions. This fact has a number of ramifications, which will be discussed shortly.

BORIS makes use of this Knowledge Dependency Graph as follows: Whenever a knowledge structure K is recognized during the parse, KS-interaction demons are spawned to determine the relationship of this structure to any other knowledge structures which have links to K within the Knowledge Dependency Graph. At the knowledge interaction level, the algorithm BORIS uses may be characterized as follows:

Knowledge Interactions Cycle:

```
LOOP
    Examine an input conceptualization
    Try to find (or create) a Knowledge Structure K
       (using memory search demons, role bindings, etc.)
    If K is found,
    Then spawn KS-interaction demons for each link
         from K to another KS in the Knowledge Dependency
         Graph to check for an interaction

    If knowledge interactions are  found,
    Then build connections between them
END-LOOP
```

Corresponding to each link in the Knowledge Dependency Graph is a group of demons responsible for checking the dependency between two corresponding knowledge sources in the graph. As a result, there are twenty-eight groups of demons dealing with knowledge structure interactions.

As we can see from the Knowledge Dependency Graph, there are a fixed number of ways in which different knowledge structures can interact with one another. This information serves as a constraint on the kinds of situations BORIS must check for during comprehension. Knowing that only a fixed number of knowledge interactions are allowed helps BORIS avoid having to test for all possible combinations.

For example, consider the dependency between ACEs and AFFECTs. What effect does this dependency have on processing?

Since ACEs are dependent on AFFECTs, whenever an AFFECT

is recognized in a narrative BORIS spawns demons to find out if this AFFECT is being MTRANSed between two characters. If this situation is true, then the demons reinterpret the AFFECT in terms of an appropriate ACE. In this way BORIS recognizes "told him not to worry" in DIVORCE-2 as ACE-REASSURANCE (see section 4.6).

Principle 16

```
+-----------------------------------+
| Knowledge structure dependencies |
| help in the recognition process.  |
+-----------------------------------+
```

Since AFFECTs only interact with ACEs, GOALs and TAUs in the Knowledge Dependency Graph, BORIS only checks three cases whenever an AFFECT arises. This serves as a constraint on processing effort and makes predictions concerning both processing and memory.

Furthermore, only a portion of the knowledge interaction demons is ever active at any one time, since the number of links emanating from a given knowledge structure is rarely more than six. By keeping the number of knowledge-structure interaction demons low, we get a very efficient system. But there are two consequences this constraint has on processing:

Consequence 1: A greater amount of processing effort will be expended on those knowledge sources with the most connections in the Knowledge Dependency Graph.

MOPs, Goals and TAUs have the greatest number of links in the Knowledge Dependency Graph. Therefore, the recognition of these structures will cause the greatest number of interaction demons to be spawned. In contrast, the mention of a PHYSICAL OBJECT will cause BORIS to check only for a possible MOP that specifies how the OBJECT is used. For instance, the mention of a phone will cause the MOP M-PHONE to be searched. On the other hand, a knowledge structure with many connections will be used most often during search and therefore will have more search heuristics associated with it.

Consequence 2: Since BORIS only checks for one fourth of all possible knowledge interactions, any story containing interactions which do not fit the ones predicted by the KS-Graph will be both a) more difficult to understand, and b) more difficult to recall.

Suppose two knowledge structures X and Z are activated during story comprehension. If there is no direct connection between them in the Knowledge Dependency Graph, then an intervening structure (or path) Y may have to be inferred in order to make the connection. The longer the path, the more difficult the inferencing process. For instance, since there are no direct connections between SCENARIOS and AFFECTS in the knowledge interaction diagram above, BORIS does not spawn demons to check for SCENARIOs when AFFECTs arise. Knowing this, we can make a number of predictions about how BORIS will behave in certain situations. Suppose BORIS reads:

> S1: John was really upset while at the restaurant.

BORIS will not be able to recall John's emotional state, nor will BORIS be able to answer the question:

> Q: How did John feel at the restaurant?

because BORIS has been told neither the goal situation which gave rise to John's AFFECT nor the event from which John's goal could be inferred. Since AFFECTs do not directly interact with SETTINGs, BORIS will never connect John's anger with John's location. As a result, BORIS will not be able to recall John's emotional state when supplied with John's location. Instead, suppose BORIS reads:

> S2: At the restaurant Bill punched John in the mouth. John became very angry.

In this case, BORIS will have no trouble recalling the answer to the question:

> Q: How did John feel at the restaurant?

Here BORIS makes use of the following knowledge interdependencies to understand the above passage:

```
SETTING -> SCENARIO -> EVENT -> GOAL -> AFFECT
```

When a new setting is recognized, BORIS spawns scenario-mapper demons (described in more detail in chapter 9) which associate that setting with any events which arise within that setting. When the punching event occurs, BORIS spawns event demons which infer the appropriate goals. In this case, a thwarted P-HEALTH goal is created. Finally, when an AFFECT reaction occurs, BORIS spawns affect demons which search for a corresponding goal situation. As a result, S2 above is understood in terms of the following connections:

```
S-0
 NODE-TYPE = MAIN-SCENARIO
 SETTING = RESTAURANT-0
 EVENTS  = (EV-PROPEL-FIST-0)
               |
               |motivation
               |
               |          affect
          P-HEALTH-0 ---------- AFF-NEG-0

RESTAURANT
     NODE-TYPE = SETTING
     SCENARIOS = (S-0)
```

This episodic memory fragment contains an access link between the RESTAURANT setting and its instantiated SCENARIO (S-0). SCENARIOs organize events (EV-PROPEL-FIST0) which are connected to goals (P-HEALTH0) by one or more intentional links (I-links).[39]

Now if BORIS is asked the question:

Q1: How did John feel at the restaurant?

BORIS again uses the same knowledge structure interdependencies, this time in order to search the memories created at understanding-time.

---

[39]I-links and SCENARIOs are discussed at length in chapters 7 and 9.

Principle 17

```
+---------------------------------------+
| Knowledge structure interdependencies |
| determine  memory  search  heuristics |
+---------------------------------------+
```

As BORIS parses question Q1, it sees that the question supplies a SETTING and requests an AFFECT. If we again examine the knowledge structure dependency graph above, we can see that there are a number of ways to get from a SETTING to an AFFECT. One path is the same as that used in understanding the passage in the first place. If this path is traversed, then BORIS will recall the fist-fight event and retrieve (or possibly reconstruct) John's emotion of anger toward Bill. This results in the response:

A1: John was angry at Bill.

The Knowledge Dependency Graph contains a number of psychological predictions as well. These predictions can be summarized as follows:

> If the Knowledge Dependency Graph is an accurate representation of the knowledge interactions which people monitor while reading narratives, then people will have difficulty recalling narratives which deviate from the KS interactions represented in the graph.

For example, the BORIS process model predicts that people will tend to forget that John was angry in a restaurant if no intervening event or goal situation is mentioned.

6.3.2 Origin of the Knowledge Dependency Graph

At this point the reader may wonder: if only one fourth of all possible interactions are used, then why was this particular subset chosen and not some other? The answer is simple:

Principle 18

```
+-----------------------------------+
| Knowledge structure interactions are |
| a  consequence  of  representational |
| dependencies.                        |
+-----------------------------------+
```

This means that the links in the Knowledge Dependency Graph are derived from structures used in representing a given source of knowledge. For example, we saw in chapter 4 that AFFECTs are represented in terms of goal situations. Since AFFECTs require reference to goals at the representational level, the recognition of an AFFECT during comprehension will cause the spawning of demons which try to find the goal(s) being implicitly (or explicitly) referenced. As a result, the representation of AFFECTs in terms of GOALs leads naturally to processing interactions between AFFECTs and GOALs during comprehension. Likewise, since each MOP is represented in terms of configurations of GOALS, PLANs, EVENTs, and SCENEs, it will be linked to these structures in the Knowledge Dependency Graph. This in turn leads to spawning demons in order to check for these dependencies. This situation is captured by the following principle:

Principle 19

```
+---------------------------------+
| Processing  control  parallels |
| memory structure interactions. |
+---------------------------------+
```

So one can predict the kinds of process interactions which will occur by knowing how different knowledge structures interact. Thus, memory interactions organize processing. On the other hand, the kinds of interactions which need to be monitored by BORIS reveal the ways in which knowledge structures depend on each other representationally.

6.4 Task Oriented Demons

In addition to categorizing demons according to the kinds of knowledge interactions they monitor, demons in BORIS may also be characterized according to the kinds of tasks they perform during narrative comprehension and question answering. These tasks are numerous and cannot all be discussed equally. (For a detailed trace of the comprehension process as applied to one story, see chapter 11). Only the more important demon tasks will be described here:

6.4.1 Role Binding and Role Checking

Whenever a conceptualization is placed into Working Memory, demons are spawned to find bindings for the roles associated with that conceptualization. For instance, the word "wrote" causes an M-LETTER MOP to be placed in Working Memory. Associated with this MOP are letter READER and WRITER roles. At least one demon is associated with each role and spawned to search Working Memory for an appropriate concept to bind to this role. Once an event has been found in episodic memory, the role bindings associated with the concept in Working Memory are matched against existing roles in episodic memory to insure that a presupposition has not been violated.

6.4.2 Memory Instantiations

Whenever a role-binding occurs in Working Memory, these bindings are used to determine whether a new or old structure is being referenced in episodic memory. Thus, role bindings provide the discriminations needed in accessing episodes in memory. If an episode can not be accessed, this indicates either that a new episode is being referenced (during story understanding), or that a presupposition has been violated (during question answering).

For example, consider the word "write". This is represented in the lexicon as:

lexicon:

```
write      (M-LETTER
              LET-WRITE * <== (EXPECT 'HUMAN 'BEF)
              LET-READER * <== ((EXPECT 'HUMAN 'AFT)
                                (PREP-OBJ 'HUMAN 'TO)
              LET-INFO * <== ...
              EVENT (EV-MTRANS-LET)
              INSTAN * <== (FIND-MOP) )
```

associated demons:

```
PREP-OBJ [Pattern, Preposition]
  Search Working Memory for Pattern
  which is object of Preposition
  When found, bind to role

EXPECT [Pattern, Direction]
  Search Working Memory for Pattern
  in the Direction specified
  When found, bind to role

FIND-MOP [mop]
  Search Episodic Memory to see if a MOP
    can be found with matching role bindings
  If not,
  Then create a new episode in memory
  Else return a referent to the episode found
```

Associated with each unambiguous lexical entry is a single conceptualization. Each unfilled role is followed by a star (*) which acts as a place-holder for a binding. Demons whose task it is to fill these roles appear after the arrow <==. Each arrow indicates where to bind the return values of the demons. Several demons may try to fill the same role. This is indicated by more than one demon following the same arrow. Demons which take parameters are enclosed within parentheses, followed by the arguments passed to them. For more detail, see [Dyer, 1982] or appendix II.

When the word "wrote" is encountered in DIVORCE-2, a

conceptualization referring to the M-LETTER MOP is build in Working Memory and role-binding demons are spawned. In this case, two activations of the EXPECT demon are spawned. The EXPECT demon knows about word order, while the PREP-OBJ demon knows about prepositional phrases. As the roles are bound, the demon FIND-MOP uses these bindings to search episodic memory for an instance of M-LETTER. Depending on whether the bindings in Working Memory match similar bindings in Episodic Memory, and whether the mode of reading is QA or SU, determines what actions are taken. These actions may be any one of the following:

1. Return a referent to an existing episode.

2. Build a new MOP (or update an old MOP) and return a referent to a new episode.

3. Generate a presupposition violation complaint.

The MOP application is discussed in more detail in chapter 8.

6.4.3 Word Sense Disambiguation

Whenever a word or phrase can refer to more than one conceptualization in the lexicon, then one must be chosen. There are two ways disambiguation can be achieved: 1) in a top-down fashion or 2) in a bottom-up fashion [Wilks, 1976].

In the top-down case, the expectation encoded in the test portion of some active demon (not spawned by the current word) uniquely matches one of the possible conceptualizations for some ambiguous word. When this happens, BORIS chooses that conceptualization as the meaning of the ambiguous word and then spawns whatever demons are associated with that conceptualization. In the bottom-up case, special demons are spawned (by the current word) whose job it is to examine memory and determine from context which conceptualization should be chosen.

Any ambiguous word may be disambiguated by either method. The particular method by which disambiguation occurs depends on the kinds of demons active in memory at any given time, and the order in which they were spawned. Consider the following sentences:

S3: John drinks gin.

S4: John plays gin.

where "gin" contains two possible meanings in the lexicon:

word   **sense**

"gin"   1.   (GAME CLASS (CARD-GAME))

          2.   (LIQUID CLASS (ALCOHOL))

The word "gin" may disambiguated either top-down or bottom-up. In the top-down case, a demon associated with INGEST (from "drinks" in the lexicon) will expect a LIQUID while the demon associated with "plays" will expect a GAME. Either way, BORIS will automatically chose the meaning which uniquely satisfies the expectation of the demon which first encounters "gin".

In the bottom-up case, when "gin" is read, a disambiguation demon is spawned. This demon will search the current context, using the following rules to select an appropriate meaning:

If the context involves INGEST
Then interpret "gin" as a LIQUID

If the context involves COMPETITIVE-ACTIVITY
Then interpret "gin" as a GAME

By either method the word will be correctly disambiguated. If a word is disambiguated in a top-down manner, then the bottom-up demons will kill themselves once they notice that disambiguation has occurred. "Gin" is disambiguated bottom-up in the following cases:

S5: The gin spilled ...

S6: The gin players...

This method has the advantage that both top-down and bottom-up processes can operate simultaneously without each getting in the way of the other.

Principle 20

```
+-----------------------------------------+
| Bottom-up and top-down processes must |
| be able to interact without conflict. |
+-----------------------------------------+
```

6.4.4 Reference

Whenever an object primitive, pronoun, relationship or proper name is encountered, reference demons are spawned. These demons may search both Working Memory and Episodic Memory to determine the referent [Shwartz, 1981]. If an old referent cannot be found then reference demons call upon tokenization functions to instantiate a new character (or object) and associate with it any relevant features.

In the case of pronominal references, the demons spawned when a pronoun is encountered may not always find the correct referent. For example, consider the following sentence from DIVORCE-2:

> S7: ... the judge would award the case to George once the judge learned that Ann had been cheating on **him.**

The referent demon associated with "him" basically searches Working Memory for the most recent character with a male gender. In this case, the demon encounters the judge, and so mistakenly thinks that "him" also refers to the judge. In fact, no local heuristic exists which will always return a correct referent. Consider the following sentence:

> S8: ... the judge would award the case to George once the judge heard the case that David would present to **him.**

Here, the word "him" does refer to the judge. Clearly, knowledge must be applied. To resolve this problem, BORIS takes the following approach:

> When a pronominal object appears, spawn local referent demons to assign a tentative referent. Select the most recent referent with matching gender and syntactic case.

The majority of the time these assignments result in correct references. But when higher level knowledge is applied and role bindings are checked, if a tentative binding violates a presupposition, then the tentative binding is rejected. For example, when BORIS reads S7 above, a referent demon tentatively assigns "him" a referent to the judge. However, once "cheating" has been interpreted (via search demons) as TAU-BROKEN-CONTRACT0 of R-MARRIAGE, the roles in TAU-BROKEN-CONTRACT0 are matched against those in Working Memory. At this point BORIS realizes that "him" must refer to George.

6.4.5 The Lexicon: An Example

The lexicon in BORIS has little resemblance to a normal dictionary. In BORIS, lexical entries point to sources of knowledge and demons. For example, consider the phrase:

...his wife Ann...

in the second paragraph of DIVORCE-2. When BORIS encounters this phrase it must infer the following:

- Ann (not George) is the character being referenced.

- George is a married man.

- The name of George's spouse is Ann.

This is accomplished by means of reference demons associated with each lexical items in the phrase. A portion of the lexicon which includes "his", "wife" and "Ann" appears below:

Sample Lexicon

```
Ann       (HUMAN GENDER (FEMALE)
                FIRST-NAME (ANN)
                LAST-NAME  * <== (LAST-NAME)
                INSTAN  * <== (CHECK-CHAR)  )


George    (HUMAN GENDER (MALE)
                FIRST-NAME (GEORGE)
                LAST-NAME  * <== (LAST-NAME)
                INSTAN  * <== (CHECK-CHAR)  )


her       (REF   CASE (POSSESSIVE)
                GENDER (FEMALE)
                INSTAN * <==  (FIND-CHAR)  )


his       (REF   CASE (POSSESSIVE)
                GENDER (MALE)
                INSTAN * <== (FIND-CHAR)   )


husband   (HUMAN
              GENDER (FEMALE)
              REL (R-MARRIAGE
                      HUSBAND * <== ((NEXT-CHAR)
                                     (REL-ROLE 'HUSBAND))
                      WIFE    * <== (POSS-REF 'FEMALE)
                      INSTAN  * <== (CHECK-REL) )
                  INSTAN * <== (INNER-INSTAN 'HUSBAND) )



roommate  (HUMAN
              REL (R-ROOMMATE
                      ROOMMATE-A * <==(POSS-REF)
                      ROOMMATE-B * <==((NEXT-CHAR)
                                       (REL-ROLE 'ROOMMATE-B))
                      INSTAN  * <== (CHECK-REL) )
                  INSTAN * <== (INNER-INSTAN 'ROOMMATE-B)  )
```

```
wife      (HUMAN
              GENDER (FEMALE)
              REL (R-MARRIAGE
                       HUSBAND  * <== (POSS-REF 'MALE)
                       WIFE     * <== ((NEXT-CHAR)
                                       (REL-ROLE 'WIFE))
                       INSTAN   * <== (CHECK-REL) )
                  INSTAN  * <== (INNER-INSTAN 'WIFE) )
```

The demons associated with the sample lexicon are briefly defined below:

Demons from Sample Lexicon

CHECK-CHAR [gender, names]
  Search Episodic Memory for a character
  with the same gender, last name and first name.
  If one is found then return its INSTAN,
  else create a new character
     with appropriate attributes.

CHECK-REL [role, rel]
  When either HUSBAND or WIFE role is bound,
  search episodic memory for the marriage.
  If found,
  Then return a referent to it
     and spawn demons to compare Working
     Memory roles with Episodic Memory roles
  Else create a new relationship
     with appropriate attributes.

FIND-CHAR [gender]
  Search Working Memory for a character
     with the same gender.
  When found, return its INSTAN.

LAST-NAME [char]
  If an unknown word immediately follows,
  Then assume it is character's last name
  and update character information.

NEXT-CHAR [char]
  If a HUMAN follows
    (or an unattached HUMAN precedes)
  Then return its INSTAN.

INNER-INSTAN [Slot]
  When the inner INSTAN of the specified
    Slot has been bound
  Then use it to bind the demon's role.

POSS-REF [gender]
  When a possessive referent is found
    with an appropriate gender,
  then return its INSTAN.

REL-ROLE [rel]
  When an appropriate relationship
    is found in Episodic memory,
  then retrieve the specified role
    from that relationship.

As BORIS reads each word in the phrase "his wife Ann" (from DIVORCE-2) one by one the associated conceptualizations are placed into Working Memory and their attached demons are spawned:

"... his"

The demon FIND-CHAR fires first and binds its INSTAN to the character George0. Now BORIS knows the referent to "his".

"wife"

Next the POSS-REF demon fires and binds the HUSBAND role with George0. Once a role in R-MARRIAGE has been bound, the demon CHECK-REL searches episodic memory to see if BORIS already knows about George's marriage. Since no marriage is recalled, an instance of R-MARRIAGE is created in Episodic Memory and instantiation demons are spawned which will update this relationship with the appropriate roles. If a marriage had been found, BORIS would have spawned demons to compare the wife role in episodic memory against the wife role supplied in working memory. At this point BORIS has a reference to a HUMAN in working memory which BORIS knows to be George's wife. However, BORIS still does not know who the wife is.

"Ann"

When this word is read, a CHECK-CHAR demon is spawned which searches episodic memory for a female character with "Ann" as a first name. Since none is recalled, CHECK-CHAR creates an instantiation of a new character (i.e. Ann0) and binds its referent to the appropriate INSTAN. Now the demon NEXT-CHAR can fire, since it has found a HUMAN following with a bound INSTAN.

At this point BORIS knows that the phrase "his wife Ann" refers to a character named Ann (rather than to George). The demon INNER-INSTAN now fires and binds its INSTAN with Ann0 also. Finally, an instantiation demon spawned by CHECK-REL notices that the WIFE role for this R-MARRIAGE is now known, so it adds this information to episodic memory. The LAST-NAME demon kills itself once it sees that the word which follows "Ann" is not a last name. BORIS has now made all of the necessary inferences and built up a marriage relationship in long-term memory. At the same time, Working Memory now holds the following conceptualization as a local context:

```
(HUMAN GENDER (FEMALE)
    REL (R-MARRIAGE
            HUSBAND (REF   CASE (POSSESSIVE)
                     GENDER (MALE)
                     INSTAN (GEORGE0))
            WIFE  (HUMAN GENDER (FEMALE)
                     FIRST-NAME (ANN)
                     LAST-NAME NIL
                     INSTAN (ANN0))
            INSTAN   (R-MARRIAGE0))
    INSTAN (ANN0))
```

This represents a reference to the female character ANN0 who is involved in the marriage relationship R-MARRIAGE0 with the character GEORGE0.

6.4.6 Theoretical Perspective

The processes just described are very general and robust. For example, the same demons are used to parse the following cases:

> From DIVORCE-1:
>   "his old college roommate Paul"
>   "Paul's wife Sarah"
>
> From DIVORCE-2:
>   "his wife Ann"
>   "her lawyer"

and other variations, such as "Paul, the husband of Sarah". There are several points to be made here:

1. All search processes are integrated.

There is no separate phase in which Working Memory is first searched, and then episodic memory is searched. Both kinds of search go on simultaneously, each relying on the results of the other and each contributing to the other. For instance, if "George's wife" were parsed a second time, after BORIS already knew that George is married, then a referent demon which searches episodic memory would return a referent to Ann0, even if the word "Ann" fails to lexically follow the phrase "George's wife".

2. Instantiation processes rely on role bindings and reference searches.

In order to create memories, existing memory must first be searched. Instantiation processes are the result of failures to recall the appropriate role bindings or referents in episodic memory.

3. Linguistic knowledge is shared whenever demons are shared.

In the past, researchers have argued against having linguistic knowledge subservient to semantic structures because that knowledge would have to be repeated for each distinct semantic structure[40] However, linguistic knowledge is not repeated in BORIS since demons are shared. Knowledge about a syntactic construct can be held in a single demon which assumes different semantic parameters.

> 4. Integrating conceptual analysis with other memory processes makes the comprehension task easier.

As a result of integrated parsing, memory structures are created "on the fly" while parsing proceeds. BORIS builds a marriage relationship in episodic memory while parsing a sentence about George catching Ann with another man in bed. In fact, the correct interpretation of the rest of the sentence relies on this marital information. If George were not married to Ann, BORIS could not infer adultery on Ann's part.

The demons which recognize adultery cannot be expected to search Working Memory for information about Ann's marital relationship, since the fact that Ann is married to George might actually have been mentioned many paragraphs earlier in a narrative. Thus, searching and building episodic structures during parsing leads to more robust parsing.

> 5. The distinction between Working Memory and Episodic Memory is essential for memory instantiation processes.

Psychological experiments indicate that human memory is divided into short-term and long-term memory [Miller, 1956]. This distinction is maintained in BORIS, but not solely for reasons of psychological validity. The distinction between a working memory (which fades after each sentence) and a long-term episodic memory is maintained in BORIS for processing convenience as well. This memory separation is required for three reasons:

---

[40]This argument has been made by ATN proponents [Woods, 1973] against word-based approaches. For example, see pp. 208-9 in [Tennant, 1981].

(1) In order to decide whether to create new events in memory, or to simply update already instantiated knowledge structures, BORIS must be able to compare the bindings, supplied by parsing the input, with the bindings already existing in episodic memory.

(2) In order to recognize that a violation has occurred, BORIS must be able to maintain a distinction between what is supplied as input versus what BORIS knows about the world in general.

(3) When parsing questions, BORIS must be able to distinguish the presuppositions in the question against the role bindings retrieved from episodic memory.

6.4.7 Reinterpretation Processes and MOP Application

When events and goals are encountered in a narrative, BORIS attempts to find higher-level knowledge structures, (such as scripts, MOPs, or TAUs) for which these conceptualizations form a single component.   The process of recognizing a Conceptual Dependency (CD) structure as part of a larger knowledge structure is termed reinterpretation.   For example, when BORIS reads in DIVORCE-1 that

> Richard picked up the phone...

conceptual analysis of these lexical items results in the following conceptualization:

> (GRASP ACTOR Richard0
>   OBJECT phone-obj0)

This primitive CD act is too "low-level" to be helpful in organizing episodic memory experiences.   People are always GRASPing things (doorknobs, soap, etc.).   Therefore, this conceptualization must be reinterpreted in terms of some higher-level memory structure that can serve as an organizer of episodes for subsequent retrieval.

Principle 21

```
+-----------------------------------------+
| Understanding an  event implies  building |
| a memory structure from   which   the event |
| can later be accessed (or reconstructed). |
+-----------------------------------------+
```

In this case, BORIS uses the following heuristic, embodied in the instantiation demon APPLY-KS:

> APPLY-KS DEMON:
> If a primitive CD ACT is encountered
> Then examine the OBJECT of the ACT
> and If the OBJECT has an associated
> script or MOP
> Then apply that script or MOP
> to the ACT

Since the physical object PHONE has the MOP M-PHONE associated with it, BORIS applies the mop M-PHONE to this GRASP event. MOP application involves a number of actions and will be described in greater detail later. Briefly, MOP application involves matching the expected events in a MOP against an event in working memory. If a match occurs, then the MOP is updated. In the case above, since it is a novel mention of M-PHONE, MOP application will also result in creating a new instantiation of M-PHONE. As a result of reinterpretation, the GRASP event is now understood as:

> (M-PHONE
> CALLER Richard0
> CALLEE nil
> EVENT (EV-MAKE-CALL))

Now that M-PHONE is instantiated in episodic memory, it can be used during the rest of the parse. So when the phrase "and dialed" is encountered in DIVORCE-1 after "picked up the phone", reinterpretation demons notice that M-PHONE is currently active and simply update the current event in M-PHONE to be EV-DIAL. In addition, demons associated with M-PHONE are spawned. Some of these demons are goal-oriented and will attempt to find out why Richard is phoning Paul. In general, event reinterpretation demons encounter the following cases:

1. If the input event is too low level to build episodic memory directly and the role bindings fail to suggest a MOP or script which can be applied, then the reinterpretation demon simply applies each active MOP from the current scenario to the input event, starting with the most recently accessed ones, until a match is found. If no match is found, then reinterpretation fails and the event is not incorporated into episodic memory.

2. If the input event is too low level but one or more role bindings suggest one or more MOPs to apply, then these MOPS are applied until a match is found.

6.4.8 Recognizing Deviations

A story understander must be able to recognize the occurrence of unexpected events, unusual situations, or deviations from the norm. Such things are what make stories both interesting and memorable.

Before an event deviation can be properly incorporated into memory, often BORIS must first recognize that a norm violation has occurred. This poses special problems. How does one recognize that an event E is a deviation of an expected event rather than some completely new event, unrelated to anything currently active in memory? For example, when the waitress knocks coke on George in DIVORCE-2, it is recognized as a deviation of an expected event (i.e. EV-SERVE-FOOD) rather than some event totally unrelated to the M-RESTAURANT context. But if BORIS attempts to simply match the spilling (i.e. a PROPEL) against expected events in M-RESTAURANT, no match will succeed. So it is important for BORIS to first realize that an unusual event has occurred; otherwise, BORIS will not know that a deviation match should be attempted between the input event and any normal events expected within the active context.

BORIS uses a number of parsing heuristics to recognize when an abnormal event may have occurred. These process rules are activated by changes in CD modifiers, such as SCALE and MODE:

Unintended Events -- Actions that are performed unintentionally are good candidates for deviation recognition. Certain words, such as "slipped", "spilled", etc. are marked as UNINTENDED actions in the lexicon. Other events are recognized as UNINTENDED through modification demons activated by such words as "accidentally".

In DIVORCE-2, for instance, the text explicitly states that "the waitress accidentally knocked a glass..." Here, "accidentally" modifies PROPEL with MODE = UNINTENDED. Associated with this mode is a deviation recognition demon. Since the ACTOR of the PROPEL has a ROLE of RT-WAITRESS, the MOP M-RESTAURANT will be chosen for MOP application. The deviation recognition demon attempts to find a matching event in M-RESTAURANT by using the following heuristic:

> Find an event in the MOP in which the ROLEs match the event in Working Memory (WM). If the ACTs fail to match, then see if the WM ACT is instrumental to an expected event in the MOP.

In the case above, since PROPEL is often instrumental to PTRANS (i. e. transfer of physical location), the input event will match as a deviation of PTRANS(food) in M-RESTAURANT.

Negative Events -- Another clue that a deviation has occurred arises when a negative event is mentioned. When we read that George did not pay the waitress for his meal we do not simply build in a data base of facts that the fact: FALSE(ATRANS George, money, waitress). Instead, we assume that something had gone wrong since it was expected that George would pay.

Negative events are the easiest to match with episodic (EP) memory. The matcher simply compares the input event against expected events in episodic memory. As the MODE = NEG is noticed violation processing is started. Examples of deviations based on MODE = NEG are:

> "Richard hadn't heard from his college roommate Paul for years."

> "Richard borrowed money from Paul and didn't pay Paul back."

"George ate and then left refusing to pay the check."

Scale Deviations -- Sometimes modifiers indicate directly that a deviation of some norm has occurred. For example, "John is fat" is represented as:

(STATE ACTOR (JOHN)
     WEIGHT (>NORM))

Not all such norm variations affect processing BORIS. But whenever the pattern >NORM occurs, deviation analysis is activated. Examples of scale deviations from DIVORCE-2 are:

"His salary from the state school system
was very small."

==> (OCCUPATION IS (TEACHER)
     EARNINGS (<NORM))

"George received a large bill in the mail."

==> (ATRANS TO (GEORGE)
     OBJECT (COST-FORM
          AMOUNT (>NORM))
     INSTRU (POSTAL))

Fleeting Events -- Various modifiers indicate that an event was expected momentarily at some point. These modifiers include: "barely", "nearly", "almost", "just missed", etc. The mention of a fleeting event usually indicates one of two situations: a) goal success was expected but unintentionally failed or b) some goal thought to have failed had not actually failed. A fleeting goal failure is recognized in DIVORCE-1 when BORIS reads:

... as Richard was driving to the restaurant he
barely avoided hitting an old man on the street.

Social Norms -- When social activities are performed, BORIS automatically performs certain bottom-up checks to determine whether a violation has occurred. These checks are made for activities that involve an unspoken agreement between individuals and/or society. For example, whenever sexual activity occurs, BORIS checks the relationship between the partners to see if a contractual rule (as in the case of marriage) has been broken. This situation arises in DIVORCE-2, for example, when George finds Ann in bed with another man. Contracts with society include legal restrictions, such as not being allowed to drink while driving. One can physically drive while intoxicated, but a violation has occurred nonetheless. So if the driver is caught in an accident while intoxicated the consequences will be more severe. The recognition of contractual violations is discussed further in chapter 8.

6.5 Summary

In this chapter we discussed the role of Working Memory and demons in a process model for narrative comprehension. In addition, we examined the kinds of tasks which must be performed by process demons during comprehension. There are two dimensions along which demons may be classified:

1. The knowledge structures they work for and the connections they form with other knowledge structures. So we have:

- GOAL/PLAN demons
- AFFECT/ACE demons
- MOP demons
- OBJECT demons
- SCRIPT/EVENT demons
- INTERPERSONAL demons
- ROLE demons
- REASONING/BELIEF demons
- THEMATIC demons
- SETTING demons

2. The kinds of tasks the demons must perform once their conditions have been satisfied. These include tasks such as:

- Finding references
- Binding roles
- Applying knowledge structures
- Checking presuppositions
- Instantiating episodes in memory
- Disambiguating word senses
- Noticing norm deviations
- Answering Questions

Most importantly, we examined the way knowledge interactions are handled in BORIS and presented a Knowledge Dependency Graph that constrains the number of interactions which must be monitored. We saw how processing control parallels memory interactions, and how these interactions determine the way in which memories are searched.

PART III. REPRESENTING AND ORGANIZING KNOWLEDGE

In PART II we argued that process knowledge is tightly coupled with representational interrelationships. Since specific processes are associated with specific knowledge structures, the rest of this thesis must explain processing on a case by case basis. The chapters which follow discuss the specifics of goals, plans, MOPs, SCENARIOs, IPTs, etc. in terms of the representations and processing tasks associated with each.

CHAPTER 7

Intentionality and MOPs

7.1 Introduction

This brief chapter provides a representational foundation for later chapters. In this chapter we present a set of intentional links, called I-links, which specify "common sense" relationships existing between goals, plans, and events [Dyer and Lehnert, 1980]. I-links provide important representational and memory functions in BORIS. They are used to 1) dynamically connect up instantiated episodic units during story understanding, 2) organize and package the internal components of knowledge structures, and 3) guide the search and retrieval of memory during question answering. These three functions will each be discussed in turn.

7.2 I-links and Episodic Memory

I-links are used to capture the motivations and intentions of narrative characters. The major I-links used in BORIS are summarized in the table below.[41] Intuitively, the desire to satisfy a goal creates an *intention* to act on the part of a character with that goal. This intention is represented by reference to a plan which, once executed, causes an event to be *realized* (instantiated). The instantiated event then *achieves* the original goal. When one character *realizes* an event, that event may *motivate* goals one the part of other narrative characters.

---

[41]Not shown in this table are links representing goal conflict, goal competition, goal concord and goal subsumption. These relationships are discussed in detail in Wilensky [Wilensky, 1978b].

```
            (E = event, G = goal, P = plan)
+-------------------------------------------------------------+
| E  forces      E | G thwarted-by  E | P realizes      E |
|    forced-by     |   motivated-by   |   blocked-by       |
|                  |   achieved-by    |                    |
|------------------------------------------------------------|
| E  motivates  G | G suspends      G | P intended-by  G |
|    thwarts       |   suspended-by   |   enabled-by       |
|    achieves      |                  |                    |
|------------------------------------------------------------|
| E  blocks      P | G intends      P | P               P |
|    realized-by   |   enables        |     --------        |
+-------------------------------------------------------------+
```

Table of I-links

I-links are grouped into pairs -- that is, for each link 'L' from node N1 to N2, there exists a corresponding link 'L-by' from N2 to N1.

Although the ultimate defense of any system of semantic categorization rests on its usefulness in processing, the meaning of each link-pair can be described intuitively, by means of examples. The examples presented below are all taken from KIDNAP-0, another story processed by BORIS. For convenient reference, KIDNAP-0 appears below in its entirety. See appendix section I.2 for BORIS question-answering behavior on KIDNAP-0.

KIDNAP-0

John left his office early Friday afternoon so he could attend a going-away party for his friend Bill. Bill had been transferred to California. When he arrived there were lots of people and plenty of beer. Three years ago Bill had borrowed $50 from John which John hoped to get back before Bill left. He was about to remind Bill about it when he was

called to the phone. It was his wife, Mary, and she
was hysterical. Mary had just received a call from
a stranger who claimed to have kidnapped their
daughter Susan. He said he would call again. John
told Mary to stay at home, keep off the phone, and
wait until he got there.

John drove home immediately. Just as he walked
in the door, the phone rang. John picked it up.
But it was only Karen, one of Mary's friends. John
told her Mary was out and hung up. Mary wanted
to call the police but John thought they should
wait. They were discussing this when Susan walked
in the door. She had stayed after school for a
gymnastics meet and taken a late bus home.
Nothing had happened to her. It was all a hoax.

What follows is a discussion of each I-link and how it is used to
connect up episodes in memory, with specific examples taken from
goals, plans, and events occurring in KIDNAP-0.

Goal Motivation -- In BORIS, events are viewed as actions
that cause state changes and goals are viewed as descriptions of
desired states. Consequently, the occurrence of an event may cause
the creation of goals in the characters affected by or involved in that
event. For example, the kidnapping of Susan (EV-KIDNAP0) by the
stranger in the story causes John to want to save Susan. This is
represented in BORIS by the following goal/event dependency:

```
                -----motivates----->
     EV-KIDNAPO                    P-HEALTHO
                <--motivated-by----
```

where P-HEALTH0 refers to John's goal of preserving Susan's health.

Goal Satisfaction -- Events can also bring about states that
are desired by one or more characters in a story. In such cases, the
event is said to have achieved the goal. For example, once Mary finds
out about Susan's kidnapping, she wants John to know about it (D-
KNOW0). To do so she calls John at the party (EV-PHONE0), and
her goal is achieved by the successful completion of the phone call:

```
        ----achieves---->
EV-PHONE0                    D-KNOW0
        <--achieved-by--
```

Phone calls by themselves do not necessarily satisfy D-KNOW goals. It is the successful transmission of the D-KNOW message from caller to intended recipient that accounts for the goal achievement.

Goal Suspension -- Whenever a high priority goal is motivated by some event, the goal holder may temporarily drop his currently active goals in order to deal with the priority goal. For example, John quits enjoying the party (G-ENTERTAIN0) and quits thinking about getting his money back from Bill (D-CONT-MONEY0) when he learns that Susan is in trouble. This situation is represented in BORIS by the suspension of John's more mundane goals due to the crisis goal:

```
        ----suspends---->
P-HEALTH0                    {E-ENTERTAIN0, D-CONT-MONEY0}
        <--suspended-by--
```

Crisis goals will intend plans even when the plans may not be well specified. For instance, we are not sure exactly what John intends to do to save Susan (and maybe neither is John), but we still know that John's actions are the result of his P-HEALTH goal.

Plan Intention -- Once a character has an active goal, he may attempt to satisfy that goal by means of a plan whose execution is intended to achieve it. For instance, at one point Mary has a goal of notifying the police (D-KNOW4), and her intended plan is to call them (MAKE-CALL4):

```
        ----intends---->
D-KNOW4                    MAKE-CALL4
        <--intended-by--
```

It doesn't matter that Mary never actually executes this plan. In fact, it is important to be able to distinguish plans as intentions-to-act from plans as the execution-of-actions in the service of goals. If Mary had actually called the police, then D-KNOW4 would also have achievement links connecting it to an instantiated phoning episode.

Enablements -- Often, enablement conditions must be satisfied before a plan can be executed. For instance, John can not enjoy the party simply by being invited to it. He must actually attend it. Otherwise John could stay at the office and still enjoy the party. This precondition on E-ENTERTAIN0 sets up a sub-goal of D-PROX0, which represents John's goal of getting to the party:

```
        ----enables---->
D-PROX0                    E-ENTERTAIN0
        <--enabled-by--
```

This proximity goal itself sets up some intended plan whose execution will satisfy the precondition:

```
        ----intends---->
D-PROX0                    Unspecified PTRANS
        <--intended-by--
```

So the connection between goals and sub-goals is mediated by enablement conditions on plans. This is necessary since understanding narratives requires the ability to fit the explicit actions of characters into the implicit intentional structures that gave rise to them.

Goal/Plan Failures -- Just as events may motivate goals, they can also thwart the achievement of goals. For instance, Karen's goal of communicating with Mary (D-KNOW3) is thwarted when John tells Karen that Mary is not home (EV-TERMINATE-CALL0):

```
                    --- thwarts --->
EV-TERMINATE-CALL                   D-KNOW3
    (John)      <--- thwarted-by --- (Karen)
```

Notice that these links say nothing about which character is aware that a goal has been thwarted. It is enough for the understander to realize that Karen's goal was not achieved and why.

If a thwarted goal serves as an enablement condition to a plan, then the plan is said to be *blocked*. For instance, Karen's call (EV-PHONE2) blocks John's plan for hearing the ransom demands:

```
                  --- blocks --->
EV-PHONE2                        ATTEND-DEMANDS0
(Karen)     <--- blocked-by ---    (John)
```

because her call has thwarted John's goal of keeping the phone line open:

```
                  --- thwarts --->
EV-PHONE2                          G-PRESERVE-CHANNEL0
(Karen)     <--- thwarted-by ---     (John)
```

where keeping the line open is an enablement condition for hearing the ransom demands:

```
                  --- enables --->
G-PRESERVE-CHANNEL0                ATTEND-DEMANDS0
                  <--- enabled-by ---
```

Event Realization -- When plans are actually executed they bring about (or help to bring about) events. For example, the phone call that John receives at the party (EV-PHONE0) is the direct result of Mary's plan to phone him (MAKE-CALL0). This is represented in BORIS as:

```
              ----realizes---->
MAKE-CALL0                       EV-PHONE0
              <--realized-by--
```

MAKE-CALL0 instantiates a plan which contains information about how to make a phone call, such as: finding the number to dial, dialing, listening to the dial tone, saying "hello", asking for the person being called, etc.

Natural Forces -- The emphasis in BORIS is on understanding the intentional relationships between the mental states of the characters and their actions. BORIS knows little about the world of

nature.   However, sometimes events are caused by other events
without intervening intentional states. In such cases, BORIS uses the
link-pair: forces/forced-by. For instance, if a hurricane blows down a
building, these two events would be related by forces/forced-by.
Recall, in KIDNAP-0, that several phone calls occur, such as:

> Just as he walked in the door, the phone rang.
> John picked it up. But it was only Karen...

What made the phone ring? Obviously we want BORIS to infer that
someone else dialed John's number on some other phone, causing
John's phone to ring.   But the relationship between John's phone
ringing and the act of dialing another phone is not mediated by any
plan or goal, so the dependency between these events is represented
as:

```
            --- forces --->
   EV-DIAL                     EV-RING
            <--- forced-by ---
```

7.3 I-link Interpretation

It is convenient to talk about what BORIS knows before reading
a narrative as its "semantic" memory, and what it constructs after
reading a narrative as its "episodic" memory.   This distinction
[Tulving, 1972] is used in the interpretation of intentional links. For
instance, an achievement link between a plan and a goal within
semantic memory means that the event realized by this plan may
achieve the goal which intended that plan. But an event has not
occurred (in episodic memory) until a realization link has been built
between   the   plan   (in 'semantic' memory)   and   its   episodic
instantiation.

So plans can not directly achieve goals in BORIS. Instead, the
execution of an intended plan brings about (or helps to bring about)
the occurrence of an event. The occurrence of this event may then
result in satisfying a character's goal. Consequently, each instantiated
goal contains a history of I-links connecting it to other goals and

events in episodic memory.   There are several reasons for setting
things up in this way:

First, BORIS can keep track of the status of any goal or plan
simply by checking these intentional links.   If a goal was marked
motivated, suspended, and finally achieved, then memory knows the
'life' of that goal.   For instance, John's goal of acquiring $50 from Bill
is first motivated by a lending event and then left in a state of
suspension by the kidnapping, while Mary's plan to call the police
never gets past the state of an intention.

Second, memory can distinguish between the intention to
achieve a goal and the intention to execute a plan to achieve a goal.
This is important in the case of fortuitously achieved goals.   In such
cases the event which achieved a goal was not realized by the intended
plan of the goal holder.   For instance, John has the goal of acquiesing
to the stranger's expected ransom demands.   However, Susan walks in
and and John's goal to save Susan is now achieved.   But John is
surprised.   Why?   The answer seems obvious enough, but how do we
represent this situation?   Here John's goal is achieved by Susan's
arrival:

```
                    ----achieves---->
        EV-ARRIVE-HOMEO                    P-HEALTHO
                    <--achieved-by--
```

However, John's plan, which was intended to satisfy his P-HEALTHO
goal, had nothing to do with the realization of Susan's arrival home.
That is why John is surprised.   By using the scheme presented here,
BORIS can represent this state of affairs.[42]

---

[42]Fortuitous goal achievement also occurs in DIVORCE-1 when Paul
unintentionally catches his wife in bed with another man.   This situation is
interpreted by TAU-HIDDEN-BLESSING (section 2.2) which makes use of these
I-links.

7.4 Packaging Knowledge with I-links

I-links do not just occur free-form in memory. Rather, I-links are used to form configurations of expectations which serve to index episodes in episodic memory. In BORIS, these configurations of knowledge are called MOPs (Memory Organization Packets) [Schank, 1982a]. An example of a MOP in KIDNAP-0 is M-BORROW, depicted graphically below:

```
                        M-BORROW

    +---------------------------------------------------+
    |  borrower                            lender       |
    |                    i                              |
    |  WANT-OBJECT.......                               |
    |  (d-cont):          :              m              |
    |          :          ASK-FOR-OBJECT.........       |
    |          : a          (mtrans)         :          |
    |          :.......                  i  CONVINCED-   |
    |                  :           ..........TO-LEND     |
    |                  :          :         (d-cont)     |
    |                  :          :                      |
    |     m ..........GIVE-OBJECT........... m           |
    |     :             (atrans)           :            |
    |     :                                :            |
    |     :                    i           :            |
    |     :            ................WANT-            |
    |     :           :               RETURNED          |
    |     :       m   :               (d-cont)          |
    |     :     .......ASK-BACK           :             |
    |     :    :        (mtrans)          :             |
    |     :    :                          :             |
    |  OBLIGATED-        i                :             |
    |  TO-RETURN..........            a   :             |
    |  (d-cont)          :                :             |
    |            GIVE-BACK................:             |
    |             (atrans)                              |
    +---------------------------------------------------+
```

By convention, the goals of each character appear along the sides of the MOP diagram, under the role played by that character. The plans and events intended by those goals are displayed in the center. Plans and events are indistinguishable until a MOP is instantiated during story understanding. Only once a plan is executed by a character does it realize an event. Thus, events are often instantiated plans or portions of plans. For simplicity, the directionality of each I-link has been left out the diagram and the I-links of motivation, achievement and intention have been abbreviated to "m", "a", and "i", respectively. For convenience, each node in a MOP contains a mnemonic name. These nodes have Conceptual Dependency information associated with them.

As we can see, M-BORROW captures the "common sense" essentials of lending: The borrower wants something (WANT-OBJECT), so he asks the lender for it (ASK-FOR-OBJECT). If the lender gives the object to the borrower, then the lender will want it back later and the borrower will feel obligated to return it (otherwise it would be a gift). When the borrower returns it (GIVE-BACK), the lender's goal to have it back (WANT-RETURNED) is achieved.

Since much of BORIS's knowledge is represented by MOPs, narrative events can become connected simply by recognizing that they match events already expected within a given MOP. This recognition process is called *MOP application*. For instance, the expectation that John will ask Bill to return the $50 is represented declaratively in M-BORROW. MOP application is discussed in the next chapter.

7.5 Using I-links to Search Memory and Answer Questions

I-links are traversed during question answering, both in order to determine the meaning of a question, and to retrieve an appropriate answer. In BORIS, search heuristics are organized solely around the knowledge interdependencies which I-links represent. Consequently, search processes can retrieve episodes without having to know the specific contents of memory. In addition, since I-links constitute a fixed set, the number of specific knowledge constructs can expand without change to retrieval rules. For example, after BORIS successfully processed DIVORCE-1, its question-answering components required no alterations when tested on DIVORCE-2.

Principle 22

```
+---------------------------------------+
| Retrieval heuristics  are  sensitive  |
| to knowledge  dependencies,  rather   |
| than to specific knowledge content.   |
+---------------------------------------+
```

7.5.1 Choosing an Appropriate Retrieval Heuristic

An appropriate retrieval heuristic must first be selected before it can be applied. In BORIS this selection process depends on a conceptual categorization scheme, developed by [Lehnert, 1978] and adapted for use here. Lehnert's system recognized 13 conceptual question types. The seven types appearing below are implemented in BORIS:

Conceptual Type	**Sample Question**
1 Causal Antecedent	Why did John go home?
2 Goal Orientation	Why did John want $50 from Bill?
3 Causal Consequent	What happened after Mary called?
4 Verification	Was Susan kidnapped?
5 Instrumental	How did John get home?
6 Concept Completion	Who called Mary?
7 Expectational	Why didn't Mary call the police?

Lehnert's six remaining question types, are currently not implemented in BORIS:

```
 8  Feature Spec        How old is Susan?
 9  Quantificational    How many people were at the party?
10  Enablement          What did John need to leave?
11  Disjunction         Did John leave or stay?
12  Judgemental         What should John do now?
13  Request             Can you pass the salt?
```

Lehnert's categorization scheme was expanded in [Kolodner, 1980] to include:

```
14  Time                When did John go home?
16  Setting             Where was Susan?
17  Identification      Who was Bill?
18  Duration            How long was John at the office?
```

Of these, BORIS currently handles: time, setting and identification questions. In addition, two new conceptual categories were added:

```
19  Event Spec          What happened at the party?
20  Affect/Empathy      How did John feel when Susan
                          came home?
                        Why did Richard congratulate Paul?
```

As each question is processed, question-answering demons are spawned to determine the conceptual category of the question. These demons are initially activated when certain question words ("who", "where", "how", "when", "did", "why", etc.) are encountered in the input.

Retrieval heuristics are also associated with question words [Dyer and Lehnert, 1982]. These heuristics check the form of the question concept in order to select an appropriate search strategy. By this point much of the search will already have been accomplished by the normal processes invoked to understand the question. In an integrated question answering system, most of the work is done while parsing the question (see chapter 5. Once the question-understanding process has returned an episodic memory referent, the retrieval of a conceptual answer usually just involves traversing a small number of I-links. Consider the following question from DIVORCE-2:

> Q: How did Ann feel when George
>   caught her cheating on him?

Here, the main effort is in understanding that the question refers to TAU-RED-HANDED0 in episodic memory. Once this has been done, AFFECT search heuristics can simply retrieve the AFFECT response associated with George's role in this TAU. For a trace of this question and others, see section 11.4.

So each search heuristic is triggered by the conceptual question type that is encountered. For instance, to answer *goal motivation* questions, BORIS retrieves the goal specified in the question and then traverses a motivated-by link to find the motivating event. In this way, the question:

> Q: Why did John want $50 from Bill?

results in the answer:

> A: Bill had borrowed $50 from John.

Enablement questions cause enablement and intention links to be examined, while *causal antecedent* questions cause intention links to be searched:

> Q: How did John get home?
> A: He drove.

> Q: Why did John drive home?
> A: To hear the ransom demands.

Expectational questions use the heuristic below:

> If the question is an expectational type
> question, and an event E is given as input
> in the question,
> Then do the following:
>   Search E for a blocked-by link.
>   Search E for a goal G which intended E,
>   and if found,
>   search G for a suspending goal G1,
>   else search G for a thwarting event E1.

This heuristic handles the following questions:

KIDNAP-0:

Q: Why didn't John stay at the party?
A: He wanted to save his daughter's life.

Q: Why didn't Karen talk to Mary?
A: John told Karen mary wasn't home.

DIVORCE-1:

Q: Why didn't Richard pay Paul the money
    he owed him?
A: Richard couldn't find Paul.

Other question-answering heuristics will be discussed on a case-by-case basis in the chapters which follow.

7.5.2 Selecting an Appropriate Answer

During answer retrieval, BORIS must determine when search processes have found the most appropriate answer and should therefore terminate. This can be difficult since goals, plans and events are all interconnected in memory by chains of I-links. For instance, how does BORIS avoid giving 'obvious' answers to questions, such as:

Q: Why did George drive home?
A: To get home.

This answer is technically correct, but it is too 'low level' to be appropriate. It has the same basis as the old joke:

> Q: Why did the chicken cross the road?
> A: To get to the other side.

Before answering a question, people perform what has been called *knowledge state assessment* [Lehnert, 1978]. They take into account what the person who is asking the question already knows. Since BORIS does not maintain information about what a questioner knows about a narrative, it can not perform knowledge state assessment in the general case. However, BORIS does perform a restricted kind of knowledge state assessment, based on the following Common Knowledge Principle:

Principle 23

```
+-------------------------------------------+
| Avoid generating answers the questioner   |
| could  have  reconstructed  on his own.   |
+-------------------------------------------+
```

which is implemented as follows:

> If an answer (ANS) to a question was arrived
> at by traversing an I-link which
> is part of BORIS's semantic knowledge,
> Then reject ANS as being too low level and
> search I-links associated with ANS
> to achieve a more informative answer.
> (If this search fails,
> Then return ANS as best one found.)

In this way, BORIS assumes that the questioner has access to the same semantic structures that BORIS accesses. Any answer retrieved by traversing general I-links in semantic memory could have been traversed also by the questioner. Such answers are therefore less appropriate since they do not supply new information to the questioner. More specifically, BORIS assumes that the questioner has access to the same semantic MOPs as BORIS. This assumption leads to the following corollary:

Mop Containment Rule

If a question refers to an event
  within a mop M,
Then avoid returning an answer which
  could be reconstructed by traversing
  I-links within the same MOP.

This principle is used to avoid generating answers such as:

DIVORCE-1:

Q: Why did Richard get a letter from Paul?
A: Because Paul wrote a letter to Richard.

Once this answer has been rejected by the Mop Containment Principle, further search will result in an answer lying 'outside' of the M-LETTER mop:

Q: Why did Richard get a letter from Paul?
A: To ask Richard to be his lawyer.

In this case, memory contains the following (simplified) structure:

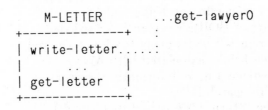

```
      M-LETTER          ...get-lawyer0
+---------------+         :
| write-letter.....:
|      ...      |
| get-letter    |
+---------------+
```

Since write-letter can be reconstructed from get-letter, and since get-lawyer lies 'outside' of M-LETTER, get-lawyer is chosen as a better answer over write-letter.

7.6 Intentionality: Related Work

In early Conceptual Dependency [Schank, 1975] theory, world knowledge was composed of states and actions. States enabled or disabled actions, while actions caused state-changes to occur. Some states were mental and could serve as reasons for actions. But mental states and goals are not necessarily the same things. A character may know, learn, or remember something without motivating a goal. Likewise, actions need not be intentional. So BORIS's I-links specify a finer 'grain' of representation along the intentional dimension. That is, causal connectives in BORIS deal mainly with the relationships between goals and plans. Furthermore, causal connectors in early Conceptual Dependency theory treated states and actions with equal importance. But in BORIS knowledge states (in contrast to goals) are only indexed under the events they enable or disable. As a result, the BORIS model predicts that states should be more difficult to recall than events. This prediction is supported in the experimental work of [Black, 1980] and [Robertson, Lehnert, Black, 1982].

The approach to intentionality in BORIS is similar to that of PAM [Wilensky, 1978b]. However, PAM processed stories by applying very general procedural rules. In contrast, BORIS uses I-links to declaratively represent many of the free-floating rules in PAM which were represented procedurally. As a result, PAM had to maintain discrimination nets of rules, each of which was chained procedurally to other rules. By representing goal-plan chains directly in MOPs, BORIS achieves many inference chains "for free" while, at the same time, avoiding the loss of intentionality[43] suffered by SAM [Cullingford, 1978]. Recently, Wilensky has argued for a declarative representation to specify goal/goal and goal/plan relationships [Wilensky, 1980a].

Finally, experimental work by Graesser on human question-answering protocols [Graesser, 1981] has lead him and his co-researchers to postulate an analogous set of intentional dependencies and associated retrieval heuristics. This parallel research provides independent evidence for the psychological plausibility of I-links,

---

[43]Differences between BORIS mops and scripts are discussed in the next chapter.

which in BORIS were developed strictly for processing reasons.

7.7 Conclusions

In this chapter we presented a system of I-links and discussed the three major functions they serve:

1. I-links provide a systematic declarative notation for representing standard goal/plan/event dependencies.

2. I-links are used to build up larger configurations of knowledge, such as MOPs.

3. Memory search heuristics make use of these I-links both during narrative comprehension and question answering.

Since goals, plans, and events are connected in a systematic way by use of a fixed set of links, search heuristics can be constructed which need not be sensitive to the specific content of each goal, plan or event. As a result, retrieval heuristics are independent of those changes to episodic memory which result from narrative comprehension processes.

CHAPTER 8

Memory Overlays with MOPs

8.1 Introduction

In this chapter we examine more closely the representation and application of MOPs in the area of narrative comprehension. In BORIS, sequences of events are handled by MOPs. So the first section of this chapter compares scripts with MOPs. The main differences are: 1) MOPs contain intentional information as to why a character performs each action in a script and 2) MOPs are built up from many different knowledge sources, each supplying its own 'perspective' from which the significance of a scriptal event can be understood outside of the current scriptal context. This approach gives BORIS a level of generality especially useful in processing norm violations when they occur within scriptal contexts.

8.2 Scripts in Review

Scripts were intended to capture situations in which behavior is so stylized that the need for complex plan or goal analysis rarely arises. A prototypical example of a script is $RESTAURANT = ENTER + BE-SEATED + WAITRESS-COMES + ORDER-FOOD + FOOD-BROUGHT + EAT-FOOD + RECEIVE-CHECK + LEAVE-TIP + PAY-BILL + LEAVE. Scripts are useful in supplying expectations during processing. These expectations represent an active context and help in such tasks as:

(1) Pronoun Resolution -- In a RESTAURANT context, clearly the "he" in "he left him a big tip" is the customer while "him" must be the waiter.

(2) Word Sense Disambiguation -- The expressions "ordered" and "to go" have very different meanings in a restaurant ("John ordered a pizza to go.") than in the military ("The general ordered a private to go.").

(3) Supplying Inferences -- Once a script is chosen, processing can proceed very efficiently, since missing information is automatically provided by the script. For example, the reader can infer that a waiter or waitress brought the food to the diner even if the text only states "When the food came, he ate it and left a big tip."

Scripts also contain one or more paths [Cullingford, 1978], each supplying a possible alternative sequence of actions to the "ghost" (or default) path [Lehnert, 1978]. An alternative path in $RESTAURANT includes leaving without paying because the food was improperly cooked. This path information is used to answer questions, such as:

Q: Why didn't John eat the hamburger?

In this case, the search heuristic starts with the 'ghost path' in which the food would have been eaten. The retrieval heuristic backs up along this path until a branch point is found. Here resides the reason:

A: The hamburger was burnt.

that an alternate path was taken. However, representing what people know about restaurants in terms of only the $RESTAURANT script is inadequate, for three reasons:

(1) Scripts were conceived as self-contained 'chunks' of knowledge. As a result, it is difficult to share knowledge across scripts. For example, a restaurant serves meals, but people also eat meals in non-restaurant situations (home, picnics). This meal knowledge should be shared with restaurant knowledge even though the meal-server in a restaurant differs from the meal-server at home.

(2) Experiences occurring within one script cannot be generalized to other relevant situations because scripts are self-contained [Schank, 1982b]. For example, the knowledge that we can refuse to pay for burnt food in a restaurant should be available in other scriptal contexts. If a mechanic fails to properly fix one's car engine, then refusing to pay should come to mind as a potential course of action. But this is impossible with scripts since refusing payment is firmly attached to $RESTAURANT (and not to $AUTO-REPAIR).

(3) Scripts lack intentionality. From a scriptal point of view, each event occurs next simply because it is the next event in the

script. Although script-based programs know that characters initiate $RESTAURANT to satisfy hunger, they do not know why any specific event within $RESTAURANT occurs. This is analogous to answering:

> Q: Why does the diner tip the waitress?
> A: I don't know. That's just what he
>   does in a restaurant after he's eaten.

Lack of intentionality has both advantages and disadvantages. It is certainly more efficient, since goals and plans do not have to be processed in order to predict what a character will do next. However, it is difficult to handle novel situations, where a character's reaction might be explainable if the underlying goals and motivations (for the expected event) were known [Wilensky, 1978b].

8.3 Multiple Perspectives with MOPs

Like scripts, MOPs encode expectations, but unlike scripts, MOPs are not isolated chunks of knowledge. Instead, each MOP in BORIS has strands [Schank, 1982a] which indicate how the MOP has been constructed from other knowledge sources. Each strand connects an event in one MOP to some event in another MOP. In this way, one or more MOPs can overlay [Dyer, 1981a] with each other. Consider the diagram below:

```
   M-SERVICE                              M-SERVICE
 (diner/owner)          M-MEAL          (diner/waitress)
+-----------+      +---------------+     +-------------+
| ARRANGE-  |      | PREPARE-FOOD.....   | ARRANGE-    |
| SERVICE   |      |             | :     | SERVICE.......
|           |      | SET-TABLE...... :   |           | :
|           |      |             | : :   |           | :
| DO-SERVICE|      | BRING-FOOD  | : :   | DO-SERVICE| :
|           |      |         :   | : :   |         : |
|           |      .......SIT   :... |   |         : |
| MAKE-     |    : |          :  : | : : | MAKE-   : |
| PAYMENT   |    : .....EAT     : | : : | PAYMENT : |
+---:-------+    :  +-----------:-+ : : | +------:----:-+
    :           :                :      :         :
    :           :                :      :         :
  s :           :                :      : ...     :
  t :           :   M-RESTAURANT :      :         :
  r :           +--------:-----------:--:-------:-------+
  a :           | diner  :: waitress :  cook : owner |  : :
  n :           |        ::          :       :       |  : :
  d :           |   *....: :         :   *..:        |  : :
  s :           |        :   *......:         :      |  : :
    :           |   *....       :                    |  : :
    :           | (order)    :         :             |  :
    :           |        :    *....                  |  :
    :           |   *......: (bring-food)            |  :
    :           |                                    |  :
    :           |   *........................        |  :
    :           | (tip)                              |
    :           |                                    |
    :......*                                         |
                | (pay-check)                        |
                +------------------------------------+

              DIAGRAM D8.1
```

   Events in **M-RESTAURANT** are overlaid with their corresponding events in **M-MEAL** and **M-SERVICE**. In this way, M-RESTAURANT can be viewed from different perspectives. From the perspective of **M-MEAL**, a restaurant is simply a setting in which

people have meals. From the perspective of M-SERVICE, the diner in
M-RESTAURANT is engaged in a service contract with the restaurant
owner. The restaurant must serve food to the diner and, in return,
the diner is expected to pay for this service. The internal structure of
M-SERVICE is illustrated below:

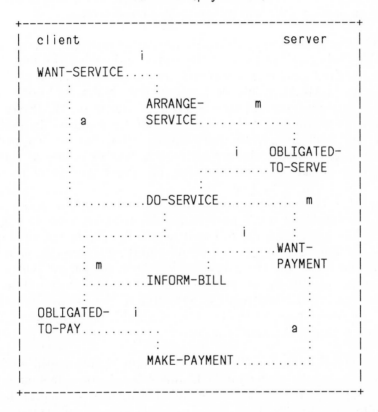

M-SERVICE above captures the following common sense
knowledge about service contracts: If a client has a goal (WANT-
SERVICE) that requires an agent, then the client can negotiate
(ARRANGE-SERVICE) with the server for service. If the server
agrees, then the server will now have the goal (OGLIGATED-TO-
SERVE) of performing the service. This goal can only be satisfied by
performing the service (DO-SERVICE). Once the service has been

performed, the client's goal is achieved. Furthermore, the realization of the service will motivate the client (OBLIGATED-TO-PAY) to pay the server for his service (MAKE-PAYMENT). If the client hasn't yet paid the server, then the server may remind the client (INFORM-BILL) of this fact. Once the client has paid the server, the server's goal for having performed the service (WANT-PAYMENT) is then achieved. Notice that the goals and events in M-SERVICE are very abstract. Any activity might constitute a service. So the specific content of M-SERVICE depends on the way in which it is instantiated during processing. We will return to this point later.

On the other hand, M-MEAL involves cooking the food, setting the table, bringing the food to the table, and eating the food. Now suppose a child goes to a restaurant for the first time. While events relating to M-MEAL would be familiar, the child would notice many novel events and try to process each in terms of M-MEAL. For instance, he would notice that it is the waitress who sets the table and brings the food in a restaurant (rather than one of his parents). Furthermore, he would also see his parents leaving money at the table and paying at the cashier. However, his understanding of these last events would simply be that "that's what one does" after eating in a restaurant. These events are harder to understand in terms of M-MEAL because they don't have analogous counterparts. It might be years before he realizes the full contractual significance of tipping and paying the bill. For instance, a friend admitted to me that as a child, she enjoyed pocketing the coins people left on restaurant tables. One day she was caught by her parents, who informed her that these coins were to reward the waitress for her service. Until this moment, in which my friend grasped the intentional significance of tipping, it had just been a "scriptal action" for her.

So children (and adults) can learn how to behave in situations without having to understand the intentional structures underlying their behavior. At this stage, a child's knowledge is 'scriptal' because the child only knows what happens next, not why it happens. At some point the child learns the significance of her actions in terms of more general structures -- i.e. structures applicable outside of the context of the script in which they first occurred. 'Payment for service' occurs in many situations, not just in RESTAURANT. The act of tipping should be understood at a more general level than just that of RESTAURANT.

Principle 24

```
+-----------------------------------+
| Memory overlays support multiple  |
| perspectives with processing at   |
| different levels of generality.   |
+-----------------------------------+
```

In DIAGRAM D8.1 (220), knowledge about a contract for service is represented by M-SERVICE. Adding this perspective to M-RESTAURANT is important since it gives BORIS the ability to generalize M-RESTAURANT knowledge in terms of more general structures. An overview of how this is accomplished is presented next.

8.4 Processing Deviations

Script-based systems represent scriptal deviations in terms of alternate 'paths'. So the restaurant script contains a BURNT-FOOD --> LEAVE-WITHOUT-PAYING path. But this approach causes a proliferation of paths in two ways: First, every possible deviation has to be anticipated and 'canned' into the script; otherwise the script would not be able to handle the deviation. Second, each service-related script ends up copying the same path. For example, in $AUTO-REPAIR there has to be a BAD-REPAIR ---> LEAVE-WITHOUT-PAYING path. By overlaying these scripts with M-SERVICE, a single deviation path: POOR-SERVICE ---> REFUSE-TO-PAY in M-SERVICE can represent deviation knowledge at a more general level. Likewise, 'payment for service' occurs in many situations, not just in $RESTAURANT. Therefore, tipping should be understood at a more general level than $RESTAURANT.

When stereotypic situations are first encountered, people form scripts for them. As they experience deviations (e.g. something goes wrong), they maintain the script (since it is efficient for processing) but create strands from the script to the knowledge structures which were needed to make sense of the deviations which occurred. Later on, when a similar deviation occurs, they can use these other knowledge structures to process the deviation.

More importantly, a deviation which has never before been encountered within that scriptal setting can be handled, as long as some strand exists from the script to a knowledge structure with information about this type of deviation. For instance, as long as we know that $MOVIE has a strand to M-SERVICE (pay-now track), the very first time the movie projector breaks, we can use our deviation path in M-SERVICE to demand a refund, even though this is a novel situation for us. In this way, only what is relevant to the situation at hand need be actively considered during processing. But when a violation occurs these alternative perspectives will be available.

Consider how BORIS processes the following fragment from DIVORCE-2:

> George was having lunch ... when the waitress accidentally knocked a glass of coke on him. George was very annoyed and left refusing to pay the check...

Briefly, an analysis of "having lunch" activates M-MEAL. When "waitress" occurs, the MOPs associated with this role are examined. If a MOP being examined has a strand to an active MOP, then it is also activated. Since there are strands from M-RESTAURANT to M-MEAL, and since M-MEAL is already active, M-RESTAURANT is activated also.[44] An interpretation of "accidentally" indicates that a violation may follow. This heuristic is based on the assumption that unintended actions usually violate scriptal expectations.

"Knocked a glass of coke on him" is analyzed in terms of the Conceptual Dependency primitive PROPEL (Object = Liquid). Given this event, BORIS tries to match it against the events expected in M-RESTAURANT. This match would normally fail, since M-RESTAURANT does not expect waitresses to PROPEL food-stuffs. However, "accidentally" has warned BORIS of a possible violation, so a violation match is attempted and succeeds (see section 6.4.8). At this point BORIS realizes that the PROPEL event is a violation of the

---

[44]In this way, BORIS avoids activating M-RESTAURANT in cases such as: "George is in love with a waitress."

event BRING-FOOD in M-RESTAURANT, rather than some event totally unrelated to M-RESTAURANT.

Now what is BORIS to do? In previous systems, there would be a path in the script for such a deviation. However, this is not the case here. When BORIS encounters a deviation, it searches the strands connected to the event where the deviation occurred. This leads to DO-SERVICE in M-SERVICE (Diagram D8.1).

Associated with M-SERVICE is general knowledge about how things may "go wrong" for each event in M-SERVICE. There are several events, such as: ARRANGE-SERVICE, DO-SERVICE, INFORM-BILL, MAKE-PAYMENT, etc. For example, the sentence:

The waitress overcharged George.

constitutes a violation of INFORM-BILL. In addition, there is knowledge about how violations may be related to one another. This knowledge is represented by these rules:

> sr1   If SERVER has done SERVICE
> badly (or not at all),
> Then SERVER should either not BILL
> CONTRACTOR or BILL for amount < NORM.

> sr2   If SERVER has done SERVICE badly
> or BILLs CONTRACTOR for amount > NORM,
> Then CONTRACTOR may REFUSE PAYMENT.

BORIS uses this knowledge to recognize the connection between the waitress' PROPEL LIQUID and George's refusal to pay a check.

Left to consider is how BORIS realizes that the violation of BRING-FOOD actually constitutes POOR-SERVICE. This is accomplished by tracking the goals of the characters. The PROPEL LIQUID on George is understood to cause a PRESERVE-COMFORT goal for George. This goal is examined by M-SERVICE, which applies the following heuristic:

> sr3   If SERVER causes a PRESERVATION
> GOAL for CONTRACTOR while
> performing SERVICE,
> Then it is probably POOR-SERVICE.

Thus BORIS uses several sources of knowledge to understand what has happened.   M-RESTAURANT supplies expectations for what the waitress should have done. Knowledge about PROPEL and LIQUIDs supplies goal information, while M-SERVICE (between waitress and diner) provides very general knowledge about how contractors will respond to poor service.

M-SERVICE is also used in processing the last paragraph in DIVORCE-2:

> A week later, George received a large bill in the
> mail from David. Was he furious!

Who does "he" refer to in "Was he furious!"?   When BORIS reads about the receipt of a bill, it matches the billing event expected in M-SERVICE. The mention of "large" indicates that the AMOUNT of the bill is greater than the norm. This constitutes a violation. In both cases:

1. Refusing to pay the waitress.

2. Receiving a large bill from the lawyer.

the processing and memory instantiations are very similar.   The episodes which BORIS instantiates to represent violations of M-SERVICE is TAU-BROKEN-SERVICE, which contains AFFECT predictions. In both cases, TAU-BROKEN-SERVICE predicts that the one experiencing the violation will react with a negative AFFECT directed at the violator. This information is used to correctly recognize that "he" refers to George.

8.5 Service Triangles

Actually, there are more service contracts active in M-RESTAURANT than appear in Diagram D8.1 above. Consider the following stories:

> S1: By the time the food came, it was cold. John
> decided not to leave a tip. He got up, paid the
> check, and left.

S2: When the food came, it tasted awful. John left
the waitress a tip, but decided to leave without
paying the bill.

These two stories can be understood only by realizing that a
diner enters into two service contracts when going to a restaurant.
The first contract is an informal one between the diner and the
waitress. The diner tips the waitress for taking his order and bringing
the food. The second contract is between the diner and the owner (or
manager) of the restaurant. So if the food is bad, but the service is
good, the diner may still tip without paying the check.

Finally, a long-term service contract exists between the owner
and the waitress. The waitress is to serve customers in turn for
payment of salary. This owner/diner contract 'dominates' the
diner/waitress contract because the waitress is acting as an agent for
the owner when she performs her service for the diner. This
dominance is represented pictorially by a service triangle:

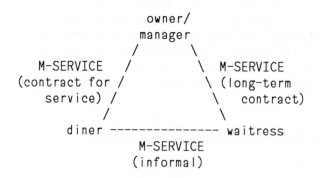

```
                         owner/
                         manager
                        /       \
        M-SERVICE      /         \  M-SERVICE
        (contract for /           \  (long-term
           service) /              \    contract)
                   /                \
           diner --------------- waitress
                   M-SERVICE
                   (informal)
```

It is important to understand the relationship between these
various service contracts. Consider the following story:

S3: When the pizza came, it had no cheese on it.
John complained to the waitress but she told him
she was busy. He threatened to complain about her
to the manager.

What is going on here? People know that when a service is not
rendered, one response can be complaining to the server. Another

response, however, is to refer directly to the dominating contract -- i.e. the one between the diner and owner. Without knowing about the service triangle active between John, the waitress, and the owner, it would be impossible to understanding why John's asking to see the manager could change the waitress' behavior.

Service triangles are very general structures and occur in many situations. For instance:

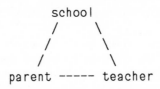

```
            school
           /      \
          /        \
         /          \
    parent ----- teacher
```

Currently, just the 'base' of the service triangle (for restaurants) is implemented in BORIS. Therefore, BORIS could handle stories such as S1 and S2, but not S3. Also, it appears that service triangles can be combined to form larger organizational structures which reveal levels of authority and responsibility. Service triangles also appear to be related to the theory of social and political 'triangles' described in [Schank and Carbonell, 1978]. Work on service triangles constitute another direction for future research.

8.6 MOP Implementation in BORIS

MOPs are used in BORIS to represent standard expectations which arise in social situations.[45] So far, we have discussed service-related MOPs in BORIS. In addition to these, MOP implementation in BORIS has concentrated on representing knowledge concerning marriage and marital disputes. This concentration is partially due to the nature of the stories processed by BORIS. The marital relationship is central in both DIVORCE-1 and DIVORCE-2. It is the

---

[45]Situations involving violations of standard expectations are represented by TAUs. See chapter 2.

breakup of this relationship that leads to legal disputes, need for lawyers, subsequent court proceedings, etc.

8.6.1 Contracts

Marriages are complex knowledge structures in that they create many social, interpersonal, affective, legal and thematic expectations. In BORIS, the relationship of marriage is represented by R-MARRIAGE, which contains both interpersonal and social dimensions. [46] When a marriage breaks up, both of these dimensions are affected. The termination of the interpersonal theme IPT-LOVERS causes emotional turmoil, such as guilt and jealousy, while the termination of the marital contract causes legal turmoil, such as alimony and custody battles. In this section we discuss the contractual aspect of marriage and how it is represented and applied in BORIS. The interpersonal dimension is discussed in chapter 10.

What BORIS knows about contracts is represented by M-CONTRACT, depicted below:

---

[46]There is also the life-theme dimension of marriage, involving courtship, engagement, the marriage ceremony itself, birth and rearing of children, etc. Life-themes are currently not dealt with in BORIS.

```
                            M-CONTRACT

    +-----------------------------------------------------+
    |                                                     |
    |   party-a                          party-b          |
    |                                                     |
    |   G-WANT-          i          i    G-WANT-          |
    |   CO-RULES-B.......        .......CO-RULES-A        |
    |       :               :    :               :        |
    |       :      m      ARRANGE-      m       :        |
    |   ...: .........  .CONTRACTS.........  :....        |
    |   :   :               :    :               :   :    |
    |   :  OBLIGATED-   i          i   OBLIGATED-  :   |
    |   :  ABIDE-BY-A...        ....ABIDE-BY-B   :   |
    |   :   :        :                 :        :   :   |
    |   :   :   m  FOLLOW-      FOLLOW-    m  :   :   |
    |   : a :      CO-RULES-A  CO-RULES-B     : a :   |
    |   :...:...:          :.........:          :...:   |
    |       :...................:                       |
    |                                                     |
    |   G-TERM-         i          i    G-TERM-          |
    |   CO-RULES-A.......        .......CO-RULES-B        |
    |       :               :    :               :        |
    |       : a             DISSOLVE-     a    :        |
    |       :...........CONTRACT...........:            |
    |       +---------------------------+                 |
    |       | AGREE-       AGREE-ON-    |                 |
    |       | TERMINATE    DIVISION     |                 |
    |       +---------------------------+                 |
    |                                                     |
    |   contractual roles:                                |
    |        SHARED resources                             |
    |        SHALTs                                       |
    |        SHALT-NOTs                                   |
    |                                                     |
    +-----------------------------------------------------+
```

M-CONTRACT captures the essential notion of interdependent cooperation: Party-a wants party-b to abide by a specified set of rules. These rules are represented by CO-RULES-B. Party-b, meanwhile, wants party-a to abide by a corresponding set of rules, designated by CO-RULES-A. Party-a convinces party-b to maintain the contract by agreeing to abide by party-b's rules and visa versa. FOLLOW-CO-RULES-A both achieves party-b's goal of G-WANT-CONTRACT-A and indirectly motivates party-b to FOLLOW-CO-RULES-B. Thus M-CONTRACT contains two agreements -- i.e. a separate set of rules for each party to follow. Furthermore, each contract is specified by three roles:

(1) SHARED: Contracts involve shared resources. In a business contract the shared resources would include the capital and products produced by the business. Two individuals who own a pizza parlor, for example, would share the building and the cooking machinery. Knowing what is SHARED is important because these are the resources which must be divided upon termination of the contract.

(2) SHALTs: Contracts specify how each party must continue to behave if the contract is to remain in force. If one party fails to perform its SHALTs, then termination of the contract becomes likely.

(3) SHALT-NOTs: Contracts also include rules which specify behavior that each party must avoid. With a SHALT, the contract is in jeopardy when one party fails to do something expected of it. With a SHALL-NOT, however, the contract is jeopardized when one party actively does something it agreed not to do.

M-CONTRACT represents what BORIS knows about contracts in general. Specific contracts contain strands which instantiate (or 'color') the various components of M-CONTRACT. For instance, a typical apartment lease would be represented as follows:

```
                    M-APT-CONTRACT

    +---------------------------------------+
    |  party-a = landlord                   |
    |  party-b = tenant                     |
    |                                       |
    |    SHARE:   NIL                       |
    |                                       |
    |    SHALTS:   landlord:                |
    |                   MAINTAIN-DWELLING   |
    |                                       |
    |              tenant:                  |
    |                   ATRANS money        |
    |                       to landlord     |
    |                       cycle:  monthly |
    |                                       |
    |    SHALT-NOTS:   tenant:              |
    |                   POSSESS pets        |
    |                   in LOC apartment    |
    |                                       |
    +---------------------------------------+
```

To maintain M-APT-CONTRACT, both the tenant and the
land-lord must abide by certain SHALTs and SHALT-NOTs. The
tenant must pay his rent every month. If the tenant acquires a pet,
then the landlord can cancel the contract. Meanwhile, the landlord
must maintain the apartment. Although the tenant uses the
apartment, he does not own it. Therefore the apartment is not a
shared resource, since it is not something that must be divided
between the landlord and the tenant when the contract expires. For
instance, when we read:

> John and his wife Mary bought a house. Years
> later they got divorced and are now fighting over
> who gets it.

we understand that the house must somehow be divided between
them. However, if we read:

> John rented an apartment from Mr. Smith. A year

later Mr. Smith evicted John and they are now fighting over who gets it.

it is more difficult to understand what's going on. This is because apartment is not SHARED. If "it" were replaced by "security deposit" then the situation would make sense.

A marriage contract is represented as follows:

```
                  M-MARITAL-CONTRACT

    +-------------------------------------------+
    |  spouse-a                    spouse-b     |
    |                                           |
    |        SHARED:  CHILDREN                   |
    |                 DWELLING                   |
    |                 VEHICLE                    |
    |                 INCOME-A                   |
    |                 INCOME-B                   |
    |                                           |
    |    SHALTS:  MAINTAIN-DWELLING              |
    |             EDUCATE-CHILDREN               |
    |                 . . .                      |
    |                                           |
    |    SHALT-NOTS:  S-SEX(spouse-a,x) or       |
    |                 S-SEX(spouse-b,x)          |
    |                   where x is neither       |
    |                   spouse-a nor spouse-b |  |
    |                                           |
    |  (Setting:  HOME                          |
    |       Ipt:  LOVERS)                        |
    +-------------------------------------------+
```

The shared resources in M-MARITAL-CONTRACT include the house, the family vehicle, and children. These are the objects which must be divided between the spouses if the marriage contract is ever terminated. When BORIS reads in DIVORCE-1:

Sarah ... wanted the car, the house, the children, and alimony.

these entities are understood together as the SHARED resources of the marriage contract, rather than four unrelated items.

BORIS knows that contracts are initiated, maintained, and later dissolved. This is important because special expectations are activated when a contract is terminated. The termination of a contract is represented by the DISSOLVE-CONTRACT node in M-CONTRACT. Dissolving a contract requires that two forms of agreement be arrived at by the parties involved:

(1) AGREE-TERMINATION: Both parties must agree to terminate the contract; otherwise, a termination-dispute may arise. For instance, this situation could have arisen in DIVORCE-1, but was eliminated by the fact that both Paul and Sarah wanted the divorce.

(2) AGREE-ON-DIVISION: Even if both parties want to terminate the contract, they may not be able to agree on how the shared resources will be divided between them. In this case a settlement-dispute will arise. This situation occurs in DIVORCE-1 when Paul informs Richard of Sarah's goals and then informs Richard:

> Paul wanted the divorce, but he didn't want to see
> Sarah walk off with everything he had.

The SHALTs in M-MARITAL-CONTRACT are complex and involve life themes (e.g. "love, honor and obey", "raise a family", "be a good parent", etc.). Currently, these are not implemented in BORIS. The major SHALT-NOT implemented in M-MARITAL-CONTRACT is termed the "sexual fidelity rule" and specifies that each spouse is restricted to having sexual relations with just the other spouse. Violation of this rule can result in a termination of the marriage. This information is necessary for BORIS to understand why George wants David to be his lawyer. In DIVORCE-2 the motivation for wanting a lawyer is never explicitly stated. Rather, the text reads:

> When he got there, he found his wife in bed with
> another man... When George found out that David
> was a lawyer, he told him all about his troubles and
> asked David to represent him in court.

Nowhere does the text state why George wants a lawyer. The reader must infer that George is going to divorce Ann. This inference comes from two sources:

1. From M-CONTRACT, BORIS knows that breaking a SHALL-NOT can lead to termination of the contract. Furthermore, disputes over contract terminations are likely and may have to be adjudicated.

2. From M-MARITAL-CONTRACT, BORIS knows that Ann has violated the terms of the contract by having had sex with someone other than her husband.

Many contracts specify the time period over which the contract is to be in effect. For example, M-APT-CONTRACT might have a default duration of one year. After that time M-APT-CONTRACT is terminated unless something is done to renew the contract. So there are two situations leading to contract terminations:

1. NORMAL TERMINATION: The contract terminates because the time period has run out, or because both parties have agreed to the termination.

2. VIOLATION TERMINATION: One party ceases to honor the contract, or has violated the rules of the contract. Hence the other party wants to terminate the contract.

When a normal termination occurs, the possibility for goal conflict can only arise over the settlement of shared resources. Some contracts, however, are set up to be permanent. M-MARITAL-CONTRACT is an example of such a contract. M-MARITAL-CONTRACT can only be terminated whenever a) both spouses mutually agree upon termination, b) one spouse forces termination upon the other, or c) a contractual violation has been committed. In either situation, the possibility of conflict is very high. This is also true for other contracts that include a great deal of shared resources.

Given knowledge about contracts in general, and about marriage contracts in particular, we are now in a position to represent divorce. "Divorce" refers to the DISSOLVE-CONTRACT node in M-MARITAL-CONTRACT which has a strand to a corresponding node in M-CONTRACT.

8.6.2 Legal Disputes

When a marriage contract breaks up, the possibility of goal conflict arises. There are two possible goal conflict situations: a) conflict over the termination of the marriage itself, and b) conflict over the division of the shared marriage resources. One situation leads to CONTESTED-DIVORCE and the other leads to CONTESTED-SETTLEMENT. When a contract termination is recognized, BORIS monitors the goals of the characters to determine whether conflict exists. If conflict is recognized, BORIS activates M-LEGAL-DISPUTE, which contains information about legal disputes. This MOP is illustrated below:

M-LEGAL-DISPUTE

```
+-----------------------------------------------------+
| litigant-a                               litigant-b |
|                                                     |
|                    exclusive                        |
| LEGAL- ...................................... LEGAL- |
| GOAL-A                      : r               GOAL-B |
|  :           m        LEGAL-       m             :   |
|  :          ...............CONFLICT.............     :   |
|  :         :                          :         :   |
|  :  CONTRACT                    CONTRACT    :   |
|  :  LAWYER-A                    LAWYER-B    :   |
|  :                                          :   |
|  :       lawyer-a          lawyer-b        :   |
|  :.....                          ......:   |
|     :  A-PETITION-     B-PETITION-     :   |
|     :  JUDGE           JUDGE           :   |
|     :       :     judge      :         :   |
|     :  m    :              : m         :   |
|     :       :...DECIDE-CASE- ..:       :   |
|     :           MERITS                 :   |
|  a  :       i       :       i      : a   |
|     :            ................        :   |
|     :       :                :         :   |
|     :  AUTH-              AUTH-         :   |
|     :....FOR-A            FOR-B........:   |
|         (thwarts LEGAL-   (thwarts LEGAL-   |
|                GOAL-B          GOAL-A)      |
|                                                     |
| setting:  COURTROOM                                 |
+-----------------------------------------------------+
```

M-LEGAL-DISPUTE captures the interactions between both litigants, their lawyers, and the judge in general legal disputes. That is, the two litigants have conflicting goals. These goals are marked as mutually exclusive. This represents the fact that the achievement of LEGAL-GOAL-A automatically results in the thwarting of LEGAL-GOAL-B and visa versa. This information is important, since often the relationship between conflicting goals is never explicitly stated, but must be inferred. For example, in DIVORCE-1, the text reads:

> With Richard there as a witness, Sarah's divorce
> case was shot. Richard congratulated Paul.

BORIS must be able to answer the following question:

> Q: Why did Richard congratulate Paul?
> A: Paul had won the case.

In DIVORCE-1, however, it is never explicitly stated that Paul has won. Instead, readers must know that Sarah's loss implies Richard's gain. Similarly, in DIVORCE-2, we read:

> ...But without a witness they had no proof and Ann
> won. David could only offer his condolences.

Again, the reader must infer from Ann's winning that George has lost.

8.6.3 The Role of Lawyer

Readers are not taken by surprise when lawyers are mentioned in the DIVORCE stories, yet the need for a lawyer must be inferred from context. Consider the following variants of DIVORCE-1 and DIVORCE-2:

> **DV-1 variant:** Not knowing who to turn to, Paul
> was hoping for a favor from the only basketball
> player he knew.

> **DV-2 variant:** When George found out that David
> was a botanist, he told him all about his troubles
> and asked David to represent him in court.

These texts make little sense because no relationship can be found between basketball players (or botanists) and legal disputes.

When "lawyer" is mentioned, BORIS examines MOPs associated with the role-theme RT-LAWYER is memory. One of these MOPs is M-REPRESENT-CLIENT, which holds information about the role lawyers play in legal disputes. Since M-LEGAL-DISPUTE is already active, and since there are strands from M-LEGAL-DISPUTE to M-REPRESENT-CLIENT, this MOP is also activated. It is illustrated below:

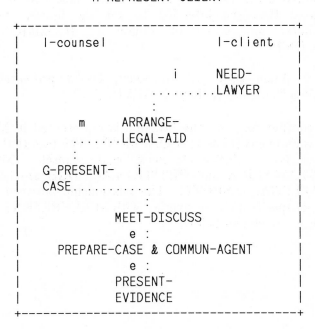

```
                    M-REPRESENT-CLIENT

        +---------------------------------------+
        |   I-counsel                 I-client  |
        |                                       |
        |                      i      NEED-      |
        |                   .........LAWYER      |
        |                      :                 |
        |          m       ARRANGE-              |
        |        .......LEGAL-AID                |
        |          :                            |
        |   G-PRESENT-    i                      |
        |   CASE...........                      |
        |                  :                     |
        |              MEET-DISCUSS              |
        |            e  :                        |
        |     PREPARE-CASE & COMMUN-AGENT        |
        |               e  :                     |
        |              PRESENT-                  |
        |              EVIDENCE                  |
        +---------------------------------------+
```

If the client needs legal counsel, then the client must contact a lawyer and get the lawyer to agree to take the case. This is done by informing the lawyer about the situation and asking the lawyer to help (ARRANGE-LEGAL-AID). Whereupon the lawyer must prepare the case by meeting with his client to discuss the case. The lawyer may also act as the client's agent in communicating the client's demands to the other litigants and hearing the their demands (COMMUN-AGENT). Finally, the lawyer must represent the client in court (PRESENT-EVIDENCE).

M-REPRESENT-CLIENT is used to connect up the various interactions between a lawyer and his client. For instance, the following portions of DIVORCE-2 are recognized in terms of M-REPRESENT-CLIENT:

When George found out that David was a lawyer, he told him all about his troubles and asked David to represent him in court... (ARRANGE-LEGAL-AID)

... David wrote to Ann, informing her that George wanted a divorce. Her lawyer called back and told David that she intended to get the house, the children and a lot of alimony... (COMMUN-AGENT)

... When they got to court, David presented George's case... (PRESENT-EVIDENCE)

Goal conflict between the litigants is represented in M-LEGAL-DISPUTE as an event (LEGAL-CONFLICT). The fact that a conflict exists causes both litigants to seek legal counsel. Notice that CONTACT-LAWYER-A and PETITION-A-JUDGE are not directly related in M-LEGAL-DISPUTE. The relationship between these two components is specified by an overlay with M-REPRESENT-CLIENT. These overlays are shown below:

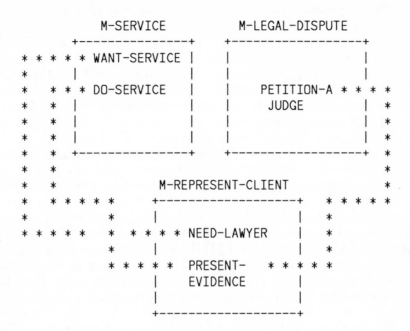

The event of PRESENT-EVIDENCE in M-REPRESENT-CLIENT is equivalent to the event of PETITION-A-JUDGE in M-LEGAL-DISPUTE. In DIVORCE-2 there are two separate M-REPRESENT-CLIENT mops which are instantiated: one for George's lawyer, the other for Ann's lawyer. In addition, an overlay exists between M-REPRESENT-CLIENT and M-SERVICE. It is M-SERVICE which supplies the expectations that the lawyers will bill their clients for services rendered.

8.6.4 Legal Reasoning

In addition to tracking the goals and plans of characters, BORIS must be able to recognize and understand restricted situations involving the use of reasoning. In BORIS, reasoning situations are processed by a specific class of mops, called reasoning mops (rM-mops). Consider the following passage from DIVORCE-2:

> David told him [George] not to worry, since the
> judge would award the case to George once he
> learned that Ann had been cheating on him.

Here, David presents George with the same reasoning he intends to give the judge. This reasoning supports David's expectation that George will win in court. The reasoning which supports David's expectation cannot be represented simply in terms of of the I-links (intention, motivation, enablement, achievement, etc.) used in BORIS to specify the other mops we have discussed. What supports David's belief is not a plan or goal, but rules concerning the weight of certain kinds of evidence in divorce cases.

Reasoning Versus Planning -- Reasons and plans are related, but not identical. Plans are intended by goals, and executed in order to achieve goals. In contrast, reasoning is used to present arguments which support or attack beliefs [Flowers, McGuire, Birnbaum, 1982]. In the class of narratives BORIS deals with, character expectations either support character decisions, or supply a basis for character actions. In DIVORCE-2, David MTRANSes to George some reasoning which supports his expectation that George will win in court. Since George does not reject David's reasoning, readers infer that both David and George believe that they will win the case.

Reasoning: Comprehension versus Generation -- BORIS recognizes the reasoning of narrative characters but cannot generate its own reasoning. This contrasts with programs such as ABDUL [Flowers, McGuire, Birnbaum, 1982] which can take a side in some argument. Unlike arguers like ABDUL, story understanders are not called upon to construct reasoning chains in order to convince an opponent of something. Instead, a story understander must deal with other issues:

1. How are reasoning situations recognized when they occur?

In BORIS, a reasoning chain is just one of many different types of knowledge which can arise in a narrative. An arguer such as ABDUL can make the assumption that everything said by an opponent will be a reasoning chain which either attacks a belief held by the program, or supports a belief of the opponent which the program has attacked. This kind of assumption, however, can not be made about the input to a narrative comprehension program, since whatever is read next may involve any one of a number of different knowledge structures. In such a task environment, simply recognizing that reasoning has occurred is a problem in itself.

2. How is the reasoning of a character parsed and understood once it is recognized as reasoning?

Although BORIS does not have to generate, agree with, or counter a reasoning chain, it must still be able to parse the lexical items which make up a reasoning chain in order to build a conceptualization of the reasoning which has occurred. For instance, how is the word "case" in DIVORCE-2 to be parsed, as in "David presented George's case" or "the judge awarded the case"? What are the conceptualizations for "had no proof" and "without a witness"? These lexical items cannot be parsed without a representation for reasoning.

3. How is reasoning knowledge represented, applied, and instantiated in memory?

Once a character's reasoning has been understood, it must be instantiated in episodic memory. This requires that reasoning be represented in some way.

4. What is the relationship between reasoning and other knowledge sources?

A character's reasoning cannot be instantiated in isolation from the rest of the narrative. It must be connected in a meaningful way to the other events in the narrative. In DIVORCE-2, for example, David's reasoning about why George would win is connected to an ACE-REASSURANCE (section 4.6) which occurs between David and George.

5. How is reasoning accessed and retrieved from memory?

To demonstrate that it has understood a narrative, BORIS must be able to answer questions about events in the narrative. Consider the following question:

Q: Why did David believe that George would win?
A: David thought that the judge would award
   the case to George because George had caught
   Ann committing adultery.

Answering it requires the retrieval of a reasoning chain from memory.

It is important to recognize and understand reasoning in narratives because of the role that reasoning plays:

> Reasoning reveals the beliefs and expectations of characters concerning future events.

As we have argued already, the most interesting events in narratives are those which violate expectations (chapters 2 and 3). A narrative comprehension program cannot recognize expectation violations when they occur unless it already knows what the expectations of the characters are. Understanding the reasoning of narrative characters helps build character expectations.

rM-JURISPRUDENCE -- In BORIS, reasoning mops contain rules which support beliefs or decisions. rM-JURISPRUDENCE organizes knowledge about legal reasoning and contains the following rules:

1. EVIDENCE rule:

> To CONVINCE someone that an event occurred, you need some form of evidence. (Saying that it is so is not enough.)

2. WITNESS rule:

> Good evidence that an event actually occurred is having an eye-witness to the event.

3. BIAS rule:

> Witnesses who have conflicts of interest are not trustworthy.

4. CONTRACT rule:

> If party A and party B have a contract and A has violated a rule of that

contract, then (all things being equal)
one should side with B.

5. DEFAULT-WIFE rule:

> All things being equal, in a divorce case
> award the house and children to the
> wife.

Some of these rules are more general than others. The
WITNESS, BIAS, and EVIDENCE rules are very general. The
CONTRACT rule applies to any contractual dispute, while the
DEFAULT-WIFE rule[47] only applies in contractual disputes involving
marriage contracts. The rules in rM-JURSIPRUDENCE are used by
BORIS to understand both David's and the judge's reasoning. David
supports his belief that George should win the case by using the
EVIDENCE, WITNESS and CONTRACT rules as follows:

CONTRACT rule applied:

> Ann has broken the sexual fidelity
> condition of the marriage contract.
> Therefore the judge should side with
> George.

EVIDENCE rule applied:

> The evidence is that Ann was in bed with
> another man.

WITNESS rule applied:

> George is an eye-witness to Ann's
> infidelity.

---

[47]Many readers of DIVORCE-1 and DIVORCE-2 commented that these stories
seemed to have been written in the 1950s. However, the issue here is not whether
the judge acted in a chauvinist manner, but what the knowledge is that would
allow a narrative comprehension program to follow the reasoning which does
occur.

These rules represent the reasoning which David presents to the judge in court. However, the judge is not convinced by David's reasoning. Instead, the judge applies both the BIAS and the DEFAULT-WIFE rules as follows:

BIAS rule applied:

Since George is the other party in the contract, George can not be the witness to a violation of the contract by Ann. Therefore, George has no evidence that Ann violated the contract.

DEFAULT-WIFE rule applied:

Since the contractual dispute involves a marriage contract, and since neither side has evidence against the other of a contractual violation, the wife receives the house and children.

In DIVORCE-1, Paul uses reasoning identical to that of David's in DIVORCE-2. In DIVORCE-1, however, the narrative ends with Paul's expectation and never reaches court. Also, both Paul and Richard caught the wife in the act of adultery. In DIVORCE-2, however, only the husband caught the wife. These differences account for the fact that the husband wins in DIVORCE-1, but loses in DIVORCE-2.

Do people use analogous rules of reasoning when reading these narratives? There is some evidence that they do. For instance, after reading the following passage in DIVORCE-1:

Then he [Paul] realized what a blessing it was. With Richard there as a witness Sarah's case was shot.

one reader remarked that Paul would have to get another lawyer to represent him when he got to court. When I asked why, I was given the following rationale:

Richard can't be Paul's lawyer since Richard must

> serve as Paul's witness in court.   Otherwise
> Richard's testimony won't be accepted by the
> judge.

It appears that this reader not only followed Paul's reasoning, but analyzed the reasoning in terms its viability, using such rules as the BIAS rule.

Organizing and Applying rM-JURISPRUDENCE -- Reasoning rules can not be applied in isolation. For one thing, some rules determine whether other rules are applicable. For instance the BIAS rule actually qualifies the WITNESS rule. Furthermore, the organization of a reasoning mop must be general enough that one character can arrive at different beliefs than another, while using the same rM-mop.   David and the judge each arrive at different conclusions even though both make use of rM-JURISPURDENCE.

In BORIS, reasoning rules are organized together in terms of a modified discrimination net [Charniak, Riesbeck, McDermott, 1980]. The non-terminal nodes in the net test for the applicability of each reasoning rule. The leaves at the end consist of the belief or decision which is supported by that path through the rules in the net. The rules of rM-JURISPRUDENCE are organized in the following manner:

rM-JURISPRUDENCE d-net:

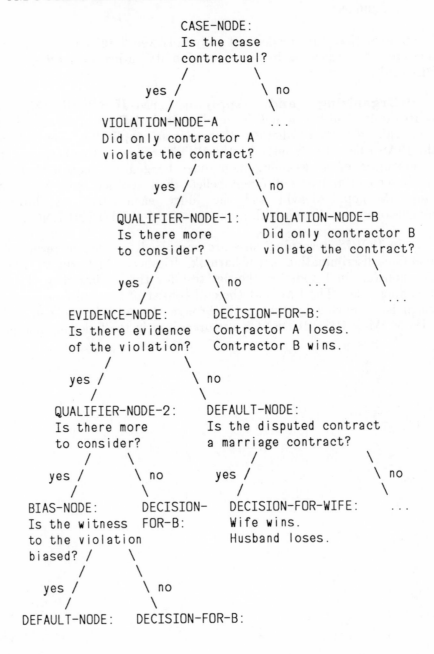

In the net above, QUALIFIER nodes perform two functions:

>   1.   QUALIFIER nodes allow rules to modify one
>   another.

QUALIFIER nodes capture the notion of testing for "all things being equal". For example, the WITNESS rule states that a witness provides evidence for a violation. However, the BIAS rule qualifies the WITNESS rule by rejecting biased evidence.

>   2.   QUALIFIER nodes allow one to terminate a
>   reasoning chain at any point and still arrive at a
>   some belief or decision.

One reason two characters may arrive at different conclusions is that one follows a reasoning chain further along than the other. A common cause of faulty reasoning is the failure to consider all of the reasoning rules that are potentially relevant. David fails to consider rules which the judge does consider.

The discrimination net representation serves two basic functions:

>   1. The net organizes reasoning rules so that BORIS
>   can know how and when each rule may be applied.

When BORIS thinks that an input may involve reasoning, it passes thruough the net whatever conceptualization the parsing process has constructed from the input.

>   2. The net serves as a declarative representation for
>   use in instantiating reasoning chains.

Once a reasoning chain has been found which matches the situation in the narrative, it must be instantiated in episodic memory. This can be accomplished by instantiating a path in the net, consisting of the following:

1. A list of the instantiated nodes in the net.

2. The character who used this reasoning.

3. The belief supported by this reasoning.

4. The status of the outcome of a reasoning chain.

5. The source of the reasoning.

For example, David's reasoning is instantiated as follows:

```
chain:   CASE-TYPE => VIOLATION-NODE-A =>
         QUALIFIER-NODE-1 => DECISION-FOR-B

reasoner:  DAVID

belief:  Judge AUTH for George in M-LEGAL-DISPUTE

outcome status:  EXPECTED

source:  ACE-REASURANCE (FROM David TO George)
```

It is important to realize the status of the outcome supported by the reasoning since one can reason about events which have not yet occurred. When David reassures George that George will win, BORIS must not mistakenly think that George has actually won the house and the children. However, once we are in court, BORIS must realize that the outcome DECISION-FOR-WIFE in the judge's reasoning has actually caused the outcome of Ann winning the house and children.

Conceptual Analysis and Reasoning -- Before an rM-mop can be applied, a conceptualization (which represents the reasoning as it appears the narrative) must be built up by parsing processes. It is this conceptualization which is then passed through a discrimination net in an rM-mop.

How is reasoning parsed? That is, how are conceptualizations involving reasoning built from lexical items and what do these conceptualizations look like? Consider the word "case". There are several ways[48] in which "case" is used:

---

[48]We leave out of this discussion the sense of CONTAINER, as in "case of beer".

(a) debater: "I disagree.
                  That is not the case."

(b) judge: "I award the case to party A."

(c) lawyer: "I'm going to present
                 the following case..."

(d) judge: "Bring in the next case."

What is the meaning of "case"? Even though we can replace:

> S1: The judge awarded **the case** to Ann.

with:

> S2: The judge awarded **the car, the house and the kids** to Ann.

we would not want to conclude that "case" refers to the objects of a dispute.

In BORIS, "case" has two possible meanings:

> 1. The instantiation of an entire mop, such as M-LEGAL-DISPUTE.

This captures the notion of "case" as an entire situation, as in (d) above.

> 2. A given chain of reasoning, including all of the facts and interpretations being handled within it.

This meaning captures the notion of "case" in (a), (b) and (c) above. "Awarding a case" then takes on the meaning: <CONVINCED-BY REASONING-CHAIN>. Likewise, "winning or losing a case" is understood by BORIS in terms of the judge being CONVINCED or not by a lawyer's reasoning chain. "Presenting a case" now means <MTRANSing a REASONING-CHAIN to someone in order to CONVINCE someone of something>. Similarly, the word "proof" can now be defines as: <a REASONING-CHAIN which CONVINCES> and "evidence" is <a RULE instantiated in a

REASONING-CHAIN>. Now we can parse:

> ... but without a witness they had no proof and
> Ann won.

to yield:

```
(LEADTO
    ANTE (MTRANS
            ACTOR (GROUP (David George))
            FROM (GROUP (David George))
            TO  (Judge)
            OBJECT (MENTAL-OBJ CLASS (REASONING)
                    ACHIEVES  (G-CONVINCE)
                    MODE (NEG))
            BLOCKED-BY (ROLE CLASS (WITNESS)
                    MODE (NEG)))
    CONSE (M-LEGAL-DISPUTE
            PARTY-B  (Ann)
            EVENT (EV-WIN-B)))
```

Why is it necessary for reasoning conceptualizations (such as the one above) to be interpreted by an rM-mop? The answer is that rM-mops supply connections within reasoning chains in much the same way that mops supply connections between goals and plans. For instance, notice that the conceptualization above states that there was no witness to Ann's violation. On the surface this statement is false, since George caught Ann in the act. (See section 2.4 for a discussion of TAU-RED-HANDED.) However, people do not stop reading at this point to complain that the narrative is contradictory. Instead, they use their legal knowledge to interpret the phrase "without a witness" to mean "without an acceptable witness". This is done by noticing that George was the witness in TAU-RED-HANDED, and then checking to see if George is associated with one of the parties in the legal dispute.

Whenever a mop is active which involves reasoning, and lexical entities are encountered which refer to reasoning, then reasoning mops are applied. For example, there are three scenes involving reasoning in M-LEGAL-DISPUTE:

1. Lawyer-a presents reasoning to the judge on his client's

behalf.

2. Lawyer-b presents his reasoning on behalf of client-b.

3. The judge may present his reasoning to support his verdict.

BORIS activates rM-JURISPRUDENCE whenever these events are expected.

Retrieving Reasoning Chains -- BORIS must sometimes access reasoning chains in order to answer questions. Consider the following question:

Q: Why did George lose the case?

While parsing this question, BORIS understands "case" to refer to a reasoning chain. The occurrence of the word "lose" causes BORIS to search for a situation involving goal competition in which the failure of the actor's goal lead to the success of the competitor's goal. A search of memory results in accessing the judge's verdict in M-LEGAL-DISPUTE. To answer this question, BORIS then uses the following retrieval rule:

rr1: If a question asks for the motivation
     underlying an event involving reasoning,
     Then search for a reasoning chain
     associated with the event.

This results in the following answer:

A: The judge believed that George
   was not an acceptable witness to Ann's
   violation of the marriage contract.

The same heuristic rule is used to answer the question:

Q: Why did David reassure George?
A: David believed that the judge
   would side with George because
   George caught Ann committing adultery.

Although story understanders are not called on to generate their own reasoning, they must be able to recognize, understand, instantiate and recall any reasoning which occurred in the narrative. This requires that general reasoning rules be represented, parsed into, applied and connected up with other active knowledge structures. Reasoning is important in narratives because it both supports and indicates the presence of character expectations and beliefs.

8.7 Conclusions

In this chapter I have discussed various problems with scripts, and suggested MOP 'overlays' as an initial solution. This overlay scheme causes equivalences to be set up between components structures in different MOPs and has three major advantages:

(1) Each knowledge structure need know only what is directly relevant to it. For example, what a waitress does is captured in M-RESTAURANT, while her reasons for doing her job are represented at the M-SERVICE level (which will handle any type of service). M-SERVICE need not be repeated for janitors, salesgirls, etc. This supports economy of storage, but more importantly, it means that any augmentation of the knowledge in M-SERVICE will automatically improve the processing ability of any MOP with strands to it.

(2) Related knowledge sources need not be activated unless something goes wrong during processing. For instance, people do not normally think of the contract between themselves and the restaurant manager unless they are having trouble with the service.

(3) A given event can be understood from several perspectives. For example, a "business lunch" involves M-MEAL, M-SERVICE, M-RESTAURANT, and M-BUSINESS-DEAL simultaneously.

Finally, we presented some of the major MOPs implemented in BORIS and showed the functions they serve in parsing, representation and search.

CHAPTER 9

A Spatial/Temporal Organization for Narratives

9.1 Introduction

We have seen that knowledge structures in BORIS serve both processing and memory functions. During processing, each knowledge structure supplies expectations for interpreting events which follow. During question answering, each knowledge structure organizes memory by supplying indices to those episodes instantiated during narrative comprehension. Each episode instantiates a portion of some knowledge structure (such as a MOP, TAU, IPT, etc.) which is then connected to other knowledge structures by means of overlays and I-links.

During narrative comprehension, BORIS imposes an additional level of organization upon narrative memory, based on setting and scene information. This level of organization is used both during comprehension and question answering. For instance, subjects who read DIVORCE-1 have no difficulty answering:

Q: What happened to Richard at home?
A: He received a letter from his old friend Paul.

even though Richard's home is never explicitly mentioned in the story. How is this accomplished? Notice that the question above fails to supply any goal, plan, MOP or TAU to serve as an index for memory search. The only access information contained within the question concerns a setting (Richard's home). To answer this question BORIS must able to a) organize episodes in terms of the settings in which they occur and b) infer settings from knowledge about narrative events. The instantiation of a spatio-temporal setting is called a scenario in BORIS and serves as a major access and organizational structure for narrative episodes [Dyer and Lehnert, 1982] [Dyer and Lehnert, 1980]. Hence, BORIS memory organization makes the following claim about human episodic memory organization:

Principle 25

```
+---------------------------------------+
| People tend  to   recall   episodes |
| in terms  of the scenarios in which |
| the episodes occurred.              |
+---------------------------------------+
```

9.2 Scenario Participant Map

During narrative comprehension, BORIS tracks the movements of characters and the contacts made between them. Whenever one or more events co-occur within the same setting, BORIS instantiates a **scenario**, of which there are three kinds:

(1) **Main Scenarios** consist of settings in which the major events of the story occur. In KIDNAP-0, for instance, both the party for Bill and John's home serve as main scenarios.

(2) **Transition Scenarios** arise whenever a character moves from one main scenario to another. In KIDNAP-0, for example, a transition scenario is built when John drives home from the party. Transitional scenarios serve to connect main scenarios, and may themselves hold episodes. In DIVORCE-1 Richard nearly runs over an old man while driving from one main scenario (Richard's home) to another (restaurant).

(3) **Mental Scenarios** come about when two characters communicate with one another across scenario boundaries. In DIVORCE-1, the content of Paul's letter forms a mental scenario.

Scenarios are organized within a Scenario Participation Map (SPM) [Dyer and Lehnert, 1980]. Below is a diagram of the scenario participant map for KIDNAP-0. Each main scenario is represented by a box. Transition scenarios are marked by D-PROX[49] goals while mental scenarios are indicated by D-KNOW goals. In addition, each scenario has episodes associated with it (not shown in the diagram):

---

[49]"Delta goals" represent desires for changes in state. States include physical proximity (D-PROX) and knowledge (D-KNOW). For more discussion of goal types, see [Schank and Abelson, 1977] or appendix II.

Scenario Participant Map for KIDNAP-0

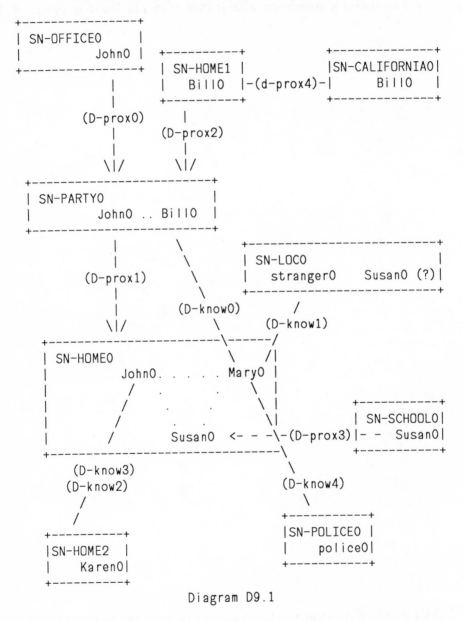

Diagram D9.1

By 'reading' the Scenario Participant Map above one can get a general idea about how episodes are interrelated in KIDNAP-0. That is, John went from an office to a party (D-prox0) which Bill also attended (D-prox2). Meanwhile, Mary was contacted by the kidnapper (D-know1). At the party, John was contacted by Mary (D-know0). Then John went home (D-prox1). At home, John was contacted by Karen (D-know2) who wanted to speak to Mary (D-know3). Mary also wanted to call the police (D-know4). Finally, Susan came home from school (D-prox3). Thus, the Scenario Participant Map serves as a mental 'map' of the story, keeping track of each setting for each character, and the contacts between them.

This map is used by a number of search heuristics. For instance, when some subjects were asked the following question about KIDNAP-0:

Q: Did John talk to Mary at the party?

they generated the following response:

A: No... Wait... Yes, on the phone.

What can explain this behavior? A natural explanation is that subjects first searched their scenario participant map and discovered that Mary was not at the party. Based on this search heuristic, the answer generated would be "no". However, another heuristic, based on MTRANS, searches those mental scenarios involving John in the party scenario. At this point, the mental scenario associated with D-KNOW0 (in diagram D9.1 above) is accessed, causing the phone conversation between John and Mary to be recalled. This recall results in the self-correcting response: "...Wait... Yes, on the phone".

9.3 Main Scenarios

Main scenarios organize episodes which occur within the same spatio-temporal setting. BORIS uses scene information is each MOP to decide when to instantiate a scenario. For example, M-LEGAL-DISPUTE contains the scenes SC-OUTSIDE-COURT and SC-COURTROOM:

```
            M-LEGAL-DISPUTE
    +--------------------+
    | SC-OUTSIDE-COURT   |
    |   meet clients     |
    |   prepare cases    |
    |                    |
    | SC-COURTROOM       |
    |   present evidence |
    |   hear verdict     |
    +--------------------+
```

As BORIS reads in DIVORCE-2:

When they got to court...

it searches for a MOP associated with the courtroom setting. Once M-LEGAL-DISPUTE is found, BORIS instantiates a new scenario with SC-COURTROOM as one of its scenes.

In general, each scene in a MOP occurs within a different physical setting. For instance, M-BORROW is divided up into the scenes SC-LEND and SC-RETURN because their associated events tend to occur at different times and places. Likewise, M-LETTER is divided up into a scene for writing the letter and a scene for receiving the letter.

Once a scenario has been created, its physical setting must be determined.[50]   If the setting is not mentioned in the text, then it must be inferred. For instance, when Richard receives a letter from Paul in DIVORCE-1, the setting (Richard's RESIDENCE) is inferred from interpersonal information.

More than one scene may be active within the same scenario. In the first paragraph of DIVORCE-2, for instance, George is involved in several scenes at once. George is a meal-eater in SC-MEAL, a diner in SC-RESTAURANT, and a homework-grader in SC-OUTSIDE-

---

[50]The same setting can appear in many scenarios.

CLASSROOM. These scenes are all part of the same scenario.

Scenarios are important because they provide contexts for search both during story understanding and question answering. Consider the following situation, in which subjects were asked the same question (in boldface below) within two distinct contextual settings. Each distinct contextual setting was created by have presented the subject with a prior question involving a different narrative setting:

CASE 1:

Prior question:

What happened at the restaurant?

creates setting context: RESTAURANT

Q: What happened to George at home?
A1: George found his wife in bed
with another man.

CASE 2:

Prior question:

What happened in court?

creates setting context: COURT

Q: What happened to George at home?
A2: George got a large bill from David
for legal services.

Subjects provide different answers to the same question, depending on the scenario that was accessed from the previous question context. Clearly, subjects use scenarios as a basis for memory search. Likewise, BORIS uses the following search rule:

ss.1 When using a scenario-based search,
start with the currently active scenario.

Scenarios also supply context during story understanding. To do
so BORIS uses the following heuristic:

ss.2 When interpreting an input event which
does not supply enough bottom-up
information to immediately access the
appropriate MOP, then search for an
applicable MOP among those associated
with the currently active scenario.

For instance, when BORIS reads that person A and person B are
socializing, it tries to find an appropriate MOP to represent this
situation. Sometimes this can be accomplished by examining the
current scenario. Consider the following situations:

S1: Bill saw John with Mary in a theater.

S2: Bill saw John with Mary in a restaurant.

Given S1 we assume that John and Mary were watching movies, while
S2 implies John and Mary were eating in a restaurant.

Using the same strategy, BORIS infers the appropriate MOP
from the following fragment of DIVORCE-1:

When Paul walked into the bedroom and found
Sarah with another man...

Notice that DIVORCE-1 never explicitly states that Sarah is having
sex with another man. This must be inferred, partly from scenario
information. Associated with BEDROOM are the activities of
sleeping, changing clothes, and having sex. Here BORIS selects SEX
because the current scenario is BEDROOM and SEX is the only
interpersonal activity which occurs within this setting.

9.4 Transition Scenarios

Whenever a character changes scenes, BORIS builds a transition scenario and adds it to the Scenario Participant Map. Within each transition scenario is a D-PROX goal of the character who initiated the scene change. Whenever a D-PROX goal is instantiated, BORIS spawns demons to discover the higher goal/plan which that D-PROX enables. For instance, in KIDNAP-0 John leaves his office in order to go to the party. John's higher goal, however, is to obtain the money that Bill had borrowed from him, and being at the party enables John to do this. BORIS uses the following rule to build an enablement link between D-PROX goals and the plans they enable:

> ss.3 When a transition scenario S2 (between main scenarios S1 and S3) is instantiated for a character C, examine the current goals of the character, along with the MOPs associated with scenario S3. If an event E in one of these MOPs can achieve a goal of C, then build an enablement link between E and C's D-PROX goal.

This rule is used to connect up the following situations:

DIVORCE-1:

> Paul agreed to have lunch with him [Richard]...
>
> ... as Richard was driving to the restaurant.

DIVORCE-2:

> George became extremely upset and felt like going out and getting plastered...
>
> At the bar...

In the first situation, Richard's goal of meeting Paul at lunch is enabled by getting to the setting of the meeting. In the second

situation, George's goal of getting drunk is enabled by getting to a
bar.

9.4.1 Recognizing Transitions

Transition scenarios are recognized in several ways. Some
MOPs, such as M-VEHICLE, are instrumental to PTRANS and
indicate directly that a transition has occurred. Othertimes, a
transition must be inferred. Consider the following fragment from
DIVORCE-2:

> At the bar... George ... asked David to represent
> him in court... Later, David wrote to Ann,
> informing her that George wanted a divorce.

The reader is never explicitly told that David and George left the bar
and are both probably somewhere else. This must be inferred from an
analysis of the word "later" and the events that follow. Likewise, a
transition scenario is inferred in the last paragraph of DIVORCE-2
from the phrase "a week later".

Transition scenarios also arise from goal situations involving D-
PROX. For example, in DIVORCE-1 Richard offers to drive Paul
home. The narrative never explicitly states that Paul agreed to be
driven home or that Richard actually drove Paul home. This must be
inferred from the mention of a new setting:

> When Paul walked into the bedroom...

Also, why aren't we bothered by this 'sudden' mention of a bedroom?
The reason is that we know Paul had a D-PROX goal of being home
in order to change his clothes, and clothes are found in bedrooms.
This situation is represented below:

```
                 achieves
    P-COMFORT <---------- CHANGE-CLOTHES
                          setting = bedroom
                          /|\
                          |enables
                          |
                         D-PROX
                          instru = M-VEHICLE
```

Consequently, scene changes make sense only in terms of the current goals of the characters and the actions which the transition will enable.

9.4.2 Accessing Transition Scenarios

Transition scenarios are clearly needed from a question-answering point of view. Consider the following KIDNAP-0 question:

Q: Why did John leave the party?

When the word "leave" is encountered, BORIS represents it in terms of PTRANS. But which PTRANS? There are numerous PTRANSes in KIDNAP-0, both explicit and implicit. For example, John PTRANSed to two phones, to a car, to numerous doors, etc. In order to find the appropriate D-PROX goal being referenced in the question, BORIS must make use of the scenario information available in the question. By using the Scenario Participant Map to 'locate' John at the party and then 'recall' where John was next, BORIS retrieves the appropriate transition scenario. Now BORIS accesses John's D-PROX goal in episodic memory. Once BORIS has this entry point, an enablement link is traversed in order to retrieve the higher goals (or plans) which caused John to want to be home.

Transition scenarios are also used to answer the following questions (from DIVORCE-1:)

Q1: How did Richard get to the restaurant?
A1: He drove.

Q2: What happened on the way to the restaurant?
A2: Richard almost hit an old man.

To answer Q1, BORIS finds the restaurant scenario. From here the transition scenario for Richard is accessed. Then the instrumental MOP associated with the transition scenario is returned. In answer Q2, BORIS searches for 'interesting' events (such as TAUs; see chapter 2) associated with the transition scenario. Notice that it would be very difficult to parse the expression "on the way" in Q2 above without a transition scenario. BORIS represents this phrase by a reference to transition scenarios.

Transition scenarios are also accessed during narrative comprehension.[51]   Consider the following example from DIVORCE-1:

> The next day, as Richard was driving to the restaurant, he barely avoided hitting an old man on the street.

The second part of this sentence has at least two possible interpretations:

1. Richard nearly had a fight with an old man.

2. Richard's car nearly hit an old man.

Upon reading the word "hitting", BORIS examines memory and finds that an M-VEHICLE transition scenario is currently active. In BORIS' semantic memory, car accidents are known to occur during transition scenarios when M-VEHICLE is the instrumental MOP. In other words, car accidents occur within driving contexts. But there is no active scenario knowledge concerning fist fights. Therefore BORIS interprets "hitting" as a vehicle accident.

---

[51]This is a natural consequence of parser integration and unification. See chapter 5.

9.5 Mental Scenarios

Mental scenarios occur whenever two characters communicate information to one another across scenario boundaries. Mental scenarios are important in text processing because they influence the application of inferences which rely on MTRANS situations. Consider the following fragment from DIVORCE-1:

> Not knowing who to turn to, he [Paul] was hoping for a favor from the only lawyer he knew.

Notice that nowhere in DIVORCE-1 is it stated that Richard is a lawyer. Yet readers commonly make this inference. How?

BORIS uses the following rule to infer Richard's occupation:

> mr1   If character C1 MTRANSes to character C2
> that C1 has a goal requiring an AGENT
> and the AGENT is never mentioned,
> Then C2 is the likely AGENT.

In order to apply this rule, BORIS must know that it is inside the mental scenario of the letter. In DIVORCE-1 we are told that Paul needs a lawyer. However, the reader is never explicitly told that Paul has MTRANSed this information to Richard. Paul's MTRANS to Richard must be inferred from the letter context. In fact, the entire second paragraph of DIVORCE-1 is governed by an implicit MTRANS:

> Unfortunately, the news was not good. Paul's wife Sarah wanted a divorce. She also wanted the car, the house, the children, and alimony. Paul wanted the divorce, but he didn't want to see Sarah walk off with everything he had. His salary from the state school system was very small. Not knowing who to turn to, he was hoping for a favor from the only lawyer he knew. Paul gave his home phone number in case Richard felt he could help.

This constitutes one giant mental scenario. Yet the reader is never told explicitly that a mental scenario has been entered. The text does not state: "Then Paul read the letter and it contained the following:" Nor are we told explicitly when this mental scenario is exited. Consequently, BORIS must employ processes to recognize when mental scenarios are entered and exited.

9.5.1 Recognizing Mental Scenarios

Mental scenarios are often recognized with the help of MOPs. In addition to the physical scenes already discussed (e.g. courtroom), some MOPs also contain mental scenes. For instance, both M-PHONE and M-LETTER contain the mental scenes SC-LETTER-INFO and SC-PHONE-CONVERSATION, respectively. In DIVORCE-1, when the letter arrives BORIS assumes that Richard will read the letter. This M-LETTER event is represented in Conceptual Dependency as:

```
(MTRANS  ACTOR letter-reader
         TO  letter-reader
         MOBJECT letter-info
         INSTRU  (ATTEND ACTOR letter-reader
                         OBJECT (eyes)
                         TO  letter-object))
```

where letter-info is a type of INFORMATION.[52]   As long as the text concerns the letter-sender, BORIS associates each piece of information in the letter with the mental scenario. In order to recognize when a mental scenario has terminated, BORIS uses the following rule:

> mr2 If a mental scenario instantiates
>   a reading scene in a MOP
>   Then exit that scenario whenever
>   the reader performs an action.

So, when BORIS reads:

---

[52]In this case, the letter-info role is bound to "news" in the sentence: "Unfortunately, the news was not good." which occurs subsequently in the text.

Richard eagerly picked up the phone and dialed.

the mental scenario created by M-LETTER is closed.

9.5.2 Accessing Mental Scenarios

Mental scenarios are useful during question answering. For instance, when BORIS is asked the following question about KIDNAP-0:

Q: Why did Mary contact John at the party?

BORIS uses the Scenario Participant Map to access SN-PARTY. Associated with SN-PARTY is a mental scenario connecting John at the party with Mary at home (see diagram D9.1 above). Also associated with this mental scenario is Mary's D-KNOW0 goal. As with transitional scenarios, an enablement link is checked in an attempt to find Mary's higher goal. In this particular case, no higher goal is found, so BORIS returns D-KNOW0 directly. This results in the response:

A: To let John know about Susan's kidnapping.

Also associated with the mental scenario is the mop that was instrumental in its creation. This MOP is accessed to answer instrumental questions:

KIDNAP-0

Q: How did Mary contact John at the party?
A: By phone.

DIVORCE-2

Q: How did David contact Sarah's lawyer?
A: By letter.

Mental and transitional scenarios share a number of features in common:

```
MENTAL:                         TRANSITIONAL:
-------                         -------------
D-goal is D-KNOW.               D-goal is D-PROX.
Enables a higher goal.          Enables a higher goal.
Connects main scenarios.        Connects main scenarios.
Activated by MTRANS.            Activated by PTRANS.
Instru = M-PHONE, M-LETTER.     Instru = M-VEHICLE, M-PLANE.
Holds ON-GOING events.          Holds PAST events and DESIRED
                                 future events.
```

Both mental and transitional scenarios connect two main scenarios by means of an instrumental MOP. Each contains a delta-goal [Schank and Abelson, 1977] which enables the achievement of some higher-level goal. Each may organize episodes. The major difference between mental and transitional scenarios is the nature of the episodes they organize. Transitional scenarios index events which occur while a character is making a scene change. In contrast, mental scenarios index either past events, or desired situations. This distinction is necessary, since BORIS must be able to tell whether an event is on-going, or simply being discussed by narrative characters.

Narratives involve character interactions. For characters to interact, they must be in either physical or channel contact with one another. Mental and transitional scenarios serve as indexing structures to those goals which depend on character interactions.

9.6 Inferring Knowledge States

BORIS does not maintain separate models of the knowledge states of each character. Consequently there is no single place in memory where everything a character knows can be found. Instead, character knowledge is inferred from both I-links (see chapter 7) and mental scenarios. I-links are used to infer knowledge states using the following rules:

rk.1   If character C has goal G
          motivated by event E
       Then C probably knows that E occurred.

rk.2 If E thwarted C's goal G
      Then C probably knows that E occurred.

rk.3 If C executed plan P to realize event E
      Then C probably knows that E occurred.

rk.4 If E executes P and P is enabled
         by mental information
      Then E probably knows that information.

Consider the following fragment from the second paragraph in
DIVORCE-1:

> Paul gave his home phone number in case Richard
> felt he could help.
>
> ... Richard eagerly picked up the phone and dialed.

Readers often can not remember whether Paul gave Richard his phone
number. In such cases they infer Richard's knowledge state from
enablement information in M-PHONE, depicted below:

M-PHONE

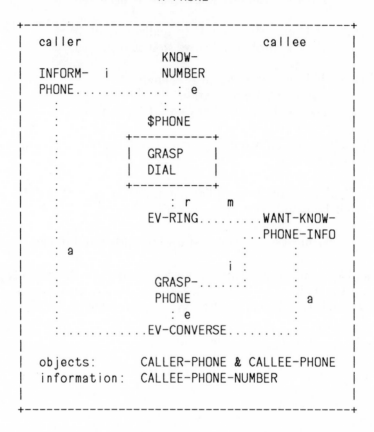

```
+-----------------------------------------------+
|  caller                         callee        |
|                      KNOW-                     |
|  INFORM-    i        NUMBER                     |
|  PHONE............. : e                         |
|    :                   : :                      |
|    :                  $PHONE                     |
|    :          +----------+                      |
|    :          | GRASP    |                      |
|    :          | DIAL     |                      |
|    :          +----------+                      |
|    :               : r     m                    |
|    :          EV-RING........WANT-KNOW-         |
|    :                        ...PHONE-INFO       |
|    : a                        :     :           |
|    :                       i  :     :           |
|    :          GRASP-......:         :           |
|    :          PHONE                : a          |
|    :            : e                 :           |
|    :...........EV-CONVERSE..........:           |
|                                                 |
|  objects:    CALLER-PHONE & CALLEE-PHONE       |
|  information: CALLEE-PHONE-NUMBER              |
|                                                 |
+-----------------------------------------------+
```

M-PHONE contains the actions performed by the caller along with the effect they have upon the receiver of the call. The caller wants to tell the callee something, so he performs a $PHONE script, a stereotypic sequence of actions including picking up the phone and dialing it. As a result, the callee's phone rings, motivating the callee to answer it and engage in a conversation with the caller.

Associated with the action of phoning is the enablement condition of KNOW-NUMBER. Since Richard actually called Paul, we can conclude (using rule rk.4 above) that Richard must have known Paul's phone number:

Q: Did Richard know Paul's number?

A1: Yes. Paul had mailed Richard his phone number.
A2: I guess so, because Richard called Paul.

Likewise, in KIDNAP-0 BORIS can infer that John knows about
Susan's kidnapping, not because BORIS maintains a list of everything
John knows, but because BORIS can recall the mental scenario in
which John was told about the kidnapping by his wife.

9.7 Inferring Temporal Relationships

People are notoriously bad at relating events in terms of their
temporal relationships.   For instance, readers of DIVORCE-1
commonly fail to recall that Richard had lunch with Paul "the next
day". Hence BORIS does not associate any explicit "time nodes" with
events.   Instead, BORIS relies on its intentional and scenario
relationships to infer temporal relationships:


```
                         Principle 26

    +---------------------------------------+
    | Temporal relationships   in  narratives |
    | are  often  inferred  from  goal, plan, |
    | and setting relationships.              |
    +---------------------------------------+
```


The following rules show how temporal information is extracted
from I-link relationships:

$$(G = \text{goals}, \; P = \text{plans}, \; E = \text{events})$$

tr.1 If G1 intends P1 which realizes E1
     and G1 was motivated by E2
  Then E1 occurred AFTER E2

tr.2 If G1 is enabled by G2
          and E1 achieved G1
          and E2 achieved G2
       Then E1 occurred AFTER E2

tr.3 If E1 motivated G1
          and E2 motivated G2
          and G2 suspended G1
       Then E1 occurred BEFORE E2

tr.4 If E2 thwarted G1
          and G1 is motivated by E1
       then E1 occurred BEFORE E2

In DIVORCE-1, for instance, Richard must have spilled the coffee on Paul before Richard offered to drive Paul home since the spilling motivated Richard to want to help Paul.

Temporal relationships are also inferred from the Scenario Participant Map, using the rule:

tr.5   If E1 occurred in scenario SN1
           and E2 occurred in scenario SN2
           and SN2 follows SN1 in the
           Scenario Participant Map
        Then E1 occurred BEFORE E2

In DIVORCE-2, for instance, George must have been grading homework before catching his wife in bed, since grading homework occurred in a prior scenario.

Question-answering protocols also supply evidence that scenarios are used when responding to certain temporal questions:

KIDNAP-0:

> Q: When did Mary call John?
> A: At the party.

DIVORCE-1:

> Q: When did Richard spill the coffee on Paul?
> A: At the restaurant.

> Q: When did Richard almost hit the old man?
> A: On the way to the restaurant.

DIVORCE-2:

> Q: When did George run into David?
> A: At the bar.

In each case above, questions that ostensibly refer to the time of an event are often answered in terms of the setting which contains that event. Subjects also answer time questions by referring to scenarios which either preceded or followed the scenario containing the event mentioned in the question:

DIVORCE-2:

> Q: When did George catch his wife in bed?
> A: After he left the restaurant.

Arguments for using intentionality and settings to represent temporal relationships are largely intuitive. It is hard to be aware of time, but easy to be aware of one's surroundings. Furthermore, settings usually carry more information about the kinds of activities which may be expected. Knowing that a character is at a bar provides numerous expectations. In contrast, knowing that it is evening (or that a week has passed) carries with it fewer and weaker expectations.

Reasoning about time and space [McDermott, 1981] [Kuipers, 1978] is very important for problem solvers. This reasoning capability need not be as sophisticated in a story understander since tracking the scenes and scene changes of the characters is usually all that is required. BORIS isn't trying to find the way to some location, notice a timing discrepancy in a murder mystery, or unravel a science fiction time-travel story [Kahn and Gorry, 1977].

9.8 Conclusions

Each event which occurs in a narrative may have one or more types of settings associated with it. These are:

- Main, such as homes, bars, and restaurants. These settings are important because they point to MOPs.

- Transitional, such as driving. Transitional scenarios are important because they indicate the initiation of new MOPs and the termination of old ones.

- Mental, such as letters, phone calls, and conversations. In BORIS, mental scenarios hold information about the knowledge states of characters, and how they acquired what they know.

We believe that scenarios provide an important organizing principle in memory. Episodes are associated with the scenarios within which they occurred, and higher level goals are accessed by means of transitional and mental scenarios. Scenarios furnish a level of representation and organization essential both during processing and retrieval.

CHAPTER 10

The Interpersonal Dimension

10.1 Principles of Interpersonal Interaction

In section 4.6 we argued that interpersonal themes (IPTs), such as IPT-FRIENDS and IPT-LOVERS, are important because they organize expectations about how one character will react to the goal situations of another character. For positive interpersonal themes, such as IPT-FRIENDS, these reactions are captured by the following principle of empathy:

```
FP-1  (IP-EMPATHY)

      Friends will    sympathize    emotionally
      with   one    another   over   each's   goal
      situations.
```

In addition to IP-EMPATHY, there are other principles of friendship:

```
FP-2  (IP-FAVOR)

      Friends are   willing   to   do   things   for
      each other.
```

```
FP-3  (IP-COMM)

      Friends like   to   keep   in touch with one
      another by  telling each   other   about
      what each   is  doing  in  life, including
      the state of their  relationships,   their
      jobs, their   recent   experiences, etc.
```

```
FP-4  (IP-SOC)

    Friends like to be in  physical  proximity
    with   one    another,  converse  with  one
    another and enjoy social events  together.
```

Whenever two characters interact, their relationship at the interpersonal level must be examined, since this level will influence the way in which events are interpreted. For instance, when readers of DIVORCE-1 are asked the question:

Q: Why did Richard and Paul meet
    at the restaurant?

their answers reveal two distinct levels of interpretation:

1. Goal/Plan Level:

A1a: To discuss the divorce case.

A1b: To help Richard prepare Paul's case
      against Sarah.

2. Interpersonal Level:

A2a: Because they had been roommates in college
      and wanted to see each other again.

A2b: They wanted to renew their friendship after
      not having seen each other for a long time.

So readers interpret the meeting at the restaurant from two different perspectives. One perspective involves the goals and plans of the characters with respect to the events in the narrative. The other perspective deals with the effects these events have on the status of their interpersonal relationships.   At the interpersonal level, the meeting at the restaurant is also serving to renew a prior friendship.

10.2 IP-FAVOR

Important character motivations will be missed if the interpersonal level is not tracked. Consider the second sentence in DIVORCE-1:

> Richard had borrowed money from Paul which was
> never paid back, but now he had no idea where to
> find his old friend.

BORIS uses its knowledge about the interpersonal relationship between Richard and Paul to interpret "borrow" at two levels:

At the goal/plan level, BORIS interprets Paul's loan of money to Richard in terms of M-BORROW, which appeared in chapter 7 and is repeated here for ease of reference:

M-BORROW

```
+--------------------------------------------------+
|  borrower                             lender     |
|                  i                               |
|  WANT-OBJECT.......                              |
|  (d-cont):         :                 m           |
|          :       ASK-FOR-OBJECT.........         |
|        : a         (mtrans)          :           |
|          :......                 i CONVINCED-    |
|                  :       ..........TO-LEND       |
|                  :       :         (d-cont)      |
|                  :       :                        |
|      m ..........GIVE-OBJECT............ m        |
|      :           (atrans)            :           |
|      :                   i           :           |
|      :            .............WANT-             |
|      :            :            RETURNED          |
|      :     m      :            (d-cont)          |
|      :  .......ASK-BACK             :            |
|      :  :      (mtrans)             :            |
|      :  :                           :            |
|  OBLIGATED-      i                   :            |
|  TO-RETURN..........                a :          |
|   (d-cont)          :                 :          |
|            GIVE-BACK...............:             |
|            (atrans)                              |
+--------------------------------------------------+
```

Recall that M-BORROW captures the essentials of lending: The borrower wants something (WANT-OBJECT), so he asks the lender for it (ASK-FOR-OBJECT). If the lender gives the object to the borrower, then the lender will want it back later and the borrower will feel obligated to return it (otherwise it would be a gift). When the borrower returns it (GIVE-BACK), the lender's goal to have it back (WANT-RETURNED) is achieved.

When a lending occurs in DIVORCE-1, BORIS activates M-BORROW, creating an expectation that the object borrowed will be returned at some point in the future. Furthermore, when BORIS reads "... was never paid back", it understands "paid back" in terms of M-BORROW and so automatically infers the missing roles of who never paid what to whom. Hence M-BORROW adequately handles processing at the goal/plan level. However, representing this situation only in terms of M-BORROW is inadequate. Consider the following story:

> **SY-1:** Kevin had borrowed $500 from Mr. Smith at the First National Bank, which he had never returned.

Although both SY-1 and DIVORCE-1 involve the lending and returning of money, they are very different in nature. For one thing, the expectations about possible consequences are very different. In SY-1, Kevin is in a lot of legal trouble and could end up in court (or ultimately, in jail). In DIVORCE-1, however, the initial consequences are interpersonal: Paul and Richard might cease being friends if Richard fails to returns what he owes. Furthermore, when readers are asked:

> Q: Why did Richard agree to be Paul's lawyer?

they usually answer:

> A: Richard owed Paul a favor because Paul had lent him money in the past.

Clearly, in SY-1 Kevin is not obligated to do anything else for Mr. Smith just because Mr. Smith has lent him money. Kevin's only obligation is to pay off his loan. Yet in DIVORCE-1 Richard feels obligated to help Paul in court (in addition to his desire to return the money he originally borrowed from Paul). How are these distinctions, between DIVORCE-1 and SY-1, to be captured?

When BORIS activates certain MOPs (such as M-BORROW) it checks the the interpersonal themes and relationships between the characters bound to the roles in the MOP. If the interpersonal relationships match the conditions of the MOP, a 'bottom-up' rule is fired, which interprets the event at an interpersonal level. In the case of M-BORROW, the recognition of IPT-FRIENDS [Richard, Paul] causes the following knowledge structure to be activated:

```
                    IP-FAVOR (1)

+---------------------------------------------------+
| person-a                         person-b         |
|                 i                                 |
| WANT-FAVOR......                  RELATIONAL-      |
|              :                i   OBLIGATION       |
|              :        ASK-FOR-FAVOR......          |
|              :        (invoke ipt)    :    : thm   |
|          :   a                  m  :   :           |
|          :...........    ...........PERSUADED      |
|              :        :   :                        |
|      m       :        :   :                        |
|     ...........DO-FAVOR                            |
|      :        (agency)                             |
|      :                                             |
+ - : - - -  - IP-FAVOR (2)  -  - -  - - - +
|     :                                             |
| RELATIONAL-              i    WANT-RETURN-         |
| OBLIGATION          ...........FAVOR               |
|                         :                :        |
| thm :     m   ASK-FOR-                   :         |
|     :     ......RETURN-FAVOR             :         |
|     :  :                      a          :         |
|   PERSUADED...... i                      :         |
|        :                                 :         |
|        DO-RETURN-                        :         |
|        FAVOR...............:             |
|        (agency)                                   |
|                                                   |
+---------------------------------------------------+
```

IP-FAVOR is a knowledge structure which represents events at the interpersonal level. That is, person-a wants person-b to do something for him (WANT-FAVOR). Person-a then tells person-b about what is desired (ASK-FOR-FAVOR). If person-b wants to maintain his relationship with person-a (RELATIONAL-OBLIGATION), he will be motivated to do the favor (PERSUADED). The relationship between RELATIONAL-OBLIGATION and

PERSUADED is represented by a thematic link.[53]   If person-b refuses person-a too many times, their relationship will suffer. Once person-b has done the favor (DO-FAVOR), person-a's goal is now achieved. In the future, if person-b ever needs person-a's to do something for him (WANT-RETURN-FAVOR), person-a will then be obligated to help out (if person-a asks for help).

Notice that IP-FAVOR is more abstract than M-BORROW. M-BORROW deals with the ATRANS [OBJECT] acts which achieve D-CONT [OBJECT] goals.   In   contrast,   IP-FAVOR   captures expectations which are more general. All we know about WANT-FAVOR is that one character has a goal which can be achieved with the help of the other character. The actual goal is not specified. This level of generality is important, since almost anything could serve as a favor. Giving a friend a lift to an airport could be a favor; house sitting could constitute a favor, etc. As a result, many MOPs may activate IP-FAVOR (based on interpersonal conditions). In contrast, IP-FAVOR can not activate mops (such as M-BORROW) since the number of potential situations would be overwhelming.

It is important that BORIS understand the lending event at both goal/plan and interpersonal levels since each level captures a different set of expectations. At the M-BORROW level, BORIS expects Richard to repay Paul the money. This expectation is rather specific and, incidentally, is never fulfilled in DIVORCE-1. At the interpersonal level, however, the expectation that Richard will help Paul is later fulfilled when Richard agrees to represent Paul in court. Furthermore, the expectation for a return-favor exists whether Richard has repaid Paul or not. Consequently, we have the following situation:

---

[53]Themes can give rise to goals, see [Wilensky, 1978b].

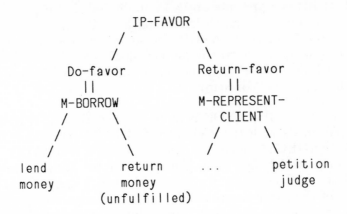

This resulting memory structure can now be used during question answering. So when BORIS is asked:

Q: Why did Richard agreed to be Paul's lawyer?

BORIS traverses the strand (see chapter 8) from a goal node within M-REPRESENT-CLIENT to the PERSUADED node in IP-FAVOR. Within IP-FAVOR, the instantiation of DO-FAVOR can be retrieved, yielding the answer:

A: Richard owed Paul a favor because Paul
had lent Richard money.

IP-FAVOR is a very general structure, and occurs commonly in narratives involving IPT-FRIENDS and IPT-LOVERS. In DIVORCE-2, for instance, after David and George accidentally run into each other at a bar, David buys drinks for George:

At the bar he ran [George] into an old college roommate David, who he hadn't seen in years. David offered to buy him a few drinks and soon they were both pretty drunk.

How is David's act to be represented? Buying a drink in a bar is represented by events in the mop M-BAR, which among other things contains the following exchange:[54]

```
(ATRANS                        (ATRANS
    ACTOR drinker                  ACTOR bartender
    FROM  drinker                  FROM bartender
    TO bartender                   TO drinker
    OBJECT money)                  OBJECT obj-drink)
```

Treating George to a drink, however, involves ATRANSing money from David to the bartender so that the bartender can ATRANS a drink, not to David, but to George. M-BAR contains knowledge about buying and drinking alcohol. The reason why David has treated George to a drink does not reside in M-BAR. The motivation for treating someone to something must be represented at the interpersonal level. The resulting structure is an overlay between IP-FAVOR with M-BAR, where the favor-giver and favor-receiver become bound with the drinker roles.

10.2.1 Returning Favors

More than one favor may be active in a narrative. In fact, this situation arises in DIVORCE-2 at the end of the third paragraph:

> ... [George] asked David to represent him in court. Since David owed George money he had never returned, he felt obligated to help out.

So two favors are active: one resulting from a prior loan of money, the other from being treated to drinks. What keeps readers from confusing these two favors and concluding that David has repaid his obligation to George, not by representing him in court, but by having bought him drinks?

There are two rules which operate in order to keep this kind of

---

[54]ATRANS represents transfer of possession. See [Schank and Abelson, 1977] or appendix II.

misinterpretation from arising:

> **FAV-P1:** Favors must be comparable in value. I.e. the goals achieved in turn for each character must be of comparable importance.

> **FAV-P2:** For x to perform a return-favor for y, x must accomplish a task for y that y CURRENTLY wants achieved.

Consider the following story:

> **SY-2:** Wally had saved Clem's life during the war. Clem decided to pay him back by buying him some drinks at the bar.

SY-2 sounds very odd. In fact, one natural inference is that Clem resents Wally for having saved his life. Although Clem's act is interpreted in terms of IP-FAVOR, it is not matched with the IP-FAVOR that Wally performed for Clem because that would violate the rule FAV-P1.

Rule FAV-P2 is sensitive to the return favor which is currently most active. Consider the following story:

> **SY-3:** When George found out that David was a lawyer, he asked David to represent him in court. Since David owed George a favor, he decided to buy George a year's supply of liquor at the bar.

SY-3 sounds odd because principle FAV-P2 has been violated. Here David is doing George a favor and the favor may be comparable in value, but it does not involve achieving any of George's currently active goals. If George had wanted lots of liquor in exchange for money lent in the past, then buying George drinks could have served as a reasonable return favor.

10.2.2 Violating Favors

When expectations are violated, they must be examined at both the goal/plan and interpersonal levels. Violations at the interpersonal level lead to changes in the status of interpersonal themes. Friends can become enemies, and in such cases, goal and empathy relationships may flip. For instance, at the end of DIVORCE-2, after George has lost the divorce case, the following situation occurs:

> A week later, George received a large bill in the mail from David. Was he furious!

Why is George furious?[55]   Readers give two different responses to this question:

A1: George had overcharged David.

A2: David thought George had agreed
to represent him in court as
a favor.

Again, we have a case where there are two perspectives concerning the same event:

1. Goal/Plan level: broken M-SERVICE

The client will be angry at the server
if server overcharges for the service,
especially if the service was bad.

2. Interpersonal level: broken IP-FAVOR

Friend-a will be angry at friend-b if
friend-a fails to do the expected
return-favor for friend-b.

---

[55]Notice that **who** is furious must be inferred. For relevant issues, see section 6.4.4 and chapter 11.

10.3 IP-COMM

In addition to helping one another, friends like to keep in touch with what the other is doing. For instance, in the fourth sentence of DIVORCE-1, Richard receives a letter:

> When a letter finally arrived from San Francisco,
> Richard was anxious to know how Paul was.

Here, the event of a letter arriving is processed in terms of M-LETTER shown below:

```
                         M-LETTER

    +-----------------------------------------------+
    |   writer                          reader      |
    |                        KNOW-                   |
    |   INFORM-        i     ADDRESS                 |
    |   LETTER............ :                         |
    |   (d-know)           : :e                      |
    |      :           $POST-LETTER                  |
    |      :           +----------+                  |
    |      :           |  WRITE   |                  |
    |      :           |  MAIL    |                  |
    |      :           +----------+                  |
    |      :              r :                        |
    |      :           EV-POST-ARRIVAL.... m         |
    |      :              (ptrans)        :          |
    |      :                              :          |
    |    : a                    i  WANT-KNOW-        |
    |      :          ...........   LETTER-INFO      |
    |      :                 :       (d-know)        |
    |      :                 :           :           |
    |      :           $READ-            : a         |
    |    :..........   LETTER............:           |
    |                  (mtrans)                      |
    |                                                |
    |   phys-objs:  LETTER-OBJ, ENVELOPE             |
    |               STAMPS, MAIL-BOX, etc.           |
    |   mental-obj: LETTER-INFO                      |
    |                                                |
    +-----------------------------------------------+
```

M-LETTER captures our common sense knowledge about letters and their use in narratives: The letter-writer wants the letter-reader to know some information (LETTER-INFO). To achieve this goal, the letter-writer performs the $POST-LETTER script, which involves writing the letter, getting an envelope, placing postage on the letter, etc. For simplicity, these actions are not shown in the diagram. When the letter-reader receives a letter in the mail[56] its arrival motivates the goal WANT-KNOW-LETTER-INFO on the part of the letter-reader. Finally, the letter-reader can achieve his goal (and the goal of letter-writer) by reading the letter.

The arrival of Paul's letter in DIVORCE-1, however, is very different from the letter in SY-4 below:

> **SY-4:** Aron received a letter from Reader's Digest, offering him a free trial subscription.

Obviously, the significance of a letter differs tremendously, depending on its contents. In cases where the contents are not immediately known, the significance of any communication can often be inferred from knowledge about its sender and the sender's relationship to the recipient. A letter from Reader's Digest is probably a bill, promotional offer, or advertisement. A phone call from the wife's lawyer in a divorce case probably concerns the wife's demands, etc.

When BORIS realizes that the letter is from Paul, it checks the interpersonal relationship between Richard and Paul. Since the letter-reader and the letter-writer are IPT-FRIENDS, the letter is interpreted as an interpersonal communication. This implies that the contents of the letter will be about Paul's life state. So when BORIS reads:

> ...Richard was anxious to find out how Paul was.

this passage is interpreted as an interpersonal goal to know Paul's life state.

---

[56]The discussion here leaves out the implicit contract between the postal service and the letter-writer, which is not implemented in the current version of BORIS.

10.4 IP-SOC and Interpersonal Stages

Interpersonal relationships are not static entities in narratives of any complexity. Relationships change over time. Characters meet, form bonds, have quarrels, break up, make reconciliations, etc. Characters may lose track of one another, only later to encounter each other by chance. Interpersonal themes never really terminate (unless a character dies). Even a friend turned enemy can become a friend again in the future. This kind of long-term information can be crucial in processing and representing narratives. Consider the following story:

> **SY-5:** Frank called his wife Nancy to tell her that he and his roommate Bob were going to show up for dinner.

People who read SY-5 commonly assume that that Frank and Nancy are probably divorced. However, when the following piece of information is added (in boldface):

> **SY-6:** Frank called his wife Nancy to tell her that he and his **old college** roommate Bob were going to show up for dinner.

readers fail to make the same inference. Why is this the case? It seems that readers are monitoring relationships in terms of both their current status and their past stages of development.

BORIS keeps track of the interpersonal stages of characters' relationships by means of the following processing structure:

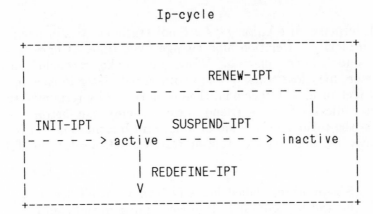

When BORIS reads about interpersonal stages, it can map these stages to the Ip-cycle associated with the particular relationship involved. For instance, the following story is almost entirely interpersonal in nature:

> **SY-7:** Hugo met a girl named Rhoda. They became good friends and saw each other every day. Then Hugo was transferred to California and they gradually lost touch. One day, Hugo got a letter from Rhoda, telling him that she was coming to California. He was very pleased. When she arrived, he took her out to dinner. Then they realized they were both in love. A few weeks later they were married.

SY-7 would be instantiated in terms of the Ip-cycle:

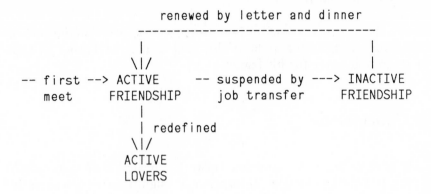

```
          renewed by letter and dinner
          ---------------------------------
              |                       |
             \|/                      |
  -- first --> ACTIVE     -- suspended by ---> INACTIVE
    meet       FRIENDSHIP     job transfer     FRIENDSHIP
               |
               | redefined
              \|/
               ACTIVE
               LOVERS
```

Associated with each node and arc in Ip-cycle are interpersonal expectations and conditions which are useful during processing. For instance, SUSPEND-IPT can be recognized whenever the following kinds of situations arise:

- Separation in time and space: "Richard hadn't seen Paul in years." (DIVORCE-1)

- Certain social events: "John was invited to a farewell party for Bill who was being transferred to California." (KIDNAP-0)

- Interpersonal conflicts: "Since Patrick and Janice had a fight Patrick has been dating Suzy instead of Janice."

What is the connection between a job transfer and a farewell party? Clearly, the connection is interpersonal, having to do with an IP-SOC initiated by one's friends in anticipation of a SUSPEND-IPT. So, SUSPEND-IPT organizes the following kinds of interpersonal goals:

- Friends like to engage in IP-SOC before a SUSPEND-IPT is to occur.

- Friends try to maintain IP-COMM when separated by distance for a period of time.

- Friends reactivate INACTIVE relationships by means of

IP-COMM and IP-SOC.

Each of these expectations arises from a desire to maintain the relationship. A character without this goal would not bother to show up at a farewell party for his friend.

10.5 Conclusions

It is clear from the question-answering behavior of readers that they are attending to the interpersonal significance of narrative events. The importance of this interpersonal level in BORIS can be seen most clearly by highlighting those fragments in the DIVORCE stories which required knowledge about interpersonal themes:

DIVORCE-1

Richard hadn't heard from his college roommate Paul for years **SUSPEND-IPT**. Richard had borrowed money from Paul ... his old friend **IP-FAVOR**. When a letter finally arrived ... Richard was anxious to find out how Paul was **IP-COMM**. Unfortunately, the news was not good **IP-EMPATHY**... Not knowing who to turn to ...Paul... was hoping for a favor **IP-FAVOR**... Paul agreed to have lunch with him **RENEW-IPT** ... Richard offered to drive him home **IP-FAVOR** ... found Sarah with another man **IPT-LOVE violation**... Richard congratulated Paul **IP-EMPATHY**... suggested that they celebrate at dinner **IP-SOC** ...

DIVORCE-2

he found his wife Ann and another man **IPT-LOVE violation** ... he ran into an old college roommate David **RENEW-IPT**, who he hadn't seen in years **SUSPEND-IPT**. David offered to buy him a few drinks **IP-FAVOR** ... Since David owed George money he had never returned, he felt obligated to help out **IP-FAVOR**

... David could only offer George his condolences **IP-EMPATHY** ... A week later, George received a large bill ... from David. Was he furious! (IP-FAVOR violation)

In order to understand complicated narratives in depth, it is important to track events at the interpersonal level. This level maintains its own perspective -- i.e. its own knowledge constructs with their associated expectations. These expectations serve to connect up events in a narrative by supplying interpersonal motivations for the actions of the characters. Furthermore, it is not enough to understand only the currently active interpersonal relationships. It is also important to follow the long-term development of interpersonal relationships.

PART IV.   SYNTHESIS -- Putting It All Together

This part contains two chapters.   In chapter 11 we examine a single story in its entirety.   As a result, an ambitious reader can get an idea of how all the processes discussed in parts I, II and III come together.   In chapter 12 we review and consolidate what has been accomplished.   This includes a discussion of current limitations in BORIS and directions for future research.

CHAPTER 11

Narrative Comprehension: A Detailed Example

11.1 Introduction

Throughout this thesis we have argued that achieving in-depth comprehension for narrative text requires the coordination, interaction, and application of numerous processes arising from many different knowledge sources. By this point the reader should have formed a clear (albeit general) notion of what is involved in narrative comprehension, based on 1) the overview presented in Parts I and II, and 2) the case by case analyses presented in Part III. Still, some readers may feel the need to see a complete example showing how each process arises and accomplishes its task.

In addition, other readers may have unanswered questions concerning certain parsing 'details' which have not been discussed elsewhere in this thesis, but which nevertheless had to be addressed at some level in order to get BORIS "to run". Such 'details' include: the disambiguation of specific words, the resolution of specific pronouns, the handling of specific syntactic constructions, etc. I have used the term 'details', not because these problems aren't interesting or important in themselves, but because no major theoretical claims are being made in this thesis concerning them. Some readers will want to know how such problems are handled in BORIS, and in doing so gain a better idea of the capabilities of the current implementation of BORIS.

This chapter contains a detailed, annotated trace of BORIS running on the entire DIVORCE-2 story, along with a few examples of BORIS answering questions concerning that story. Annotations are used both to clarify the trace and to describe various heuristic solutions to those issues which were not central enough in this thesis to deserve stand-alone treatment. The narrative trace is followed by selected question-answering traces and a description of BORIS implementation "specs", such as: the number of demons, vocabulary size, CPU time, etc.

11.2 Caveats

A complete, verbatim trace describing everything BORIS does while reading DIVORCE-2 and answering questions takes up over 300 single-spaced pages. This includes demons being spawned, described, fired, and killed, along with all memory instantiations, bindings, and resulting inferences. Much of this information is designed mainly to aid those working directly with the program. Therefore, the trace has been edited in a number of ways:

1. For sake of brevity, only highlights are shown. In addition, the trace starts out in relatively great detail, but gradually becomes sketchier. The assumption is that the reader will be able to fill in subsequent gaps by imagining the recurrent application of those processes shown at the beginning of the trace. Likewise, the conceptual structures which are built later on in the trace are shown in a more simplified format as the trace proceeds.

2. For clarity, demons have been given mnemonic names and the descriptions of most demons have been simplified. For instance, the condition which determines when a demon kills itself is not described.

3. In the verbatim trace, when a demon is spawned a description of the process rule it embodies is output. In this edited trace, subsequent instantiations of the same demon will not include this redundant process description, unless some additional aspect of the demon is being exercised.

4. Only those demons are shown which actually "fire" during the comprehension of DIVORCE-2. Demons which check for situations not occurring in DIVORCE-2 have been left out of the trace. Also, some demon parameters have been omitted in cases where it is clear which conceptual structure the demon is associated with.

5. I have chosen to omit certain low-level aspects of comprehension, such as the creation of tokens for object primitives.

6. Where the analysis is too lengthy to explain and has already been covered in detail elsewhere, I simply refer the interested reader to that corresponding section in the thesis.

7. Since the knowledge structures used in Episodic Memory are describe throughout the thesis, in the trace presented here I only show a tiny fraction of the Episodic Memory which is being built. Instead, I rely on the parse result left in Working Memory to give the reader a notion of what corresponding structures have been created in Episodic Memory.

Other than these edits, I have kept as close as possible to the verbatim trace produced by BORIS and demo-ed at the seventh IJCAI in Vancouver [Dyer, Wolf, Korsin, 1981]. For the reader who wants to know more about what the demons and the BORIS lexicon actually look like, see section 6.4, or see [Dyer, 1982] for an implementation description of a micro version of the BORIS parser.

11.3 Annotated Narrative Trace

The trace appears below. Much of it is designed to be self-explanatory. When a demon is spawned, a description of the demon's task appears immediately after it. The spawning, execution and killing of each demon is shown toward the beginning.

Comments which have been added to the trace appear after the bar symbol "|". Demon activations have the format: DEMONm/n = (demon-name parameters ...) where m/n indicates that the demon is attached to concept CONm in *wm* (Working Memory), with n specifying a particular demon instantiation. The format for conceptual dependency structures is: (dependency role filler ... role filler). If a filler receives a binding, it is indicated by the arrow <-- . When annotations discuss a specific topic, a topic heading appears right after the point in the trace where that topic arises.

11.3.1 PARAGRAPH-1

(BORIS DIVORCE-2) | invokes BORIS to read narrative

Processing sentence: GEORGE WAS HAVING LUNCH WITH ANOTHER
TEACHER AND GRADING HOMEWORK ASSIGNMENTS WHEN THE WAITRESS
ACCIDENTALLY KNOCKED A GLASS OF COKE ON HIM *PERIOD*

```
GEORGE ==> Adding:  CON0 to *wm*
    CON0 = (HUMAN FIRST-NAME (GEORGE) GENDER (MALE) INSTAN INSTAN0)
    Spawning:  DEMON0/0 = (FIND-CHAR CON0)
        If character CHAR exists with matching GENDER and FIRST-NAME
        Then return CHAR found,  Else create a new CHAR
    Executing:  DEMON0/0 = (FIND-CHAR CON0)
        Creating character:  GEORGE0 in EP memory
        INSTAN0 <-- GEORGE0
    Killing:  DEMON0/0
```

Here, CON0 holds what BORIS knows about the word "George"
while GEORGE0 points to whatever BORIS builds up in Episodic
Memory about the narrative character George.

```
WAS ==> Adding:  CON1 to *wm*
    Spawning priority:  DEMON1/0 = (DISAMBIG-AUX CON1)
        If ACT follows with TIME = PAST,
        Then interpret CON as VOICE = PASSIVE
        Else modify ACT with TIME = PAST
        If PROGRESSIVE follows Then ignore
```

Auxiliaries and Passive Voice -- Role filling demons check
for the existence of a passive voice in Working Memory and alter their
actions accordingly. For example, if a demon wanting to fill an
ACTOR slot notices a passive voice, it ceases to look before the ACT
and instead looks for the object of a "by".[57]

---

[57]Passive voice does not occur in DIVORCE-2, so it does not appear in the
trace.

```
HAVING ==> Springing Morphology Trap:  ING
               Using word HAVE with PROGRESSIVE root
           Closing Morphology Trap: ING
   Executing:  DEMON1/0 = (DISAMBIG-AUX CON1)
      Ignoring CON1
   Killing:  DEMON1/0
```

Morphological Endings and Role Bindings -- BORIS must
notice morphological endings. For instance, the progressive form of
"have" usually indicates a social interaction rather than possession.
Examples are: "having a friend over", "having a party", "having a
fight", "having a conversation", etc.

```
LUNCH ==> Adding:  CON4  to *wm*
   CON4 = (M-MEAL EATER-A  EATER-A0  EVENT  EVENT0
                  EATER-B  EATER-B0  INSTAN INSTAN0)
   Spawning:  DEMON4/0 = (FIND-MOP CON4)
       If MOP known but CON roles do not match EP roles
       Then (1) Instantiate new MOP with new roles
            (2) Spawn demon to update event in MOP
   Spawning:  DEMON4/1 = (EXPECT EATER-A0 HUMAN BEFORE)
       If HUMAN found BEFORE
       Then bind EATER-A0 with HUMAN found
   Spawning:  DEMON4/2 = (EXPECT-PREP EATER-B0 HUMAN WITH)
       If HUMAN found modified by preposition: WITH
       Then bind EATER-B0 with HUMAN found
   Executing:  DEMON4/1 = (EXPECT EATER-A0 HUMAN BEFORE)
       EATER-A0 <-- CON0
   Killing:  DEMON4/1
   Executing:  DEMON4/0 = (FIND-MOP CON4)
       Creating:  M-MEAL0 bound to INSTAN0
       Spawning:  DEMON4/3 = (UPDATE-EVENT)
           If HAVE precedes
           Then (1) Set EVENT to main event in MOP
                (2) Update scenario map
                (3) Spawn any associated demons
       Spawning:  DEMON4/4 = (EP-ROLE-CHECK)
           If any role is bound to CON4
           Then build corresponding role in EP memory
   Killing:  DEMON4/0
   Executing:  DEMON4/3 = (UPDATE-EVENT)
       EVENT0 <-- EV-INGEST in M-MEAL0
       Creating Scenario:  S0
```

```
Killing: DEMON4/3
Executing:  DEMON4/4 = (EP-ROLE-CHECK)
    Building EATER-A0 role in EP memory
```

Knowledge based on word order is captured by the direction in which EXPECT demons search Working Memory. These demons can look either to the left (BEFORE) or to the right (AFTER) of the conceptualization to which each demon is attached. Conceptualizations can directly refer to MOPs. In such cases the EP-ROLE-CHECK demon is spawned to bind roles in EP memory as each role is bound in Working Memory by EXPECT demons.

```
WITH ==>  Adding:  CON5 to *wm*
    Spawning priority: DEMON5/0 = (MODIFY-PREP PP WITH)
        If HUMAN1 follows and HUMAN2 precedes
        Then spawn demons to determine social activity
```

Prepositions -- Prepositions are treated much like adjectives. For instance, "with a fat man" is parsed as: (HUMAN GENDER (MALE) WEIGHT (>NORM) PREP-OBJ (WITH)). In BORIS syntactic information is not treated in any special way differing from other, more semantic-oriented information. This is in contrast with systems which treat syntax as an autonomous distinct entity.[58]

```
ANOTHER ==>  Adding:  CON6 to *wm*
    Spawning priority: DEMON6/0 = (NEW-TOKEN)
        If PP found, Then mark it: TOKEN = NEW
    Spawning:  DEMON6/1 = (ADD-FEATURES)
        If ROLE-THEME follows and is socializing
            with preceding MOP-ROLE in Episodic Memory
        Then infer that HUMAN bound to MOP-ROLE
            has same ROLE-THEME feature.

TEACHER ==>  Adding:  CON7 to *wm*     | NEW-TOKEN fires
```

---

[58]For a discussion of the relationship of syntax to semantics and the position taken by the "Yale Approach" to natural language, see [Schank and Birnbaum, 1982].

```
   Creating:  RT-TEACHER0 with  ROLE-THEME RT-TEACHER
      << rt-demon fires >>       CLASS  HUMAN
Executing:  DEMON6/1 = (ADD-FEATURES)
   Updating:  GEORGE0 with  ROLE-THEME RT-TEACHER
Killing:  DEMON6/1
Executing:  DEMON5/0 = (MODIFY-PREP PP WITH)
   Setting heuristic:  M-MEAL implies activity INGEST
Killing:  DEMON5/0
Executing:  DEMON4/2 = (EXPECT-PREP EATER-B0 HUMAN WITH)
   EATER-B0 <-- RT-TEACHER0
Killing:  DEMON4/2
Executing:  DEMON4/5 = (EP-ROLE-CHECK)
   Building EATER-B0 role in EP memory
```

Building and Updating Tokens -- The appearance of "another" blocks the role-theme demon from first searching EP memory for a prior referent, causing a new role-theme to be instantiated immediately. See section 5.4 for more discussion on "another".

```
AND ==> Adding:  CON8 to *wm*
   Spawning priority:  DEMON8/0 = (DISAMBIG-AND)
      If preceding conceptualization is an EVENT E1
        and what follows is an EVENT E2
      Then interpret CON as (*CONJUNCT*)
      Else spawn GROUPER demon
```

Conjunctions -- If "and" is interpreted as a conjunct, then it indirectly affects the behavior of other demons. For example, in the sentence "John hit Bill and ran away" an ACTOR demon associated with "ran" will return the ACTOR of "hit" when it can not find a HUMAN in between PTRANS ("ran") and the conjunct.

The other use of "and" is to indicate groups, as in "John, Bill, and Mary went to the movies." In this case, *CONJUNCT* (and also *COMMA*) spawn demons to build: (GROUP MEMBERS (John Bill Mary)) as the ACTOR in the event.

```
GRADING ==> Springing Morphology Trap:  ING
               Using word GRADE with PROGRESSIVE root
            Closing Morphology Trap: ING
```

```
CON10 = (EVALUATE EVALUATOR EVALUATOR0  EVENT EVENT1
                    OBJECT  OBJECT0  INSTAN  INSTAN1)
Spawning:  DEMON10/0 = (EXPECT EVALUATOR0 HUMAN BEFORE)
Spawning:  DEMON10/1 = (EXPECT OBJECT0 WORK-OBJ AFTER)
Spawning:  DEMON10/2 = (FIND-MOP CON10)
    If MOP for EVENT not known and OBJECT of EVENT
      has MOP associated with it
    Then apply MOP to EVENT (i.e. match MOP-events against
      EVENT and if successful, reinterpret EVENT as an
      event in the MOP).
Executing:  DEMON8/0 = (DISAMBIG-AND)
    CON8 = (*CONJUNCT*)
Killing:  DEMON8/0
Executing:  DEMON10/0 = (EXPECT EVALUATOR0 HUMAN BEFORE)
    EVALUATOR0 <-- CON0   | When EXPECT demon encounters
Killing:  DEMON10/0       | *CONJUNCT* while searching *wm*
                          | for an actor it returns the actor
                          | of event preceding *CONJUNCT*
```

HOMEWORK ASSIGNMENTS
```
    ==> Recognized phrase: HOMEWORK ASSIGNMENT
    CON11 = (WORK-OBJ MOP (M-EDUCATION))
    Executing:  DEMON10/1 = (EXPECT OBJECT0 WORK-OBJ AFTER)
        OBJECT0 <-- CON11
    Killing:  DEMON10/1
    Executing:  DEMON10/2 = (FIND-MOP CON10)
        Applying:  M-EDUCATION to CON10
        Reinterpret CON10 as:
            (M-EDUCATION  TEACHER (CON0)  STUDENT STUDENT0
                          EVENT (EV-GRADE)  INSTAN (M-EDUCATION0))
        Updating Scenario: S0
    Killing:  DEMON10/2
```

MOP Application -- Here, the M-EDUCATION mop is found
by noticing that the **OBJECT** of **EVALUATE** is an object-primitive
associated with the mop M-EDUCATION.   As a result, M-
EDUCATION is applied to EVALUATE and a match is found in M-
EDUCATION. An inference arising from this match is that George is
a teacher, but this inference has already been made by the demon
associated with "another".

WHEN ==> Adding: CON12 to *wm*
```
    CON12 = (*EVENT*)
```

```
THE WAITRESS ==>  Adding:  CON13 to *wm*
          Creating:  RT-WAITRESS0 with GENDER FEMALE
    Spawning:  DEMON13/0 = (FIND-RT-MOP CON13)
        If an RT has an uninstantiated MOP M1 associated with it
          and there is an instantiated MOP M2 with strands to M1
        Then instantiate M1
    Executing:  DEMON13/0 = (FIND-RT-MOP CON13)
        Creating:  M-RESTAURANT0
        Updating Scenario S0 with SETTING RESTAURANT
    Killing:  DEMON13/0
```

Articles, RTs, and MOP strands -- Articles, such as "the", "an", and "a" are essentially ignored by BORIS. Articles need not be processed since BORIS searches Episodic Memory everytime a PP (picture producer) [Schank, 1973] is mentioned. Whether "a waitress" or "the waitress" is read, BORIS must search memory to decide whether to instantiate a new character or return a referent to an existing character. Articles are used in the recognition of phrases, however. For instance, "a living" means OCCUPATION while "the living" refers to ANIMATE HUMANs.

Role-themes in BORIS are used to suggest MOPs for MOP application. The occurrence of RT-WAITRESS here suggests that M-RESTAURANT be applied. Since M-MEAL is active and has strands to M-RESTAURANT, M-RESTAURANT becomes active also. See section 8.4.

```
ACCIDENTALLY ==> Springing Morphology Trap:  LY
                    Using word ACCIDENTAL with ADVERBIAL root
                Closing Morphology Trap: LY
    Spawning priority:  DEMON14/0 = (MODIFY-MODE ACT *UNINTENDED*)
        If ACT follows,
        Then modify with MODE UNINTENDED


KNOCKED ==> Springing Morphology Trap:  ED
                Using word KNOCK with PAST root
            Closing Morphology Trap: ED
    CON16 = (PROPEL ACTOR ACTOR0 OBJECT OBJECT1 TO TOO)
    Executing:  DEMON14/0 = (MODIFY-MODE ACT *UNINTENDED*)
        Updating:  CON16 with MODE *UNINTENDED*
    Killing:  DEMON14/0
    Spawning:  DEMON16/0 = (EXPECT ACTOR0 HUMAN BEFORE)
```

```
Spawning: DEMON16/1 = (EXPECT OBJECT1 PHYS-OBJ AFTER)
Spawning: DEMON16/2 = (EXPECT-PREP TOO HUMAN ON)
Spawning: DEMON16/3 = (FIND-MOP CON16)
     If ACT is *UNINTENDED*
     Then attempt violation match if mop application fails
Executing:  DEMON16/0 = (EXPECT ACTOR0 HUMAN BEFORE)
     ACTOR0 <-- RT-WAITRESSO
Killing:  DEMON16/0
```

Priority Demons and Unintended Acts -- In general, the most recently spawned demons are executed first. Demons spawned with priority, however, execute before other demons. Most modification demons have priority over mop-application demons, since those demons will want to have access to any modifications before searching memory. So "accidentally" will modify "knocked" before demons associated with "knocked" can execute. For discussion of unintended events, see section 6.4.8.

```
A GLASS ==> Adding: CON17 to *wm*
     Spawning:  DEMON17/0 = (DISAMBIG-MEASURE CON17)
          If followed by a LIQUID
          Then CON = MEASURE,  Else CON = MATERIAL

OF COKE                    | Preposition "of" modifies "coke"
     CON19 = (LIQUID CLASS (COKE) PREP-OBJ (OF))
     Executing:  DEMON17/0 = (DISAMBIG-MEASURE CON17)
          CON17 = (MEASURE OBJECT (LIQUID CLASS (COKE)))
     Killing:  DEMON17/0
     Executing:  DEMON16/1 = (EXPECT OBJECT1 PHSY-OBJ AFTER)
          OBJECT1 <-- CON17
     Killing:  DEMON17
```

Object Primitives and Pronoun Reference -- BORIS must know about PROPELing LIQUIDs. This includes inferring that the OBJECT of the PROPEL will be wet (not shown here). This information is held in discrimination nets associated with both LIQUID and PROPEL and is applied by FIND-MOP.

```
ON HIM ==> Adding: CON21 to *wm*
     CON21 = (HUMAN GENDER (MALE) CASE (OBJECT) INSTAN INSTAN6)
     Spawning:  DEMON21/0 = (BIND-REF MALE)
```

```
        If HUMAN found with correct GENDER and CASE
        Then bind CON with it
Executing:  DEMON21/0 = (BIND-REF MALE)
        Reference found is GEORGE0
Killing:  DEMON21/0
Executing:  DEMON16/2 = (EXPECT-PREP TOO HUMAN ON)
        TOO <-- GEORGE0
Killing:  DEMON16/2
```

Pronouns are bound tentatively by reference demons, which search Working Memory for the last HUMAN with an appropriate GENDER and CASE. If the binding formed in Working Memory does not match a memory structure in Episodic memory, then the tentative binding is ignored. See section 6.4.4.

```
*PERIOD* ==> Adding:  CON22 to *wm*
    Executing:  DEMON16/3 = (FIND-MOP CON16)
        Since match fails and MODE is *UNINTENDED*,
            check for deviation.
        TAU recognition:
            PROPEL LIQUID UNINTENDED motivates P-COMFORT goal
                in TAU-REG-MISTAKE with SCHLMOZL = RT-WAITRESS0
                                        SCHLEMIEL = GEORGE0
        Since ACTOR is ROLE-THEME, check RT-MOP M-RESTAURANT
            and MOP STRANDS for violation information

        EVENT is violation of EV-BRING-FOOD in M-RESTAURANT
        EVENT is violation of EV-DO-SERVICE in M-SERVICE

        VIOLATION found on EV-DO-SERVICE
        Creating:  TAU-BROKEN-SERVICE0 with EVENT BAD-SERVICE0
        Updating scenario: S0 with TAU-BROKEN-SERVICE
    Killing:  DEMON16/3   | other demons kill themselves also
```

Recognizing Deviations -- This specific case of spilling and TAU-REG-MISTAKE is described in section 8.4.

```
Result of parse:

    (M-MEAL EATER-A (HUMAN NAME (GEORGE)
                           GENDER (MALE)
```

```
                            INSTAN (GEORGE0))
            EATER-B (HUMAN RTS (RT-TEACHER0)
                           PREP-OBJ (PREP IS (WITH))
                           INSTAN (RT-TEACHER0))
            EVENT (EV-EAT-MEAL)
            INSTAN (M-MEAL0)))

      (M-EDUCATION TEACHER (HUMAN NAME (GEORGE)
                                 GENDER (MALE)
                                 INSTAN (GEORGE0))
                STUDENT NIL
                EVENT (EV-PREPARE-CLASS)
                INSTAN (M-EDUCATION0))

   (TAU-REG-MISTAKE
         REG-MISTAKE (PROPEL
                   ACTOR (HUMAN GENDER (FEMALE)
                                RTS (RT-WAITRESS)
                                INSTAN (RT-WAITRESS0))
                   OBJECT (MEASURE
                           OBJECT (LIQUID CLASS (COKE))
                           INSTAN (OBJ-PRIMITIVE0))
                   TO  (HUMAN GENDER (MALE)
                              CASE (OBJECT)
                              INSTAN (GEORGE0))
                   MODE (*UNINTENDED*))
         INSTAN (TAU-REG-MISTAKE0))
```

Sentence Endings and Parse Results -- Many demons kill themselves if they encounter a *PERIOD* without having found what they were looking for. Hence the number of active demons usually remains small.

After BORIS has parsed a sentence, it goes through Working Memory and prints out all "top-level" CON cells. These are the cells which have not been bound to any role within another concept. During output, each role filler is recursively replaced by the structure bound to it.

At this point, Episodic memory contains an instantiated scenario with pointers to M-EDUCATION0, M-MEAL0, M-RESTAURANT0, M-SERVICE0, TAU-BROKEN-SERVICE0, and TAU-REG-MISTAKE0. George plays a role in each. He is a meal eater, a restaurant patron, a contractor for service, a shlimazel who is wet, and a homework grader. All of these roles are associated with the same scenario. Furthermore, the role-themes of teacher and waitress have been built, along with the relations of husband and wife in R-MARRIAGE0.

An I-link (chapter 7) has also been built between the PROPEL and George's P-COMFORT goal. In addition, access links have been built to all of these knowledge structures for use during subsequent comprehension and question-answering.

```
Processing    sentence:  GEORGE  WAS  VERY  ANNOYED  AND  LEFT
REFUSING TO PAY THE CHECK.
```

GEORGE WAS | Builds CON23 and CON24

```
VERY ==> Adding CON25 to *wm*
    Spawning priority: DEMON25/0 = (MODIFY-SCALE (STATE ACT) >NORM)
        If a STATE or ACT is found
        Then modify with SCALE >NORM
```

```
ANNOYED ==> Adding CON26 to *wm*
    CON26 = (AFFECT CHAR CHAR0  STATE (NEG)  TOWARD TOWARD0
                     EVENT EVENT0  G-SITU G-SITU0
                     SCALE  (>NORM))   | Scale added by DEMON25/0
    Spawning:  DEMON26/0 = (EXPECT-PREP TOWARD0 HUMAN (AT WITH))
    Spawning:  DEMON26/1 = (EXPECT CHAR0 HUMAN BEFORE)
    Spawning:  DEMON26/2 = (EXPECT EVENT0 ACT)
    Spawning:  DEMON26/3 = (EXPLAIN-AFFECT CON26)
        Search memory for a TAU or goal situation which
        is compatible with the affective state and character
        If the affect can be reconstructed from a TAU or goal
        Then ignore. Else instantiate this affect
    Executing:  DEMON26/1 = (EXPECT CHAR0 HUMAN BEFORE)
        CHAR0 <-- CON23
    Killing:  DEMON26/1
    Executing: DEMON26/3 = (EXPLAIN-AFFECT CON26)
        Search for explanation of the NEG AFFECT
        Check tau: TAU-BROKEN-SERVICE0 for agreement
        :::>> AFFECT agreement found
    Killing: DEMON26/3
```

Affect Handling -- Both TAU-BROKEN-SERVICE and TAU-REG-MISTAKE predict that George will be mad at the waitress.

Since characters can feel more than one AFFECT at a time, BORIS quits processing an AFFECT when the first TAU is found whose affect information matches this AFFECT in Working Memory.

```
AND
LEFT ==> Adding:  CON28 to *wm*
    Spawning:  DEMON28/0 = (DISAMBIG-PTRANS CON28)
        If BODY-PART, AREA or PREP-OBJ = OF follows
        Then interpret as SPATIAL RELATION
        Else interpret as PTRANS

REFUSING ==> Adding: CON30 to *wm*  | Morphology:  REFUSE + ING
    Spawning priority:  DEMON30/0 = (MODIFY-MODE ACT NEG)
    Executing:  DEMON28/0 = (DISAMBIG-PTRANS CON28)
    CON28 = (PTRANS ACTOR ACTOR2  FROM FROMO
                    TO TO2   PROX-GOAL PROX-GOALO)
    Spawning:    |   Role-binding demons
    Spawning:  DEMON28/4 =  (TRANSITION-SCENARIO CON28)
        Build a transition scenario and  spawn demons
        to find the motivation for this change of setting
```

Transition Scenarios -- BORIS doesn't realize that a change of setting has occurred until "left" is disambiguated by noticing that "refusing" is not a body part (e.g. as in "left hand"), area ("left side") or preposition ("to the left of center"). At this point BORIS builds a transition scenario with an unknown destination.

*TO PAY THE CHECK *PERIOD**

```
    CON32 = (ATRANS ACTOR HUMO OBJECT OBJECT2
                    FROM HUMO TO TO3
                    MODE (NEG)   |  added by DEMON30/0 ("refusing")

    Executing:  DEMON32/5 = (FIND-MOP CON32)
        Noticing MODE NEG
        Using OBJECT information to select mop:  M-RESTAURANT
        Finding  Deviation Match with EV-PAY in M-RESTAURANT
        Searching Deviation Information ==> none found
        Searching strands
        Searching Deviation Information  ==> EV-DENY-PAY in M-SERVICE
        Finding TAU-BROKEN-SERVICE
        Instantiating BAD-SERVICE ---motivates---> EV-DENY-PAY
```

```
Killing:  DEMON32/5
```

Deviation Matching -- Deviation matching is relatively easy in the MODE NEG case. MOP application simply ignores the MODE until a match is found; in this case, with EV-PAY in M-RESTAURANT. Since the MODE is NEG, an expectation failure has occurred. (After all, one is expected to pay for one's meal in a restaurant.) Now BORIS looks for deviation information to explain this expectation failure. For more discussion, see section 6.4.8.

```
Processing sentence:  HE DECIDE TO DRIVE HOME TO  GET  OUT  OF
HIS WET CLOTHES *PERIOD*
```

HE DECIDED TO DRIVE HOME

```
Result of parse:

    (GOAL ACTOR (HUMAN GENDER (MALE) INSTAN (GEORGE0))
          OBJECT OBJECT3)
                 |
               CON37 = (M-DRIVE
                         DRIVER (HUMAN GENDER (MALE)
                                        INSTAN (GEORGE0))
                         PASSINGER NIL
                         DESTINATION (SETTING CLASS (RESIDENCE)
                                              INSTAN (SETTING1))
                         EVENT (EV-DRIVE)
                         INSTAN (M-DRIVE0)
                         PREP-OBJ (PREP IS (TO))))

    Spawning:  DEMON37/6 = (D-PROX-ENABLES CON37)
        If an ACT at the DESTINATION SETTING
          of a transition scenario is enabled
          by that SETTING
        Then build an ENABLES link between the
          GOAL achieved by the ACT and the
          D-PROX goal in the transition scenario
```

The mop M-DRIVE spawns demons which search for a transition scenario to update (or create). At this point BORIS knows how George will get home, but not why he's going home.

TO GET OUT OF HIS WET CLOTHES *PERIOD*

```
Result of Parse:

   CON42 = ($CHANGE-CLOTHES
           INSTAN ($CHANGE-CLOTHES0)
           CHANGER (HUMAN GENDER (MALE)
                         INSTAN (GEORGE0))
           OLD-CLOTHES (PHYS-OBJ  CLASS (CLOTHING)
                         OWNER (GEORGE0)
                         INSTAN (PHYS-OBJ1) STATE (WET))
           EVENT (EV-CHANGE-CLOTHES)
           PREP-OBJ (PREP IS (TO)))

   Spawning:  DEMON42/5  = (FIND-INTENTION  CON42)
        If ACT in this CON normally achieves
          GOAL G and G is active
        Then build INTENTIONAL links between ACT and G
```

BORIS recognizes "get out of" as a phrase. BORIS then spawns a disambiguation demon which checks for the object of that phrase. CLOTHING suggests the $CHANGE-CLOTHES script.

D-PROX Enablement -- When DEMON37/6 fires, it notices that $CHANGE-CLOTHES is enabled by D-PROX(home). That is, one can not change clothes without first being in a setting where one's clothes are found. At this point BORIS knows why George wanted to be at home.

DEMON42/5 is spawned to try and explain why George is changing his clothes. Clothes are usually changed because they are uncomfortable (P-COMFORT goal) or dirty (P-APPEARANCE goal) [59] In this case, George has a P-COMFORT goal active, so an INTENDs link is built between P-COMFORT0 and $CHANGE-CLOTHES0.

---

[59]Clothes are also changed as an enablement for a social activity. For example, pajamas enable sleeping and football uniforms enable playing football. This knowledge is currently not implemented in BORIS.

11.3.2 PARAGRAPH-2

Processing sentence: WHEN HE GOT THERE *COMMA* HE   FOUND   HIS
WIFE ANN AND ANOTHER MAN IN BED *PERIOD*

WHEN HE GOT THERE | New scenario S2 is built.

COMMA | Noticed by demons which search Working Memory
    CON51 = (*BOUNDARY*)

HE FOUND HIS WIFE ANN | R-MARRIAGE built (section 6.4.5)

AND ANOTHER MAN
    CON59 = (HUMAN GENDER (MALE) INSTAN INSTAN18)
    Executing: DEMON58/0 = (NEW-TOKEN)
    Executing: DEMON59/0 = (BIND-REF MALE)
        Creating: HUMAN0
    Executing: DEMON57/3 = (GROUPER) | spawned by DISAMBIG-AND
        Interpreting AND as GROUP
        Spawning: DEMON57/4 = (INFER-SOC-ACTIVITY)
            If ACTIVITY unknown but SETTING known,
            Then infer ACTIVITY from SETTING
    Killing: DEMON57/3

Inferring Social Activities -- The word "another" insures
that a new character will be instantiated for "man".   This is
important if BORIS is to infer adultery later on.   When BORIS
notices two characters together, it assumes they are engaged in some
kind of social interaction and tries to find out what it is.   The only
social activity inferable from a SETTING of BED is sex.   See section
9.3.

IN BED
    CON61 = (SETTING IS (BED))
    Executing: DEMON57/4 = (INFER-SOC-ACTIVITY)
        Inferring ACTIVITY = M-SEX
        Firing BOTTOM-UP RELATIONSHIP check
            Inferring TAU-BROKEN-CONTRACT (MARRIAGE)
                VIOLATION: Sex-fidelity
            Spawning: DEMON57/5 = (BROKEN-CONTRACT-AWARENESS)
                If other PARTY in CONTRACT is aware of
                    VIOLATION and VIOLATION is on-going

```
                    Then infer TAU-RED-HANDED
        Killing:  DEMON57/4
*PERIOD*
```

Bottom-up Inferences -- Whenever BORIS instantiates a knowledge structure, it executes functions associated with it. These functions may spawn demons. In this case, the event EV-SEX causes BORIS to perform a bottom-up check on the relationship between the sexual partners. When a contractual violation is found, another bottom-up check is performed to see if the other partner in the contract is aware of the violation. The processing is similar to that of TAU-BROKEN-SERVICE (RESTAURANT). That is, BORIS looks for violation information under MARRIAGE. When none is found, BORIS chases strands to M-CONTRACT. Here is information that tells BORIS to look for the effect this violation has on the other contract holder. See section 8.6.1.

```
Result of parse:

    (ATTEND ACTOR (HUMAN GENDER (MALE)
                         INSTAN (GEORGE0))
           OBJECT (EYES)
           TO (M-SEX SEX-PARTNER-A (HUMAN INSTAN (HUMAN0))
                    SEX-PARTNER-B (HUMAN GENDER (MALE)
                                        INSTAN (HUMAN3))
                    INSTAN (M-SEX0)
                    EVENT (EV-SEX)))
```

Working Memory becomes inaccessible as new sentences are parsed. Episodic Memory now contains a BEDROOM scenario in which TAU-RED-HANDED occurred over TAU-BROKEN-CONTRACT (MARRIAGE) due to M-SEX violating the SEX-FIDELITY rule in the contract. In this scenario, Sarah plays the following roles: DECEIVER in TAU-RED-HANDED, CONTRACT-BREAKER in TAU-BROKEN-CONTRACT, SEX-PARTNER-A in M-SEX, and WIFE in R-MARRIAGE. George plays the roles of HUSBAND in R-MARRIAGE, CONTRACT-VICTIM in TAU-BROKEN-CONTRACT and WITNESS in TAU-RED-HANDED.

```
Processing  sentence:   GEORGE BECAME EXTREMELY UPSET AND FELT
```

```
LIKE GOING OUT AN GETTING PLASTERED *PERIOD*
```

GEORGE BECAME EXTREMELY UPSET

```
    Executing: DEMON66/3 = (EXPLAIN-AFFECT CON26)
        Search for explanation of the NEG AFFECT
        Check tau: TAU-BROKEN-CONTRACT0 for agreement
        :::>> AFFECT agreement found
    Killing: DEMON66/3
```

This AFFECT is handled in the same way "George was very annoyed" was handled in the first paragraph.

AND FELT LIKE | recognized as phrase: FELT LIKE
```
    CON67 = (GOAL ACTOR ACTOR7 OBJECT OBJECT5)
```

GOING OUT | recognized as phrase: GO OUT
```
    CON69 = (PTRANS ACTOR ACTOR8 FROM FROM2
                      TO TO7  PROX-GOAL PROX-GOAL2)
```

AND GETTING PLASTERED | recognized phrase: GET PLASTERED
```
    CON72 = (M-IMBIBE-ALCOHOL BOOZER BOOZER0 EVENT EVENT7
                              INSTAN INSTAN21)
    Spawning:  DEMON72/5 = (ACT-STATUS-CHECK)
        If CON is an ACT1 modified by "ING" (or by PREP-OBJ = TO)
          and CON is preceded by GOAL (or GOAL ACT2 *CONJUNCT*)
        Then mark ACT1 as an intended plan (vs an actual event)
    Executing:  DEMON72/5 = (ACT-STATUS-CHECK)
        EVENT7 marked as intended
    Executing:  DEMON72/4 = (UPDATE-EVENT)
        Instantiating goal:  G-BE-INTOXICATED in M-IMBIBE-ALCOHOL
        Executing BOTTOM-UP Inferences:
            Building AFFECT link between:
            G-RELIEVE-TENSION in M-IMBIBE-ALCOHOL and
            NEG AFFECT in TAU-BROKEN-CONTRACT(MARRIAGE)
```
PERIOD

Goals/Plans versus Events -- It is important to distinguish goals and plans from actual events. In BORIS, events are realized by the execution of a plan which is intended by some character to achieve an active goal. In the trace above, the text states only that George wanted to get drunk, not that he actually got drunk. Intentional states may never come about. This is in contrast to actual events.

Whenever BORIS comes upon a progressive or infinitival ACT, a demon is spawned to determine whether the ACT constitutes an actual event, or is simply an intentional state of a character. In order to realize that "getting plastered" is not yet an event, the demon ACT-STATUS-CHECK searches for a GOAL. ACT-STATUS-CHECK correctly recognizes the following kinds of intentional situations:

> "John felt like killing Mary"
> (vs "John killed Mary").

> "John wanted to kiss Betty"
> (vs "John kissed Mary").

In order to recognize "getting plastered" as an intention, ACT-STATUS-CHECK must know about conjunctive constructions, since "felt like" is immediately followed by "going out".

AFFECT links -- M-IMBIBE-ALCOHOL contains the information that people get drunk to reduce the SCALE of an AFFECT. When the goal G-BE-INTOXICATED is instantiated, a bottom-up check is made to see if the BOOZER has a strong positive (or negative) AFFECT active. If so, BORIS infers that the character's desire for intoxication is a result of his affective state.

11.3.3 PARAGRAPH-3

```
Processing sentence:  AT THE BAR HE RAN INTO  AN  OLD  COLLEGE
ROOMMATE DAVID *COMMA* WHO HE HADN'T SEEN IN YEARS *PERIOD*
```

AT THE BAR | New main scenario is built along with M-BAR
   CON75 = (SETTING IS (BAR) MOP (M-BAR))
   Executing: DEMON74/6 = (D-PROX-ENABLES CON74)
      Inferring: D-PROX to BAR enables G-BE-INTOXICATED
       | For description of DEMON74/6, see DEMON37/6

HE
RAN INTO
   Spawning DEMON77 = (DISAMBIG-RAN-INTO CON77)
      If actor is VEHICLE or SCENARIO is TRANSITIONAL

```
with VEHICLE instrument,
Then interpret CON as M-VEHICLE-ACCIDENT
Else If object is REL or IPT HUMAN
      Then interpret CON as interpersonal
        activity RENEW-IPT
```

Phrases and Noun Groups -- In BORIS, phrases are distinguished from words. A phrase is an idiom or stylized expression [Becker, 1975]. Here, "ran into" is treated as a phrase because splitting up the words can change its meaning. For example, "George ran into David at the bar" has a very different meaning from "George ran David into the bar".

AN OLD COLLEGE ROOMMATE DAVID
```
    Spawning:  DEMON78/0 = (DISAMBIG-OLD CON78)
       If REL or IPT follows
       Then modify it with STATUS (PAST)
       Else If HUMAN or PHYS-OBJ follows
         Then modify it with AGE > NORM
    Spawning:  DEMON79/0 = (DISAMBIG COLLEGE)
       If REL or IPT follows
       Then modify it with ERA = COLLEGE
       Else interpret CON as (INSTITUTION MOP (M-EDUCATION)
                                          CLASS (COLLEGE))
```
COMMA

In contrast to Gershman's parser [Gershman, 1980], which entered a special processing state for noun groups, the BORIS parser relies on disambiguation demons to handle noun groups properly. In the case above, "old college roommate" could mean:

1. x's roommate from an old college.
2. a college roommate who is old.
3. a roommate during a past college era.

In the trace above, the demon DISAMBIG-OLD cannot modify "college" until DISAMBIGUATE-COLLEGE has fired. When DISAMBIG-COLLEGE fires, it will interpret "college" as a modifier of "roommate". Therefore, when DISAMBIG-OLD finally fires, it will correctly modify "roommate" instead of modifying "college". See section 6.4.5.

```
WHO ==> Adding:  CON83 to *wm*
   CON83 = (HUMAN SPEC (*?*) INSTAN INSTAN27)
   Spawning:  DEMON83/0 = (FIND-REF HUMAN BEFORE)
   Spawning:  DEMON84/1 = (FILL-ACT-SLOT  AFTER)
      If ACT follows and ACTOR slot is not filled
      Then bind this CON to the ACTOR slot
      Else bind this CON to the OBJECT slot
```

Question words -- The mode of processing (QA versus SU) determines whether or not BORIS treats "who" as the initiation of a question. See section 5.4.2.

```
HE HADN'T SEEN IN YEARS  |  Morphology:  HADN'T as HAD NOT
   CON87 = (ATTEND ACTOR ACTOR10 TO TO9)
   Spawning:  DEMON87/0 = (DISAMBIG-SEE CON87)
      If OBJECT of ATTEND is a REL or IPT
      Then reinterpret ATTEND as IP-SOC
         and spawn interpersonal demons
   Executing: DEMON87/0 = (DISAMBIG-SEE CON87)
      Reinterpreting CON87 as:  IP-SOC
      BOTTOM-UP inference:
         If MODE = NEG and DURATION > NORM
         Then infer IP STATUS = SUSPENDED in PAST
*PERIOD*
```

The Interpersonal Level -- MTRANS-related words like "seen" and "heard from" cause demons to search for interpersonal units in memory. Once an interpersonal unit is recognized, its status is checked. See section 10.3.

```
Processing sentence:  DAVID OFFERED TO BUY HIM  A  FEW  DRINKS
AND SOON THEY WERE BOTH PRETTY DRUNK *PERIOD*
```

```
DAVID OFFERED  |  "offer" is x MTRANSing goal to be y's agent
   CON93 = (MTRANS ACTOR X3 FROM X3 OBJECT OBJECT9   TO TO6
                 (D-AGENCY OBJECT OBJECT10 FOR FOR0))
      Spawning:  DEMON93/7 = (CHECK-FAVOR CON93)
         If ACTOR and TO have a positive IPT
         Then search for and infer IP-FAVOR
```

Whenever an AGENCY structure is encountered, interpersonal demons check for any motivations or consequences at the interpersonal level.

TO BUY HIM A FEW DRINKS

Result of parse:

```
(MTRANS ACTOR David0
        FROM David0
        TO George0
        OBJECT (D-AGENCY
                    OBJECT (M-EXCHANGE
                                EXCHANGER-A David0
                                OBJECT-A  (MONEY)
                                EXCHANGER-B  NIL
                                OBJECT-B (LIQUID
                                                CLASS (ALCOHOL)))
                FOR George0))

Executing:  DEMON95/5 = (FIND-MOP CON95)
    Finding STRANDS from M-EXHANGE to M-BAR
    Instantiating EV-BUY-ALCOHOL in M-BAR
Executing:  DEMON93/7 = (CHECK-FAVOR CON93)
    Inferring:  IP-FAVOR
```

The M-EXCHANGE mop holds two ATRANSes. Whenever a MOP is instantiated, search demons check for strands to active MOPs. If such strands are found, then the active MOP is updated. In this case, M-EXCHANGE has strands to M-BAR which is active. So the event EV-BUY-DRINKS in M-BAR is instantiated.

From the perspective of M-BAR, David has simply bought drinks. However, when CHECK-FAVOR examines the interpersonal relationship between George and David, it infers (at the interpersonal level) that David is doing George a favor. This means that George owes David a return favor of the same kind. See section 10.2.

AND SOON THEY WERE BOTH PRETTY DRUNK *PERIOD*

Group References and Physical States -- BORIS

instantiates EV-INTOXICATED0 in M-IMIBIBE-ALCOHOL0. As a result, George's goal of G-BE-INTOXICATE0 is now achieved. Furthermore, when the demon EP-ROLE-CHECK notices that the BOOZER role is bound to GROUP (David George), it spawns demons to instantiate a new M-IMIBIBE-ALCHOL1 and EV-INTOXICATED1 for David. Thus, the rule:

> If a GROUP with members M1...Mn
>   fills the ACTOR role in a MOP
>   which does not take GROUP bindings
> Then instantiate MOPs for each GROUP member

is embedded within the BORIS role-binding mechanism.

```
Processing sentence:  WHEN GEORGE FOUND OUT THAT DAVID  WAS  A
LAWYER *COMMA*  HE  TOLD HIM ALL ABOUT HIS TROUBLES AND ASKED
DAVID TO REPRESENT HIM IN COURT *PERIOD*
```

WHEN GEORGE FOUND OUT THAT DAVID WAS A LAWYER *COMMA*

```
Result of parse:

    (MBUILD ACTOR George0
            OBJECT (EQUIV ACTOR David0
                          ROLE (HUMAN INSTAN (David0)
                                      RTS (RT-LAWYER))))
```

HE TOLD HIM ALL ABOUT HIS
TROUBLES
```
    CON123 = (P-GOAL TAU TAU2  AFFECT (NEG) ACTOR ACTOR70)
    Spawning: DEMON123/3 = (FIND-TAU-AFFECT-GOAL INSTAN90)
        If violation of ACTOR's goal situation found
        Then bind it to TAU
```

```
Result of parse:

    CON118 = (MTRANS
                ACTOR George0
                OBJECT (P-GOAL TAU (TAU-BROKEN-CONTRACT0)
                               AFFECT (NEG)
                               ACTOR (GEORGE0))
                TO David0)

    Executing:  DEMON118/5 = (FIND-MOP CON118)
```

```
      BOTTOM-UP inference:
          If x MTRANS goal G TO y
             and IPT(x,y) is not NEG
             and y's Role-theme achieves goals of type G
          Then activate MOP M  associated with y's RT
             and apply it
      Reinterpreting:  CON118 as EV-TELL-PROBLEM
          in M-REPRESENT-CLIENT
  Killing:  DEMON118/5
```

Bottom-up MTRANS Rules and Mental Objects

-- Whenever BORIS encounters an MTRANS, it applies bottom-up rules to try to select an appropriate MOP to apply. In this case, M-REPRESENT-CLIENT is activated because George has told David about a goal which can be achieved by a lawyer.

*AND ASKED DAVID TO REPRESENT HIM IN COURT *PERIOD**
```
  | builds MTRANS of GOAL of AGENCY
```

This directly matches EV-ASK-AID in the mop M-REPRESENT-CLIENT which was just activated. Since M-REPRESENT-CLIENT is the OBJECT of an MTRANS, the scenario demons refrain from inferring a new scenario of COURTROOM. All instantiation demons make sure that the context is not mental before they attempt to instantiate an ACT as actually having happened.

```
Processing sentence:  SINCE DAVID OWED  GEORGE  MONEY  HE  HAD
NEVER RETURNED *COMMA* HE FELT OBLIGATED TO HELP OUT *PERIOD*
```

SINCE
```
    CON135 = (LEADTO ANTE ANTE5 CONSE CONSE5)
```

DAVID OWED GEORGE MONEY
```
    CON137 = (M-BORROW EVENT (EV-LEND-OBJ) ...)
    Executing:  DEMON137/6 = (RT-CHECK-FAVOR)
        Inferring IP-FAVOR from Role-theme information
    Killing:  DEMON137/6
```

*HE HAD NEVER RETURNED *COMMA**
```
    CON144 = (ATRANS ACTOR George0
                     OBJECT (PHYS-OBJ NAME (MONEY)
```

```
                                    INSTAN (PHYS-OBJ2))
                        FROM George0
                        TO NIL
                        MODE (NEG))
          Executing:  DEMON144/5 = (FIND-MOP CON144)
             Noticing MODE NEG
             Using RECENCY to select mop:  M-BORROW
             Finding  Deviation Match with EV-RETURN-OBJ in M-BORROW
             Searching Deviation Information ==> none found
             Searching strands
             Searching Deviation Information
                 ==> BAD-OBLIG in M-OBLIGATION
             Finding TAU-BROKEN-OBLIGATION
          Killing:  DEMON144/5
```

Negative Events -- The processing here is similar to that of "refusing to pay" in paragraph one. Whenever an event with a MODE NEG is encountered it is matched against a MOP and then strands are chased to find deviation information. From TAU-BROKEN-OBLIGATION BORIS can infer that David feels guilty.

HE FELT OBLIGATED TO HELP OUT *PERIOD*

```
Result of parse:

    (LEADTO ANTE (M-BORROW INSTAN (M-BORROW0)
                        LENDER George0
                        BORROWER David0
                        LEND-OBJECT (PHYS-OBJ NAME (MONEY)
                                                INSTAN (PHYS-OBJ2))
                        EVENT (EV-LEND-OBJ))
              CONSE (GOAL ACTOR David0
                        OBJECT (M-REPRESENT-CLIENT
                                INSTAN (M-REPRESENT-CLIENT0)
                                EVENT (EV-TAKE-CASE)
                                L-CLIENT NIL
                                LAWYER David0
                                PREP-OBJ (PREP IS (TO)))))
```

Favors -- Since BORIS has already inferred IP-FAVOR from M-BORROW, the above sentence is processed rather easily. The word "obligated" has demons which search for an active goal. The phrase "help out" spawns a demon to find George's agency goal. The rule used is:

> If x wants y to be x's agent
>   and y owes a return favor
> Then infer that y will
>   agree to be an agent

Since EV-TAKE-CASE satisfies an agency goal, it matches the event EV-RETURN-FAVOR in IP-FAVOR1. EV-TAKE-CASE does not match IP-FAVOR0 (buying the drinks) because it is not of the same magnitude. See 10.2.

11.3.4 PARAGRAPH-4

Instrumental MTRANS MOPs -- Some MOPs are instrumental to MTRANS. Examples of these are M-PHONE and M-LETTER.

```
Processing sentence:  LATER *COMMA* DAVID WROTE TO ANN *COMMA*
INFORMING HER THAT GEORGE WANTED A DIVORCE *PERIOD*
```

*LATER *COMMA* | Builds a new scenario node

*DAVID WROTE TO ANN *COMMA* | Node updated as a MENTAL scenario
```
    Spawning:  DEMON158/6 = (FIND-HIGHER-D-KNOW-GOAL)
        If x MTRANS goal G to y
        Then build ENABLEMENT between D-KNOW in M-LETTER and G
```

*INFORMING HER THAT GEORGE WANTED A DIVORCE *PERIOD**

```
Result of parse:

    (M-LETTER
        INSTAN (M-LETTER0)
        EVENT (EV-MTRANS-LETTER)
        LET-OBJ (LETTER)
        LET-INFO (M-REPRESENT-CLIENT
                    INSTAN (M-REPRESENT-CLIENT0)
                    EVENT (EV-INFORM-OPPONENT)
                    OPPONENT  Ann0
                    LAWYER David0
```

```
              L-CLIENT George0
              LEGAL-GOAL (GOAL
                              ACTOR George0
                              OBJECT (R-MARRIAGE
                                            INSTAN (R-MARRIAGE0)
                                            STATUS (TERMINATED))))
        LET-WRITER David0
        LET-READER George0
        PREP-OBJ (PREP IS (TO)))
```

Legal Disputes -- The mop M-REPRESENT-CLIENT contains information about what RT-LAWYERs do. This includes MTRANSing information to and from legal opponents. When MTRANS mops are instantiated here, they are treated as enablements for MTRANS events in M-REPRESENT-CLIENT.

Once David tells Ann that George wants a divorce, the mop M-LEGAL-DISPUTE is instantiated with the LEGAL-GOAL being the goal to terminate the marriage. M-LEGAL-DISPUTE is instantiated by a bottom-up rule associated with the event EV-INFORM-OPPONENT in M-REPRESENT-CLIENT.

```
Processing sentence: HER LAWYER CALLED BACK  AND  TOLD  DAVID
THAT  SHE  INTENDED  TO GET THE HOUSE *COMMA* THE CHILDREN AND
ALOT OF ALIMONY *PERIOD*
```

HER LAWYER | New RT-LAWYER1 and M-REPRESENT-CLIENT1 built
              | because M-LEGAL-DISPUTE is already active.

CALLED BACK | Recognized as phrase: CALL BACK

AND TOLD DAVID THAT SHE INTENDED TO
              | Builds (MTRANS TO David0 OBJECT (GOAL...))

GET ==> Adding: CON183 to *wm*
     Spawning DEMON183 = (DISAMBIG-GET CON183)
        If "HOME" follows, then build D-PROX goal
        If PHYS-OBJ follows, then build D-CONT goal
        If PHYS-STATE follows, then build D-STATE goal

*THE HOUSE *COMMA* THE CHILDREN AND ALOT OF*
     *ALIMONY *PERIOD**
     CON185 = (GROUP INSTAN (GROUP2)) | Done by GROUPER demon

Result of parse:

```
(M-PHONE
    INSTAN (M-PHONE0)
    CALLER Rt-lawyer0
    CALLEE NIL
    CALL-INFO (M-REPRESENT-CLIENT
                INSTAN (M-REPRESENT-CLIENT1)
                EVENT (EV-INFORM-OPPONENT)
                OPPONENT David0
                LAWYER  Rt-lawyer0
                L-CLIENT  Ann0
                LEGAL-GOAL (D-CONT
                            ACTOR Ann0
                            OBJECT (GROUP
                                     INSTAN (GROUP2))))
    PHONE-OBJ (PHONE)
    EVENT (EV-MAKE-CALL))
```

When Ann's lawyer is mentioned, a new M-REPRESENT-CLIENT1 is instantiated. This happens because M-LEGAL-DISPUTE is already active and expects two lawyers, one for each legal party in the dispute.

M-LETTER is dealt with in the identical way that M-PHONE preceding it was dealt with. In each case, the reason for the communication (i.e. the higher goal) is found and associated with the mental scenarios built by each mop. In addition, the goals communicated in M-LETTER0 and M-PHONE0 each match a LEGAL-GOAL in M-REPRESENT-CLIENT. The occurrence of MTRANS mops, such as M-LETTER and M-PHONE, causes BORIS to examine the message contained within the mop, and try to match that message to other, already active, knowledge structures.

Furthermore, from contractual knowledge BORIS knows that George and Ann have goal conflict over the SHARED-POSSESSIONS in M-MARRIAGE-CONTRACT. From OBJECT knowledge, BORIS recognizes GROUP2 as the SHARED-POSSESSIONs in M-MARRIAGE-CONTRACT. For discussion on contracts, see 8.6.1.

Processing sentence: WHEN GEORGE HEARD THIS *COMMA* HE WAS

```
VERY WORRIED *PERIOD*
```

*WHEN GEORGE HEARD THIS *COMMA**
```
    CON195 = (MBUILD
                ACTOR George0
                OBJECT (M-REPRESENT-CLIENT
                            LEGAL-GOAL (D-CONT
                                            ACTOR Ann0
                                            OBJECT (GROUP
                                                        INSTAN (GROUP2))))
                        INSTAN (M-REPRESENT-CLIENT1)))
```

*HE WAS VERY WORRIED *PERIOD**
```
    Executing:  DEMON201/5 = (EXPLAIN-AFFECT CON201)
        If CHAR expects possible goal failure,
        Then find (or infer) a P-GOAL that
            is active in the current scenario.
        Inferring:  P-LIFESTYLE-A0
    Killing:  DEMON201/5
```

```
Result of parse:

    (AFFECT CHAR George0
            STATE (NEG)
            E-MODE (EXPECTED)
            G-SIT (FAILURE GOAL (P-LIFESTYLE-A0))
            SCALE (>NORM))
```

Processing AFFECTs -- When a character is "worried", affect demons try to find the P-GOAL which is active. If a P-GOAL is not active in the current scenario, then the demon tries to infer a goal from the currently active MOPs. The inference rule which fired above is:

> If MOP involves **GOAL CONFLICT** between x and y
> and x has **NEG AFFECT** with goal failure expected
> Then infer P-GOAL for x from success of y's goal

Using this rule, BORIS infers P-LIFESTYLE-A0 since this is the goal which George will have if Ann achieves her D-CONT goal.

```
Processing sentence:  HE DIDN'T EARN MUCH AT THE   JUNIOR   HIGH
```

```
SCHOOL *PERIOD*
```

HE DIDN'T | Morphology: DIDN'T as DID + NOT

EARN MUCH AT THE
```
    CON206 = (OCCUPATION ...)
    Spawning DEMON206/6 = (UPDATE-ROLE-THEME CON206)
        If any information in CON is not in EP memory
        Then update RT in EP memory with new info.
```

JUNIOR HIGH SCHOOL | Recognized as phrase in lexicon.

Result of parse:

```
    (OCCUPATION IS (RT-TEACHER1)
               ACTOR George0
               SALARY (AMOUNT IS (>NORM))
               SETTING (INSTITUTION MOP (M-EDUCATION)
                                   CLASS (JUNIOR-HIGH)
                                   INSTAN (INSTITUTION0)
                                   PREP-OBJ (PREP IS (AT)))
               MODE (NEG))
```

Updating Role Themes -- BORIS doesn't do much with this sentence, other than to update role-theme information about George.

```
Processing sentence:  DAVID TOLD HIM NOT TO WORRY *COMMA*
SINCE THE JUDGE WOULD AWARD THE CASE TO GEORGE ONCE HE LEARNED
THAT ANN HAD BEEN CHEATING ON HIM *PERIOD*
```

DAVID TOLD HIM
```
    CON214 = (MTRANS ...)
```

*NOT TO WORRY *COMMA**
```
    Spawning:  DEMON218/7 = (ACE-CHECK CON218)
        If an AFFECT is the OBJECT of an MTRANS
        Then attempt ACE recognition
    Executing:  DEMON218/7 = (ACE-CHECK CON218)
        Reinterpreting CON as ACE-REASSURANCE
        Spawning:  DEMON214/7 = (FIND-SUPPORT CON214)
            If a LEADTO structure with MODE EXPECTED
               is encountered
            Then find an appropriate REASONING MOP
               and apply that MOP to it
```

```
Result of parse:

     (ACE-REASSURANCE INSTAN (ACE-REASSURANCE0)
                      REASSURER David0
                      WORRIER George0
                      G-SITU (P-LIFESTYLE-A0)
                      SUPPORT  SUPPORT0)
```

Building ACEs -- Whenever an AFFECT is recognized, BORIS spawned an ACE-CHECK demon to see if the AFFECT is an expression of empathy between two characters. See section 4.6.

Reasoning and Beliefs -- Since ACE-REASSURANCE involves a belief (i.e. a character's expectation about a future outcome), a demon is spawned to look for reasoning to support this belief. Since reasoning often involves rules concerning causality, the reasoning demon looks for causal patterns (e.g. LEADTO) in Working Memory.

SINCE
```
     CON220 = (LEADTO ANTE ANTE2  CONSE2 CONSE2)
     Spawning:  DEMON220/0 = (FIND-ANTECEDENT CON220 ANTE2)
        If an EVENT, STATE or GOAL follows
        Then bind it to ANTE
     Spawning:  DEMON220/1 = (FIND-CONSEQUENT CON220 CONSE2)
        If an unbound EVENT, STATE or GOAL precedes
        Then bind it to CONSE
        Else search for CONSE binding after next clause boundary
```

Causal Structures -- When these demons fire, they build (LEADTO ANTE X CONSE Y) from the following kinds of linguistic constructions:

> "Since X, Y."
> "Y, because X."
> "Without X, Y."

THE JUDGE | Role-theme RT-JUDGE0 is built.

WOULD
```
    Spawning priority:  DEMON222/0 = (MODIFY-MODE ACT EXPECTED)
```

AWARD THE CASE TO GEORGE
```
    CON223 =  (AUTH ACTOR Rt-judge0
                    TO George0
                    OBJECT (MENTAL-OBJ CLASS (REASONING))
                    MODE (*EXPECTED*))

    Executing:  DEMON223/5 = (FIND-MOP CON223)
        Using Role-theme information in ACTOR slot
        Matches EV-WIN-A in M-LEGAL-DISPUTE
        Instantiating EV-WIN-A0 with MODE *EXPECTED*
            BOTTOM-UP rule:
                Since AUTH in M-LEGAL-DISPUTE is
                often supported by reasoning, spawn
                reasoning demon
                Spawning:  DEMON223/6 = (FIND-SUPPORT CON223)
    Killing:  DEMON223/5
```

The event of the judge AUTHorizing matches the event of George winning in M-LEGAL-DISPUTE. (For explanation of social acts, such as AUTH, see [Schank and Carbonell, 1978].)

Future Events -- BORIS treats all future events as expectations, since future events may actually never come about. Since the event has not occurred, no courtroom scenario (with the judge giving his verdict) is built yet.

ONCE | treated like "since"
```
    CON227 = (LEADTO ANTE ANTE3 CONSE CONSE3)
```

HE LEARNED
```
    CON229 = (MBUILD ...)
```

THAT ANN HAD BEEN | "had been" is recognized as a phrase.

CHEATING ON | Also recognized as entry in phrasal lexicon.
```
    Spawning:  DEMON236/0 = (DISAMBIG-VIOLATION CON236)
        Search EP memory for a TAU involving a contractual
        violation with the correct role bindings and
        return a referent to it
```

HIM | Is tentatively bound to RT-JUDGE0 by a reference
| demon. This binding is rejected once DEMON236/0
| finds TAU-BROKEN-CONTRACT0
PERIOD

```
    Executing:  DEMON223/6 = (FIND-SUPPORT CON223)
        Applying reasoning mop RM-JURISPRUDENCE
        Finding reasoning chain in d-net
        Instantiating RM-JURISPRUDENCE0
              with chain  REASONING0
    Killing:  DEMON223/6

    Executing:  DEMON214/7 = (FIND-SUPPORT CON214)
        Applying reasoning mop RM-JURISPRUDENCE
        Finding instantiated chain REASONING0
    Killing:  DEMON214/7

Result of parse:

    (LEADTO
      ANTE (LEADTO
            ANTE (MBUILD
                    ACTOR Rt-judge0
                    OBJECT (TAU-BROKEN-CONTRACT
                                INSTAN (TAU-BROKEN-CONTRACT0)))
            CONSE (M-LEGAL-DISPUTE
                    INSTAN (M-LEGAL-DISPUTE0)
                    EVENT (EV-WIN-A)  | Judge AUTHs for George
                    LD-VERDICT (MENTAL-OBJ
                                CLASS (REASONING))
                    LD-PARTY-A  George0
                    LD-JUDGE  Rt-judge0
                    MODE (*EXPECTED*)))
      CONSE (ACE-REASSURANCE
                INSTAN (ACE-REASSURANCE0)
                REASSURER (HUMAN4)
                WORRIER (GEORGE0)
                G-SIT (P-LIFESTYLE-A0)
                SUPPORT (REASONING0))
```

Reasoning About Contracts -- There are two reasoning processes spawned in the above trace. One is associated with ACE-REASSURANCE. The other is attached to the AUTH event in M-LEGAL-DISPUTE, in which the judge gives support for his verdict.

The demons spawned (bottom-up) from M-LEGAL-DISPUTE actually instantiate the reasoning chain which the demon spawned by ACE-REASSURANCE ends up finding in Episodic Memory. For more discussion on reasoning, see 8.6.4.

11.3.5 PARAGRAPH-5


```
Processing sentence:   WHEN  THEY  GOT TO COURT *COMMA* DAVID
PRESENTED GEORGE'S CASE *COMMA* BUT WITHOUT A WITNESS THEY HAD
NO PROOF AND ANN WON *PERIOD*
```

*WHEN THEY GOT TO COURT *COMMA** | `Builds transition/main`
                                    `scenarios.`

Courtroom Scenario -- The mention of a setting alone is not enough to cause a new scenario to be created. The sentence "George asked David to represent him in court." mentions the courtroom setting. Since this setting occurs within an MTRANS of a GOAL no scenario is built. Whenever a PTRANS occurs, however, a transition scenario is created. Furthermore, "got to" indicates that the D-PROX has been achieved, so a main scenario is built also.


```
Processing  sentence:   DAVID  PRESENTED GEORGE'S CASE *COMMA*
BUT WITHOUT A WITNESS THEY HAD NO PROOF AND ANN WON *PERIOD*
```

DAVID PRESENTED
    `CON248 = (MTRANS ...) | spawns demon expecting REASONING`

GEORGE'S | `Morphology spawns demon to add POSSESSIVE`

*CASE *COMMA**
```
    Spawning:  DEMON252/0  = (DISAMBIG-CASE CON252)
        If PHYS-OBJs follow with PREP-OBJ OF modifying it
        Then interpret CON as CONTAINER
        Else If context contains legal mops
              Then interpret CON as REASONING
                  and spawn demon POSS-ACTOR to find
                  out the ACTOR of the REASONING  by
                  looking for a POSSESSIVE HUMAN

    Executing:  DEMON248/5 = (FIND-MOP CON248)
```

```
        Found match with EV-PETITION-A in M-REPRESENT-CLIENT0
        BOTTOM-UP:
            Spawning:  DEMON248/6 = (FIND-SUPPORT CON248)
    Killing:  DEMON248/5
```

BUT
```
    CON254 = (*VIOLATION*)
```

WITHOUT A WITNESS THEY HAD NO PROOF
```
    CON255 =  (LEADTO ANTE (ROLE CLASS (WITNESS)
                                  STATUS (UNAVAILABLE))
                     CONSE (MENTAL-OBJ CLASS (REASONING)
                                      GOAL (PERSUADE)
                                      MODE (NEG)))


    Executing: DEMON248/6 = (FIND-SUPPORT CON248)
        Applying REASONING MOP RM-JURISPRUDENCE
            Found reasoning chain REASONING1
    Killing:  DEMON248/6
```

Petitioning The Judge -- By passing CON255 through the reasoning mop RM-JURISPRUDENCE BORIS realizes that George is rejected on the grounds of being a biased witness. See section 8.6.4.

AND ANN WON
```
    CON264 = (COMPETITION ACTOR-A Ann0
                          ACTOR-B NIL
                          ACHIEVEMENT ACHIEVEMENT0)
    Spawning DEMON264/0 = (FIND-COMPETITION CON64)
        Search EP memory for goal competition MOP
        between ACTOR and another character.
    Executing:  DEMON264/0 = (FIND-COMPETITION CON64)
        Found M-LEGAL-DISPUTE0
        Instantiating: EV-WIN-B0
            BOTTOM-UP:  Inferring  G-POSS-A0
                            THWARTED-BY EV-WIN-B0
            BOTTOM-UP:  Noticing MODE *EXPECTED*
                        on EV-WIN-A0
                        Building TAU-BROKEN-REASSURANCE0
                        EV-FAIL VIOLATES REASONING0
                        AFFECTS:  REASSURED = ANGER, SURPRISE
                                  ASSURER = GUILT, SURPRISE
*PERIOD*
```

Failed Expectation -- BORIS knows that a COMPETITION implies both a goal failure and a goal success. Whenever a goal failure occurs, BORIS checks to see if there is a character expectation associated with the status of that goal. If the actual status does not match the expected status, then BORIS recognizes that an expectation violation has occurred.

```
Processing sentence:  GEORGE ALMOST HAD A FIT *PERIOD*
```

GEORGE
ALMOST | Adds SCALE information
HAD A FIT | Recognized as entry in phrasal lexicon
    Spawning: DEMON269 = (DISAMBIG-FIT CON269)
        If context is MEDICAL,
        Then interpret as DISEASE-ATTACK
        Else If context is TAU with AFFECT SURPRISE
            Then interpret with TAU

```
Result of Parse:

    (AFFECT CHAR George0
            STATE (NEG)
            E-MODE (UNEXPECTED)
            SCALE (>NORM)
            G-SITU (G-WANT-POSS-A0)
            MODE (NEG SCALE (LESS-NORM)))
```

AFFECT Disambiguation -- Like other words, affect descriptors may have to be disambiguated. In this case, a context search reveals a match between a possible meaning of "had a fit" and an affect reaction predicted by an active TAU.

```
Processing sentence:   DAVID  COULD  ONLY  OFFER  GEORGE  HIS
CONDOLENCES *PERIOD*
```

DAVID
COULD ONLY | ignored
OFFER | builds MTRANS of GOAL
HIS
CONDOLENCES | builds ACE and spawns demons to find actor

```
                    | (ie ACTOR of an MTRANS or POSSESSIVE referent)
*PERIOD*

Result of parse:

    (ACE-COMMISERATION
         INSTAN (ACE-COMMISERATION0)
         COMMISERATOR David0
         SUFFERER George0   | found by searching EP memory
         G-SIT (G-WANT-POSS-A0))
```

Another ACE -- Here, "offer" is parsed as an MTRANS (involving AGENCY) and "condolence" directly activates ACE-COMMISERATION. Associated with this ACE are demons which search for a goal failure on the part of the SUFFERER. The goal which is failed for George0 is G-WANT-POSS-A0 in M-LEGAL-DISPUTE. This is George's desire for the family possessions associated with the marriage contract.

11.3.6 PARAGRAPH-6

```
Processing sentence:  A WEEK LATER *COMMA* GEORGE  RECEIVED  A
LARGE BILL IN THE MAIL FROM DAVID *PERIOD*
```

*A WEEK LATER *COMMA** | Builds new scenario node

GEORGE RECEIVED
```
    CON283 = (ATRANS ...)
```

A LARGE BILL | "bill" is disambiguated as a COST-FORM
```
               | which has a role link to M-SERVICE
    CON286 = (PHYS-OBJ CLASS (COST-FORM)
                       INSTAN (PHYS-OBJ4)
                       SCALE (GREATER-NORM)))
```

```
    Executing:  DEMON286/3 = (FIND-MOP CON32)
         Noticing SCALE violation
         Using OBJECT information to select mop:  M-SERVICE
         Instantiating M-SERVICE1
              with strands from M-REPRESENT-CLIENT0
         Finding  Deviation Match
              with EV-SEND-BILL in M-REPRESENT-CLIENT0
```

```
EVENT is violation of EV-BILL in M-REPRESENT-CLIENT
EVENT is violation of EV-SEND-BILL in M-SERVICE

VIOLATION found on EV-DO-SERVICE
  Creating:  TAU-BROKEN-SERVICE1 with EVENT BAD-BILL
Killing:  DEMON286/3   | other demons kill themselves also
```

A Final Violation -- Demons associated with ATRANS notice the COST-FORM and search M-SERVICE for a match with the recipient in the ATRANS being the CLIENT in M-SERVICE. A match is found with EV-SEND-BILL in the M-SERVICE1 between George and David. BORIS knows to instantiate M-SERVICE1 since a) M-REPRESENT-CLIENT0 is active, b) COST-FORM has been mentioned, and c) M-REPRESENT-CLIENT has a strand to M-SERVICE. This last violation is handled in the way the spilling incident was handled in paragraph one.

```
IN THE MAIL  |  Recognized as entry in phrasal lexicon.
    Spawning: DEMON288/0 = (DO-M-LETTER CON288)
        If preceding ATRANS found
        Then instantiate M-LETTER
          and spawn a demon to search
          for a higher level motivation

FROM DAVID *PERIOD*

Result of parse:

    (M-REPRESENT-CLIENT
         INSTAN (M-REPRESENT-CLIENT0)
         EVENT (EV-SEND-BILL)
         L-FEE (PHYS-OBJ NAME (BILL)
                         CLASS (COST-FORM)
                         INSTAN (PHYS-OBJ4)
                         SCALE (GREATER-NORM))
         L-CLIENT George0
         LAWYER David0)

    (M-LETTER
         INSTAN (M-LETTER1)
         EVENT (EV-POSTAL)
         LET-WRITER David0
```

```
LET-READER George0)
```

Another Letter -- The phrase "in the mail" causes BORIS to realize that George has received a letter from David. Since BORIS already knows the contents of the letter, BORIS simply builds a link between the goal of sending the letter and the goal of billing the client, which is the reason why the letter was sent. BORIS can use this link later if asked: "How did David inform George of the bill?"

```
Processing sentence:  WAS HE FURIOUS *EXCLM*
```

WAS | In QA mode this would indicate a VERIFICATION
        | question but since the mode is SU,
        | the sentence is treated rhetorically.
HE
FURIOUS
```
    CON294 =  (AFFECT CHAR George0
                      STATE (NEG)
                      SCALE (>NORM))
              G-SITU (FAILURE GOAL (P-FINANCES0))
```
EXCLM

Rhetorical Sentence, Referent Binding, Final AFFECT -- The QA demon associated with "was" is sensitive to processing mode. The referent demon associated with "he" builds a tentative binding with David. This is rejected, however, once a match is found between this AFFECT and TAU-BROKEN-SERVICE1. The goal which is violated here is a P-FINANCES goal due to a BAD-BILL. The processing of this AFFECT is similar to the case in paragraph one. The exclamation mark is essentially ignored.

11.4 Question-Answering Traces

Since questions are parsed by the same processes which parse narratives, only the differences are highlighted here for the traces covering question-answering.

In BORIS, answer retrieval demons are spawned whenever WH-words (such as: "who", "what", "how", "where", "why", etc.) are encountered at the beginning of a clause boundary. In addition to determining the type of conceptual question being asked [Dyer and Lehnert, 1982] [Lehnert, 1978], these demons carry out the following retrieval tasks:

1. WHO and WHAT spawn demons to search for role bindings and events in memory.

2. WHY spawns demons to chase I-links. For example, if a question refers to an event, as in "Why did George go home?" then retrieval over I-links will yield the answer: "To change his clothes."

3. WHERE and WHEN spawn demons which search the scenario map.

4. HOW spawns demons which traverse instrumental and affective links.

5. WAS and other auxiliaries spawn verification demons which return an elaboration on a "yes" or "no" answer.

For more details, see section 7.5.

11.4.1 Event Specification Questions

BORIS uses various heuristics when searching for events. One main organizer of events in memory is the Scenario Participant Map (chapter 9). If a setting is supplied in an event specification question, search demons will make use of this.

```
Q: What happened at the restaurant?

WHAT
    CON300 = (*?* INSTAN INSTAN51)
    Spawning: DEMON300/0 = (LIFE-THEME-QUES CON300 INSTAN121)
    Spawning: DEMON300/1 = (EVENT-QUES CON300 INSTAN121)
        If an EVENT follows
        Then bind this CON to it
            and spawn event specification demons
```

HAPPENED

```
    CON301 = (EVENT TYPE (*IMPORT*)
                    IS IS40
                    SETTING SETTING12
                    OBJECT OBJECT20)
    Spawning: DEMON301/0 = (PREP CON301 SETTING12 AT SETTING)
        Search for a SETTING which is object
        of preposition AT

    Executing: DEMON300/0 = (EVENT-QUES CON300 INSTAN121)
        IS40 <-- CON300
        Spawning: DEMON301/1 = (ANS-EVENT CON301)
            If a SETTING is mentioned and
              TYPE = *IMPORT*
            Then search scenario map for TAU-related events
    Killing: DEMON300/0
```

AT THE RESTAURANT

```
    CON304 = (SETTING CLASS CLASS20
                      INSTAN (SETTING0))

    Executing: DEMON301/1 = (ANS-EVENT CON301)
        :::>> SO Found
              Appropriate TAU EVENTS in SO Found
    Killing: DEMON301/1
```

QMARK

Result of parse:

```
    (EVENT TYPE (*IMPORT*)
           IS (*?* INSTAN (*LIST* BAD-SERVICE0 REFUSE-PAY0))
           SETTING (SETTING CLASS (RESTAURANT)
                            INSTAN (SETTING0)
                            PREP-OBJ (PREP IS (AT)))
           OBJECT NIL)
```

Conceptual answer of question: (BAD-SERVICE0 REFUSE-PAY0)
Calling BORIS Generator:

THE WAITRESS SPILLED COKE ON GEORGE AND HE REFUSED TO PAY THE
CHECK.

The TYPE of an event determines whether normal or interesting
events are sought in memory. If the question had requested normal

events, as in:

Q: What was George doing at the restaurant?

then the answer would have been:

A: He was eating lunch and grading homeworks.

11.4.2 Affective Reaction Questions

Characters can experience a number of different affective reactions throughout a narrative. Therefore, a question requesting an affective reaction must supply information which can help BORIS find the appropriate affect. This information may include SETTING, EVENT, GOAL or TAU information. For instance, SETTING information is supplied in the question:

Q: How did George feel at the restaurant?

Consider the following question:

Q: How did Ann feel when George caught her cheating on him?

Here BORIS is supplied with a TAU-related event. As a result, most of the search is done while the word "caught" is being parsed:

HOW
```
    Spawning: DEMON312/0 = (QUANT-QUES CON312 HOW M3)
    Spawning: DEMON312/1 = (QUAL-QUES CON312 HOW M4)
    Spawning: DEMON312/2 = (INSTRU-QUES CON312 HOW M2)
    Spawning: DEMON312/3 = (AFFECT-QUES CON312 HOW M1)
        If an AFFECT is encountered
        Then use SETTING, EVENT, GOAL or TAU
            in question as access to AFFECT
```

The word "how" can indicate a number of different conceptual question categories. For instance: "How did George get home?" requests instrumental information while "How much did George pay the waitress?" requests information concerning quantity. Consequently "how" must spawn demons which examine the rest of the question in order to determine the kind of retrieval heuristics to employ.

DID ANN
FEEL | The word "feel" is also ambiguous

```
    Spawning: DEMON315/0 = (TOUCH-FEEL CON315 FEEL M2)
    Spawning: DEMON315/1 = (GOAL-FEEL CON315 FEEL M3)
    Spawning: DEMON315/2 = (AFFECT-FEEL CON315 FEEL M1)
        If a PHYS-OBJ or EVENT follows
        Then interpret "feel" as an AFFECT
```

WHEN

```
    CON316 = (*EVENT*)
    Executing: DEMON315/2 = (AFFECT-FEEL CON315 FEEL M1)
        CON315 = (AFFECT STATE STATE65
                         ACTOR ACTOR70
                         EVENT EVENT80)
```

GEORGE CAUGHT HER

```
    CON317 = (TAU-RED-HANDED
                   RH-WITNESS      George0
                   RH-PERPETRATOR Ann0
                   EVENT    EVENT81
                   INSTAN   INSTAN156)

    Spawning: DEMON317/5 = (FIND-TAU-EVENT RH-VIOLATION)
        Search Episodic Memory for a TAU-RED-HANDED event
        with matching role bindings
    Executing: DEMON317/5 = (FIND-TAU-EVENT RH-VIOLATION)
        Finding TAU-RED-HANDED0 with event RH-VIOLATION0
    Killing: DEMON317/5
    Executing: DEMON315/2 = (AFFECT-FEEL CON315 FEEL M1)
        Using TAU-RED-HANDED0
        :::> Finding Affect AF-SURPRISE0
    Killing: DEMON315/2
```

CHEATING ON | Recognized as a phrase
*HIM *QMARK**

```
    CON319 = (*CHEAT-VIOLATION*
                     PARTY-A Ann0
                     PARTY-B George0)
```

```
Spawning: DEMON319/5 = (DISAMBIG-VIOLATION CON319)
    Search Episodic Memory for a TAU involving cheating
    with matching role bindings

Conceptual answer of question:  (AF-SURPRISE0)
Calling BORIS Generator:


SHE WAS SURPRISED.
```

Notice that BORIS knows the answer to the question once DEMON315/2 fires. (See chapter 5 for effect of integration on Q/A.) This occurs at the point that BORIS has parsed "How did Ann feel when George caught her..." Thus, the phrase "cheating on him" is somewhat superfluous and only serves a purpose for presupposition checking.

11.4.3 Causal Antecedent Questions

For many questions, the major portion of the memory search is done as a side-effect of the processes involved in trying to understand the question. Consider the question below:

Q: Why did George tell David his troubles?

The word "tell" indicates an MTRANS. The word "troubles" refers to a P-GOAL of David. The hard work here is finding a MOP which matches this event in memory. This work is done as a side-effect of understanding the question. Once an event has been located, the answer can be quickly retrieved by traversing the I-links supplied in the mop M-REPRESENT-CLIENT. Below is the trace of this question:

```
WHY
    CON325 = (LEADTO ANTE (*?*)
                      CONSE CONSE7)
    Spawning: DEMON325/0 = (SUBST-INTERFERE CON325)
    Spawning: DEMON325/1 = (ANS-LEADTO-AFF CON325)
    Spawning: DEMON325/2 = (SHORT-QUES CON325)
    Spawning: DEMON325/3 = (ANS-LEADTO CON325)
        If a MOP event is found
        Then search I-links for causal motivation
```

```
Spawning: DEMON325/4 = (EXP-B CON325 CONSE7 CD-KS AFT)
    If a CD knowledge structure follows
    Then bind it to CONSE
```

Different search heuristics must be used, depending upon what information is supplied in the rest of the question. For instance, if the question is simply "Why?", then the demon SHORT-QUES will use the previous question and answer as a source of information for subsequent memory search and retrieval. This kind of situation occurs as follows:

> Q: Who wrote to Ann?
> A: David.
> Q: Why?

Other demons, such as SUBST-INTERFERE, perform retrieval on expectation violation questions [Lehnert, 1978], such as:

> Q: Why didn't George pay the waitress?

In such cases the event mentioned in the question never occurred in the narrative, so search processes must differ.

DID GEORGE TELL DAVID

```
CON328 = (MTRANS ACTOR  George0
                 FROM   George0
                 MOBJECT MOBJECT30
                 TO     David0)
Executing: DEMON325/4 = (EXP-B CON325 CONSE7 CD-KS AFT)
    CONSE7 <-- CON328
Killing: DEMON325/4
Killing: DEMON325/0
Killing: DEMON325/1
Killing: DEMON325/2
```

*HIS TROUBLES *QMARK **
```
CON331 = (P-GOAL ACTOR  George0
                 INSTAN INSTAN195
                 AFFECT AFFECT11)
```

```
Executing:  DEMON328/3 | binds P-GOAL as MOBJECT of MTRANS
```

```
        MOBJECT30 <-- CON331
   Killing:  DEMON328
```

At this point there is no more information in the question. Meanwhile a FIND-MOP demon associated with the MTRANS has failed in its attempt to use its role bindings to suggest indices into memory. Therefore, it applies all active MOPs in Episodic Memory until a match is found.

```
Searching MOP M-BORROW0 for a matching event
   :::>> NONE FOUND
Searching MOP M-REPRESENT-CLIENT0 for a matching event
   :::>> Match found with event EV-TELL-PROBLEM

   CON328 = (M-REPRESENT-CLIENT
                        INSTAN INSTAN196
                        EVENT EVENT125
                        LAWYER T0121
                        LEGAL-PROBLEM MOBJECT30)
```

BORIS now knows that the MTRANS conceptualization refers to an event in M-REPRESENT-CLIENT0. At this point the demon ANS-LEADTO fires, and the mop M-REPRESENT-CLIENT0 supplies the goal which motivated this MTRANS.

```
Result of parse:

   (LEADTO
      ANTE (*?*)
      CONSE (M-REPRESENT-CLIENT
                INSTAN (M-REPRESENT-CLIENT0)
                EVENT (EV-TELL-PROBLEM)
                LAWYER David0
                LEGAL-PROBLEM (P-GOAL
                                   ACTOR George0
                                   INSTAN (TAU-BROKEN-CONTRACT0)
                                   AFFECT (NEG))
                L-CLIENT George0))

Conceptual answer of question:
   (M-REPRESENT-CLIENT0 GOAL (G-NEED-LAWYER))
```

Calling BORIS Generator:

GEORGE WANTED DAVID TO BE HIS LAWYER.

Once BORIS understands the question in terms of its episodic memory referent, the retrieval of the conceptual answer is relatively straightforward.

11.4.4 Presupposition Violations

When a referent to a MOP event is recognized, the roles bound to that event in working memory are compared against the corresponding roles in episodic memory. If a discrepancy is found during QA, then a complaint is generated (see section 5.5). The demon which compares bindings for potential presupposition violations is called PRES-CHECK, and is shown in the trace below.

Q: Why did George write to Ann?

WHY
```
    CON337 = (LEADTO ANTE ANTE11
                     CONSE CONSE11)
```
DID GEORGE
WRITE
```
    CON340 = NIL | "write" can be a letter or a publication
    Spawning: DEMON340/0 = (AUTHORSHIP CON340 WRITE M1)
    Spawning: DEMON341/1 = (LET-WRITE CON340 WRITE M2)
```

TO ANN | now BORIS knows that it is a letter
```
    Executing: DEMON340/1 = (LET-WRITE CON340 WRITE M2)
        CON340 = (M-LETTER INSTAN INSTAN133
                           EVENT EVENT35
                           LETTER-OBJ LETTER-OBJ1
                           LETTER-INFO LETTER-INFO1
                           LET-WRITER LET-WRITER1
                           LET-READER LET-READER1)
        Spawning: DEMON340/2 = (FIND-MOP CON340 INSTAN133)
        Spawning: DEMON340/3 = (EXP-C LETTER-INFO1 (ACT MOP TAU) AFT)
        Spawning: DEMON340/4 = (EXP-A LET-WRITER1 HUMAN BEF)
        Spawning: DEMON340/5 = (EXP-A LET-READER1 HUMAN AFT)
        Spawning: DEMON340/6 = (PREP-AO LET-READER1 TO HUMAN)
    Killing: DEMON340/1
```

```
Killing: DEMON340/0 = (AUTHORSHIP CON339 WRITE M1)
```

As various demons fire, roles are bound. There is no point in comparing roles against episodic memory until a referent to a MOP is found in episodic memory. Once M-LETTER0 is found, PRES-CHECK demons are spawned to make sure that presuppositions are fulfilled.

```
        CONSE11 <-- CON340
        LET-WRITER1 <-- CON339
        INSTAN133 <-- (M-LETTER0)

   Spawning: DEMON340/7 = (PRES-CHECK CON340 LET-WRITER1)
   Spawning: DEMON340/8 = (PRES-CHECK CON340 LET-READER1)
   Spawning: DEMON340/9 = (PRES-CHECK CON340 LETTER-OBJ1)
   Spawning: DEMON340/10 = (PRES-CHECK CON340 LETTER-INFO1)

   Executing: DEMON340/7 = (PRES-CHECK CON340 LET-WRITER1)
        :::> Role Disagreement Found
                EP Memory has HUMAN4
                PRESUPPOSITION was GEORGE0
                For the ROLE of LET-WRITER
   Killing: DEMON340/7

Result of parse:

   (LEADTO ANTE (*?*)
           CONSE (M-LETTER INSTAN (M-LETTER0)
                           EVENT (EV-MTRANS-LETTER)
                           LETTER-OBJ (LETTER)
                           LETTER-INFO NIL
                           LET-WRITER George0))

Conceptual answer of question:
    (DISAGREE MEM (HUMAN4) QUES (GEORGE0)
              ROLE (LET-WRITER))
Calling BORIS generator:

IT WASN'T GEORGE, IT WAS DAVID WHO WROTE TO ANN.
```

Instead of trying to answer this question, BORIS generates information about the presupposition violation which was encountered.

11.4.5 Empathy Related Questions

BORIS uses it knowledge of ACEs to answer questions about empathetic reactions on the part of one character for another. For instance, BORIS knows that ACE-REASSURANCE is supported by a reasoning chain. Therefore, a question of the form: (LEADTO ANTE (*?*) CONSE (ACE-REASSURANCE)) will cause search demons to find the associated reasoning chain, as in:

> Q: Why did David reassure George?
> A: David believed the judge would award
>   the case to George because Ann had
>   broken the marriage contract.

In contrast, ACE-COMMISERATION is motivated by a thwarted goal. Therefore, a question of the form: (LEADTO ANTE (*?*) CONSE (ACE-COMMISERATION)) will cause search demons to look for this motivating goal. However, these search heuristics can not be applied unless the question is understood in terms of an ACE. So understanding a question at the right level is the key to being able to answer it. Below is a trace of a question involving empathy:

```
Q: Why did David console George?

WHY DID DAVID
CONSOLE
    CON417 = (ACE-COMMISERATION INSTAN INSTAN166
                                COMMISERATOR COMMISERATOR1
                                SUFFERER SUFFERER1
                                G-SIT G-SIT6)
    Spawning: DEMON417/0 = (FIND-MOP CON417 INSTAN166)
    Spawning: DEMON417/1 = (EXP CON417 COMMISERATOR1 HUMAN BEF)
    Spawning: DEMON417/2 = (EXP CON417 SUFFERER1 HUMAN AFT)
    Spawning: DEMON417/3 = (FIND-G-SIT CON417 G-SIT6 SUFFERER)
        Search for a P-goal or matching TAU affect

        COMMISERATOR1 <-- CON416
        INSTAN166 <-- (ACE-COMMISERATION0)
        CONSE16 <-- CON417
GEORGE *QMARK*
```

```
        SUFFERER1 <-- CON418

    Executing: DEMON417/3 = (FIND-G-SIT CON417 G-SIT6 SUFFERER)
        G-SIT6 <-- (G-WANT-POSS-A0)
    Killing: DEMON417/3
    Executing: DEMON414 = (ANS-LEADTO-MOP CON414)
        :::> Answer with Goal Situation of ACE
Result of parse:

    (LEADTO
        ANTE (*?*)
        CONSE (ACE-COMMISERATION
                        INSTAN (ACE-COMMISERATION0)
                        COMMISERATOR David0
                        SUFFERER George0
                        G-SIT (G-WANT-POSS-A0)))

Conceptual answer of question:   G-WANT-POSS-A0
Calling BORIS Generator:

BECAUSE GEORGE LOST HIS FAMILY POSSESSIONS.
```

Once BORIS interprets the question in terms of ACE-COMMISERATION, it is relatively easy to a) find an episodic memory referent and b) apply associated retrieval heuristics to find a conceptual answer.

11.5 English Generation

The BORIS generator (BORGEN) is an adaptation (by Steve Harley) of the system GEN, written by Rod McGuire at Yale [McGuire, 1980]. Currently BORGEN is used to generate English for conceptual answers produced by BORIS during question-answering. The abridged trace below produces an English response to the question:

Q: What happened at the restaurant?

in section 11.4.

```
Calling BORIS Generator:

  popping !PS = (D-PH PRD)
 =>((!S (D-PH) 'BAD-SERVICE0) AND (!S (D-PH) 'REFUSE-PAY0))
  !S of: (D-PH) following path: ((QUOTE BAD-SERVICE0))
    to: BAD-SERVICE0  MOTIVATES REFUSE-PAY0
   =>((!D PHL) D-MODE (!D LEX VERB) (!PHROBS !CPZN NIL))
    !D following (SUBJECT)
      D-SUBJ setting !SUBJECT to (SC0-ROLE2)
      !D following (FIRST-NAME)
      !S of: (D-PH) following path: (RTS)
        to: (RT-WAITRESS0)
THE WAITRESS ...
      popping !PS = ((!UP BAD-SERVICE0)
                       (D-MODE (!D LEX VERB) (!PHROBS !CPZN NIL))
                       ...)
      popping !PS = ((D-MODE (!D LEX VERB) (!PHROBS !CPZN NIL))
                       (!UP (*LIST* BAD-SERVICE0 REFUSE-PAY0)) ...)
     =>(!AF *DIST)  -- waiting for an IS-VERB to appear
        popping !PS = ((((!D LEX VERB) (!PHROBS !CPZN NIL))
                         (!UP (*LIST* BAD-SERVICE0 REFUSE-PAY0))...)
      !D following (LEX VERB)
        =>(D-PROPEL)
"SPILLED" ...
      popping !PS = ((!PHROBS !CPZN NIL)
                       (!UP (*LIST* BAD-SERVICE0 REFUSE-PAY0))...)
     =>((!S (D-PH) OBJECT)
        (ON (!S (D-PH) TO))
        (D-PASSIVE-ACTOR)
        (!PHROBS G-S (ACTOR TO OBJECT)))
      !S of: (D-PH) following path: (OBJECT)
        to: (LIQUID0)
COKE ...
      popping !PS = (((ON (!S (D-PH) TO))
                       (D-PASSIVE-ACTOR)
                       (!PHROBS G-S (ACTOR TO OBJECT)))
                       (!UP (*LIST* BAD-SERVICE0 REFUSE-PAY0)) ...)
ON ...
      popping !PS = (((!S (D-PH) TO)
                       ((D-PASSIVE-ACTOR)
                        (!PHROBS G-S (ACTOR TO OBJECT))) ...)
      !S of: (D-PH) following path: (TO)
        to: (SC0-ROLE0)
        !D following (FIRST-NAME)
GEORGE ...
      popping !PS = (((D-PASSIVE-ACTOR)
```

```
                      (!PHROBS G-S (ACTOR TO OBJECT)))
                      (!UP (*LIST* BAD-SERVICE0 REFUSE-PAY0)) ...)
   popping !PS = ((AND [!S (D-PH) 'REFUSE-PAY0]) PRD)
AND ...
   popping !PS = (((!S (D-PH) 'REFUSE-PAY0) PRD)
   !S of: (D-PH) following path: ((QUOTE REFUSE-PAY0))
     to: REFUSE-PAY0    VIOLATES  EV-MAKE-PAYMENT0
     =>((!D PHL) D-MODE (!D LEX VERB) (!PHROBS !CPZN NIL))
     !D following (PHL)
       D-SUBJ setting !SUBJECT to (SCO-ROLE0)
HE ...
     popping !PS = ((D-MODE (!D LEX VERB) (!PHROBS !CPZN NIL))
                      (!UP (*LIST* BAD-SERVICE0 REFUSE-PAY0)) ...)
     =>(!AF *DIST)  -- waiting for an IS-VERB to appear
     !D following (LEX VERB)
       =>(!V REFUSE TO PAY)
"REFUSED" TO PAY ...
     popping !PS = ((!PHROBS !CPZN NIL)
                      (!UP (*LIST* BAD-SERVICE0 REFUSE-PAY0)) ...)
     =>(((!S (D-PAY-BILL) OBJECT) (!PHROBS G-S (OBJECT)))
       !S of: (D-PH) following path: (NAME)
         to: CHECK   PHRASE    (THE CHECK)
         =>((D-PH) (!UP (PHYS-OBJ0)))
THE CHECK ...
     popping !PS = (((!PHROBS G-S (OBJECT))
                      (!UP (*LIST* BAD-SERVICE0 REFUSE-PAY0)) ...)
   popping !PS = (PRD)
PRD ...
```

```
THE WAITRESS SPILLED COKE ON GEORGE AND HE REFUSED
TO PAY THE CHECK.
```

BORGEN produces an English response to a question in a left-to-right order by traversing CD structures. For more information concerning generation, see [Lehnert, Dyer et al., 1980].

11.6 BORIS Implementation Specs

BORIS is written in TLISP, a version of YALE-UCI-RUTGERS LISP [Meehan, 1979] running on a TOPS-20. Its lexicon currently contains approximately 300 words and 20 phrases. Since BORIS is largely an experimental prototype, little effort has gone into enlarging its vocabulary beyond those words directly used for DIVORCE-1, DIVORCE-2, and for generation.

The BORIS core image, not including TLISP itself, takes up about 120,000 CONS cells in order to maintain the lexicon, knowledge structures and all demon instantiations. This could be reduced considerably if special storage management techniques were to be employed.

The size of episodic memory after narrative comprehension depends on how interesting the narrative was. A highly reconstructable story will take up less memory while a narrative containing many violations will contain more memory instantiations. Episodic memory of DIVORCE-2, for example, takes up an addition 35,000 CONS cells. This figure would be much smaller if the BORIS system selectively REMOBed portions of Working Memory as they are incorporated into Episodic Memory.

BORIS contains over 100 demons. During comprehension, approximately 5 demon instantiations are spawned per word. For instance, over 1000 instantiated demons are spawned throughout the reading of DIVORCE-2. It is hard to compare the number of rules embodied in these demons with, say, the number of rules in PAM [Wilensky, 1978b]. This is because many of the rules contained procedurally in PAM are encoded declaratively in BORIS' I-links and strands. When a demon traverses these links, it is in essence executing what was in PAM a procedural inference rule.

As an in-depth understander BORIS is a relatively fast and efficient system. For example, it takes BORIS approximately 20 minutes (real-time) to both read DIVORCE-2 and answer around 30 questions. CPU time for DIVORCE-2 alone is 300 seconds. BORIS takes about 10 CPU seconds per question, which includes understanding the question, searching memory, retrieving an answer, and generating a response in English. If the BORIS program were compiled, these times could be improved by a factor of 2 or more.

CHAPTER 12

Future Work and Conclusions

12.1 Review

This thesis has presented a theory of in-depth understanding for narratives, embodied in a program called BORIS. What insights have we gained in our experience with BORIS? At this point it is appropriate to review major claims and principles regarding both memory and processing for narrative comprehension in the BORIS model.

TAUs play fundamental memory and processing roles for understanding narratives in depth.

TAUs represent situations involving planning failures and supply error avoidance and recovery advice for future planning. This advice is often expressed in terms of an adage, which often captures the moral or point of a story and accounts for what makes some narratives memorable.

Since TAUs represent abstract planning situations, a number of stories from widely varying contexts may be indexed in terms of the same TAU. As a result, the recognition of a TAU in one context may lead to the recall of a similar TAU in another context. This is important since it makes plans which have only been used in one context available in other contexts. Thus TAUs account for one class of cross-contextual remindings which arise during narrative comprehension.

Because TAUs deal with failure situations, TAU recognition processes are activated when goal, plan, and expectation failures occur. The recognition of specific TAUs is based upon 11 planning metrics which account for the reasons why plans fail.

> **Parsing processes are integrated with episodic memory search and instantiation processes during both narrative comprehension and question answering.**

In this thesis, parsing and memory manipulation functions are viewed as two sides of the same coin -- parsing organizes memory search while memory structures direct parsing processes. This point of view has two major consequences for question answering.

First, the processes of question answering can lead to episodic memory modifications. This "Loftus effect" for narrative text arises as a natural consequence of processing integration.

Second, in an integrated system, most of the memory search is performed while understanding a question. As a result, the answers to questions are often known before the question has been completely parsed.

12.2 Was Building BORIS Worth It?

There are three reasons why it has been important to implement the theories presented here. These reasons are not restricted to the BORIS project, but have potential application to any cognitive science project:

> (1) BORIS program implementations have sometimes uncovered important theoretical consequences which had not been anticipated.

This happened rarely, but really made programming efforts worth while when it did. For instance, we did not foresee that parser unification and integration (as described in chapter 5) would lead to episodic memory modifications during question answering. This "Loftus effect" [Loftus, 1979] for narratives was a nice result, since it showed for the first time that the Loftus effect is not just some isolated psychological aberration, but arises as a natural consequence of processing integration. In this case it was a processing consideration which provided the basis for re-examining and re-evaluating an experimentally observed phenomenon. Yet it is doubtful whether this result would have been discovered if the programming effort had not been made.

In fact, much of the theory presented in this thesis arose from problems encountered while trying to build a running program. For instance, the theory of TAUs was initially developed to deal with representational problems encountered in the second paragraph of DIVORCE-1. Likewise, the AFFECT/ACE system in BORIS came about in an effort to handle certain passages in DIVORCE-1 involving emotional descriptors.

> (2) The BORIS program has served both as a source
> and object of experimentation.

Since BORIS attempts to model cognitive processes, design decisions during program implementation have often served as directions for the design of psychological experiments. For instance, the invention of TAUs (initially created to handle processing and memory needs) naturally sparked questions concerning their psychological plausibility, and this lead to a number of experimental results [Seifert, 1981] [Seifert et al., 1982]. The discovery of episodic memory modifications during question answering in BORIS resulted in experiments on Loftus effects for narratives [Lehnert, Black, Robertson, 1982] [Robertson, Lehnert, Black, 1982].

On the other hand, the results of psychological experiments and human protocols has directed a number of design decisions concerning program implementation. For instance, experiments by Black [Black, 1980] indicate that information concerning actions dominates state information in human memory for narratives. As a result, BORIS only instantiates action-oriented information and relies upon reconstructive processes to infer corresponding state information.[60]
Similarly, the theory of MOPs [Schank, 1982b] was developed initially in response to experiments [Bower, Black and Turner, 1979]

---

[60]For example, BORIS need not instantiate the fact that a narrative character x knows y's phone number when BORIS can infer this fact from an episode in which x had called y.

regarding memory confusions not predicted by Schank's scripts.

> (3) BORIS implementations reveal both the strengths and weaknesses of current theoretical constructs and consequently guide directions for future research.

Programs which model cognitive processes in artificial intelligence are usually very complicated. Consequently, one can not predict the ways in which such programs will behave. The only way to learn whether a given theoretical construct will work within a larger processing framework is to construct a model, run it on a computer, and find out. The way a program breaks down can tell us a lot about what to do next.

Whenever theoretical constructs are programmed, it becomes clear how well (or how badly) these theoretical notions differ from the reality of making them work in a computer program. In going through this implementation exercise it becomes very clear to the programmer where he has been forced to kludge, how badly he has kludged, at what level he has kludged, etc. A thesis emphasizes the positive -- the reader is told about what worked, what was systematic, what was elegant, etc. But, in addition, the program builder is left with a mental 'map' of all the weaknesses in his system -- where the solutions work poorly, where the system is most fragile, where it fails outright, etc. What the program builder has learned here is most important in the long run, since each of these "failure points" will serve as a basis for future research. A program can be worth its weight in gold as a generator of new research topics. In the next section we will discuss current limitations of BORIS and directions for future work.

12.3 Future Research on TAUs

Numerous directions exist for research in the area of narrative themes. Major research directions include a) the learning and acquisition of TAUs, b) the generation and translation of TAUs, and c) the relationship between TAUs and analogical structures.

TAU Acquisition -- In any given culture, adages refer to the most common planning-failure situations which arise. Being able to plan 'correctly' implies having indexed experiences under the same set of TAUs shared by other members of that culture. During our lives we encounter many situations which are highly personal in nature. If a TAU does not already exist to handle it, then one must be learned. In fact, becoming an expert in a given domain implies having acquired a set of TAUs, each with its own "personal adages" (or planning heuristics) adapted specifically to that domain. The number of TAUs in memory, therefore, is open-ended and depends on the types of planning situations experienced, and the types of failures encountered.

The more TAUs a person has learned, the more potential failures he can either avoid or recover from, and the more experienced he will be. Children do not have as rich a set of TAUs built up; therefore, they can not understand the more complicated reasons for their failed plans. By the time one is an adult, one knows all the common adages of one's culture, along with many personal planning heuristics geared toward recurring idiosyncratic situations.

How might a new TAU be learned? First, the failure which occurs should be novel. Consider, for example, the following experience:

PALIMONY

> Actor Marvin dated Michelle for years, but never married her. After they broke up, Michelle took Marvin to court, claiming that she should be treated as his wife, and receive alimony. She won a settlement of over $100,000 from Marvin.

Here Marvin has experienced a major goal failure. But what types of planning advice can be drawn from his experience? This depends on what Marvin believes is the source of the failure. For example, any one of the following "personal adages" could be constructed:

1. Try to settle disputes out of court.

2. Don't get involved with women.

3. Beware of an implicit legal contract arising from an informal relationship.

4. Be sure to sign a pre-nuptial contract before you start living with someone.

It seems clear that 3 and 4 are 'more reasonable' lessons to be drawn than 1 and 2. But how do we know this? This question is a complex one, since the lesson one draws from an experience is mitigated by other knowledge sources. If Marvin had been to court many times and had always lost, then 1 might very well be a reasonable lesson to learn. Both 3 and 4 seem related to one another. However 3 is more general, telling us to avoid an abstracted situation, but without telling us how, while 4 gives a specific plan which can be used to avoid the specific failure which occurred.

The reason 2 is bad is because it is too general an avoidance heuristic.

So we have two principles:

(A) If the adage is too specific to
        the current situation,
      Then it will not be useful in similar,
        but slightly different situations.

(B) If the adage is too general,
      Then it will be applied in too many cases.

Marvin would be suffering from (A), for example, if he only worried in the future about dating a woman with dark hair because Michelle had dark hair.

If the experience is indexed under a general TAU, that is not as bad, since it can always be refined further. For example, the following adage might remind Marvin of his **PALIMONY** experience:

Adg: Hell hath no fury like a woman scorned.

The more general the TAU, the more cases in which its avoidance/recovery heuristics will be available. The optimal strategy, therefore, is to attempt to generalize planning experiences.[61] In this way, the specific planning heuristics associated with the PALIMONY, such as:

> Beware of marriage obligations arising from informal lover relationships.

are available at the level of the specific goal which failed, while the more abstract planning situation can still be available at a more general level.

For example, while reading the PALIMONY story, some individuals experienced the following remindings:

LENT CAR

> Years ago I lent my car to an old college friend. He smashed into the backend of a car stopped at a traffic light. The driver ended up suing, not my friend, but *me* because I happened to be the owner of the car.

SQUATTERS' RIGHTS

> I heard of a man who owned a lot of land. A group of people decided to live on his land. The owner was a kind man so never asked them to leave. After a few years, to his surprise he found out that they now had a legal claim to his land as squatters, and he ended up losing his land in court.

If the planning failure were only indexed in terms of the specific content of PALIMONY, it would have been impossible for LENT CAR or SQUATTERS' RIGHTS to have come to mind.

What is shared between these episodes is a generalization of the planning heuristics learned from PALIMONY:

---

[61]A Madison Avenue company now exists which provides a "Palimony Prevention Kit" to those who want to avoid contract failures arising from informal living arrangements.

TAU-IMPLICIT-CONTRACT

x enters into an informal cooperative
    relationship with y
    (for mutual goal satisfaction)
x is not careful about implicit
    contractual obligations arising
    from this informal agreement
x suffers a failure arising
    from the unforseen contract

I am not aware of any adage which characterizes TAU-IMPLICIT-CONTRACT. Nonetheless, it is also a TAU. The reason that it lacks a common adage is simply that most people do not commonly encounter such a planning failure. Those that do, however, will have built such a TAU, and be sensitive to the possibility of such implicit unwanted contracts. Marvin will undoubtedly be reminded of PALIMONY the next time he begins living with another woman.[62] Whether LENT CAR would remind him of PALIMONY would depend on the level at which he generalized the PALIMONY experience in the first place.

TAU Generation and Translation -- Currently, the BORIS English generator makes use of mainly MOPs and Conceptual Dependency primitives for generation. For the most part TAUs are used in generating responses to questions about unusual events and strong affects. However, future work should allow BORIS to generate adages from TAUs. For example, in answer to the question: "What is a moral of this story?" a response from a story indexed under TAU-HIDDEN-BLESSING would be: "Every cloud has a silver lining."

TAUs are often expressed by adages which share little or nothing of content with the stories indexed beneath the associated TAU. Hence, the expression of a given TAU can not rely on narrative content. This fact makes the problem of translating a theme into another language an interesting one because it may involve no words or context in common. For instance, the translation of "Hiding your

---

[62]When the woman tennis player Billy Jean King was sued by her lesbian lover for alimony, several TV announcers mentioned that they were reminded of the Lee Marvin case, and began to refer to King's situation as "galimony".

head in the sand" in chinese is "Covering your ears when you steal the town bell".   The translation of "The blind leading the blind" in chinese is "Swimming across the river on a clay buddha".[63]   The only way such adages could be translated into another language is for the translator to access the appropriate abstract theme (i.e. the TAU) which both adages refer to.

Metaphors, Analogies, and TAUs -- TAUs also seem to underlie at least one aspect of metaphoric or analogical processing. If we look at the verbatim text of adages, we see that many are based on physical situations which correspond metaphorically to the abstract configurations captured in their associated TAUs. For instance, the adage fragments below each contain physical objects intended to correspond to goal/plan situations:

> "frying pan and fire"
> "pot and black kettle"
> "spilt milk"
> "burning a bridge"
> "eggs in one basket"

The key idea in TAUs is that they represent abstract generalizations about planning situations. When a narrative is characterized in terms of a TAU, the metaphoric mapping which exists between the concrete adage and the associated TAU becomes available. That is, the metaphoric mapping between the physical objects in the adage and the corresponding entities in the narrative are mediated through the TAU which generalizes each of them. For example, the adage:

> Adg: Don't throw rocks if you live
>   in a glass house.

is mapped to a TAU as:

---

[63]Thanks to C. J. Yang for having suggested these examples.

```
         adage                    TAU
         -----                    ---

     throw rocks      -->    counter-plan P of x
                             against y

      living in       -->    p-goal situation G
                             of x active

     glass house      -->    G vulnerable
                             to counter-plan P
                             of y against x
```

Later, when a related story at the thematic level is generalized to the same TAU and the adage comes to mind, the corresponding metaphoric mapping appears to the reader to have been made between the narrative and the adage which came to mind. However, the real process involved one of recognizing the correct TAU. From that point on, the correspondence between the TAU and the adage is already available. Hence TAUs account for one type of metaphoric phenomena.

Finally, it is interesting to note that many parables, jokes, and fables both describe planning errors and give advice on how to plan at a very general level (e.g. the parable of the good Samaritan; the fable of the fox and the crow, etc.) Jokes serve to ridicule and point out improper plans (e.g. the story of the drunk and the lamppost). Many parables involve "life plans" and general attitudes toward various abstract situations. For example, one recurring theme is that of pyrrhic victories. Finally, such structures often provide support for belief systems (religious, political, etc.) and other systems for life-long ethical attitudes and moral behavior. All of these structures constitute unexplored areas awaiting future research.

12.4 Future Work on Processing Integration

Much work remains to be done exploring in more detail the

interactions between the seventeen different knowledge sources used in BORIS. Also, more research is needed in improving the program's use of overlays and multiple perspectives, and in expanding the system's inferencing capability, including the ability to recover from erroneous inferences [Granger, 1980a] [Granger, 1980b] during parsing. Most important are experiments dealing with interactions between parsing processes and other episodic memory manipulations.

Major directions for research include a) integrated generation, b) reconstructive memory processes, and c) narrative/narrative interactions.

Integrated Generation -- While parsing has become integrated and unified, the process of language generation in BORIS occurs only after a complete conceptual answer has been constructed. But people often start generating English before a complete conceptualization has been formed. A more integrated generator would give BORIS the ability to generate "introspective protocols" of its own answer retrieval processes. What remains difficult in this case is the generation of appropriate transition expressions to make the fragmentary output appear "smooth". But this fact again argues for a merging of generation processes with other memory inference, search and understanding processes. Therefore, another direction of research involves integrating the generation of answers (during question answering) with the search processes used to find (or reconstruct) the answer.

Reconstuctive Memory Processes -- In this thesis we discussed some memory modifications which arose during question-answering in BORIS, and which resulted from parsing unification and integration. Furthermore, we argued that Loftus effects depend upon a reconstructive memory. Consequently, a key research direction involves modeling reconstructive search strategies for narrative memory.

Some work on reconstructive search has been done already in the area of long-term memory for personal experiences [Kolodner, 1980] [Kolodner, 1981]. Kolodner argues that long-term memory is organized around differences. Similar experiences become "mushed" and inaccessible -- i.e. they can only be recalled reconstructively, Only the deviations lead to unique memories. Hence the recognition of norm violations becomes a key component in any reasonable theory of narrative comprehension and narrative memory.

Facilities in BORIS for processing norm violations are still very primitive. For instance, subjects who read DIVORCE-1 are often bothered by the fact that the lawyer got drunk while on a legal case and also by the fact that the client had allowed a drunk to drive him home. These two violations of social norms are essentially ignored by BORIS (to the extent that no special processing is invoked). In contrast, such events are usually of interest to human readers because they know that intoxicated individuals commonly violate norms of behavior. In fact, any knowledge structure can be violated:

```
Structures:  M-LETTER, IP-COMM

Violation:   John threw the letter from
             Mary away without reading it.
```

What happens when any given expectation is violated, and at what point are violations recognized during processing? These are difficult problems, and both depend upon the nature of the violation. For instance, violations concerning beliefs may need to be treated differently from violations involving social roles, interpersonal themes or other knowledge sources [Abelson, 1979]. Consider the subtleties in parsing the word "only" below, which appears in paragraph five of DIVORCE-2 and is essentially ignored in the current implementation of BORIS:

> David told George not to worry since the judge would award the case to George once he learned that Ann had been cheating on him.

> ... without a witness they had no proof and Ann won. George almost had a fit. David could **only** offer George his condolences.

Here subjects felt that "only" conveyed an attitude of cynicism and sarcasm concerning David's incompetence as a lawyer. In contrast, when character beliefs and expectations were altered as follows:

> David warned George that he thought the judge might reject George's testimony and side with Ann.

> ... without a witness they had no proof and Ann
> won. George almost had a fit. David could **only**
> offer George his condolences.

subjects then interpreted "only" to mean sincerity on David's part.
Clearly, the effect of "only" during processing depends on the
plausibility of character expectations and beliefs. When these beliefs
are violated, the underlying reasoning is re-examined. As a result,
sarcasm is recognized. The problems touched upon in these examples
need to be addressed, and constitute areas for future research.

Narrative/Narrative Interactions -- A current theory on
reminding [Schank, 1982a] [Schank, 1982b] argues that the memory of
a prior narrative should aid in processing a similar narrative. Right
now, BORIS maintains an episodic memory for only one narrative at a
time. How should question answering and story understanding
processes behave in a multi-narrative episodic memory environment?
What would happen if BORIS were to read DIVORCE-2 in the
context of DIVORCE-1?

Subjects who had read DIVORCE-1 in the past were reminded
of it upon reading DIVORCE-2 and later showed certain memory
confusions during recall and summarization tasks. Clearly, subjects
were accessing and applying episodes from DIVORCE-1 while
processing DIVORCE-2. In fact, they could not help but be reminded
of the prior divorce story. But before we can develop a theory of
processing many narratives that access similar knowledge structures, it
will be necessary to examine the memories of people who have read
narratives sharing related episodic structures. Our intuitions and
experience tell us that people will demonstrate memory confusions,
and where this is the case, we would like BORIS to do the same.
Hopefully, such research will tell us more about the processes of
indexing and accessing narratives when remindings are occurring.

12.5 Final Retrospection

There is still along way to go before computers will be able to
intelligently read and comprehend a full-length literary novel. Before
this can happen, much more needs to be known about human episodic
memory structures for narratives. What does human memory "look

like" after reading *The Hardy Boys, Lord of the Flies,* or *Crime and Punishment*? Humans are the only information processing devices capable of such text understanding feats, so clearly more psychological experiments and human protocols on episodic memory and text comprehension processes are in order before tasks of such magnitude can be adequately addressed.

In commercially available expert systems and in other areas of computer science, programs are viewed as solutions to problems. This is not the case in cognitive modeling (especially in natural language domains). No program exists which constitutes a solution to 'the natural language problem', so every natural language program is by nature a 'failure'. Consequently, what's interesting about computer programs which model cognitive processes are their potential for on-going experimental study and continuing development. This point of view ("program as experimental object") is very different from that of "program as solution".

What stands out in our experience with BORIS? One striking fact is the sheer complexity of understanding natural language text. People do not appreciate this complexity because they handle everyday language comprehension tasks with unconscious ease. Almost anyone can engage in a conversation, argue over a point, discuss a newspaper article, enjoy a fictional novel, etc. Everyday language comprehension tasks are not considered expert skills, as are chess playing, medical diagnosis, symbolic integration, etc. Yet expert programs exist in commercial use. Natural language systems, however, have yet to hold up their end in a mundane conversation, or read a well-known short story.

This fact no longer seems paradoxical when we accept the notion that natural language tasks exercise fundamental cognitive processes much more basic (and therefore potentially much more difficult) than tasks which only experts can handle. Experience with BORIS lends ample support to this point of view. BORIS's major contribution lies in its role as both a source and testing ground for theoretically interesting issues concerning fundamental cognitive abilities.

I. APPENDIX: Narratives and Sample Q/A

I.1 Narrative: KIDNAP-0

John left his office early Friday afternoon so he could attend a going-away party for his friend Bill. Bill had been transferred to California. When he arrived there were lots of people and plenty of beer. Three years ago Bill had borrowed $50 from John which John hoped to get back before Bill left. He was about to remind Bill about it when he was called to the phone. It was his wife, Mary, and she was hysterical. Mary had just received a call from a stranger who claimed to have kidnapped their daughter Susan. He said he would call again. John told Mary to stay at home, keep off the phone, and wait until he got there.

John drove home immediately. Just as he walked in the door, the phone rang. John picked it up. But it was only Karen, one of Mary's friends. John told her Mary was out and hung up. Mary wanted to call the police but John thought they should wait. They were discussing this when Susan walked in the door. She had stayed after school for a gymnastics meet and taken a late bus home. Nothing had happened to her. It was all a hoax.

I.2 Question-Answering: KIDNAP-0

```
Why did John go to the party?
HE WANTED TO HAVE A GOOD TIME AND HE WAS
BILL'S FRIEND AND HE WANTED TO GET 50
DOLLARS BACK FROM HIM.
```

Why did John leave the party?
HE WAS WORRIED ABOUT SUSAN.

Why?
SUSAN WAS KIDNAPPED.

What happened to John at the party?
HE GOT A CALL FROM MARY.

Why did Mary call John at the party?
SHE WANTED TO TELL HIM ABOUT SUSAN'S
KIDNAPPING.

Why did John want money from Bill?
HE BORROWED 50 DOLLARS FROM HIM.

Why didn't John talk to Bill?
HE WAS MORE WORRIED ABOUT SUSAN.

Who called John at home?
KAREN.

Why?
SHE WANTED TO TALK TO MARY.

Was Karen upset?
NO, SHE DID NOT KNOW ABOUT SUSAN'S
KIDNAPPING.

Did John kidnap Susan?
NO. HE WAS HER FATHER.

Where was Susan?
SHE WAS ATTENDING A GYMNASTICS MEET.

What happened when Susan came home?
JOHN WAS RELIEVED THAT SHE WAS SAFE.

I.3 Narrative: DIVORCE-1

Richard hadn't heard from his college roommate Paul for years. Richard had borrowed money from Paul which was never paid back, but now he had no idea where to find his old friend. When a letter finally arrived from San Francisco, Richard was anxious to find out how Paul was.

Unfortunately, the news was not good. Paul's wife Sarah wanted a divorce. She also wanted the car, the house, the children, and alimony. Paul wanted the divorce, but he didn't want to see Sarah walk off with everything he had. His salary from the state school system was very small. Not knowing who to turn to, he was hoping for a favor from the only lawyer he knew. Paul gave his home phone number in case Richard felt he could help.

Richard eagerly picked up the phone and dialed. After a brief conversation, Paul agreed to have lunch with him the next day. He sounded extremely relieved and grateful.

The next day, as Richard was driving to the restaurant he barely avoided hitting an old man on the street. He felt extremely upset by the incident, and had three drinks at the restaurant. When Paul arrived Richard was fairly drunk. After the food came, Richard spilled a cup of coffee on Paul. Paul seemed very annoyed by this so Richard offered to drive him home for a change of clothes.

When Paul walked into the bedroom and found Sarah with another man he nearly had a heart attack. Then he realized what a blessing it was. With Richard there as a witness, Sarah's divorce case was shot. Richard congratulated Paul and suggested that they celebrate at dinner. Paul was eager to comply.

I.4 Question-Answering: DIVORCE-1

What happened to Richard at home?
RICHARD GOT A LETTER FROM PAUL.

Who is Paul?
RICHARD 's FRIEND.

Did Richard want to see Paul?
YES, RICHARD WANTED TO KNOW HOW PAUL WAS.

Had Paul helped Richard?
YES, PAUL LENT MONEY TO RICHARD.

Why didn't Richard pay Paul back?
RICHARD DID NOT KNOW WHERE PAUL WAS.

How did Richard feel when the letter appeared?
RICHARD FELT GLAD BECAUSE PAUL AND HE
WERE FRIENDS.

What was the letter about?
PAUL AND SARAH WERE GETTING A DIVORCE.

Did Paul write Sarah?
NO, IT WASN'T SARAH, IT WAS RICHARD
WHO GOT THE LETTER.

Why was Paul upset about the divorce?
PAUL AND SARAH WERE FIGHTING OVER
THE FAMILY POSSESSIONS.

What did Paul do for a living?
PAUL WAS A TEACHER.

What did Sarah want?
SARAH WANTED TO HAVE THE CAR AND THE HOUSE AND
THE KIDS AND THE ALIMONY.

Why did Paul write to Richard?
PAUL WANTED RICHARD TO BE HIS LAWYER.

Why did Richard call Paul?
RICHARD WANTED TO ARRANGE A MEETING WITH PAUL.

Did Richard contact Paul?
YES. RICHARD CALLED PAUL.

How did Richard contact Paul?
BY PHONE.

How did Paul feel when Richard called?
PAUL WAS HAPPY BECAUSE RICHARD AGREED TO BE
PAUL'S LAWYER.

Why did Richard eat out with Paul?
RICHARD WANTED TO DISCUSS THE DIVORCE CASE
WITH PAUL.

What happened to Richard on the way
to the restaurant?
RICHARD ALMOST RAN OVER AN OLD MAN.

Why did Richard get drunk?
RICHARD WAS UPSET ABOUT ALMOST RUNNING OVER
THE OLD MAN.

What happened at the restaurant?
RICHARD SPILLED COFFEE ON PAUL.

How did Richard feel when the coffee spilled?
RICHARD WAS UNHAPPY.

How did Paul feel?
PAUL WAS MAD AT RICHARD.

Why did Richard spill the coffee?
RICHARD WAS DRUNK.

How did Richard get drunk?
HE DRANK ALCOHOL.

When was Richard drunk?
AT THE RESTAURANT.

When did Richard almost hit the old man?
WHILE RICHARD WAS DRIVING TO THE RESTAURANT.

Where did Richard have lunch with PAUL?
AT A RESTAURANT.

Why did Richard drive Paul home?
SO PAUL COULD CHANGE HIS CLOTHES.

What happened to Paul at home?
PAUL CAUGHT SARAH COMMITTING ADULTERY.

How did Paul feel?
PAUL WAS SURPRISED.

Why was Paul surprised when he got home?
PAUL CAUGHT SARAH COMMITTING ADULTERY.

Why did Sarah lose her divorce case?
SARAH COMMITTED ADULTERY.

Why did Richard congratulate Paul?
PAUL WON THE DIVORCE CASE.

I.5 Narrative: DIVORCE-2

George was having lunch with another teacher and grading homework assignments when the waitress accidentally knocked a glass of coke on him. George was very annoyed and left refusing to pay the check. He decided to drive home to get out of his wet clothes.

When he got there, he found his wife Ann and another man in bed. George became extremely upset and felt like going out and getting plastered.

At the bar he ran into an old college roommate

David, who he hadn't seen in years. David offered to buy him a few drinks and soon they were both pretty drunk. When George found out that David was a lawyer, he told him all about his troubles and asked David to represent him in court. Since David owed George money he had never returned, he felt obligated to help out.

Later, David wrote to Ann, informing her that George wanted a divorce. Her lawyer called back and told David that she intended to get the house, the children and a lot of alimony. When George heard this, he was very worried. He didn't earn much at the junior high school. David told him not to worry, since the judge would award the case to George once he learned that Ann had been cheating on him.

When they got to court, David presented George's case, but without a witness they had no proof and Ann won. George almost had a fit. David could only offer George his condolences.

A week later, George received a large bill in the mail from David. Was he furious!

I.6 Question-Answering: DIVORCE-2

What did George do for a living?
GEORGE WAS A TEACHER.

Where did George have lunch?
AT THE RESTAURANT.

What was George doing at the restaurant?
GEORGE AND A TEACHER WERE EATING A MEAL
AND HE WAS GRADING HOMEWORK.

What happened at the restaurant?
THE WAITRESS SPILLED COKE ON GEORGE
AND HE REFUSED TO PAY THE CHECK.

How did George feel at the restaurant?
GEORGE WAS ANGRY BECAUSE THE WAITRESS
SPILLED COKE ON HIM.

How did the waitress feel at the restaurant?
THE WAITRESS REGRETTED THAT SHE SPILLED COKE
ON GEORGE.

Why did George go home?
GEORGE WANTED TO CHANGE CLOTHES.

How did George get home?
GEORGE DROVE.

Why didn't George pay the check?
BECAUSE THE WAITRESS SPILLED COKE ON GEORGE.

Why was George upset?
BECAUSE THE WAITRESS SPILLED COKE ON HIM.

How did Ann feel when George caught her
cheating on him?
SHE WAS SURPRISED.

Why did George want to get drunk?
HE WAS UPSET BECAUSE HIS WIFE WAS CHEATING
ON HIM.

Who was David?
GEORGE'S COLLEGE ROOMMATE.

Why did David buy George drinks?
BECAUSE THEY WERE FRIENDS.

What did David do for a living?
HE WAS A LAWYER.

Did George borrow money from David?
NO. IT WASN'T GEORGE WHO BORROWED MONEY,
IT WAS DAVID.

Why did George tell David his troubles?
GEORGE WANTED DAVID TO BE HIS LAWYER.

Why did David feel obligated to help out George?
HE WANTED TO RETURN A FAVOR BECAUSE HE OWED
GEORGE MONEY.

Why did George write to Ann?
IT WASN'T GEORGE, IT WAS DAVID WHO WROTE
TO ANN.

Did George want a divorce?
YES. GEORGE CAUGHT ANN CHEATING ON HIM.

Why did Ann's lawyer phone David?
HE WANTED TO INFORM DAVID THAT ANN WANTED
THE HOUSE, THE CHILDREN, AND ALIMONY.

Why did David reassure George?
DAVID BELIEVED THAT THE JUDGE WOULD AWARD
THE CASE TO GEORGE BECAUSE ANN HAD BROKEN
THE MARRIAGE CONTRACT.

What happened at court?
THE JUDGE AWARDED THE CASE TO ANN.

How did George feel about the verdict?
GEORGE WAS SURPRISED BECAUSE ANN WON.

Why did George lose the case?
GEORGE DID NOT HAVE A WITNESS TO
THE VIOLATION.

How did David feel about the verdict?
DAVID FELT GUILTY BECAUSE HE HAD TOLD
GEORGE THAT HE WOULD WIN.

Why did David console George?
BECAUSE GEORGE LOST THE FAMILY POSSESSIONS.

Why did David send George a bill?
DAVID REPRESENTED HIM IN COURT.

How did George feel when he received the bill?
GEORGE WAS ANGRY AT DAVID.

Why?
BECAUSE THE BILL WAS TOO LARGE.

I.7 Major DIVORCE Knowledge Structures

MOPs	Scripts
M-BAR	$CHANGE-CLOTHES
M-BORROW	$CALL
M-CONTRACT	$SEX
M-EDUCATION	$WRITE
M-LEGAL-DISPUTE	
M-MARITAL-CONTRACT	Settings
M-MEAL	
M-REPRESENT-CLIENT	BAR
M-RESTAURANT	BEDROOM
M-SERVICE	COURTROOM
M-LETTER	HOME
M-PHONE	RESTAURANT
	ROADWAY

Reasoning

rM-JURIS-PRUDENCE

Interpersonal

IPT-LOVERS
IPT-FRIENDS
IP-FAVOR
RENEW-IPT
SUSPEND-IPT

TAUs

TAU-BROKEN-SERVICE
TAU-BROKEN-CONTRACT
TAU-CLOSE-CALL
TAU-DIRE-STRAITS
TAU-HIDDEN-BLESSING
TAU-RED-HANDED

ACEs

Commiseration
Felicitation
Reassurance

Physical Objects

ALCOHOL
CAR
CLOTHES
LETTER
LIQUID
MONEY
PHONE

Relationships/Roles

R-MARRIAGE
R-ROOMMATES
RT-JUDGE
RT-LAWYER
RT-TEACHER

Affects

gratitude
relief
anger
surprise, etc.

(Most goals, plans, events are associated with MOPs)

II. APPENDIX: CD, Goals, Plans, Scripts

This appendix provides a brief introduction to Conceptual Dependency (CD) theory, as originally developed in [Schank, 1973] [Schank, 1975] and expanded in [Schank and Abelson, 1977].

II.1 CD: Primitive ACTs

Conceptual Dependency (CD) is a system designed to represent the meanings of sentences by decomposing them into a small number of primitive "acts". In Conceptual Dependency theory, sentences with identical meaning will have the same underlying conceptual representation, regardless of differences in grammatical form or language used. A basic premise of Conceptual Dependency theory is that meaning arises from a combination of memory search, planning, and inference. Only a small fraction of meaning is actually conveyed directly by those lexical items which explicitly appear in a given sentence.

For example, when we read:

S1:   John bought a television.

we understand a great number of things, including:

1.   There was another individual involved.
2.   John gave money to this individual.
3.   This individual gave a TV to John
       in exchange for John's money.
4.   John bought the TV in order to watch shows
       on it, probably for his own enjoyment.
5.   John probably bought the TV at a store.
6.   The individual at the store no longer
       has possession of the television.
6.   John will plug the TV in at home, etc.

Most of this information does not appear in S1 above. Furthermore, people draw the same conclusions even when presented with a completely different sentence, such as:

S2: A TV set was sold to John.

By mapping grammatically and lexically distinct utterances to their underlying conceptualizations, the processes of inference and memory search are simplified. For example, the inference that John now owns the TV can be made independently of whether the word "bought", "sold", "got", "took", "gave", "paid", or "acquired" was used.

Below are the eleven primitive "acts" of CD theory. Associated with each act are a number of case-frames, including: actor, recipient, optional object, direction, and instrumental cases. These case-frames hold expectations for what conceptualizations should follow. Such expectations are useful in language analysis processes, such as word sense disambiguation and pronoun reference.

1. ATRANS -- the transfer of possession. For example, both sentences S1 and S2 would be represented in terms of two ATRANSes:

```
(ATRANS              (ATRANS
   ACTOR John           ACTOR individual
   OBJECT money         OBJECT TV
   FROM  John           FROM  individual
   TO individual)       TO John)
```

2. PROPEL -- the application of a physical force. Such actions as throwing, hitting, falling, pulling, kicking, shoving all involve PROPEL.

3. PTRANS -- the transfer of physical location. For example, the actions of driving, flying, taking a bus or train, walking all result in a change of location. PROPEL may be instrumental to PTRANS and PTRANS may be instrumental to ATRANS, as in the case where John gives Mary a ball as a present by throwing it to her.

4. INGEST -- when an organism takes something from outside its environment and makes it internal. Acts of INGEST are breathing, eating and smoking. For example, when a CD parser reads: "John smokes pot",

the lexical item "smokes" is represented as the INGEST of some GASEOUS-OBJECT. The CD parser then uses its expectation for GASEOUS-OBJECT to choose MARIJUANA-FUMES over COOKING-UTENSIL as the meaning of "pot".

5. EXPEL -- the opposite of INGEST. Examples of EXPEL are sweating, crying, defecating, spitting, etc.

6. MTRANS -- the transfer of mental information from one individual to another. The acts of speaking, talking, reading, sign language all involve MTRANS. When MTRANS occurs between distinct parts of of the same individual's memory, then the notions of remembering, forgetting, learning, recalling can be represented.

7. MBUILD -- thought processes which create new conceptualizations from old ones. Acts of deciding, concluding, realizing, considering and imagining all involve MBUILD.

8. MOVE -- The movement of a bodypart of some animate organism. Actions such as waving, throwing, dancing, jumping all involve MOVE. For example, "walking" is represented as a PTRANS accomplished by an instrumental MOVE of LEGS.

9. GRASP -- the act of physically contacting an object, usually by MOVE arm/hand. The acts of grabbing, holding and hugging involve the primitive act of GRASP.

10. SPEAK -- any vocalization. The act of MTRANS is usually accomplished by people through the instrumental act of SPEAKing.

11. ATTEND -- the act of directing a sense organ. Hearing someone involves ATTENDing one's ears toward the sounds being made by that individual. For example, when we read that John "listened to" a guitar, we realize that he was ATTENDing to the *sounds* being made by the guitar, not to the guitar itself. This realization is important because, for one thing, it supports the inference that some (unmentioned) individual must actually be

playing the guitar.

II.2 Goals and Plans

Conceptual Dependency theory is adequate for representing mundane physical actions. However, most actions are part of larger plans in the service of higher-level goals, and much of the comprehension process involves recognizing what goals and plans are being employed. Below are listed a number of goals used in CD theory:

1. S-goals -- Satisfactions goals arise from the need to satisfy recurring bodily desires. S-goals include: S-SEX, S-HUNGER, S-SLEEP, and S-THIRST.

2. D-goals -- Delta goals represent desires for a change in state. States may be mental, such as the need to know something (D-KNOW), or physical, the desire to change one's location or proximity to something (D-PROX), or the desire to gain control of something (D-CONT) or someone (D-SOCCONT), as in a kidnapping.

3. E-goals -- Entertainment goals. For example, one may go to a restaurant with a friend to satisfy an E-COMPANY entertainment goal rather than to satisfy S-HUNGER. Other e-goals include E-TRAVEL and E-EXERCISE.

4. A-goals -- Achievement goals involve the long-term attainment of social status or position. Examples of a-goals are A-GOOD-JOB and A-SKILL.

5. P-goals -- Preservation goals are those goals which become active only when threatened. For instance, one does not normally think of one's health unless one is sick, injured, or threatened with injury. In addition to P-HEALTH, other preservation goals are: P-COMFORT, P-APPEARANCE and P-FINANCES.

For each goal there are a number of plans which may be used to achieve it. Plans contain preconditions which must be satisfied before the plan can be invoked. For example, common plans for achieving D-CONT (control of an object) include:

1. ASK -- Ask the person who has the object to give it to you. This plan may work if the owner is a friend.

2. INFORM-REASON -- Try to convince the owner why there is a good reason that you should have the object.

3. BARGAIN -- Offer to exchange some object in your possession for the desired object. This includes buying the object.

4. THREATEN -- Tell the owner that you will cause some harm to him if he does not give you the desired object.

5. OVERPOWER -- Take the object from him by force.

6. STEAL -- Gain control of the object through theft.

A precondition for ASK, INFORM-REASON, BARGAIN, THREATEN and OVERPOWER is to be in physical proximity of the owner of the desired object, or to have a link for MTRANS (e.g. a phone). A precondition for STEAL is to be within physical proximity, not of the owner, but of the desired object itself.

II.3 Scripts

Detailed planning is not always needed. Often, actions are part of a large sequence of stereotypic actions (in a given culture) and may have no directly associated goal. An example of a stereotypic action sequence is that of a marriage ceremony, including the throwing of rice. In addition to ceremonies, many service contracts involve a stereotypic action sequence. For instance, going to a movie includes: buying a ticket, giving the ticket to the doorman, getting a ripped ticket in return, going to the candy counter, entering the theater, sitting down, watching the movie, and leaving through the doors marked "exit". In addition to $MOVIE, examples of other scripts are: $RESTAURANT, $AUTO-REPAIR, $BUS-RIDE, $AIRPLANE-RIDE, and $GROCERY-SHOPPING.

Associated with each script are roles and props. For instance, roles in $GROCERY-SHOPPING include the shopper, the meat-cutter, and the cashier. Props include the groceries, check-out counter, and grocery cart. By organizing CD acts within a single script, the problem of inference is greatly reduced. For instance, the inference that John PTRANSed FOOD to the CART can be made simply by virtue of the fact that $GROCERY-SHOPPING is active.

III. APPENDIX: McDYPAR -- A Demon Parser

III.1 Introduction

McDYPAR is a micro version of DYPAR (Dyer's Parser), an expectation-based conceptual parser[64] currently being used at the Yale Artificial Intelligence lab. The description which follows is divided into five sections: 1) a general description of how McDYPAR works, 2) some background comparing DYPAR with its predecessors and discussing its current use at Yale, 3) a sample lexicon for McDYPAR, including a detailed trace of McDYPAR parsing a single sentence, 4) a documented listing which shows how McDYPAR is implemented in TLISP, and 5) a series of exercises designed to transform McDYPAR into a system with the capabilities of DYPAR.

III.2 An Overview of McDYPAR

McDYPAR parses a sentence in a left-to-right manner. As it encounters each word, it saves the "meaning" of that word in a Working Memory and "spawns" demons which represent expectations -- either for what has already occurred, or for what *may* occur next. Demons are active processes which "wait" until their conditions are satisfied, whereupon they "fire" and cause various structures to be connected together. Unlike syntactic parsers, the result of a McDYPAR parse is intended to capture the *conceptual* content of a sentence.

The best way to become familiar with McDYPAR is by means of an example. We will parse the sentence: "Mary said John ate an apple." Therefore, assume we have the following words in our (informal) lexicon below, where each word has an associated conceptual representation:

---

[64]Special acknowledgements go to Tom Wolf for helping to edit DYPAR down into the micro version (McDYPAR) presented here.

III.2.1 An Informal Lexicon

```
Word        Representation
----        --------------


Mary        (HUMAN NAME (MARY)
                    GENDER (FEMALE))



said        (MTRANS ACTOR  X <== demon:
                                    expect to have already
                                    heard of the human who
                                    is performing this act
                        OBJECT * <== demon:
                                    expect to hear about
                                        some action, state, or goal
                        FROM  X
                        TO   * <== demon:
                                    expect that the human
                                    receiving the message
                                    will be the object of the
                                    preposition "to")



John        (HUMAN NAME (JOHN)
                    GENDER (MALE))



ate         (INGEST ACTOR * <== demon:
                                    expect to have already
                                    heard of the human who
                                    is performing this act
                        OBJECT * <== demon:
                                    expect to hear next of
                                        the food being ingested)

an          NO ENTRY
```

```
apple     (FOOD TYPE (APPLE))
```

As you can see, each conceptual representation has the following structure:

```
concept = (HEAD SLOT GAP  <== demons
                SLOT GAP  <== demons
                  . . .
                SLOT GAP)
```

where HEAD may be a Conceptual Dependency (CD) [Schank and Abelson, 1977] act (such as MTRANS, INGEST, ATRANS, etc.); where SLOT indicates a role (such as ACTOR, OBJECT, etc.), and where GAP may be either a variable, or a "*" (or recursively, another conceptual representation with its own HEAD, SLOTs, GAPs, and demons). The formal syntax for word senses is specified in the documentation to the McDYPAR code in section III.5.2.

The GAP is a place-holder for where bindings will occur. Pointing at each GAP (via an arrow) are one or more demons. In the informal lexicon above, these demons have been described simply in English. In a moment we will see how demons are actually defined.

When a GAP is indicated by "*", this means that we do not care what the GAP is called, and McDYPAR will automatically make up a name based upon the SLOT preceding it. When the GAP is specified by a variable, then McDYPAR will make sure that any other GAP indicated by the same variable will receive the same binding. For example, both the ACTOR and the FROM slots in the MTRANS above have the same GAP "X", so they will receive the same binding when the attached demon fires.

As each word is processed, its associated concept is placed in Working Memory (WM) and the demons associated with its SLOTs are "spawned" (i.e. activated). If the expectation of the demon is fulfilled, then whatever fulfilled it is bound to the GAP which the demon was pointing at with an "<==".

In some cases, a demon will "fire" (i.e. satisfy its expectation) immediately. For example, the demon associated with the ACTOR slot in the MTRANS concept above will fire immediately. However, the demon associated with the OBJECT slot in the INGEST concept above will have to wait until the next word is processed. In some cases, a demon's expectation may never be fulfilled. For example, in the sentence "Mary said John ate an apple" the TO slot in the MTRANS does not receive a binding. It is because demons have to wait for possible future situations that the processes they model cannot be handled by simply executing functions. Thus, demons are a way of implementing delayed processes.

The following diagram shows how the GAPs are linked up after all of the appropriate demons have fired for the sentence "Mary said John ate an apple". The reader should compare the bindings in the diagram below with the demon descriptions in the lexicon above in order to see how each binding was formed. These bindings are indicated by dotted lines.

III.2.2 A Parse Result in Working Memory

```
                              . . . . . . . . . . . . . . . . . . . . .
    . . . . . . . . . . . . . . . . . . . .      . . . .   :  . . . . . . . . . . . . . .      :      . . . .
    :                         :  :      :                       :              :      :  :
    CON0            CON1      :  :   CON2             CON3            :      :  CON4
    |               |         :  :    |               |               :      :  |
    (HUMAN          (MTRANS   :  :   (HUMAN           (INGEST          :      :  (FOOD
    NAME (MARY)     ACTOR X0  :         NAME (JOHN)    ACTOR ACTOR0 :     TYPE
    GENDER (FEMALE) OBJECT OBJECT0  GENDER (MALE))  OBJECT OBJECT1)  (APPLE))
                    FROM   X0
                    TO   TO0)
```

If we look at Working Memory above, we will notice that only CON1 does **not** have a dotted line leading into it. Therefore, CON1 must be the "highest level" concept, since it is not bound to any GAP within some other conceptual fragment. Starting with CON1, if we recursively replace each GAP with the CON bound to it, we get the following complete conceptualization:

```
(MTRANS ACTOR  (HUMAN  NAME (MARY)
                       GENDER (FEMALE))
        OBJECT (INGEST ACTOR (HUMAN NAME (JOHN)
                                     GENDER (MALE))
                       OBJECT (FOOD TYPE (APPLE)))
        FROM (HUMAN  NAME (MARY)
                     GENDER (FEMALE))
        TO  NIL)
```

where **TO** is **NIL** since its expectation was never fulfilled.

As we can see from the result of the parse above, all conceptualizations in McDYPAR have the following recursive form:

```
con  =   NIL  or
         (HEAD)  or
         (HEAD SLOT con

                ...
          SLOT con)
```

Now that we have explained what conceptual structures look like in Working Memory, we have only to describe the relevant syntax and semantics of demons in McDYPAR.

III.2.3 Demon Syntax and Semantics

Demons have the following form:

```
(DEMON  name
   (COMMENT  (TEST "comments")
             (ACT  "comments"))
    (PARAMS   sequence-of-parameters)
    (SHARE    sequence-of-variables)
    (KILL   sequence-of-lisp-expressions )
    (TEST   sequence-of-lisp-expressions )
```

```
(+ACT    sequence-of-lisp-expressions )
(-ACT    sequence-of-lisp-expressions ))
```

A demon is made up of a group of "segments". Each segment begins with a keyword (e.g. COMMENT, PARAMS, SHARE ...). Each segment is completely optional and segments may appear in any order. The semantics of each segment is described below:

COMMENT: This segment is used both to document a demon, and to serve as an automatic explanation of how the parse is proceeding. Whenever a demon is spawned, the comments in this segment are printed out.

PARAMS: When a demon is "interpreted", its arguments are bound to its parameters. Parameters may appear in TEST, KILL, +ACT and -ACT segments. (Demon interpretation is described below.)

SHARE: Shared variables are initialized to NIL automatically. Whenever a variable is given a value in one segment which is subsequently accessed in another segment, then that variable must be marked as SHARE.

KILL: If the last lisp expression in this segment evaluates to non-NIL then the demon is "killed" (i.e. permanently removed from consideration for interpretation). A missing KILL segment is equivalent to (KILL NIL). The KILL segment is evaluated before TEST or ACT segments.

TEST: The result of the TEST segment is the last expression executed within this segment. It is bound to the local (i.e. implicitly SHAREd) variable TEST (so that the result can be referred to later). If the TEST evaluates to non-NIL, then the +ACT is fired. Otherwise the -ACT is fired. A missing TEST segment is equivalent to (TEST T).

+ACT: After +ACT is evaluated, the entire demon is automatically killed.

-ACT: If there is a -ACT segment and it is evaluated, then the demon is automatically killed. If the TEST segment evaluated to NIL and there was no -ACT, then the demon remains alive.

All demons are interpreted whenever a new word is processed. McDYPAR is designed so that any demon which can "fire" will do so an soon as it is able to. The interpretation of a demon is described via the "pidgin" LISP below:

```
(COND  [ KILL exists and evals to non-NIL
             => kill demon ]

       [ TEST missing or
         TEST exists and evals to non-NIL
             => bind result of TEST to variable TEST
                eval +ACT
                kill demon ]

       [ -ACT exists
             => eval -ACT-part
                kill demon ])
```

Now we are ready to write a demon. Let us choose the demon associated with the OBJECT slot in the INGEST from the lexicon given earlier. The lexical entry for "ate" will now contain the name of a demon (which we will call "EXPECT-HEAD"):

```
(INGEST  ACTOR *
         OBJECT * <== (EXPECT-HEAD 'FOOD))
```

We will define this demon as follows:

```
(DEMON EXPECT-HEAD
    (COMMENT (TEST "expect a con with a given head"
                   "  to occur later in the sentence")
             (ACT  "link this con to my gap"))
    (PARAMS MYCON MYGAP DESIRED-HEAD)
    (KILL (EVAL MYGAP))
    (TEST (SEARCH '(LAMBDA (CON)
                      (EQ (HEAD CON) DESIRED-HEAD))
              MYCON  NIL  'AFT))
    (+ACT (LINK MYCON MYGAP TEST)))
```

All of this needs some explanation: Let us consider in detail how demons are processed and what these particular segments mean.

Spawning A Demon

Initially, when a conceptual representation is added to Working Memory, its associated demons are "spawned". Spawning a demon consists of building a structure (called a D-FORM) which holds an instantiation of that demon, containing: a) the name of the demon and b) any arguments it needs in order to perform its task. These arguments usually include:

1. The CON in Working Memory that the demon is associated with.

2. The GAP that the demon will fill.

3. A description of what the demon expects and possibly the direction in Working Memory to search.

In the case above, McDYPAR will automatically create the following D-FORM:

DEM0 = (EXPECT-HEAD CON3 OBJECT1 FOOD)

which means: 1) DEM0 is an instantiation of the demon EXPECT-

HEAD, 2) DEM0 is attached to CON3 in Working Memory, 3) DEM0 has an expectation for FOOD, and 4) if this expectation is fulfilled then DEM0 will bind it to OBJECT1.

Notice that CON3 and OBJECT1 are nodes appearing in the Working Memory diagram shown earlier. These are passed to DEM0 when McDYPAR processes the "<==" in the lexicon. The last argument, FOOD, is passed explicitly to DEM0 via the expression: "(EXPECT-HEAD 'FOOD)" in the lexicon. At interpretation time, these arguments will be bound to the variables in the PARAMS segment above. In addition, since demon arguments are evaluated at spawning time, the argument FOOD had to be quoted in the lexicon (under the entry "ate").

Given this D-FORM, McDYPAR now has everything it needs in order to interpret DEM0. Also, it should be clear that several instantiations of EXPECT-HEAD may be active at once, each with its own set of arguments. In this case, EXPECT-HEAD represents an expectation for FOOD to occur. In another situation, EXPECT-HEAD could be used to represent an expectation for the recipient of an object, as in "John gave Mary a ..." and would appear in a lexicon under "gave" as follows:

```
gave     (ATRANS ACTOR X
                 OBJECT *
                 TO * <== (EXPECT-HEAD 'HUMAN)
                 FROM X)
```

Now that we have seen a few uses of EXPECT-HEAD, we are ready to examine the definition of EXPECT-HEAD above, in order to see how DEM0 would be interpreted:

First, the parameters MYCON, MYGAP and DESIRED-HEAD are passed the values: CON3, OBJECT1, and FOOD, respectively. Second, the KILL segment is interpreted.

Killing a Demon

Each demon is in charge of determining its own time of death. By seeing if MYGAP already has a value, DEM0 can find out if some other demon has already done the same job. This approach has two advantages:

1. Several demons can work for the same GAP without getting in each other's way -- each communicating with the others,indirectly, through shared arguments (such as MYGAP in this case).

2. Demons do not have to be responsible for, or know about each other. The advantage of this arrangement is in reduced combinatorial complexity. Consider what could happen if demons had to decide when to kill other demons: For instance, suppose demons D1, D2, D3, and D4 were all trying to fill the same gap (each representing different expectations). In this case D1 would have to kill D2, D3, and D4 if it successfully fired first. Likewise, D2 would have to know to kill D1, D3, and D4, if it had fired first, and so on. This combinatoric explosion is avoided in McDYPAR.

Testing A Demon

Next, the TEST segment is evaluated. Although the TEST segment may contain any LISP code, in the demon EXPECT-HEAD it consists of a call to the McDYPAR function SEARCH. SEARCH, which returns a CON in Working Memory as its value, takes the following four parameters:

1. A lambda expression (or function) of one argument. This expression is applied to Working Memory until a CON is found which satisfies the lambda expression.

2. A CON which indicates where to start the search.

3. A lambda expression (or function) of one argument which indicates when to give up the search. An argument of NIL means to give up when there are no more CONs to be examined.

4. A direction to search in -- either BEF (before) or AFT (after) the MYCON in Working Memory.

When the TEST is satisfied, the variable TEST will receive the result of the TEST segment as its value, and if TEST = non-nil, then the +ACT segment will be executed.

The +ACT in this case is: "(LINK MYCON MYGAP TEST)". The McDYPAR function LINK binds the appropriate GAP with the CON which was found, and, in addition, creates back pointers from the CON-found to the GAP which the CON-found is now a part of. Finally, since one of its ACT segments has fired, the demon is automatically killed. The result of all of this will be to bind OBJECT1 with CON4.

III.2.4 Demon Trees

In McDYPAR, demons may themselves spawn other demons. This is a very powerful capability, since it allows for the construction of "demon trees". In order for a demon to spawn other demons, it must execute the following command:

```
(SPAWN    CON    demon-form ... demon-form)
```

where each demon-form is a list consisting of the name of a demon and its arguments. The CON specifies which CON in Working Memory the spawned demons are to be associated with.

Below is a schematic example of a possible "demon tree" of expectations. That is, when EXP-A fires, it also spawns EXP-B and EXP-C, which represent yet other expectations, and so on:

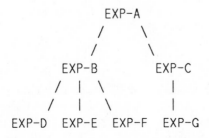

This discrimination tree of demons would be produced in McDYPAR as follows:

```
(DEMON  EXP-A
  (PARAMS MYCON ...)
  (TEST ...)
  (+ACT ... (SPAWN MYCON  (EXP-B  ...)
                          (EXP-C  ...))  ...)))

(DEMON EXP-B
  (PARAMS ...)
  (TEST ...)
  (+ACT  (SPAWN MYCON  (EXP-D ...)
                       (EXP-E ...)
                       (EXP-F ...))))
(DEMON EXP-C

    ...
  (+ACT (SPAWN MYCON  (EXP-G ...))))

(DEMON EXP-D ...)
(DEMON EXP-E ...)
(DEMON EXP-F ...)
(DEMON EXP-G ...)
```

In addition to binding GAPs, demons can perform many other tasks. For example, when a word has more than one possible meaning, the CON loaded in Working Memory is set to NIL. Then one or more disambiguation demons are spawned, whose job it is to decide which meaning that CON should receive (so that its associated GAP demons can then be spawned).

In general, demons usually perform the following tasks:

1. Bind a GAP with some other CON in Working memory.

2. Modify another CON by attaching new information to it. For instance, modification of a CON will occur when parsing the phrase "red apple". In this case a demon

associated with the concept for "red" will attach "COLOR (RED)" to the concept for "apple".

3. Spawn other demons (possibly with new arguments).

4. Disambiguate the CON it is associated with. An example of disambiguation appears in the detailed trace in section III.4.

In addition, demons may be written to:

1. Perform intelligent error correction.

2. Interpret the testing and execution of other demons.

3. Search and construct long-term memory structures -- as for use in a story understanding system.

4. Pass messages to communicate with other demons.

Demons may communicate with each other, but only in the following restricted ways: a) the demon passes arguments to another demon that it is spawning, b) the demon looks at the bindings that other demons have placed on a GAP, and c) the demon places messages on its CON so that other demons may read them.

III.3 Background

DYPAR was originally written in the spring 1979 as an extension to and improvement on McELI [Riesbeck and Schank, 1981], an expectation-based based parser which implemented expectations by means of "requests" [Riesbeck, 1978]. In contrast, DYPAR models expectations by means of processes called "demons". DYPAR-style demons are less constrained than McELI-style requests and DYPAR is similar in spirit to another parser at Yale, called CA [Birnbaum and Selfridge, 1981].

For those readers familiar with McELI, the list below describes, in general terms, some of the improvements which DYPAR-style demons offer over McELI-style requests, and thereby gives some indication of what motivated the creation of DYPAR. Many of the observations which follow have appeared elsewhere and the interested reader should consult [Gershman, 1980] [Birnbaum and Selfridge, 1981].

1. Unlike McELI requests, McDYPAR-style demons have names. Therefore a single demon can be "factored out" and reused in more than one place, simply by referring to its name.

2. Unlike requests in both McELI and CA, McDYPAR-style demons may also take parameters. Thus, many instantiations of the same demon may be active at the same time and a single demon may represent a CLASS of requests.

3. In McELI, requests are organized by means of a stack. This is more efficient, but it is also too restrictive. If the top request fails to "fire", then those requests lying beneath it can not be considered. Therefore everything grinds to a halt. This never happens in DYPAR, since all demons are considered.

4. In McELI, expectations which are order independent cause a combinatoric explosion in the number of branches to specify in a request tree. For example, if A, B, C can occur in any order in a sentence, then with a stack we need the following type of request tree structure:

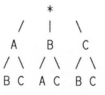

```
          *
       /  |  \
      A   B   C
     / \ / \ / \
     B C A C B C
```

Since demons in McDYPAR "come and go" dynamically, their tree structures rarely get very complicated. In contrast, it is difficult to write McELI-style requests to handle such cases as: "John gave Mary a book", "A book John gave Mary", "John gave a book to Mary", etc.

5. McDYPAR has a Working Memory (WM). It is a doubly-linked queue which can be searched in either direction and which allows ease of insertion and deletion. Since McELI does not have a

working memory, it must maintain a pre-parse request for the type of sentence it expects. Therefore, although McELI could handle "Mary said John walked home.", it could **not** handle "John walked home, said Mary." because the "said Mary" could not have been expected by "walked".

6. McDYPAR is more "bottom-up" than McELI. For example, McELI would parse "John walked home yesterday." by having "walked" expect to hear mention of the time of the action. In contrast, a DYPAR demon associated with "yesterday" would attach a time modification to whatever was the current action. In this way, an expectation for a modifier of the time (of an action) arises only when a time modifier is actually mentioned in the input.

7. McDYPAR uses dynamically created atoms to represent the "gaps" where bindings are to occur. In contrast, McELI uses global variables for GAPs.[65] Therefore, two occurrences of "told" in "John told Mary that Fred told her Bill was sick." will cause the bindings set up by the first "told" to be clobbered by the bindings from the second "told".

8. In McDYPAR, the order in which modifiers occur during parsing is unimportant. This allows modifications to occur on concepts which have already been bound to other concepts. For example, suppose we parse "John walked home yesterday..." as:


```
(PTRANS ACTOR John
        TO   home
        TIME (YESTERDAY))
```


Now suppose the next word encountered is: "afternoon". We'd like to be able to modify (YESTERDAY) to be (YESTERDAY PORTION (AFTERNOON)) without knowing that YESTERDAY is already bound inside a PTRANS. We'd also like the TIME slot in the PTRANS automatically updated as YESTERDAY is updated. This is what happens in DYPAR since, unlike McELI, bindings occur only

---

[65]This is not a problem in ELI.

between atoms. That is, the gap for TIME is TIME0, which is bound
to CON3, where CON3 = (YESTERDAY). When CON3 is updated
to (YESTERDAY PORTION (AFTERNOON)) by a demon associated
with "afternoon", any atom whose value is CON3 (such as TIME0)
will become automatically updated.

9. DYPAR has morphology and "phrasal lexicon" features. (See
exercises in section III.6.)

10. In general, there are two ways to disambiguate a word with
multiple possible senses: 1) **explicitly** -- by attaching to the word
one or more demons (or requests) whose job it is to search memory
and decide which sense is correct, or 2) **automatically** -- by letting
the active context (i.e. the expectations represented by other demons
already spawned) determine which sense is correct.   McELI's
automatic disambiguation feature works by examining the current
request at the top of its stack whenever an ambiguous word is
encountered. This has two weaknesses: First, the ambiguous word
must be disambiguated **at the moment** that it is encountered. Thus,
McELI can **automatically** disambiguate: "strike" in "The union
called a strike." vs "The umpire called a strike." since "umpire" and
"union" supply active expectations (each for a different kind of strike)
at the moment the word "strike" is encountered. So the correct
meaning can be selected by choosing the meaning preferred by the
active expectation.   However, McELI can **not** automatically
disambiguate "strike" in "The strike was called by the union." vs
"The strike was called by the umpire." since the active context needed
occurs AFTER the word "strike" has appeared. Second, McELI-style
automatic disambiguation requires being able to "read" the LISP-
code which implements the expectation which the top request
represents.   This is very difficult and requires that requests be
represented in a non-procedural manner. In contrast, DYPAR does
not have these weaknesses. For a description of how automatic
disambiguation is implemented in DYPAR, see exercise number 9. in
section III.6.

All of the features mentioned above (except for 9 and 10) are
also included in the micro version of DYPAR. The reader should
recognize that any production-style parser (such as McELI, CA or
DYPAR) provides only a bare "skeleton" for managing the control
and execution of dynamic processes (in our case, demons). Therefore,
the bulk of the parser will reside in those demons which represent the
expectations associated with entries in the lexicon. These demons

have to be written by whoever wants to use the parser. The more 'sophisticated' the demons, the more robust the parser. It is in writing such demons that the most interesting issues and problems will arise.

As such, DYPAR provides the foundation upon which the BORIS story understanding and question answering system at Yale has been built. In BORIS, DYPAR demons associated with lexical entries search not only Working Memory, but an Episodic Memory, which represents the story as understood up to that point in the processing. This results in a complete integration of both parsing and memory search processes, thus making memory available in parsing.

III.4 A Detailed Trace, With Associated Lexicon and Demons

III.4.1 Execution Trace

What follows is the output produced verbatim by McDYPAR when parsing the sentence: "John picked up the ball and put it in the box". In the trace, the binding of GAPs is indicated by " <-- ". The rest is almost self-explanatory. The demons and lexical items which appear in this trace are defined immediately after the trace.

```
*(PARSE '(JOHN PICKED UP THE BALL AND DROPPED IT IN THE BOX))


---------------------------------
Processing word: JOHN
---------------------------------
    Adding to *wm*: CONO
        CONO = (HUMAN NAME NAMEO
                      GENDER GENDERO)
    Spawning: DEMO = (SAVE-CHARACTER CONO)

        ======================= DEMO =======================
        T:
        A: Bind the MYCON to the MOST-RECENT-CHARACTER, if there is
            no LOCAL-CHARACTER bind the MYCON to it also
        =========================================================
```

```
    Executing: DEMO = (SAVE-CHARACTER CONO)
    Killing: DEMO = (SAVE-CHARACTER CONO)


--------------------------------
Processing word: PICKED
--------------------------------

    Adding to *wm*: CON1
        CON1 = NIL
    Spawning: DEM1 = (PICK-UP? CON1)


        ======================= DEM1 =======================
        T: If the next word is UP ...

        A: Set the MYCON to the grasp configuration
        ====================================================


    Spawning: DEM2 = (DECIDE? CON1)


        ======================= DEM2 =======================
        T: Search for a person or a physical object after the MYCON

        A: Set the MYCON to the decision configuration
        ====================================================



    Executing: DEM1 = (PICK-UP? CON1)
    Spawning: DEM3 = (EXP CON1 HO HUMAN BEF)


        ======================= DEM3 =======================
        T: Search for a CONCEPT with one of the given CLASSES in the
            given DIRECTION until a boundary is reached.

        A: The CONCEPT is bound to the given GAP.
        ====================================================


    Spawning: DEM4 = (EXP CON1 XO PHYS-OBJ AFT)


        ======================= DEM4 =======================
        T: Search for a CONCEPT with one of the given CLASSES in the
            given DIRECTION until a boundary is reached.

        A: The CONCEPT is bound to the given GAP.
        ====================================================


        CON1 = (GRASP ACTOR HO
```

```
                        OBJECT X0
                        INSTR INSTR0)
        Killing: DEM1 = (PICK-UP? CON1)


        Executing: DEM3 = (EXP CON1 H0 HUMAN BEF)
             H0 <-- CON0
        Killing: DEM3 = (EXP CON1 H0 HUMAN BEF)
        Killing: DEM2 = (DECIDE? CON1)


    ----------------------------------
    Processing word: UP
    ----------------------------------

        Adding to *wm*: CON2
            CON2 = NIL
        Spawning: DEM5 = (IGNOR CON2)


        Executing: DEM5 = (IGNOR CON2)
        Killing: DEM5 = (IGNOR CON2)


    ----------------------------------
    Processing word: THE
    ----------------------------------

        Adding to *wm*: CON3
            CON3 = NIL
        Spawning: DEM6 = (IGNOR CON3)


        Executing: DEM6 = (IGNOR CON3)
        Killing: DEM6 = (IGNOR CON3)


    ----------------------------------
    Processing word: BALL
    ----------------------------------

        Adding to *wm*: CON4
            CON4 = (PHYS-OBJ CLASS CLASS0
                             NAME NAME1)
        Spawning: DEM7 = (SAVE-OBJ CON4)


            ========================= DEM7 =========================
            T:
            A: Bind the MYCON to the MOST-RECENT-OBJECT
            =======================================================


        Executing: DEM7 = (SAVE-OBJ CON4)
        Killing: DEM7 = (SAVE-OBJ CON4)
```

```
    Executing: DEM4 = (EXP CON1 XO PHYS-OBJ AFT)
        XO <-- CON4
    Killing: DEM4 = (EXP CON1 XO PHYS-OBJ AFT)


--------------------------------
Processing word: AND
--------------------------------

    Adding to *wm*: CON5
        CON5 = (*CONJ*)
    Spawning: DEM8 = (IGNOR CON5)

    Executing: DEM8 = (IGNOR CON5)
    Killing: DEM8 = (IGNOR CON5)


--------------------------------
Processing word: DROPPED
--------------------------------

    Adding to *wm*: CON6
    Spawning: DEM9 = (EXP CON6 ACTORO HUMAN BEF)

        ======================= DEM9 =======================
        T: Search for a CONCEPT with one of the given CLASSES in the
           given DIRECTION until a boundary is reached.

        A: The CONCEPT is bound to the given GAP.
        ====================================================


    Spawning: DEM10 = (EXP CON6 THGO PHYS-OBJ AFT)

        ======================= DEM10 ======================
        T: Search for a CONCEPT with one of the given CLASSES in the
           given DIRECTION until a boundary is reached.

        A: The CONCEPT is bound to the given GAP.
        ====================================================


    Spawning: DEM11 = (PREP CON6 TOO (IN INTO ON) (HUMAN PHYS-OBJ) AFT)

        ======================= DEM11 ======================
        T: Search for a CONCEPT with one of the given CLASSES and
           preceded by one of the given PREPOSITIONS

        A: The CONCEPT is bound to the given GAP.
        ====================================================


    CON6 = (PTRANS ACTOR ACTORO
```

```
                        OBJECT THG0
                        TO TO0
                        INSTR INSTR1)
```

```
    Executing: DEM9 = (EXP CON6 ACTOR0 HUMAN BEF)
        ACTOR0 <-- CON0
    Killing: DEM9 = (EXP CON6 ACTOR0 HUMAN BEF)
```

Processing word: IT

```
    Adding to *wm*: CON7
        CON7 = NIL
    Spawning: DEM12 = (FIND-OBJ-REF CON7)
```

```
            ======================= DEM12 =======================
            T:
            A: Set the MYCON to the most recently mentioned object
            =====================================================
```

```
    Executing: DEM12 = (FIND-OBJ-REF CON7)
        CON7 <-- CON4
    Killing: DEM12 = (FIND-OBJ-REF CON7)
```

```
    Executing: DEM10 = (EXP CON6 THG0 PHYS-OBJ AFT)
        THG0 <-- CON7
    Killing: DEM10 = (EXP CON6 THG0 PHYS-OBJ AFT)
```

Processing word: IN

```
    Adding to *wm*: CON8
        CON8 = (PREP IS ISO)
    Spawning: DEM13 = (INS-AFT CON8 (PHYS-OBJ SETTING) PREPOBJ)
```

```
            ======================= DEM13 =======================
            T: Search for a CONCEPT with one of the given CLASSES

            A: Insert the given SLOT with the MYCON as its GAP into
                the CONCEPT.
            =====================================================
```

Processing word: THE

```
    --------------------------------
        Adding to *wm*: CON9
            CON9 = NIL
        Spawning: DEM14 = (IGNOR CON9)


        Executing: DEM14 = (IGNOR CON9)
        Killing: DEM14 = (IGNOR CON9)


    --------------------------------
Processing word: BOX
    --------------------------------

        Adding to *wm*: CON10
            CON10 = (PHYS-OBJ CLASS CLASS1
                             NAME NAME2)


        Executing: DEM13 = (INS-AFT CON8 (PHYS-OBJ SETTING) PREPOBJ)
            CON10 <-- (PHYS-OBJ CLASS CLASS1
                             NAME NAME2
                             PREPOBJ CON8)
        Killing: DEM13 = (INS-AFT CON8 (PHYS-OBJ SETTING) PREPOBJ)


        Executing: DEM11 = (PREP CON6 TOO (IN INTO ON) (HUMAN PHYS-OBJ) AFT)
            TOO <-- CON10
        Killing: DEM11 = (PREP CON6 TOO (IN INTO ON) (HUMAN PHYS-OBJ) AFT)



Result of parse:

        (GRASP ACTOR (HUMAN NAME (JOHN)
                           GENDER (MALE))
               OBJECT (PHYS-OBJ CLASS (GAME-OBJ)
                               NAME (BALL))
               INSTR (MOVE ACTOR (HUMAN NAME (JOHN)
                                       GENDER (MALE))
                          OBJECT (FINGERS)
                          TO (PHYS-OBJ CLASS (GAME-OBJ)
                                     NAME (BALL))))


        (PTRANS ACTOR (HUMAN NAME (JOHN)
                            GENDER (MALE))
                OBJECT (PHYS-OBJ CLASS (GAME-OBJ)
                                NAME (BALL))
                TO (PHYS-OBJ CLASS (CONTAINER)
                            NAME (BOX)
                            PREPOBJ (PREP IS (IN)))
                INSTR (PROPEL ACTOR (GRAVITY)
```

```
                    OBJECT (PHYS-OBJ CLASS (GAME-OBJ)
                                   NAME (BALL))))
```

*

III.4.2 Sample McDYPAR Lexicon

The lexicon below has enough in the way of word definitions to parse the sentence traced above. Words with preferred meanings (i.e. marked by DEF) are placed immediately in Working Memory and their GAP-filling demons are spawned. When a word is ambiguous, however, a CON cell bound to NIL is place in Working Memory and disambiguation demons are spawned.

```
(WORD JOHN
   DEF      (HUMAN NAME    (JOHN)
                   GENDER (MALE))

   DEMONS   (SAVE-CHARACTER)
]


(WORD PICKED
   DEMONS   ((PICK-UP?)(DECIDE?))

   M1     (GRASP ACTOR  H <==(EXP 'HUMAN 'BEF)
                 OBJECT X <==(EXP 'PHYS-OBJ 'AFT)
                 INSTR  (MOVE  ACTOR H
                               OBJECT (FINGERS)
                               TO  X))

   M2     (MBUILD ACTOR  * <==(EXP 'HUMAN 'BEF)
                  MOBJ   (POSS ACTOR  * <==(EXP 'HUMAN 'BEF)
                               OBJECT * <==(EXP '(HUMAN PHYS-OBJ)
                                                         'AFT)))
]


(WORD UP
   DEMONS   (IGNOR))
```

```
(WORD THE
   DEMONS   (IGNOR))


(WORD BALL
   DEF      (PHYS-OBJ CLASS (GAME-OBJ)
                      NAME  (BALL))

   DEMONS   (SAVE-OBJ))


(WORD AND
   DEF      (*CONJ*)

   DEMONS   (IGNOR))


(WORD DROPPED
   DEF   (PTRANS ACTOR * <==(EXP 'HUMAN 'BEF)
                 OBJECT THG <==(EXP 'PHYS-OBJ 'AFT)
                 TO   *  <==(PREP '(IN INTO ON) '(HUMAN PHYS-OBJ)
                                                       'AFT)
                 INSTR  (PROPEL ACTOR (GRAVITY)
                                OBJECT  THG)))


(WORD IT
   DEF      NIL

   DEMONS   (FIND-OBJ-REF))


(WORD IN
   DEF      (PREP IS (IN))

   DEMONS   (INS-AFT '(PHYS-OBJ SETTING) 'PREPOBJ))


(WORD BOX
   DEF      (PHYS-OBJ CLASS (CONTAINER)
                      NAME  (BOX)))
```

III.4.3 Associated Demon Definitions

```
~ Searches for a concept with one of the given classes
~ in the given direction.
~ The found concept is bound to the given gap.
~ Search stops at a boundary (such as a clause or end of sentence)
(DEMON EXP    ~ search within boundary
  (PARAMS MYCON MYGAP CLASSES DIR)
  (COMMENT (TEST "Search for a CONCEPT with one of the given CLASSES"
                 "in the  given DIRECTION until a boundary is reached.")
           (ACT "The CONCEPT is bound to the given GAP."))
  (KILL   (EVAL MYGAP))
  (TEST   (SEARCH '(LAMBDA (CON)
                     (AND (NOT (EQ CON MYCON))
                          (CLASS? (HEAD CON) CLASSES)))
                  MYCON 'STOP-AT-CONJ DIR))
  (+ACT   (LINK MYCON MYGAP TEST)))


~ Stops at a boundary and returns the local character if the boundary
~ is a conjunctive. This is done to handle elisions.
(DE STOP-AT-CONJ (C)
  (OR (AND (CLASS? (HEAD C) '*CONJ*) ~ created by conjuncts/punctuation
           (COND [(CLASS? 'HUMAN CLASSES) => *LOCAL-CHAR*]
                 [T]))
      (CLASS? (HEAD C) 'BOUNDARY)))


~ Saves actors in global variables for pronoun reference.
(DEMON SAVE-CHARACTER
  (PARAMS MYCON)
  (COMMENT (ACT "Bind the MYCON to the MOST-RECENT-CHARACTER, if there"
               "  is no LOCAL-CHARACTER bind the MYCON to it also"))
  (+ACT (SETQ *MOST-RECENT-CHAR* MYCON)
        (AND  (NULL *LOCAL-CHAR*)
              (SETQ *LOCAL-CHAR* MYCON))))


~ Disambiguation for  "pick up"
~ Note:  doesn't consider case of "John picked a girl up at a bar."
(DEMON PICK-UP?
  (PARAMS MYCON)
  (COMMENT (TEST "If the next word is UP ...")
           (ACT "Set the MYCON to the grasp configuration"))
```

```
        (KILL (EVAL MYCON))
        (TEST (EQ *NEXT-W* 'UP))    ~ this allows limited 'look-ahead' ability
        (+ACT (CON-SET MYCON (GET 'PICKED 'M1))))


~ Disambiguation for "pick" to mean "choose" in the sense of "deciding"
(DEMON DECIDE?
    (PARAMS MYCON)
    (COMMENT
        (TEST "Search for a person or a physical object after the MYCON")
        (ACT  "Set the MYCON to the decision configuration"))
    (KILL (EVAL MYCON))
    (TEST (SEARCH '(LAMBDA (CON)
                        (AND (NOT (EQ CON MYCON))
                            (CLASS? (HEAD CON) '(HUMAN PHYS-OBJ))))
                MYCON NIL 'AFT))
    (+ACT (CON-SET MYCON (GET 'PICK 'M2))))


~ Put an IGNOR property on the concept (to indicate that it has
~ been processed and can be ignored)
(DEMON IGNOR
    (PARAMS MYCON)
    (+ACT (PUTPROP MYCON T 'IGNOR)))


~ Saves objects in a global variable for pronoun reference.
(DEMON SAVE-OBJ
    (PARAMS MYCON)
    (COMMENT (ACT "Bind the MYCON to the MOST-RECENT-OBJECT"))
    (+ACT (SETQ *MOST-RECENT-OBJ* MYCON)))


~ In the trace, prepositions are treated like modifiers.
~ E.G. "with Mary" causes the concept for "Mary" to be 'modified'
~ by "PREP-OBJ prep". Demons sensitive to prepositions can then search
~ for a CLASS of object modifiers by prepositions.
~ (This is not the only way to do it, of course.)
(DEMON PREP
    (PARAMS MYCON MYGAP PREPS CLASSES DIR)
    (COMMENT
        (TEST "Search for a CONCEPT with one of the given CLASSES and "
                " preceded by one of the given PREPOSITIONS")
        (ACT "The CONCEPT is bound to the given GAP."))
    (KILL (EVAL MYGAP))
    (TEST (PREP-SEARCH MYCON PREPS CLASSES DIR))
```

```
    (+ACT (LINK MYCON MYGAP TEST)))


~ (all search functions should be defined in terms of the
~ McDYPAR function SEARCH)
(DE PREP-SEARCH (MYCON PREPS CLASSES DIR)
    (SEARCH '(LAMBDA (C)
                (AND (NOT (EQ C MYCON))
                     (CLASS? (HEAD C) CLASSES)
                     (COND [(ATOM PREPS) =>
                            (EQ (PATH '(PREPOBJ IS *) C)
                                PREPS)]
                           [=> (MEMQ (PATH '(PREPOBJ IS *) C)
                                     PREPS)])))
            MYCON NIL DIR))


(DEMON FIND-OBJ-REF
   (PARAMS MYCON)
   (COMMENT (ACT "Set the MYCON to the most recently mentioned object"))
   (+ACT (SET1 MYCON *MOST-RECENT-OBJ*)))


~ This demon performs modifications on other concepts in WM
~ by adding a new SLOT GAP pair to it
(DEMON INS-AFT
   (PARAMS MYCON CLASSES SLOT)
   (COMMENT (TEST "Search for a CONCEPT with one of the given CLASSES")
            (ACT "Insert the given SLOT with the MYCON as its GAP into"
                 " the CONCEPT."))
   (TEST  (SEARCH '(LAMBDA (CON)
                      (AND (NOT (EQ CON MYCON))
                           (CLASS? (HEAD CON) CLASSES)))
                  MYCON NIL 'AFT))
   (+ACT (SET1 TEST (APPEND (EVAL TEST) (LIST SLOT MYCON)))
         (PUTPROP MYCON (LIST TEST SLOT) 'INSIDE)))
```

III.5 McDYPAR As Implemented In TLISP

The code which appears below is implemented in TLISP, a version of LISP originally implemented at Stanford University, and subsequently modified and extended by the University of California at

Irvine, Rutgers University, and Yale. The interested reader, who is already familiar with LISP, can refer to [Meehan, 1979] for a description of UCI-Rutgers LISP. Readers who lack familiarity with programming languages and want an simplified introduction to LISP can read [Weissman, 1967]. Programmers unfamiliar with LISP can read [Winston and Horn, 1981].

A number of macros are available in TLISP and appear in the code for MCDYPAR below. These macros include: LOOP, FOR, LET, and the readmacros "?" and "'".

LET is used to create local variables and takes the form:

```
(LET  [var-1 val-1
        ...
       var-n val-n]
   sequence-of-expressions)
```

which is equivalent to:

```
( (LAMBDA (var-1 ... var-n)
      sequence-of-expressions)
   val-1 ... val-n )
```

LOOP can be represented in terms of PROG with GO but they both provide structured looping capabilities without the need for GOTOs. For instance, (LOOP (DO (code))) is equivalent to (PROG L (code) (GO L)). Exits to LOOP are provided by the keywords WHILE and UNTIL. Variables within the loop can be initialized by use of INITIAL.

The function FOR replaces all mapping functions. For instance, (FOR (x IN '(A B C)) (DO (PRINT x))) is equivalent to (MAP (FUNCTION PRINT) '(A B C)). The expression (FOR (x IN '(A B C)) (SAVE x)) returns the list (A B C) and so is equivalent to (MAPCAR (FUNCTION CAR) '(A B C)).

Readmacros provide the ability to execute user-defined functions at read time. For instance, the readmacro "'" inserts "QUOTE" before its argument, so 'DOG will become (QUOTE DOG) at read time.

A complete discussion of LET, FOR, LOOP, and readmacros appears in [Charniak, Riesbeck, McDermott, 1980], along with their implementation.

One final note: In TLISP, if a function is passed fewer arguments than the number of parameters specified in it definition, then the remaining parameters are automatically bound to NIL, so given the definition (DE FOO (X Y Z) ...) an invocation (FOO 'BAZ) causes X to be bound with BAZ while Y and Z are bound with NIL.

```
~*********************************************************************
~                    McDYPAR        (version 1, JAN '81)
~*********************************************************************

~ makes sentence available for parsing. loops through word tasks and
~ demon tasks, printing out the result at the end of the sentence.
~ set up as tasks so they can be altered dynamically
(DE PARSE (SENTENCE)
  (SETQ *S* SENTENCE)
  (INIT-GLOB)                   ~initialize global variables
  (LOOP
     [INITIAL *GO-ON*  T] ~get it started
     [WHILE *GO-ON* ]     ~set to nil by some process to stop parsing
                          ~(usually will be end of sentence)
     [DO (WORD-TASKS) (DEMON-TASKS)])
  (FIN)                     ~print the resulting parse
  (ASCII 0) )               ~return nothing


~ initialize global control variables
(DE INIT-GLOB ()
  (SETQ *CURR-W* NIL)             ~ the current word being parsed
  (SETQ *DEMON-FIRED* NIL)        ~ set to T every time a demon fires
  (SETQ *CURR-DEMON* NIL)         ~ demon currently executing
  (SETQ *MOST-RECENT-OBJ* NIL)  ~ most recently mentioned object
  (SETQ *MOST-RECENT-CHAR* NIL)~ most recently mentioned character
  (SETQ *LOCAL-CHAR* NIL)         ~ local actor
  (SETQ *WM* NIL) )               ~ working memory (a QUEUE of cd-atms)
```

```
~ this readmacro causes ?... in BUILDs occuring below to
~ be replaced by (*VAR* ...) during read-time (i.e. dskin time)
(DRM /? (LAMBDA ()
           (LIST '*VAR* (READ) ~ readmacro used in BUILD function


~ outputs top level con structures in wm once the parse is done
~ this function choses only the highest level CONs in memory
~ (ie ones that are not INSIDE other concepts)
(DE FIN ()
   (PRETTY
     (LOOP [INITIAL CON *WM*
                     UNUSED NIL]
           [UNTIL (NULL CON)]
           [DO (AND (NOT (GET CON 'INSIDE))
                    (NOT (GET CON 'IGNOR))
                    (PUSH CON UNUSED))]
           [NEXT CON (GET CON 'BEF)] ~ since *wm* points to a queue
           [RESULT UNUSED])))


~ pretty first expands each cd-atm and then prints it
~ OUT is an augmented MSG function.  The keyword CD tell OUT
~ to pretty-print the object assuming a McDYPAR concept-sytax.
~ In general, (OUT flag ...)  is equal to  (AND flag (MSG ...))
(DE PRETTY (L)
   (OUT |PO T T T "Result of parse: " T)
   (FOR (CON IN L)
        (DO (OUT |PO T 4 (CD (EXPAND CON)) T))))
```

III.5.1 Word Tasks

```
~ updates and loads each new word
(DE WORD-TASKS ()
   (SETQ *PREV-W* *CURR-W*)
   (SETQ *CURR-W* (POP *S*))
   (SETQ *NEXT-W* (CAR *S*))
   (COND [(NULL *CURR-W*) => (SETQ *GO-ON* NIL)] ~ stop parsing at end
         [ => (RUN-WORD *CURR-W*)])  )


~ runs word if it has been defined
(DE RUN-WORD (WORD)
   (OUT |P T T "------------------------------"
           T "Processing word: " WORD
```

```
            T "-------------------------------")
    (COND
        [(GET WORD 'WORD)        ~ if it is a word
          => (LOAD WORD)]        ~ load word definition
        [ => (OUT |P " -- is ignored")]])))
```

III.5.2 Code To Handle Declarative Notation For Word Senses

```
~ load the word into working memory spawning any demons and setting the
~ definition if it is known.
(DE LOAD (WORD)
    (LET [CON (ADD-WM (NEWSYM CON))
         DEF (GET WORD 'DEF)
         DEM (GET WORD 'DEMONS)]
        (COND
            [DEF =>                ~ if there is an unambiguous definition ...
              (SET CON
                   (SPLIT-CONFIG CON DEF))]~ then set the concept to that def
            [=> (SET CON NIL)])            ~ else set it to nil
        (OUT |P T 8 CON " = " (CD (EVAL CON)))
        (AND DEM (SPAWN-DFORMS CON DEM)))) ~ if there are demons spawn them


~ places a con at front of the queue, with bef and aft pointers set
~ bef points to all con atoms occurring before this con in time
~ aft = all occurring later in time
(DE ADD-WM (CON)
    (OUT |P T 4 "Adding to *wm*: " CON)
    (PUTPROP CON *CURR-W* 'WORD)              ~ save word that caused this
    (COND [(NULL *WM*) => (SETQ *WM* CON)] ~ if this is the first word
          [ => (PUTPROP CON *WM* 'BEF)     ~ then initalize wm
               (PUTPROP *WM* CON 'AFT)
               (SETQ *WM* CON)]) )


~ A word definition in the lexicon should be in configuration form.
~ A configuration (config) is a CD structure with any gap-filling
~ demons  associated with it.  The syntax for specifying a config is:
~    config --> NIL | (pred) | (pred  slot-name  spec
~                                           ...
~                                      slot-name  spec)
~    spec -->   config | gap-atom [ <==(gapdform ... gapdform) ]
~    gap-atom --> atom |  *
```

```
~
~  where: (1) | means "or"
~          (2) pred and slot-name are atoms
~          (3) gapdform is a demon-form missing
~                 the con and gap arguments
~          (4) [] indicates optionality
~          (5) * indicates that the gap-node receives
~                 the associatedslot-name as its newsym name


~ separates demons from config and returns the appropriate
~ structure with gap-atoms created, etc
(DE SPLIT-CONFIG (CON CONFIG)
   (AND CONFIG
        (CONS (CAR CONFIG) (SPLIT-REST CON (CDR CONFIG)))))


~ split-rest takes a list of form:  (slot filler ... slot filler)
~ where each filler may be followed by:  <== (-dform-)
~ It returns a singly atomized structure.
(DE SPLIT-REST (CON  REST)
   (LOOP [INITIAL STRUC NIL      ~ frame with newsym-ed gaps
                  SLOT NIL       ~ ie slot-name or <==
                  FILLER NIL     ~ ie *, atom, or (-dform-)
                  GAP  NIL       ~ name to replace * with
                  DFORMS NIL]    ~ gap filling demon forms
         [WHILE REST]
         [DO (SETQ SLOT (POP REST))
             (SETQ FILLER (POP REST))
             (SETQ STRUC (APPEND1 STRUC SLOT))  ~ slot-names are copied
             (COND [(NULL FILLER)    => (EMPTY-GAP)]
                   [(CONSP FILLER)   => (CONFIG-GAP)]
                   [(EQ FILLER '*)   => (*-GAP)]
                   [(LITATOM FILLER) => (ATM-GAP)])]
         [NEXT STRUC (APPEND1 STRUC GAP)]
         [RESULT STRUC] ))


~ if the gap position is NIL,
~ then create a gap-node with the value NIL
(DE EMPTY-GAP ()
   (SETQ  GAP (EVAL (LIST 'NEWSYM SLOT)))
   (SET GAP NIL))


~ if the gap position holds an embedded structure
```

```
~ then recursively spawn any demons for that structure
(DE CONFIG-GAP ()
   (SETQ  GAP (EVAL (LIST 'NEWSYM SLOT)))
   (SET GAP (SPLIT-CONFIG CON FILLER)))


~ if the gap position holds a  "*"
~ then it must have "<==" and demons following, so spawn these demons
(DE *-GAP ()
   (SETQ  GAP (EVAL (LIST 'NEWSYM SLOT)))
   (SET GAP NIL)
   (POP REST) ~ ignore "<=="
   (SETQ DFORMS (POP REST)) ~ get demons and spawn them
   (SPAWN-DFORMS CON DFORMS GAP))


~ if the gap position holds an atom
~ then  it may or may not be followed by demons
~    if demons do follow it,
~    then save the atom so that other references to it get the same GAP
(DE ATM-GAP ()
   (COND
       [(EQ (CAR REST) '<==)  ~ is followed by demons
         => (SETQ GAP (EVAL (LIST 'NEWSYM FILLER)))
            (SET GAP NIL)
            (PUSH (CONS FILLER GAP) *GAP-ALIST*)
            (POP REST)  ~ remove " <== "
            (SETQ DFORMS (POP REST))
            (SPAWN-DFORMS CON DFORMS GAP)]
       [ => (SETQ GAP (CDR (ASSOC FILLER *GAP-ALIST*)))
            (OR GAP (SETQ GAP FILLER))]))


~ holds a list of the gap names
(DV *GAP-ALIST* NIL)
```

III.5.3 Demon Management

```
~ Currently, go thru each con in *wm*, testing all the demons of each.
~ If any demon fires, then (after all have been tested) go back thru
~ con atms again (since one firing might allow a previously tested demon
~ to now fire)
(DE DEMON-TASKS ()
   (LOOP
      [INITIAL *DEMON-FIRED*  T]    ~get it started
      [WHILE *DEMON-FIRED* ]
      [NEXT  *DEMON-FIRED*  NIL]    ~reset for each loop
```

```
        [DO (EXAMINE-ALL-D-AGENDAS *WM*)]))


(DE EXAMINE-ALL-D-AGENDAS (CON)
  (LOOP [WHILE CON]
        [DO (FOR (D-ATM IN (GET CON 'D-AGENDA))  ~ examine one d-agenda
            (DO (SETQ *CURR-DEMON* D-ATM)
                (RUN-DEMON-ATM D-ATM CON)))]
        [NEXT CON (GET CON 'BEF)]))
```

III.5.4 Demon Interpreter Functions

```
~   Note:  variables that the Killpart wants to pass to testpart
~          or that testpart wants passed to  actpart ,etc.
~          should be marked SHARE and then just SETQ-ed
~   Note:  an empty test part is equivalent to (TEST T)
(DE RUN-DEMON-ATM (D-ATM CON)
  (LET [D-FORM (EVAL D-ATM)]    ~ d-form is named demon
    (LET [D-NAME (CAR D-FORM)
          ARGUMS (CDR D-FORM)
          D-BODY NIL]
      (SETQ D-BODY (GET D-NAME 'DEMON))
      (PARAM-ENVIRON D-NAME D-BODY ARGUMS  D-ATM CON))))


~ set up parameter environment
~ (if you don't understand apply# and lambda, read
~ Artificial Intelligence Programming by
~ by Charniak, McDermott, and Riesbeck  or any book on LISP
~ Or, if you want a formal treatment, read about
~ Alonzo Church's 'Lambda Calculus')
~ Once params have been bound with values from argums,
~ then share-environ is executed within this binding environment
(DE PARAM-ENVIRON (D-NAME D-BODY ARGUMS D-ATM CON)
  (COND
    [ARGUMS
      => (LET [PARAMS (CDR (ASSOC 'PARAMS D-BODY))]
           (APPLY#
             (LIST 'LAMBDA PARAMS
                          '(SHARE-ENVIRON D-NAME D-BODY D-ATM CON))
             ARGUMS))]
    [ => (SHARE-ENVIRON D-NAME D-BODY D-ATM CON)]))

~ set up shared variable environment and
```

```
~ initialize them to nil
~ note:  (apply# (lambda args ...)) causes args to each get nil
~            when apply# is missing its second argument.
(DE SHARE-ENVIRON (D-NAME D-BODY D-ATM CON)
   (LET [SHARE-VARS (CDR (ASSOC 'SHARE D-BODY))]
      (COND
         [SHARE-VARS
            => (APPLY#
                  (LIST 'LAMBDA SHARE-VARS
                     '(RUN-DEMON D-NAME D-BODY D-ATM CON)))]
         [ => (RUN-DEMON D-NAME D-BODY D-ATM CON)])))


~ actually interprets the demon keyword-parts
(DE RUN-DEMON (D-NAME D-BODY D-ATM CON)
   (LET [KILL-PART (ASSOC 'KILL D-BODY)
         TEST-PART (ASSOC 'TEST D-BODY)
         +ACT-PART (ASSOC '+ACT D-BODY)
         -ACT-PART (ASSOC '-ACT D-BODY)
         TEST NIL]  ~ so +act-part can refer to result of test-part
      (COND
         [(AND KILL-PART (EVAL (CONS 'DO (CDR KILL-PART))))
            => (KILL-DEMON D-ATM CON)]
         [(OR (NULL TEST-PART)   ~ empty test-part same as: (test t)
              (AND (SETQ TEST (EVAL (CONS 'DO (CDR TEST-PART))))))
            => (OUT |P T T 4 "Executing: " D-ATM " = " (EVAL D-ATM))
               (EVAL (CONS 'DO (CDR +ACT-PART)))
               (KILL-DEMON D-ATM CON)]
         [(AND -ACT-PART (NULL TEST))   ~ test-part evaled to nil
            => (OUT |P T T 4 "Executing -ACT of " D-ATM " = " (EVAL D-ATM))
               (EVAL (CONS 'DO (CDR -ACT-PART)))
               (KILL-DEMON D-ATM CON)])))


~ if the test is true always kill the demon
(DE KILL-DEMON (D-ATM CON)
   (OUT |P T 4 "Killing: " D-ATM " = " (EVAL D-ATM))
   (LET [DFORMS (GET CON 'D-AGENDA)]
      (SETQ DFORMS (REMOVE1ST D-ATM DFORMS))  ~ remove the demon
      (SETQ *DEMON-FIRED* T)    ~ at top level call demon tasks again
      (PUTPROP CON DFORMS 'D-AGENDA)))


~ returns a list with first elem at top level removed
(DE REMOVE1ST (ELEM L)
   (LET [RESTL (MEMBER ELEM L)]
```

```
        (COND [RESTL => (APPEND (LDIFF L RESTL) (CDR RESTL))]
              [ => L ]
]
```

III.5.5 Functions to Spawn Demons

```
~ form is:  (SPAWN con  dform-1... dform-n )
~ where con is an atom, and dform is a named demon:
~      (name arg-1...arg-n)
~ spawn does the following:
~      a. replaces the args in a dform  with their values
~      b. creates a d-atom whose value is the new dform
~      b. pushes each d-atom onto a d-agenda under a specified con
~   NOTE:  spawn should be called from user defined demons.
~          spawn-dforms is called at word definition time.

(DF SPAWN ($GRP)
  (LET [CON (EVAL (CAR $GRP))
        DFORMS (CDR $GRP)]
    (FOR (DFORM IN DFORMS) (DO (SPAWN-DFORM CON DFORM)))))


~ adds in the mycon and mygap for spawning
~ when the demon occurs after a "<==" in a word sense
(DE SPAWN-DFORMS (CON DFORMS GAP)
  (AND (ATOM (CAR DFORMS))  (SETQ DFORMS (LIST DFORMS)))
  (FOR (DFORM IN DFORMS)
    (DO (LET [HEAD (CAR DFORM)
             ARGS (COND [GAP =>    ~ evaluates args at spawn-time
                              (APPEND (BUILD '((QUOTE ?CON) (QUOTE ?GAP)))
                                      (CDR DFORM))]  ~ to be evaled
                        [=> (APPEND (BUILD '((QUOTE ?CON)))
                                    (CDR DFORM))])]
        (SPAWN-NAME CON HEAD ARGS)))))


~ like spawn-dforms except mycon and mygap assumed already
~ inserted in body.  this function is called in SPAWN
(DE SPAWN-DFORM (CON DFORM)
  (LET [HEAD (CAR DFORM)
        BODY (CDR DFORM)]
    (COND
```

```
           [(GET HEAD 'DEMON) => (SPAWN-NAME CON HEAD BODY)]
           [ => (OUT |P T 4 "Dform not spawned since name: "
                          HEAD " undefined")]])))


~ eval args and form their vals into a new dform with name at head
~ then put d-atom into a d-agenda on the con
(DE SPAWN-NAME (CON HEAD ARGS)
  (COND
     [(NULL (GET HEAD 'DEMON))
       => (OUT |P T 4 HEAD " not spawned since undefined")]
     [ => (LET [NEW-ARGS  (FOR (ARG IN ARGS) (SAVE (EVAL ARG)))]
            (LET [D-ATOM (NEWSYM DEM)]
              (SET D-ATOM (CONS HEAD NEW-ARGS))
              (OUT |P T 4 "Spawning: " D-ATOM " = " (EVAL D-ATOM))
              (PRINT-COMMENT (GET HEAD 'DEMON) D-ATOM)
              (D-AGENDIZE D-ATOM)))]))


~ The agendas are currently just lists
~ Push the demon onto the agenda
(DE D-AGENDIZE (D-ATOM)
   (PUTPROP CON (CONS D-ATOM (GET CON 'D-AGENDA)) 'D-AGENDA))
```

III.5.6 Functions to Define Words and Demons

```
~ template for word:
~   (WORD   name
~       DEF        config
~       DEMONS     dforms
~       M1         config
~          ...
~       Mn         config   )
~
~  NOTE: If the word is unambiguous its config  should  be  put  in
~        the def field.  If it is ambiguous, the configs associated
~        with the various  meanings  should  be  placed  in  fields
~        m1 - mn with the def field remaining blank.

(DF WORD (L)
  (LET [NAME (POP L)]
    (PUTPROP NAME T 'WORD)     ~ indicates item is defined as a word
    (LOOP [INITIAL INDIC NIL   ~ put all the properties on the word
                   VAL NIL ]
```

```
            [WHILE L]
            [DO (SETQ INDIC (POP L))
                (SETQ VAL (POP L))
                (COND [(EQ INDIC 'VALUE) => (SET NAME VAL)]
                      [ => (PUTPROP NAME VAL INDIC)])])]
            [RESULT NAME])))
```

```
~ Function to define demons.
~ <The user can add any other keywords, but they are ignored by the
~  demon interpreter>
(DF DEMON (L)
  (LET [NAME (CAR L)]
    (PUTPROP NAME (CDR L) 'DEMON)
    NAME))
```

III.5.7 Standard Utility Functions Used By Demons

```
 ~ Binds a GAP with a CON in Working Memory and
~ marks the CON as INSIDE the MYCON associated with this GAP
~ During tracing, prints: "GAP <-- CON " when the binding occurs.
(DE LINK (MYCON MYGAP CON-FOUND)
  (AND MYGAP
    (LET [MYSLOT (SLOT MYGAP MYCON)]
      (AND (LITATOM CON-FOUND)
           (PUTPROP CON-FOUND (LIST MYCON MYSLOT MYGAP) 'INSIDE))
      (SET1 MYGAP CON-FOUND))))
```

```
~ Sets the CON to the appropriate meaning when
~ disambiguation has occurred.
(DE CON-SET (MYCON MEANING)
   (SET MYCON (SPLIT-CONFIG MYCON MEANING))
   (OUT |P T 8 MYCON " = " (CD (EVAL MYCON))))
```

```
~ returns non-nil if atm is a member of class (searches recursively
~ thru atm's classes for this class)
(DE CLASS? (ATM CLASS)
  (COND
     [(CONSP ATM) => (OUT T T "CLASS? expects atomic 1st arg")]
     [(AND ATM (COND [(CONSP CLASS) => (MEMQ ATM CLASS)]
                     [=> (EQ ATM CLASS)]))]
     [(LET [CLASSES (GET ATM 'CLASS)]
```

```
          (OR (FOR (CL IN CLASSES)
                  [WHEN (CLASS? CL CLASS)]
                  [STOP])
              (FOR (NEXT-CLASS IN CLASSES)
                   (WHEN (CLASS? NEXT-CLASS CLASS))
                   (STOP)) ]
]


~ path is used to selectively examine the contents of
~ conceptual structures in Working Memory.
~ It allows the user to ignore the fact that
~ all the bindings are done via atoms.
~ E.g.  given X = (INGEST ACTOR (HUMAN NAME (JOHN)
~                                       GENDER (MALE))
~                        OBJECT (FOOD TYPE (LOBSTER)))
~ Then (PATH '(ACTOR NAME) X) returns (JOHN)
~ and  (PATH '(OBJECT TYPE *) X) returns LOBSTER
(DE PATH (L CD)
  (COND [(NULL CD) => NIL]
        [(ATOM CD) => (PATH L (EVAL CD))]
        [(NULL L) => CD]
        [(ATOM L) => (OUT |P T T "PATH expects 1st arg to be a list")]
        [(EQ (CAR L) '*) => (CAR CD)]
        [ => (PATH-REST L (CDR CD))]
]


(DE PATH-REST (L RV-LIS)
  (LET [VAL (CADR (MEMQ (CAR L) RV-LIS))]
    (COND [VAL => (PATH (CDR L) VAL)]
]



~ this function is to be used in place of LIST when building CDs
~ that have many constants and few variables
~ e.g. (LIST 'PTRANS 'ACTOR X 'OBJECT Y 'TO (LIST 'PERSON 'NAME Z))
~ is the same as:
~        (BUILD '(PTRANS ACTOR ?X OBJECT ?Y TO (PERSON NAME ?Z))
(DE BUILD (CD)
  (COND [(ATOM CD) => CD]
        [(IS-VAR CD) => (EVAL (CADR CD))]
        [ => (CONS (BUILD (CAR CD))
                   (BUILD (CDR CD))) ]
]


~ this function is used with the ? readmacro appearing
~ at the beginning of the code
```

```
(DE IS-VAR (X)
  (AND (CONSP X) (EQ (CAR X) '*VAR*)))


~ expand replaces every gap with its value
(DE EXPAND (CD)
  (COND [(NULL CD) => NIL]
        [(ATOM CD) => (EXPAND (EVAL CD))]
        [ => (CONS (CAR CD) (EXPAND-SF (CDR CD)))]
]

~ expand-sf expects a list of slot-fillers
(DE EXPAND-SF (SF)
  (LOOP [INITIAL ANS NIL]
        [UNTIL (NULL SF)]
        [NEXT ANS (APPEND1 ANS (POP SF))            ~ slot
              ANS (APPEND1 ANS (EXPAND (POP SF)))] ~ filler
        [RESULT ANS]
]


~ eg given cd-atm = (head slot fil slot fil ...), returns head
(DE HEAD (CD)
  (COND [(NULL CD) => NIL]
        [(ATOM CD) => (HEAD (EVAL CD))] ~ in case is atomized
        [ => (CAR CD)]
]

~ given slot-name and cd, returns the top-level gap-name
~ of that slot-name (NOT the gap value)
(DE GAP (SLOT CD)
  (COND [(NULL CD) => NIL]
        [(ATOM CD) => (GAP SLOT (EVAL CD))]
        [ => (LET [REST (MEMBER SLOT CD)]
              (CADR REST))]))


~ given a gap (NOT the gap value) and a cd,
~ returns the top-level slot-name that has
~    gap-name associated with it
(DE SLOT (GAP CD)
  (COND [(NULL CD) => NIL]
        [(ATOM CD) => (SLOT GAP (EVAL CD))]
        [ => (LET [REST (MEMBER GAP (REVERSE CD))]
              (CADR REST))]))
```

III.5.8 Search Utilities

```
~ SEARCH takes four parameters:
~ 1. what to look for:          a fcn-name or lambda-exp of one arg
~ 2. where to start looking:    a con atm (or variable *wm*)
~ 3. when to give up looking:   a fcn-name of lambda-exp of one arg
~ 4. what direction to look in: BEF or AFT
~ NOTE: a. it tries 3. on a con atm first, and then tries 1.
~         b. it quits if runs out of atms to look at
~ It returns either NIL, or a con atm found
(DE SEARCH (TEST-FCN START STOP-FCN DIR)
  (COND [(NULL DIR) => (SETQ START *WM*) ~ default start is *wm*
                       (SETQ DIR 'BEF)]) ~ default direction is before
  (LOOP [INITIAL FOUND NIL
                 PTR   START]
        [UNTIL (OR (NULL PTR)
                   (AND STOP-FCN
                        (LET [ST-VAL (APPLY# STOP-FCN (LIST PTR))]
                          (COND [(EQ ST-VAL T)]
                                [ST-VAL => (SETQ FOUND T) ~ for result
                                           (SETQ PTR ST-VAL)]))))]
        [UNTIL
          (SETQ FOUND (APPLY# TEST-FCN (LIST PTR)))]
        [NEXT PTR (GET PTR DIR)]
        [RESULT (AND FOUND PTR)]))


~ Look for class throughout wm
(DE FIND-WM (CLASS MYCON)
  (SEARCH '(LAMBDA (CON)
             (AND (NOT (EQ CON MYCON))
                  (CLASS? (HEAD CON) CLASS)))
          *WM* NIL 'BEF))
```

III.5.9 Tracing Functions

```
(DV |P  T) ~ flags for tracing parser fcns, demons, setql, set1
(DV |PO T) ~ flags for printing resulting parser output
(DV |C  T) ~ flags for demon comment message

~ like set but used for tracing
(DE SET1 (A B)
  (SET A B)
  (OUT |P T 8 A " <-- " (CD B))
```

```
   B
]

~ prints out the comment field of a demon
(DE PRINT-COMMENT (BODY D-ATM)
  (LET [COMMENT (CDR (ASSOC 'COMMENT BODY))]
    (AND |C COMMENT
      (LET [TEST (CDR (ASSOC 'TEST COMMENT))
            ACT  (CDR (ASSOC 'ACT COMMENT))]
        (OUT |C T T 8 "========================= " D-ATM
                    " =========================="
              T 8 "T:")
        (FOR (STRING IN TEST)
          [DO (OUT |C (T 13) STRING T)])
        (OUT |C T 8 "A:")
        (FOR (STRING IN ACT)
          [DO (OUT |C (T 13) STRING T)])
        (OUT |C 8 "=========================="
                  "=============================" T)))))


~ ********************* END CODE ****************************
```

III.6 Exercises

The following exercises involve extending McDYPAR in various directions in order to approach the capabilities of DYPAR. Each of these exercises can easily grow into large projects, depending upon the interests of the students, the problems they encounter, and the generality of their solutions.

Before attempting these exercises, it is assumed that the student has gained some familiarity with McDYPAR by writing new demons and word definitions for its lexicon in order to parse sentences similar to the one given in the trace. Here are a few suggestions:

```
1. John gave Mary a book.
   --> (ATRANS ACTOR (HUMAN NAME (JOHN)
                            GENDER (MALE))
```

```
              OBJECT (PHYS-OBJ TYPE (BOOK))
              TO (HUMAN NAME (MARY)
                        GENDER (FEMALE))
              FROM (HUMAN NAME (JOHN)
                        GENDER (MALE)))
```

2. Fred told Mary that John eats lobster.
```
   --> (MTRANS
          ACTOR (HUMAN NAME (FRED)
                      GENDER (MALE))
          OBJECT (INGEST ACTOR (HUMAN NAME (FRED)
                                     GENDER (MALE))
                         OBJECT (FOOD TYPE (LOBSTER)))
          FROM  (HUMAN NAME (FRED)
                      GENDER (MALE))
          TO  (HUMAN NAME (MARY)
                      GENDER (FEMALE)))
```

In the exercises which follow, many semantic representations
(which McDYPAR should produce for each sentence) have **NOT** been
specified. Instead, it has been left up to the student to decide upon a
representation which seems appropriate. This has been done since the
issue of what constitutes an appropriate representation is too
complicated to be discussed here.

1. Add morphological analysis to McDYPAR so that regular
   suffixes can be handled. **MORPHOLOGY** should
   function as follows:

   a. If a word is not recognized, then morphological
      analysis will try to break up the word into a
      recognizable ROOT and ENDING. (This can be
      done efficiently by using a discrimination tree
      where each path in the tree represents a particular
      suffix.) If successful, the meaning of the ROOT is
      added to Working Memory and any demons
      associated with both the ROOT and the ENDING
      are spawned. You will have to decide how the
      demons associated with the ENDING will modify

the meaning of the ROOT.

b. Some standard suffixes to handle are: "ed", "ly", "es", "ing", "able", "ness".   For example, "walked" would be defined as follows:

```
(WORD WALK
    <ptrans configuration + demons> )

(SUFFIX ED
    <demons to add  TIME = (PAST)
     to the meaning associated with
     the ROOT if the ROOT's meaning
     is a CD act>   )
```

c. Augment MORPHOLOGY so that it handles doubled consonants and silent "e", as in "hopped" and "hoped". (Is there anything which can be done about irregular verbs? How do people handle them?)

2. Some people have argued that parsing does not always occur at a word-for-word level [Becker, 1975].   Rather, language is full of larger phrases which are parsed as single units.

a. Add an EXPRESSION feature to McDYPAR so that idiomatic expressions can be parsed directly, thus creating a "phrasal lexicon". Examples of expressions are: "had a fit", "bumped into", "walked out on", "who to turn to", "in case". E.g. if you enter the following into the lexicon:

```
(EXPRESSION (HAVING A FIT)
    <definition + demons>   )
```

then, when McDYPAR encounters this expression

in the input, it will treat it as a single unit, creating a single conceptualization in Working Memory.

b. Augment the EXPRESSION feature so that MORPHOLOGY operates while the expression is being processed. Thus, "having a fit" would be recognized even though only "have a fit" was entered in the lexicon.

3. Give McDYPAR the capability to handle simple modifiers. One way to do this involves writing a single demon which attaches any modifier to whatever object follows. This demon should be spawned whenever a modifier is encountered. Test your demon on the following examples:

```
a. "the red book" --> (PHYS-OBJ
                           TYPE (BOOK)
                           COLOR (RED))


b. "a fat old man" --> (HUMAN
                           AGE (GT-NORM)
                           WEIGHT (GT-NORM))


c. "an afternoon picnic" --> (MEAL TIME
                                  (GT-12OCLOCK))
```

Should the same demon be able to handle all of these examples?

4. Implement a PASSIVE capability, so that McDYPAR can handle such things as "The apple was eaten by John." There are numerous ways in which this can be accomplished.

a. One way is to associate a demon with auxiliary verbs. This demon would expect a CD act with TIME = (PAST). If this expectation were fulfilled, then the auxiliary would be marked PASSIVE. Demons associated with CD acts would have to check for PASSIVE before deciding, for example, whether to fill an ACTOR slot with the subject or with the object of a "by".

b. Another way involves associating a demon with past participle forms of verbs (and/or with the suffix "ed"). If an auxiliary verb were found in Working Memory, then "passive demons" would be spawned.

c. Other methods involve letting the demons bind the ACTOR and OBJECT slots "as normal" and then have a demon switch the bindings once the passive construction has been recognized.

d. Test your implementation of passive on such examples as: "Mary was given a book by John." and "A book was given Mary by John."

5. Add pronoun reference demons to McDYPAR so that it can handle such examples as:

a. "John went home. He kissed his wife Ann."

b. "John told Bill that he was hungry."

c. "Bill was hit by a car. John saw that he was bleeding."

What problem do you encounter in b and c? Is there a general solution to this problem?

6. Augment McDYPAR so that it can handle a variety of complex sentences, involving conjunctions, subordinate clauses, etc. Make such your system can handle the following example: (which will appear later)

"George was having lunch at a restaurant
when the waitress spilled coffee on him."

7. Noun groups pose a special problem. For example, if GRASP simply has a demon expecting a physical object, then "John picked up the phone book." will be parsed to (GRASP OBJECT (PHONE)) with the word "book" left over. Therefore, add a feature so that noun groups can be parsed before demons "outside" the noun group get a chance to inadvertently bind their gap to the wrong object. Try your solution out on the following kinds of examples:

    a. "John picked up a phone book."

```
where "phone" is defined as  (PHYS-OBJ
                                  TYPE (PHONE))
      "book"       "        (PHYS-OBJ
                                  TYPE (BOOK))
but "phone book" results in:
      (PHYS-OBJ TYPE (BOOK)
            ENABLES ($PHONE-CALL))
```

    b. "John threw a dog biscuit
        at the Italian store window."

```
where "dog bone" parses to something like:
      (FOOD
          TYPE (BUISCUIT)
          ENABLES (S-HUNGER
                      ACTOR (ANIMAL
                                TYPE (DOG))))
```

```
and "clothing store window" parses
      to something like:
      (PHYS-OBJ
          TYPE (WINDOW)
          PART-OF
              (STRUCTURE
```

```
TYPE (STORE)
PRODUCT
    (PHYS-OBJ
        TYPE (CLOTHES))))
```

Should these noun groups have been defined as EXPRESSIONs? Should "high school sorority play" also be an EXPRESSION?

8. Define demons for wh-words, such as "why", "who", "how" and "where" so that McDYPAR can answer simple questions. Try it out on the following examples:

```
story:   "John went home because
          he was tired."

a.   Q:  Who went home?
     A:  John.

b.   Q:  Where did John go?
     A:  Home.

c.   Q:  Why did John go home?
     A:  John was tired.
```

The answers generated need not be in English. Instead, the question-answering demons can produce CD structures as output. For example, the answer to c. might simply be: "S-SLEEP".

9. In general, there are two ways that words cn be disambiguated: 1) Each word can have one of more demons associated with it, whose job it is to perform the disambiguation. 2) An **automatic** disambiguation feature can make use of the current context (i.e. the active demons). These two approaches do not have to be conflicting.

a. Write a disambiguation demon associated with "shot" in order to handle the following cases:

```
"The gun shot Mary."
    --> (PROPEL OBJECT (BULLETS)) etc.

"The camera shot Mary."
    --> ($TAKE-PICTURE ...) etc.
```

b. Make sure your demon can handle cases in which the disamiguation must be delayed until a sufficient context is available, as in:

```
"Mary was shot by a gun."
"Mary was shot by a camera."
```

c. The particular sentence "The camera shot Mary." actually represents a "garden path" case. That is, many people assume that "shot" meant with a gun, and then must correct their error upon hearing "camera". Therefore, as a variation, write an error correction demon that overrides the preferred meaning of "shot" when a garden path has occurred.

10. Implement a GENERAL disambiguation feature, in which expectations associated with "gun" and "camera" **automatically** cause McDYPAR to select the correct meaning of "shot" for storage into Working Memory. For instance, the mention of "gun" will cause a demon to expect a (PROPEL OBJECT (BULLET)) rather than $TAKE-PICTURE. Since McDYPAR will notice that the active context prefers (PROPEL OBJECT (BULLET)), this meaning of "shot" will be chosen. Notice that this general mechanism can operate alongside the specific disambiguation demon(s) written for exercises a and b. If the automatic mechanism fails, then (hopefully) the specific disambiguation demons will succeed. In DYPAR,

this general mechanism is implemented basically by altering the function SEARCH (since every demon uses SEARCH to scan Working Memory). When SEARCH encounters an ambiguous word in Working Memory, it automatically examines the possible meanings for that word. If one can be uniquely chosen, then that meaning is automatically placed in to Working Memory (and its associated demons spawned). In this way, the expectation associated with "gun" causes "shot" to be disambiguated. At the same time, "shot" can have its own disambiguation demons directly associated with it.

11. Augment McDYPAR with a primitive story memory so that it can handle more than one sentence at a time. Then give it the sentence in exercise 6 followed by: "George drove home to change his clothes." Before attempting this project, make sure you have a thorough familiarity with the material covered in this book.

    a.   Your resulting story memory should capture the following information:

- George was eating at a restaurant
- A waitress spilled coffee on George.
- George's clothes were wet.
- George wanted dry clothes.
- George wanted to be home.
- George left the restaurant.
- George drove home.
- George was at home.
- George changed his clothes.
- George was no longer wet.

    b. Use your question-answering capability to answer the following questions:

Q: What happened at the restaurant?
A: The waitress spilled coffee on George.

```
Q:  Why did George go home?
A:  So George could change his clothes.

Q:  How did George get home?
A:  George drove.
```

Now you're on your own. Happy parsing!

References

Abelson, R. P. The Structure of Belief Systems. In Schank and Colby (Eds.), *Computer Models of Thought and Language*, San Francisco: W. H. Freeman, 1973.

Abelson, R. P. Differences Between Belief and Knowledge Systems. *Cognitive Science*, 1979, **3**(4).

Anderson, J. R. and Bower, G. *Human Associative Memory*. Wash. D.C.: Winston-Wiley, 1973.

Anderson, J. R. *Language, Memory and Thought*. Hillsdale, NJ: Erlbaum, 1976.

Austin, J. L. *How To Do Things With Words*. Cambridge, MA: Harvard University Press, 1975. Second edition.

Bach, K. and Harnish, R. M. *Linguistic Communication and Speech Acts*. Cambridge, MA: MIT Press, 1979.

Bartlett, R. *Remembering: A Study in Experimental and Social Psychology*. MA: Cambridge University Press, 1932.

Becker, Joseph. The Phrasal Lexicon. In *Theoretical Issues in Natural Language Processing*, Cambridge, MA, 1975.

Birnbaum L. and Selfridge M. Conceptual Analysis of Natural Language. In R. Schank and C. Reisbeck (Eds.), *Inside Computer Understanding: Five Programs Plus Miniatures*, Hillsdale, NJ: Lawrence Erlbaum, 1981.

Black, J. B. Memory for State and Action Information in Narratives. In *21st Annual Meeting of the Psychomomic Society*, 1980. Held in St. Louis, Missouri.

Bower, G. H., Gilligan, S. G. and Monteiro, K. P. Selectivity of Learning Caused by Affective States. *Journal of Experimental Psychology: General*, 1981, **110**(4).

Bower, G. H., Black, J. B., and Turner, T. J. Scripts in Memory for Text. *Cognitive Psychology*, 1979, **11**, 177-220.

Carbonell, Jaime G. *Subjective Understanding: Computer Models of Belief Systems.* Technical Report 150, Yale University. Department of Computer Science, 1979. Ph.D. Dissertation.

Charniak, E., Riesbeck, C. K., and McDermott, D. V. *Artificial Intelligence Programming.* Hillsdale, NJ: Lawrence Erlbaum, 1980.

Charniak, Eugene. *Toward a Model of Children's Story Comprehension.* PhD thesis, Artificial Intelligence Lab. M.I.T., Boston MA, 1972.

Charniak, Eugene. Organization and Inference in a Frame-Like System of Common Sense Knowledge. In R. Schank and B. Nash-Webber (Eds.), *TINLAP-1: Theoretical Issues in Natural Language Processing*, distributed by ACL, 1975.

Charniak, Eugene. On the Use of Framed Knowledge in Language Comprehension. *Artificial Intelligence*, 1978, **11**(3).

Cofer, C. N. *Motivation and Emotion.* Glenview, Ill: Scott, Foresman & Co., 1972.

Colby, K. M. Simulations of Belief Systems. In Schank and Colby (Eds.), *Computer Models of Thought and Language*, San Francisco: W. H. Freeman, 1973.

Colby, K. M. *Artificial Paranoia.* NY: Pergamon Press, 1975.

Colby, K. M. Modeling a Paranoid Mind. *The Behavioral and Brain Sciences*, 1981, **4**(4).

Cullingford, R. E. *Script Application: Computer Understanding of Newspaper Stories.* Technical Report 116, Yale University. Department of Computer Science, 1978. Ph.D. Dissertation.

Cullingford, R. E. SAM. In R. C. Schank and C. K. Reisbeck (Eds.), *Inside Computer Understanding: Five Programs Plus Miniatures*, Hillsdale, NJ: Lawrence Erlbaum, 1981.

Davis, R. and King, J. An Overview of Production Systems. *Machine Intelligence*, 1977, **8**.

Davitz, J. R. *The Language of Emotion*. NY: Academic Press, 1969.

DeJong II, Gerald F. Prediction and Substantiation: A New Approach to Natural Language Processing. *Cognitive Science*, 1979, **3**, 251-273.

DeJong II, Gerald F. *Skimming Stories in Real Time: An Experiment in Integrated Understanding*. Technical Report 158, Yale University. Department of Computer Science, 1979. Ph.D. Dissertation.

Dennett, Daniel C. *Brainstorms: Philosophical Essays on Mind and Psychology*. Montgomery, VT: Branford Books, 1978.

Dreyfus, H. L. *What Computers Can't Do: A Critique of Artificial Reason*. NY: Harper and Row, 1972.

Dyer, Michael G. and Wendy G. Lehnert. *Organization and Search Processes for Narratives*. Technical Report 175, Yale University. Department of Computer Science, 1980.

Dyer, Michael G. and Lehnert, Wendy G. Question Answering for Narrative Memory. In J. F. Le Ny and W. Kintsch (Eds.), *Language and Comprehension*, Amsterdam: North-Holland, 1982. (in press).

Dyer, Michael G., Wolf, Thomas C., and Martin Korsin. BORIS -- An In-Depth Understander of Narratives. In *Proceedings of the Seventh International Joint Conference on Artificial Intelligence*, 1981. (program demo).

Dyer, Michael G. $RESTAURANT Revisited or 'Lunch with BORIS'. In *Proceedings of the 7th International Joint Conference on Artificial Intelligence*, August 1981. Held in Vancouver, BC.

Dyer, Michael G. The Role of TAUs in Narratives. In *Proceedings of the Third Annual Conference of the Cognitive Science Society*, August 1981. Held at Berkeley, CA.

Dyer, Michael G. Integration, Unification, Reconstruction, Modification: An Eternal Parsing Braid. In *Proceedings of the Seventh International Joint Conference on Artificial Intelligence,* 1981.

Dyer, Michael G. DYPAR -- A Demon-Based Parser. In *Processes of Thought and Language,* 1982. by Wendy G. Lehnert (in preparation).

Dyer, Michael G. The Role of Affect in Narratives. *Cognitive Science,* 1983.in press.

Flowers, M., McGuire, R., and Birnbaum, L. Adversary Arguments and the Logic of Personal Attacks. In W. Lehnert and M. Ringle (Eds.), *Strategies for Natural Language Processing,* Hillsdale NJ: Lawrence Erlbaum, 1982.

Gershman, A. V. *Knowledge-Based Parsing.* Technical Report 156, Yale University. Department of Computer Science, 1980. Ph.D. Dissertation.

Goldman, N. Conceptual Generation. In *Schank, Conceptual Information Processing,* pp 289-371, NY: American Elsevier, 1975.

Graesser, A.C. *Prose Comprehension Beyond the Word.* NY: Springer-Verlag, 1981.

Granger, Richard H. (Jr). *Adaptive Understanding: Correcting Erroneous Inferences.* Technical Report 171, Yale University. Department of Computer Science, 1980. Ph.D. Dissertation.

Granger, Richard H. (Jr). When Expectation Fails: Towards a Self-Correcting Inference System. In *Proceedings of the First National Conference on Artificial Intelligence,* Stanford, CA: 1980.

Izard, C. E. *The Face of Emotion.* NY: Appleton-Century-Crofts, 1971.

Izard, C. E. *Human Emotions.* NY: Plenum Press, 1977.

Johnson, Steven C. Hierarchical Clustering Schemes. *Psychometrika,* 1967, **32**(3).

Kahn, K. and Gorry, G. Mechanizing Temporal Knowledge. *Artificial Intelligence*, 1977, **9**(1).

Kolodner, Janet L. *Retrieval and Organizational Strategies in Conceptual Memory: A Computer Model*. Technical Report 187, Yale University. Department of Computer Science, 1980. Ph.D. Dissertation.

Kolodner, Janet L. Organization and Retrieval in a Conceptual Memory for Events (or CON54, Where are you?). In *Proceedings of the 7th International Joint Conference on Artificial Intelligence*, 1981. Held at the University of British Columbia, Vancouver Canada.

Kuipers, B. Modeling Spatial Knowledge. *Cognitive Science*, 1978, **2**(2).

Lebowitz, Michael. *Generalization and Memory in an Integrated Understanding System*. Technical Report 186, Yale University. Department of Computer Science, 1980. Ph.D. Dissertation.

Lehnert, W. G. and Burstein, M. H. The Role of Object Primitives in Natural Language Processing. In *Proceedings of the 6th International Joint Conference on Artificial Intelligence*, 1979.

Lehnert, W. G. and Robertson, S. P. Memory Modification During Question Answering. In *Text Comprehension Symposium at the Deutsches Institut fur Fernstudien an der Universitat Tubingen*, 1981. University of Tubingen, W. Germany.

Lehnert, W. G., Black, J. and Robertson, S. P. Memory Interactions During Question Answering. In Mandle, Stein, and Trabasso (Eds.), *Aspects of Text Comprehension*, (in press), 1982.

Lehnert, W. G., Dyer, M. G., Johnson, P. N., Yang, C. J. and S. Harley. *BORIS -- An Experiment in In-Depth Understanding of Narratives*. Technical Report 188, Yale University. Department of Computer Science, December 1980.

Lehnert, W. G., Dyer, M. G., Johnson, P. N., Yang, C. J. and S. Harley. BORIS -- An In-Depth Understander of Narratives. *Artificial Intelligence*, 1982.

Lehnert, Wendy G. *The Process of Question Answering.* Hillsdale, New Jersy: Lawrence Erlbaum, 1978.

Lehnert, W. G. Representing Physical Objects in Memory. In M. D. Ringle (Ed.), *Philosophical Perspectives in Artificial Intelligence,* Atlantic Highlands, NJ: Humanities Press, 1979.

Lehnert, W. G. Affect and Memory Representation. In *Proceedings of the Third Annual Conference of the Cognitive Science Society,* Berkley, California: 1981. (Major Address).

Lehnert, Wendy G. Plot Units and Narrative Summarization. *Cognitive Science,* 1982.(in press).

Lehnert, Wendy. Plot Units: A Narrative Summarization Strategy. In Lehnert and Ringle (Eds.), *Strategies for Natural Language Processing,* Hillsdale, NJ: Lawrence Erlbaum, 1982. (in press).

Loftus, E. F. Leading Questions and the Eyewitness Report. *Cognitive Psychology,* 1975, **7**.

Loftus, E. F. *Eyewitness Testimony.* Cambridge, MA: Harvard University Press, 1979.

Mandler, G. *Mind and Emotion.* NY: John Wiley, 1975.

Mandler, G. Affect, Emotion, and Other Cognitive Curiosities. In *Proceedings of the Third Annual Conference of the Cognitive Science Society,* Berkley, CA: 1981. (Major Address).

Marslen-Wilson, W., Tyler, L. and Seidenberg, M. Sentence Processing and the Clause Boundary. In W. Levelt and G. Flores d'Arcais (Ed.), *Studies in the Perception of Language,* NY: John Wiley and Sons, 1978.

McCawley, J, D. *Adverbs, Vowels, and Other Objects of Wonder.* Chicago, Illinois: University of Chicago Press, 1979.

McDermott, Drew. *A Temporal Logic for Reasoning about Processes and Plans.* Technical Report 196, Yale University. Department of Computer Science, 1981.

McGuire, R. Political Primaries and Words of Pain. 1980. Unpublished Manuscript, Department of Computer Science. Yale University.

Meehan, J. R. *The New UCI LISP Manual.* Hillsdale, NJ: Lawrence Erlbaum, 1979.

Miller, George A. The Magic Number Seven, Plus or Minus Two: Some Limits on Our Capacity for Processing Information. *Psychology Review*, 1956, **63**, 81-97.

Minsky, M. A Framework for Representing Knowledge. In P. Winston (Ed.), *The Psychology of Computer Vision*, NY: McGraw-Hill, 1975.

Minsky, M. Frame-System Theory. In P. Johnson-Laird and P. Wason (Eds.), *Thinking: Readings in Cognitive Science*, MA: Cambridge University Press, 1977.

Newell, A. Production Systems: Models of Control Structures. In W. C. Chase (Ed.), *Visual Information Processing*, NY: Academic Press, 1973.

Rieger, Charles J. III. Conceptual Memory and Inference. In Schank (Ed.), *Conceptual Information Processing*, pp 157-288, NY: American Elsevier, 1975.

Riesbeck C. K. and Schank R. C. *Comprehension by Computer: Expectation-Based Analysis of Sentences in Context.* Technical Report 78, Yale University. Department of Computer Science, 1976.

Schank R. C. and C. K. Riesbeck (Eds.). *Inside Computer Understanding: Five Programs Plus Miniatures.* Hillsdale, NJ: Lawrence Erlbaum, 1981.

Riesbeck, Christopher K. Conceptual Analysis. In Schank (Ed.), *Conceptual Information Processing*, pp 83-156, NY: American Elsevier, 1975.

Riesbeck, C. K. An Expectation-Driven Production System for Natural Language Understanding. In D. A. Waterman and F. Hayes-Roth (Eds.), *Pattern-Directed Inference Systems*, NY: Academic

Press, 1978.

Robertson, S. P., Lehnert, W. G. and Black, J. B.   Alternations in Memory for Text by Leading Questions. In *Meeting of the American Educational Research Association*, NY: 1982.

Robinson, J. A. Sampling Autobiographical Memory. *Cognitive Psychology*, 1976, **8**.

Roseman, Ira. Cognitive Aspects of Emotion and Emotional Behavior. 1979. Yale Psychology Dept.   Paper read at 87th Annual Convention of the American Psychological Association in NYC.

Roseman, Ira. *Cognitive Aspects of Discrete Emotions*. PhD thesis, Yale University, 1982. (in preparation).

Schachter, S. and Singer, J. E.   Cognitive, Social and Physiological Determinants of Emotional State. *Psychological Review*, 1962, **69**.

Schachter, S.   The Interaction of Cognition and Physiological Determinants of Emotional State. In Spielberger, C. D. (Ed.), *Anxiety and Behavior*, NY: Academic Press, 1966.

Schank, Roger and Abelson, Robert. *Scripts, Plans, Goals, and Understanding.*   Hillsdale, NJ: Lawrence Erlbaum, 1977. The Artificial Intelligence Series.

Schank, R. C. and Birnbaum L. Memory, Meaning, and Syntax. In T. Bever and L. Miller (Eds.), *Cognitive, Philosophical, Computational Foundations of Language*, (in press), 1982.

Schank, R. C. and J. G. Carbonell, Jr.   *Re: The Gettysburg Address. Representing Social and Political Acts.*   Technical Report 127, Yale University. Department of Computer Science, 1978.

Schank, R. C. and J. G. Carbonell, Jr.   Re: The Gettysburg Address. Representing Social and Political Acts. In N. Findler (Ed.), *Associative Networks*, NY: Academic Press, 1979.

Schank, R. C., Lebowitz, M., and Birnbaum, L. An Integrated Understander. *American Journal of Computational Linguistics*, 1980, **6**(1).

Schank, R. C.   Identification of Conceptualizations Underlying Natural Language. In Schank and Colby (Eds.), *Computer Models of Thought and Language*, San Francisco: W. H. Freeman, 1973.

Schank, Roger C. (Ed.). *Conceptual Information Processing.* NY: American Elsevier, 1975. Fundamental Studies in Computer Science, Volume 3.

Schank, R. C. Interestingness: Controlling Inferences. *Artificial Intelligence*, 1979, **12**(3).

Schank, Roger C.   Language and Memory. *Cognitive Science*, 1980, **4**(3).

Schank, Roger C. Failure-Driven Memory. *Cognition and Brain Theory*, 1981, **1**.

Schank, Roger C. Reminding and Memory Organization: An Introduction to MOPs. In W. Lehnert and M. Ringle (Eds.), *Strategies for Natural Language Processing*, Hillsdale NJ: Lawrence Erlbaum, 1982. (in press).

Schank, Roger C. *Dynamic Memory: A Theory of Reminding and Learning in Computers and People.* NY: Cambridge University Press, 1982.

Searle, J. R. *Speech Acts.* NY: Cambridge University Press, 1969.

Seifert, C., Abelson, R., McKoon, G., Ratcliffe, R. and M. Dyer. Thematic Structures in Text Processing (unpublished manuscript). 1982. Psychology Dept. Yale University.

Seifert, Colleen. Preliminary Experiments on TAUs (unpublished manuscript). 1981. Psychology Dept. Yale University.

Shwartz, S. *The Search for Pronominal Referents.* Technical Report 10, Cognitive Science Program. Department of Computer Science. Yale University, 1981.

Sloman, A. and Croucher, M.   Why Robots will have Emotions. In *Proceedings of the 7th International Joint Conference on Artificial*

Intelligence, August 1981.   Held in Vancouver, BC.

Small,   Steven. Viewing   Word   Expert   Parsing   as   Linguistic Theory. *Proceedings of the 7th International Joint Conference on Artificial Intelligence*, August 1981.Held in Vancouver, BC.

Spiro, Rand J., Esposito, J., Vondruska, R. J.   The Representation of Derivable Inofrmation in Memory: When What Might Have Been Left Unsaid is Said. In *TINLAP-2: Theoretical Issues in Natural Language Processing.*, pp 226-231, University of Illinois at Urbana-Champaign,   1978.   Sponsored   by   Association   for   Computing Machinery.

Strongman, K. T. *The Psychology of Emotions.*   NY: John Wiley, 1978. Second Edition.

Sussman, G. J. *A Computer Model of Skill Acquisition.*   NY: American Elsevier, 1975.

Tennant, H. *Natural Language Processing.*   NY: Petrocelli Books, 1981.

Terr, Lenore C. Psychiatric Trauma in Children: Observations Following the Chowchilla School-Bus Kidnapping. *American Journal of Psychiatry*, 1981, **Jan.**

Tulving, E.   Episodic and Semantic Memory. In E. Tulving and W. Donaldson (Eds.), *Organization of Memory*, NY: Academic Press, 1972.

Tyler, L. and Marslen-Wilson, W. The On-line Effects of Semantic Context on Syntactic Processing. *Journal of Verbal Learning and Verbal Behavior*, 1977, **16.**

Waterman, D. A.   and   Hayes-Roth,   F. (Eds.). *Pattern-Directed Inference Systems.*   NY: Academic Press, 1978.

Weissman, C. *LISP 1.5 Primer.*   Belmont, CA: Dickenson Publishing, 1967.

Wilensky, Robert. Why John Married Mary: Understanding Stories Involving Recurring Goals. *Cognitive Science*, 1978, **2**(3).

Wilensky, Robert. *Understanding Goal-Based Stories.* Technical Report 140, Department of Computer Science. Yale University, 1978. Ph.D. Dissertation.

Wilensky, Robert. *Meta-Planning: Representing and Using Knowledge About Planning in Problem Solving and Natural Language Understanding.* Technical Report Memo. No. UCB/ERL M80/33, Electronics Research Lab. College of Engineering, University of California, Berkley., 1980.

Wilensky, Robert. *Points: A Theory of Story Content.* Technical Report Memo. No. UCB/ERL M80/17, Electronics Research Lab. College of Engineering, University of California, Berkley., 1980.

Wilks, Y. Parsing English I and II. In E. Charniak and Y. Wilks (Eds.), *Computational Semantics*, Amsterdam: North-Holland, 1976.

Winograd, Terry. *Understanding Natural Language.* NY: Academic Press, 1972.

Winston, Patrick H. and B. K. P. Horn. *LISP.* Reading, Mass.: Addison-Wesley Publishing Co., 1981.

Woods, W. A. Progress in Natural Language Understanding -- An Application to Lunar Geology. *Proceedings of the National Computer Conference*, 1973.

Zajonc, R. B. Feeling and Thinking: Preferences Need No Inferences. *American Psychologist*, 1980, **35**(2).

Index